INFORMATION SYSTEMS DEVELOPMENT
AND DATA MODELING
Conceptual and Philosophical Foundations

T0275761

INFORMATION SYSTEMS DEVELOPMENT AND DATA MODELING

Conceptual and Philosophical Foundations

Rudy Hirschheim
University of Houston

Heinz K. Klein
State University of New York, Binghamton

Kalle Lyytinen
University of Jyväskylä

CAMBRIDGE
UNIVERSITY PRESS

Published by the Press Syndicate of the University of Cambridge
The Pitt Building, Trumpington Street, Cambridge CB2 1RP
40 West 20th Street, New York, NY 10011-4211, USA
10 Stamford Road, Oakleigh, Melbourne 3166, Australia

©Cambridge University Press 1995

First published 1995

Library of Congress cataloguing in publication data available

British Library cataloguing in publication data available

ISBN 0 521 37369 7 hardback

Transferred to digital printing 2003

Table of Contents

Preface

Though the fields of information system development, in general, and data modeling in particular — the topics of this book — have amassed an impressive amount of research knowledge during the past two decades, they currently lack a global perspective and interpretation. In this context we define information systems development as the application of information technologies (computers and telecommunications) to solve and address problems in managing and coordinating modern organizations. Data modeling is concerned with describing, organizing and analyzing the properties of the 'rawware' of information systems — data. A wealth of research in these fields has produced an astonishing array of empirical results and practical insights, conceptual and terminological diversity and confusion, and a large suite of tools and methods. But as many researchers and practioners alike feel, these form an isolated, disjoint, and often contradictory amalgam of knowledge. In such a situation, the synthesis of the existing knowledge is at least as valuable as the addition of more detail in the form of further empirical results, new methods and tools, and refinements in vocabulary, etc. The need for synthesis to decrease the confusion in the area has motivated us to write this book: we seek out the principal, contradictory lines of research in information systems; describe and interpret them and their results in a way which does not deny or hide their differences, but in fact highlights the differences; and thereby hope to make these lines of research understandable. At the same time we strive to shed light on similarities where they exist and to discuss possible directions for improvement.

To accomplish our task, we need an intellectual tool to penetrate beneath the 'surface structure' of individual pieces of IS research and to organize them in some intelligible manner. We believe we have found such a tool in the form of a philosophical framework for analyzing the assumptions which guide different lines of research on IS and which points out the ways in which each line of research is somehow limited but at the same time brings order into chaos by making visible which assumptions make the approaches so different and what the implictions for adhereing to alternative assumptions are. We point out that all systems development methodologies make implicit assumptions which we feel may be problematic. Let us take a concrete example. Most (but not necessarily all) modeling techniques focus on functions, data or objects as elementary building blocks. The implict and/or explicit underlying assumptions are that:

(1) these building blocks exist in the world (realism) and

(2) there is an objectively definable set of things whose definition is inde-
     pendent of the perceptions of the developer (objectivism).

The implication of the first assumption is that it is the developer's job
to 'find' those objects as though they were the treasures of a sunken ship
washed up on shore just waiting to be picked up by the first one to come
along. The implication of the second assumption is that any two developers
should come up with the same model (because they will find the same
treasures) and if there are differences they are resolvable. If two developers
do see things differently, assumption (2) suggests that one developer is not
seeing the application as clearly as the other, or that one developer is simply
not as good as the other.

As our analysis reveals alternative standpoints are possible as well. What
if the objects are not given, but are to be constructed out of the pieces on
the shore with the flotsam and jetsam of many cultures (the different user
languages and views)? What if there are no universals, e.g. what are shells
to one culture is money to another? Thinking along such lines, in this book
we shall show:

(1) that most studies on information systems development rely on a specific
     standpoint which we call here a functionalist world view,

(2) that this view amounts to a distinct philosophical position, and

(3) this position is problematic in understanding and engaging in many
     facets of systems development.

If this point is accepted, then it is logical to ask what alternative philosophical positions are possible and what their implications for systems development and data modeling could be.

It will turn out that at least four philosophical positions can be discerned
in the literature and these can account for many of the contradictory results
and insights in the field. Researchers or practitioners adhering to different
philosophical positions simply see different objects on the beaches (or should
we say in the trenches) while developing information systems. This observation sets the principal agenda for this book: to define the fundamental
philosophical positions, and to explain how they apply to systems development in general and data modeling in particular. The refinement of these
issues form the core of our argument in this book. This will be a long and
involved argument, like a long and winding road with many paths, but we
have found it rewarding though difficult at times to navigate. We hope that
many readers will enjoy the same experience, and that they will never see
the same beach again after closing this book.

Rudy Hirschheim, Heinz Klein, Kalle Lyytinen
Houston, Owego and Hong Kong

Acknowledgements

This book has been both a physical and metaphorical journey for us. It has been an intellectual journey as well. Physically, it started out over 7 years ago in London and then Oxford, but has wound its way through places such as San Francisco, Owego, Jyväskylä, Lovanger, Houston, Ehringerfeld, Aalborg, Boston, Copenhagen, New York, Buffalo, Enschede, Orlando and Hong Kong. Over the years we have had many deep philosophical discussions, some of which have led to considerable disagreement, others which have resulted in the three of us uttering in unison 'ah ha'. No matter what the outcome, these philosophical discussions were always intellectually inspiring.

We learned a lot in writing this book. But it wasn't easy. Not much attention has been given in the literature to the kind of philosophical analysis of an applied field such as Information Systems. We felt like a voice in the wilderness when we first started with this book. Metaphorically, we had to find a path through the wilderness which would lead us to furtile grounds to satisfy our intellectual hunger. In this way, we came to know many interesting places which are not commonly visited by IS researchers. In our search for intellectual sustenance, we were delighted to find a few kindred spirits (or travel companions so to speak) who also tried to articulate the most fundamental assumptions on which the discipline of IS in general or ISD in particular rests. Among these kindred spirits we include Boland's (1979): 'Control, Causality and Information System Requirements,' Winograd and Flores' (1986) 'Understanding Computers and Cognition', Iivari's (1991) 'Paradigmatic Analysis of ISD', Dahlbom and Mathiassen's (1993) 'Computers in Context', and Ehn's (1988) 'Work-Oriented Design of Computer Artifacts'.

Behind every significant journey is a large cast of supporting characters helping with the journeys' organization and execution. These individuals give advice, warn of dangers, point to fruitful avenues and offer the weary travellers physical and emotional sustenance. We owe a great deal of thanks to many people who supported us in our endeavor; who sacrificed much while we spent many days sequestered away writing the manuscript. First, we would like to thank our respective families; their support and understanding during the seven years is gratefully appreciated. Next, Cambridge University Press and especially David Tranah must be thanked for their extreme patience and unwavering support. It would have been so easy for them to say: 'look guys, enough is enough'. But they didn't, and we sincerely appreciate their understanding. Next, Jaana Porra, provided a most penetrating and thorough critique of the entire manuscript. In doing so, she highlighted numerous oversights and misconceptions. Juhani Iivari, Duane Truex and John Haynes helped in commenting on selected sections of earlier versions of the book. Their comments helped make the book more coherent and readable. Ronald Stamper graciously helped make material available on LEGOL/NORMA. This allowed us to have a much better understanding of this interesting rule-based data modeling approach. Similarly, Jan Stage provided missing information on the Professional Work Practices approach. Winnie White at the University of Houston was most helpful in compiling the bibliography, tables and figures for the book. We would also like to acknowledge the financial support from the Academy of Finland, Danish Natural Science Research Council, and the Information Systems Research Center of the University of Houston. Lastly, our respective University departments both directly and indirectly supported our intellectual and physical travels. We gratefully acknowledge the financial and collegial support of the School of Management (SUNY-Binghamton), Department of Computer Science and Information Systems (University of Jyväskylä) and College of Business Administration (University of Houston). Thanks to all of you.

1
Introduction

1.1 Background

It is a truism to say that computers have become ubiquitous in today's organizations. Since their application in administrative data processing in the mid-1950s, they have become one of the key instruments for improving the formal information processing activities of organizations. In less than four decades, computer-based information systems (IS) have evolved from supporting back office, already formalized, systems such as payroll, to penetrating the entire organization. New applications and technologies have emerged with great fanfare, and the enthusiasm for information systems continues to run high. Indeed, many enthusiasts conceive of information technology as the primary vehicle for organizational problem-solvers, increasing an organization's capacity to cope with external and internal complexity and improve its performance. Nor is there any doubt that information systems will play an even more vital role in tomorrow's organization.

The development of these information systems has received considerable attention in both the popular and academic literature. New methods for designing systems, new approaches for analysis, new strategies for implementing the developed systems, and the like, have proliferated over the past 30 years. Yet, a majority of information systems design approaches conceive of information systems development (ISD) with the assumption that they are technical systems with social consequences. This leads one to focus on IS design problems as problems of technical complexity. Proponents of this view assume that IS development problems can largely be resolved by more sophisticated technical solutions (tools, models, methods and principles).

In recent years, however, there has been a growing interest in viewing IS as social systems that are technically implemented. They serve as the agent for significant social interactions which implies their connection to human communication through the medium of language. Contrary to 'second wave technologies' (i.e. matter and energy transforming machines; *cf.* Toffler 1980), information technology is by its very nature a social technology because its existence depends on social institutions like language, the legitimation and control of power and other forms of social influence, and other norms of behavior. The proponents of this view also claim that in fact all technological solutions are social solutions. As a consequence they regard IS design problems as dealing primarily with social complexity and only secondarily with technological complexity. We can conclude that such a socially informed view of IS assumes that all technical designs constitute

1

interventions in the social institution.

The 'paradigm shift' implied by the above has led to the proposal of new 'social approaches'. Most of these have come from academia but have not yet been widely employed in practice. An interesting feature in these new approaches is the bewildering variety of views and processes they propose in dealing with IS as a social design problem. This suggests that 'social complexity' should be distinguished from 'technical complexity' because the former is of a different sort and more ambiguous (Weinberg 1981). Accordingly the IS design problem is a far more complex phenomenon than is realized in most cases, because it affects the conditions of human existence in similar ways as law making or other social institutions. Yet the mainstream literature continues to deal with it as a one-dimensional technological issue.

It is our contention that all involved in the framing of IS development bring to bear certain assumptions and beliefs about what is 'social', and that it is these assumptions which generate the variety of design approaches. The diverse assumptions and beliefs about the nature of IS have led to methodological pluralism in the IS research community (Mumford *et al.* 1985; Nissen *et al.* 1991). This pluralism can be said to reflect the multidimensional nature of complexity of ISD that cannot be reduced to any type of well-defined technical complexity. In other words, the complexity of IS development cannot be captured in some formal model and finally resolved through improved formalisms.

An interesting question arises immediately. Can this type of social complexity be analyzed and can we systematically trace its origins? We believe that it can be done but it requires a different type of inquiry than is usually followed in circles that regard IS design problems as mainly technical problems. Simply put, we do not need more refined mathematical theories, models or new sophisticated technologies. Instead, what we need is the ability to pose and debate — in a critical manner — traditional philosophical questions in the context of IS design that have been the subject of discourse by philosophers and social thinkers. At the same time it requires critical assimilation and acquaintance with problems and questions addressed in the mainstream of social theory and philosophy so that the latter can be used to speak to the issues that are relevant in IS development.

To address these issues, we engage in a critical analysis of assumptions and beliefs about the nature of social phenomena as revealed in a number of design methods and approaches that have been proposed for ISD. In more specific terms we shall conduct a critical analysis of systems development methods and methodologies that have emerged during the last two decades. We interpret methods and methodologies here quite broadly as any process oriented prescriptions of how to go about developing an information system. In this sense our analysis covers process models, methods and tools, and ways to organize systems development (e.g. participation). A more detailed analysis of these concepts is provided in chapter 3. Another target of our examination is those methods that focus on describing, organizing and analyzing data that are stored and manipulated in the IS. This area, in general, is denoted as data modeling. A more detailed description of the pertinent data modeling concepts is provided in chapter 3. The reason for choosing this as a specific area of interest in our book is that data modeling deals with concepts like information, knowledge, meaning, and language which cannot be handled without explicit (or implicit) recourse to philosophical analysis. We believe that this type of analysis can serve two important goals:

(1) to systematically trace the complexity of IS design problems and methods into a set of beliefs and assumptions about the nature of 'social' reality (and social knowledge), and

(2) to point out some principal alternative approaches in which IS design and data modeling problems can be framed depending on the assumptions and beliefs about the nature of social reality.

1.2 Purpose of the Book

It is our contention in writing this book that it is not possible to develop information systems without bringing to the development task a set of implicit and explicit assumptions. The most basic assumptions concern the nature of the world around us (ontological assumptions) and how one inquires or obtains knowledge about the world around us (epistemological assumptions). Different sets of assumptions are likely to yield very different approaches to information systems development. Yet, this kind of philosophical analysis of an applied field is a genre which has not received much attention in the IS literature. We do, however, note a few kindred companions who have tried to articulate the fundamental assumptions on which the discipline of IS in general or ISD in particular rests. Among these kindred spirits are Boland (1979), Iivari (1991), Dahlbom and Mathiassen (1993), Winograd and Flores (1986), Ehn (1988), and Floyd *et al.* (1992).

For whatever reason the number of studies of this genre is small, and since its beginning the field of IS has not spent much effort to explore the different sets of assumptions which consciously and unconsciously influence systems developers as reflected in their use of preferred methods and tools. The closest representative of this genre is perhaps Dalhbom and Mathiassen (1993) who tried to capture the issues emerging from the controversy between technical enthusiasts and social critics in information systems under the headings of mechanism and romanticism. From the romantic perspective, change is unpredictable and beyond human control, the expression of hidden and unknowable forces. The mechanist, on the other hand, believes in the power of good representations to predict and control social change. In this book, we shall build on different distinctions. Some of the key issues which we shall address include: what is the nature of social reality and social causation; how can we obtain information about it; what is the relationship between the inquirer and the object of inquiry in a social context;

what is the meaning of meaning and how is it created through language; what are the fundamental values that are guiding IS development in practice (Kling 1978; Mowshowitz 1984; Burns 1981) and those underlying different methodologies (Klein and Hirschheim 1991), and finally: does the concept of rational choice extend to value questions, or are value choices merely a matter of faith and politics? (*cf.* Klein and Hirschheim 1993). By looking at different answers to these questions in social theory and philosophy we believe that we can shed light on the social complexity in IS development. In short, some of the origins of this complexity can be found in the eyes of the beholder, i.e. with what type of assumptions and beliefs he or she approaches the social reality of IS design.

This is a different answer than usually adopted in the IS research literature. Instead, it is usually taken for granted that there exists only one set of fundamental assumptions which are essentially the same for all. But is this true? The purpose of the book is to explore this belief and expose it as misguided. There is simply more than one set of assumptions guiding systems development and which have commonly been taken for granted. They are associated with the 'paradigm' of functionalism. The purpose of this book is to explain this in more detail, and in particular we focus on the following three claims:

(1) There are fundamentally different sets of assumptions about the nature of the world and how one obtains knowledge of it which have important implications for both information systems development and use. In this book we limit our discussion to IS development. In fact, we will show it is possible to see four different sets of assumptions yielding four paradigms of ISD, one of which is functionalism. Moreover, each paradigm has its own way of looking at information systems; highlighting certain aspects of the IS, and de-emphasizing others.

(2) It is possible to see in the literature that radically different approaches exist to information systems development which are influenced by these paradigms. However the understanding of these different approaches has suffered because much of this literature is not well-documented, and hence not easily accessible. Also, the language of some of the literature is impenetrable without some understanding of philosophical principles. Therefore, a second purpose of this book is to provide a survey of this literature, articulating and clarifying its underlying, different philosophical assumptions. This is necessary for interpreting the diverse streams of research on information systems development.

(3) The relative inaccessibility of much of the literature informed by alternative paradigms has produced an imbalance in the way the field is defined. This bias has led to the overlooking of important issues: for example as IS are widely perceived as providing effective representations of organizational reality for the purpose of organizational control

and problem solving, alternative paradigms highlight the information systems' role in the process of social reality construction through sense-making, or their contribution to the improvement to arguments in the organizational discourse with possible implications for emancipation. Depending on which issue is defined as the principal project goal, a rather different approach to ISD will be appropriate. If it turns out that the most popular approaches follow the tenets of only one paradigm, an imbalance arises.

We believe this book is a first step toward correcting the intellectual imbalance of the field in that we focus on those approaches informed by alternative paradigms which have received insufficient attention in the refereed research literature. Our book is more than an intellectual exercise as it contributes to emancipation: the book may help the IS community to question the legitimacy of its current practices and resulting social arrangements.

We would like to acknowledge that this book is not meant as a contribution to philosophy, but rather its purpose is much more modest: to simply supply the current state of discussion in information systems with a broad philosophical basis.

1.3 Goals and Organization of the Book

More specifically, the principal goals of this book are:

(1) to develop a philosophical and conceptual foundation to analyze and discuss representative ISD and data modeling approaches. This foundation is based on recent debates in the philosophy of science and language and it helps to clarify the conceptual foundations upon which all development approaches rest.

(2) To suggest a way to analyze systems development and data modeling approaches which is consistent with the proposed conceptual foundation. This is based on a systematic analysis of several development approaches and data modeling schools in which the concepts of systems development and data modeling are elaborated and refined.

(3) To provide a useful inventory of archetypical development approaches and their conceptual and philosophical foundations. In particular we want to point out what the main underlying theoretical underpinnings in current ISD approaches are and what areas of ISD are less developed and in need of further refinement.

(4) To develop a critical synthesis of the current philosophical debate about IS.

(5) To examine the implications of this debate for possible theoretical improvements in future approaches to ISD and data modeling.

Our grand goal in writing this book is to show that the IS community cannot remain aloof from the philosophical controversies that have washed

over social research during the last two decades. There is much to be learned
from the serious scholarly work in social theory and philosophy — an issue
that has been largely overlooked by the IS community as pointed out above.
At the same time the scholarly work in social theory and philosophy teaches
us that IS research is basically a study of our (possible) social conditions (of
knowing and communicating) that is inspired and supported by the immense
potential of information technology. The application of social theory and
philosophy to social research in general, and IS research in particular, is
beneficial because it permits us to be much more realistic about the potential
and the likely impacts of information technology. It also helps us to become
critically aware of the limitations of all of our approaches in the face of the
pluralistic and complex reality of ISD.

To address these goals we shall organize our argument in terms of eight
chapters which address the following five topics. The principal dependencies
between these five topics are outlined in figure 1.1:

I   Chapter 2 introduces some basic definitions and a historical perspective
      of the fundamental subject matter of this book, namely alternative
      approaches to ISD and data modeling.

II   Chapter 3 lays the philosophical and conceptual foundations which are
      fundamental for the structure of the remainder of the book, i.e. the
      paradigms.

III   Chapters 4 and 5 apply the notion and conceptual foundations associ-
      ated with paradigms to the analysis of ISD methodologies.

IV   Chapters 6 and 7 apply the notion and conceptual foundations associ-
      ated with paradigms to the analysis of data modeling approaches.

V   Chapter 8 summarizes our study, and considers the implications of our
      ideas on IS research and practice.

The following presents a more detailed outline of each chapters' purposes
and motivations:

Chapter 2's purpose is to inform the reader of our view of information systems development. We define the key concepts of ISD by abstracting from
its historical evolution without reference to their paradigmatic assumptions.
These are presented in more detail in chapter 3. The concepts defined in this
chapter are used throughout the book. An additional purpose of the chapter is to reveal the breadth of alternative approaches to ISD (including data
modeling) in their historical context. It is necessary to provide an overview
of the various approaches that have been proposed for systems development
because a subsequent chapter (chapter 3) provides a comprehensive classification scheme for alternative systems development approaches. Without
this chapter, the classification would lack a critical historical perspective.
Furthermore, the historical review of the evolution of systems development
approaches provides the broader picture by which the selection of certain
approaches for detailed discussion done in subsequent chapters (chapters

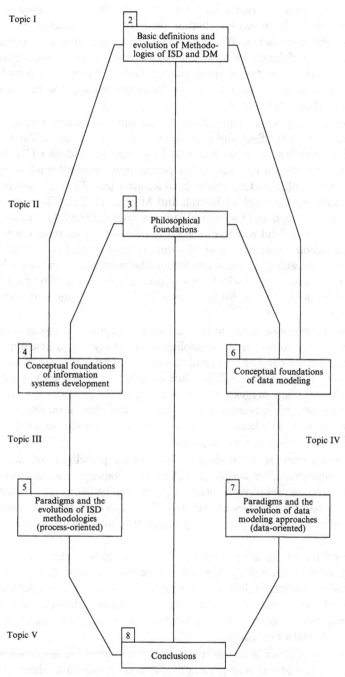

Figure 1.1: Grouping of chapters into five topic areas

5 and 7) becomes meaningful. The selection and discussion of the chosen approaches illuminates critical features of the classification scheme. In particular, chapter 2 introduces a distinction between 'process-oriented' and 'data-oriented' approaches. When we speak about information systems development methodologies we are primarily referring to process-oriented approaches and these are taken up chapters 4 and 5. When we speak of data modeling approaches we are referring to data-oriented approaches; these are discussed in chapters 6 and 7.

Chapter 3's purpose is to introduce our classification scheme which is the core of our view of the field and provides the plot for the book. We contend that such a classification scheme should be grounded in ideas which have a long standing tradition and the philosophical analysis of alternative epistemologies and ontologies. Our choice is to adopt a paradigmatic assumption analysis following the work of Burrell and Morgan (1979). The notion of a paradigm is explained and four paradigms are distinguished. Our proposal is that they offer a fruitful way to classify approaches to systems development. The classification allows one to see the unique features and contributions of alternative approaches. It leads one to see the significance of radically different approaches, some of which may appear idiosyncratic. The paradigms lay the philosophical basis for analyzing both process- and data-oriented approaches.

Chapter 4's purpose is to apply the four paradigms of chapter 3 to ISD without reference to specific methodologies. We apply the philosophical basis of the previous chapter to reveal the content and structure of different methodological approaches to ISD. Each paradigm portrays ISD in different ways. Each paradigm suggests preferred interpretations of the key concepts presented earlier and imposes a specific bias on our view of information systems development. The bias is explained for each paradigm in terms of key actors, narrative, plot and assumptions.

Chapter 5's purpose is to show how the four paradigms of chapter 3 apply to a representative sample of ISD methodologies excluding data modeling. The paradigmatic assumptions of each methodology are stated and their strengths and weaknesses explored. The chapter shows the value of a paradigmatic assumption analysis by suggesting how methodologies could be improved.

Chapter 6's purpose is to apply the four paradigms of chapter 3 to data modeling without reference to specific approaches. It shows how paradigms portray data modeling in different ways. In order to explain the bias that different paradigms impose on data modeling, it discusses the epistemological, ontological, social context, and representational assumptions of alternative approaches to data modeling.

Chapter 7's purpose is to discuss several data modeling approaches and their relationship to different paradigms. This corresponds to chapter 5 but instead, covers data modeling approaches. Its primary contribution is that it draws attention to radically different approaches to data modeling which are relatively unknown and deserve more attention. It also provides a critical evaluation of alternative approaches of data modeling.

Chapter 8's purpose is to return to the stated goals of the book and critically review how they have been met. A secondary purpose is to ask the question: 'what, if anything, should now happen?'. We conclude our analysis with the provocative question: why is it that most of academic research, ISD approaches arising from academia, and the teaching of university students has been confined to the domain of functionalism, when practitioners have for some time, evidently, embraced selective insights from multiple paradigms.* If this is so, the next step for the practitioner is to continue to draw on alternative paradigmatic foundations more consciously and systematically. For academia, our question implies the need to distribute its effort in research and teaching in a more balanced way; that is, to give equal attention to the different insights emanating from each paradigm. For example, one might consider what each paradigm implies for prudent information systems policies; however, this is a matter for another book. Stay tuned . . .

---

* Episkopou (1987) and Baskerville (1991) provide empirical evidence to the claim that practitioners, in applying the different methodologies, have intuitively acted in a way which was consistent with insights drawn from different paradigms. Apparently, some practitioners in applying a methodology, feel uncomfortable with its intrinsic underlying assumptions; if so, they bend them to better fit their own orientations. This might lead to, for example, producing a social relativist interpretation to some of the features of a functionalist methodology and vice versa.

2

Definition and Evolution of Information Systems Development Methodologies and Data Modeling

2.1 Introduction

The purpose of this chapter is two-fold: firstly, the chapter suggests a set of terms and concepts to describe and converse about information systems development which is independent of any particular or preferred way of dealing with it. Not surprisingly, as the IS field evolved, many different and sometimes inconsistent uses of terms to describe key notions appeared. For example, the part of the organization that is targeted for change through an IS development project is variably referred to as utilizing system, domain of change, target system, or universe of discourse. We shall use the term object system to cross-relate these terms coming from different sources. The concepts proposed in this chapter were selected with two requirements in mind:

(1) they should be maximally consistent with the literature base; and

(2) they should serve as a compass directing us deeper into the underlying philosophical issues often ignored in the literature on ISD.

Secondly, the chapter provides a brief overview of the history of information systems development and data modeling. This analysis serves as a historical background for understanding the origins (genealogy) of theoretical concepts and definitions offered in the chapter. It also provides the historical context for the more detailed treatment of specific systems development methodologies in chapter 5 and the analysis of data modeling approaches in chapter 7. Though methodologies and modeling are important parts of the evolution of IS, a full historical treatment of IS is beyond our scope here (but see Dickson 1981; Couger 1982 and Friedman and Cornford 1989).

To meet the challenge of keeping the historical review concise, the following treatment uses a broad brush to highlight the fundamental features which characterize important directions among the hundreds of methodologies that have been proposed over the years. History is, of course, too complex for any single taxonomy to do justice to its richness. As will be seen, the grouping of the methodologies into 'generations' is inspired by certain theoretical and philosophical principles discussed in later chapters of the book, particularly those associated with paradigmatic assumptions (see chapters 4, 5 and 7). The following discussion of the methodologies suggests a possible, but by no means absolute, ordering and the placement of specific methodologies is open to debate. Our discussion of the evolution of data modeling as well as its chronological placement, is also subject to debate.

Before embarking into a more detailed and conceptual discussion of information systems we shall introduce some rudimentary and widely accepted characterizations of the terms associated with information systems development. These will provide a first level understanding of the area which we shall further elaborate upon later in this chapter.

Traditionally, an *information system* has been defined in terms of two perspectives: one relating to its function; the other, to its structure. From a structural perspective (see e.g. Davis and Olson 1985), an information system consists of a collection of people, processes, data, models, technology and partly formalized language, forming a cohesive structure which serves some organizational purpose or function. From a functional perspective (see e.g. Langefors 1973, Goldkuhl and Lyytinen 1982a,b), an information system is a technologically implemented medium for the purpose of recording, storing, and disseminating linguistic expressions as well as for the supporting of inference making. Through performing these elementary functions, IS facilitate the creation and exchange of meanings that serve socially defined purposes such as control, sense-making, and argumentation (i.e. the formulation and justification of claims). In either of these two perspectives on information systems, it should be noted that humans are included within its boundaries which means that the services provided by an IS in part depend upon human capabilities and contributions.

In the widely accepted meaning, *systems analysis* is the process of collecting, organizing, and analyzing facts about a particular IS and the environment in which it operates. *Systems design* is the conception, generation and formation of a new system. It usually builds upon the understanding gained through systems analysis. *Systems development* encompasses the complete range of activities involved in the process of building (including both analysis and design), implementing and maintaining an information system. There is great variation as to which detailed activities are actually performed during systems development, the sequence in which they are performed, when they are performed and by whom they are performed, the documentation produced from each, and the extent to which they are prescribed and formalized. There are historical and cultural reasons for such variation. The field has also seen a long series of attempts to achieve greater understanding of these processes through formalization and description in order to gain better control of systems development. Such attempts have resulted in what are currently called *information systems development methodologies*. ISD methodologies are usually understood as sets of methods, tools, techniques, and models that are available to assist the developer. A 'technique' is defined as a way of accomplishing a task. Techniques fundamentally rely on human skills. A 'method' is a well-defined description of a technique. A method is always documentable whereas a technique need not be. A 'tool' is a specific object employed in the use of a particular method or technique which exists independently from the methods or techniques that use it. Because this book focuses on systems development, and data modeling which is a critical part of ISD, we discuss these terms in more detail below.

2.2 Basic Terminology

2.2.1 Introductory concepts and terms

In order to introduce some background for interpreting the more detailed and jargon-laden discussion of ISD in subsequent chapters, this section introduces some core concepts of the IS literature. As noted above information systems organize, store, retrieve and process data. These basic functions are reflected in the term 'data processing system'. As these systems evolved, new functions were added: improving organizational control and human understanding. Hence arose the claim that computer-based systems can provide information and knowledge. For certain types of systems it is of often claimed that they can help to solve problems or make decisions. Many types of decisions can be completely automated. If taken literally these are ambitious claims. What is an informed attitude towards evaluating them? To answer this we need to have some common understanding of what we mean by data, codes, information, beliefs, knowledge, and wisdom.

2.2.1.1 Codes and data

The basis for all communication, technically, biologically or socially, are invariances encoded in some medium. We call such invariances *codes*. The Morse alphabet or DNA are examples of codes. Computers basically process invariances that are coded as bit patterns, not unlike the Morse alphabet. In a more limited way, (biological) viruses also process invariances in reproducing themselves. *Data* are invariances with potential meaning to someone who can interpret them. In many situations, standard schemes of interpretation are taken for granted among communities sharing data, e.g. tax advisors are expected to interpret tax data in a fairly standard way.

There is, however, a great difference between recognizing and transforming invariances to recognizing and creating meaning. Therefore it is not surprising that major controversy exists as to whether IS are merely cleverly engineered technical means of conveying data (storing, transporting and transforming invariances) and consist merely of computer hardware and software, or if they include formal and informal organizational arrangements ('orgware') which interpret data to create and share meanings. In the latter case IS include social interaction networks, such as reporting channels or informal communication groups which interpret the results of computer processing, for example by taking into account meanings from rumors and other types of soft information. In this activity, computers may again be used in various ways, e.g. hypothetical calculations are performed in a spreadsheet, related data retrieved from a database or e-mail is used to keep in touch with a wide variety of people. If IS are narrowly defined as technical means for dealing with invariances consisting only of hardware and software, many researchers would question if they can even recognize information or knowledge, let alone provide it. Hence an ever growing number of researchers define IS as social interaction systems and see computers merely as an effective means to proliferate and change the quality of social interaction. From this perspective, IS are technically mediated social interaction systems aimed at creating, sharing and interpreting a wide variety of meanings.

2.2.1.2 Meaning vs. invariances

Contrary to some writings in artificial intelligence and the IS literature, we take the attitude that by themselves *invariances* have no intrinsic meaning just as 'paper' acquires meaning as money only through social conventions. If some invariances, as the letters in this book, assume meaning it is only through the interpretation of the human recipient. We do not follow the suggestion that the meaning of an invariance is identical with the behavior it produces. This does not adequately account for the possibility that the meaning can be freely renegotiated: as meaning comes first and behavior follows the former should not be equated with the latter. The interpretation is a creative act and no two interpretations are ever quite the same. Hence *meanings* are in the eye of some human beholder(s). If a machine were able to translate this book from English into Chinese, it would do so by processing invariances in accordance with elaborate rules and not by understanding the meaning in English and then re-expressing it in Chinese. If a human would follow merely the translation rules of the machine and arrive at a translation in this way, s/he could do so without learning Chinese (or English) and consequently we would not say that this person 'understands' Chinese. Neither would s/he understand the meaning of this book merely by virtue of following the translation rules.

Through social communication we may be able to exchange and share meanings, albeit only imperfectly. Meaning is related to human understanding: through meaning we make sense of our feelings, thoughts and the world around us. Understanding meaning expressed in language is tied to basic human experiences (Dreyfus 1982) or 'forms of life' as Wittgenstein (1958) refers to them in his *Philosophical Investigations*.

Invariances can be transmitted in many forms: as scents (e.g. the sex hormones of Japanese beetles) or other chemicals (e.g. genetic codes), electromagnetic light waves (e.g. letters or gender markings on birds), pressure waves (mating calls of deer or the spoken word), or electrical currents. It is useful to distinguish between invariances that occur naturally (such as bird markings) and invariances that are created by humans for some purpose, such as traffic signs, letters or graphics. If there is a given set of signs that are encoded as a standardized set of invariances we speak of an alphabet and the rules of mapping the signs to the invariances are called a code. Typically the elements of an alphabet can be combined into more complex signs such as a no parking sign followed by a time table. In IS, we are particularly interested in standardized signs which are interpreted in similar ways by a community of users. Business data are such a standard set of signs which are expected to convey the same or at least similar meanings to a user community.

2.2.1.3 Data vs. information and knowledge

Data must not be confused with information. In everyday life, *data* correspond to stating something (be it true or not) while *information* corresponds to speech acts which convey intentions. Hence items of information are meanings that are intended to influence people in some way. If I say 'it is raining today' I make a statement and as such it is data. If this statement is said with the intention of a warning to keep you inside or to get you to fetch an umbrella, it is a speech act to convey information (which need not necessarily be true even though a truth claim is implied). Alternatively the statement could have been said to correct your opinion of today's weather (as in a reply to 'nice weather today!' 'No, today it is raining'): it then is a speech act which makes an explicit truth claim and is information to influence you. Following Habermas' *Theory of Communicative Action*, in principle there are four types of speech acts (*cf.* Dietz and Widdershoven, 1992): To get someone to accept something as true (assertions about the external world, also called constativa), to get someone to do something (orders, imperativa), to appeal to others to obey accepted social norms (regulativa), and to express how one feels or thinks (expressiva).

Information need not necessarily be true, people sometimes try to get their way by being deceptive. If beliefs are stated about a subject with legitimate claims to truth or correctness, they are called *knowledge*. The difference between opinions or beliefs and knowledge is that the reasons or grounds supporting the truth claims of knowledge have been approved by some qualified elite and therefore at the present time are taken to be beyond questioning for practical purposes (over time knowledge changes). Historically it was held that knowledge is that which is certain to be true and therefore will not change. But this had to weaken as we mortals can never be sure of any truth claim. In modern society, different elites decide on different truth claims: the justice system on legal claims, the medical establishment on the correctness of cures, the scientific establishment on matters of fact, and the managerial establishment on matters of prudence in administration and so forth.

From these definitions it follows that computers by themselves do not process knowledge. They may process certain kind of invariances and rules which encode the knowledge of a subset of experts at a certain point in time. But computers do not 'know' that they utter truth claims and hence they cannot 'know' anything about the validity or doubtfulness of the grounds of these truth claims. Only the humans which feed the computer one set of invariances and interpret the resulting outputs with understanding can know. If we include humans in the definition of IS (computer-based communities or social institutions), then IS can obviously create meanings, produce information and evaluate knowledge claims. If IS are artificially limited to the technical vehicles of automated processing, they know no more about information and knowledge than a desk calculator knows about arithmetic or an automatic function integrator 'knows' about calculus.

2.2.1.4 Knowledge vs. wisdom

Certain kinds of knowledge are sometimes referred to as prudence or *wisdom*. Wisdom arises from well-reflected rules and policies for conducting human affairs, namely those which have proven effective by long personal experience. Wisdom cannot be acquired from books alone. It may be said that good management requires wisdom, i.e. knowledge about people as can be acquired only over a life time through a mixture of reflection and experience. As computers cannot participate in human affairs and reflect about experiences as we do, they cannot acquire wisdom. We do not see any evidence that computers can accumulate knowledge in a way similar to humans who can validly claim to be 'knowledgeable'. However, if information systems are seen as interacting people armed with computers, they can possibly make wise decisions; also the way in which an IS was designed can embody more or less wisdom just as a body of law or the consitution of government may embody wise choices about how to regulate human affairs.

2.2.2 Basic terminology for IS

This section will elaborate a set of basic terms about IS development which we use throughout the book. We describe the key features of information systems development by postulating that ISD is form of object system change. This helps to outline the features of object systems by noting their content and representation forms, and to define the concept of a systems development methodology as a social institution (knowledge plus resources) which conditions and guides the perception, analysis, synthesis, evaluation and implementation of object system changes.

2.2.2.1 Definition of information systems development as object system change

We shall suggest a definition of information systems development that is general enough to allow us to understand systems development broadly, yet specific enough to shed light on its essential aspects. We define information systems development as (Welke 1983): a *change process* taken with respect to *object systems* in a set of *environments* by a *development group* to achieve or maintain some *objectives*.

The essential components of this definition are illustrated in figure 2.1 and reviewed below in more detail.

Object systems consist of phenomena 'perceived' by members of the development group. What is 'perceived' is either given as a reality independent of the observer, or socially constructed through sense-making and institutionalized conventions. This points us to fundamentally different philosophical positions on the nature of reality and human inquiry which will

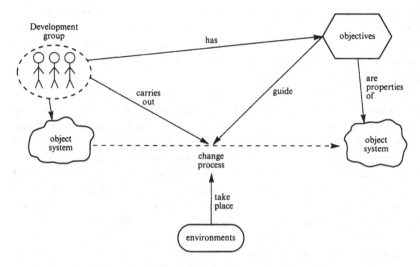

Figure 2.1: Information systems development

be taken up in chapter 4. In any case, object systems identify a target of change. In general, there is more than one object systems which a development group can identify. Object systems are often related, so that a change in one can induce a change in others. Members' perceptions of object systems need not coincide. This raises the issue of how to handle ambiguous or even conflicting views of object systems throughout systems development. Object systems should be further characterized in terms of their underlying concept structure, representation form, ontology, and epistemology. These are discussed in more detail below in the section on features of object systems.

Change process is an event in which phenomena, i.e. objects, properties and their relationships in object systems, come into being as a result of a development group's deliberate action. The change process is further characterized by intentionality, intersubjectivity and uncertainty.

Information systems development is intentional, to the extent it reflects a planned change. It is based on developers' intentions to change object systems towards desirable ends. Intersubjectivity means that the change process is founded on recognition of phenomena by more than one participant and on mutual understandings and coordination of participants' actions. Systems development is not just an artificial intervention because it is always embedded in a social and cultural milieu entailing many uncertainties. Therefore, the change process is not a deterministic one. For example, developers are often uncertain whether the planned intervention can be carried out, and whether the resulting object systems will have the desired properties.

In general, we shall distinguish three types of uncertainty: means uncertainty, effect uncertainty and problem uncertainty. The first type deals with situations in which developers are unsure whether certain means can achieve a desired end-state. The second type reflects situations in which developers are unsure of whether the end-state will have the desired properties. An intervention can coproduce changes that are incongruent or even conflicting with its stated ends. Problem uncertainty arises from the developers' need to choose which of several object systems they ought to approach and which of many possible changes are needed to remedy a problematic situation. This type of uncertainty may lead to 'errors of the third kind', i.e. solving the wrong problem (Mitroff 1980).

Environments should be viewed as 'webs of conditions and factors' which surround development processes (*cf.* Kling and Scacchi 1982). Environments include labor, economy, technology, application, external and normative environments. They exert influence on development activities, organization, outcomes, and so on.

The notion of a *development group* entails that systems development is carried out by a formally organized group. It has similarities with social institutions (Robey and Markus 1984): it sets mutual expectations; it punishes and gives rewards; it consists of positions and roles filled by people, and so on. A development group can organize itself in alternative ways by specifying the set-up of its positions, roles, authority structures and decision-making rights (Scacchi 1985). Note how this view of the development group differs from the classical view of IS development which still prevails in the software engineering literature, where the nature of systems development is seen more as a technical than social process.

Intentions in systems development are expressed by *objectives*. These are related to general value-orientations and represent what 'one ought to do' or 'what is good' (Klein 1984; Klein and Hirschheim 1993). Objectives have several features that must be kept in mind when studying IS change:

(1) they can be implicitly imposed, for example, by the methods used, or they can be explicitly agreed upon through an open negotiation, or imposed by fiat;

(2) they can be clear or vague (ill-defined);

(3) they can be uni- or multi-functional;

(4) they can be conflictual or a-conflictual.

The components of the definition of systems development form a complicated 'web' of social, technological, and cultural phenomena. The components are not independent of each other, nor are they completely dependent. Rather, we can speak of the totality in which components' features are defined by their interactions with other components — they are thus emergent. A detailed specification of one component is a case of a constrained choice: a choice with regard to one component constrains our freedom to choose the others, for example, identified object systems are constrained largely by pursued objectives. Usually, a major part of these interactions are prefixed by a systems development methodology as will be shown below.

The complexity of perceptions and human interaction in object systems raises the participation issue. Participation can be seen in at least three ways:

(1) as an expediency either to collect needed information or overcome potential resistance to change;

(2) as a prerequisite for creating shared meanings in social reality construction; and

(3) as a moral right to exert influence upon one's destiny in a pluralist society.

While these three views of participation are not necessarily mutually exclusive, they can be linked to different core assumptions about the nature of ISD as a technical, sense-making, or rational argumentation process, and as a political process. As will be seen in chapter 4, these three roles of participation are associated with differing research communities adhering to conflicting beliefs and research methodologies or 'paradigms'.

Features of object systems

Several, even overlapping, object systems can be generated during systems development. These are determined by underlying concept structures and theories. Such mental structures can be used to classify, explicate and give order to phenomena perceived during the ISD. For example a computer system could be viewed as a set of physical states, logical circuitry or a computation process. Many factors affect the construction of concept structures that lead us to identify object systems in systems development: prior experiences, other mental constructs (i.e. familiar analogies) and acquired habits. Vitalari (1984, 1985), for example, noted that experienced and successful analysts perceive the political aspects in systems development while less experienced practitioners do not. Systems development environments and the composition of development groups also have an impact of shared mental models. But the most influential factor is likely to be that of a systems development methodology which is discussed in section 2.2.2.2.

Object systems have a variety of other properties, which are illustrated in figure 2.2. No object system is objectively given (Checkland 1981). Rather people have viewpoints which enable them to perceive object systems. These viewpoints are determined by the concept structures that are applied to make sense of the development phenomena Hence, the notion of the object system and its dependency on the developers' mental models (concept structures) indicates the open-ended, situation-dependent and cyclical nature of IS intervention because the concepts may change due to learning or other influence. Usually, the initial change intervention is motivated by the initial perception of some deficiency in the recognized object system and this perception is strongly influenced by the language which is used by those articulating the deficiency. However, during the development process, language and perceptions are in a constant flux. This insight comes from philosophical hermeneutics (*cf.* Gadamer 1976; Bleicher 1980) which insists that all our understanding begins with some preconceived notions or 'prejudices' to be refined through repeated cycles of interpretations. In each interpretation cycle the understanding shifts and with it the way language is used to articulate the current understanding.

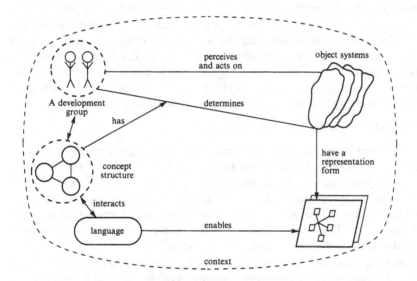

Figure 2.2: Object systems in systems development

Object system classes

One way to classify object systems in systems development is to focus on the general property of the object system the developer wants to target. Three principal perception schemes have dominated the ways in which object systems have been perceived in systems development, these are: *static*, *dynamic* and *hybrid*. Each of these has, to some extent, independently developed its own terminology which the following relates to our fundamental concepts of an object system and its features, particularly in terms of modeling constructs.

Typical of dynamic modeling is the view underlying the transform analysis of the family of structured methodologies based on *processes* (DeMarco 1978; Gane and Sarson 1979; Weinberg 1980). According to DeMarco's version of process representation, the object system is seen as a set of processes connected through data flows which they transform and pass on. A process is anything that transforms data by either changing the format or content of data. If processes are not completely synchronized data are held in stores in between two or more processes. There are always some processes that receive data input from the environment and others that deliver data to the environment after transformation. The environment is represented globally by labeling specific sinks and sources that provide or receive data.

In static modeling, the object system is perceived as a set of static units (or *entities*) which are connected through relationships. Each unit has a set of distinguishing features or properties which are represented as attributes. In hybrid modeling, the object system is perceived as consisting of discrete actors (or *objects*) each of which reacts to stimuli and has a limited view of the system environment. Hence an actor 'knows' something about the kind of stimuli it can receive and the ways it can react: therefore an actor encapsulates its knowledge of the environment in the form of predefined ways of knowing its environment together with a selected set of reaction schemes. The object systems in hybrid models consist of populations of actors which together form the perceived object system behavior.

Representation forms of object systems

Systems developers must find an explicit representation for object systems after they have been identified to communicate it to others and themselves in the development group. Object systems can be represented in multiple ways. Examples of representation forms are free-form text, semiformal notation such as structured English, graphical descriptions, and formal mathematical notations. The chosen representation form depends primarily on the concept structure and its degree of accuracy and formality.

Applying representation forms results in 'object system representations' which correspond to 'information systems models' as used in some parts of the IS and software engineering literature. Object system representations can serve different purposes during the course of ISD: descriptive, predictive, prescriptive, interpretive, and reconstructive.

Philosophical aspects of object systems

Because object systems are not known *a priori* to systems developers but become understood through inquiry, the following two basic issues are important:

(1) the nature of what is investigated (ontology); and

(2) the nature of human knowledge and understanding that can possibly be acquired through different types of inquiry and alternative methods of investigation (epistemology).

Both of these are taken up in some detail later in the book. Ontology is concerned with the fundamental units which are assumed to exist in the object system: the basic stuff that is 'seen'. It can be composed of hard, tangible structures with a concrete material base (realism), or it can be composed of malleable, vague phenomena, which are socially constructed through an intellectual or cultural base of values and concepts (nominalism or idealism).

The epistemological dimension reflects how developers inquire into object systems and see phenomena in them. It affects the format in which the knowledge ('perception') of the object system is represented. There are two positions: the first postulates that all knowledge can be expressed in statements of laws and facts that are positively corroborated by measurement (positivism); the second denies the possibility of positive, observer-independent knowledge, and instead emphasizes sympathetic reason in understanding phenomena (anti-positivism). This leads to the further question of whether an abstract representation of object systems is a sufficient base to inform judgements in ISD or whether design judgements need to be supported by hands-on, concrete experiences. The viewpoint that the power of abstraction is very limited in informing human judgement and should be replaced by concrete experiences (interacting with the world) has been proposed originally by philosophical pragmatism (*cf.* Peirce 1960). In ISD, it has been promulgated by the evolutionary systems development or prototyping school which is discussed in chapter 4.

The three object system classes as discussed above (i.e. process, entity and object) can be used with different ontologies and epistemologies. All three can be interpreted as identifying actually existing elements of the world (realism) or as constructs guiding the social construction of reality (nominalism or idealism). The details of the object system classes are explored in chapters 4 through 7. It should be noted that the notions of ontology and epistemology require a more comprehensive treatment, because they relate to the most fundamental assumptions shared by a research community. These assumptions play a critical role in the way the ontological units (i.e. processes, data and objects or more generally, any object system instance) are used in systems development. Therefore a systematic treatment of ontological and epistemological assumptions should precede the details of object system class analysis. Such a treatment is provided in chapter 3 under the philosophical notion of 'paradigm'.

2.2.2.2 *Definition of information systems development methodology*

The predisposition to believe in the power of methodologies comes from Descartes who proposed that truth is more a matter of proper method than genial insight or divine inspiration. From Descartes' influental writings the concept of methodology entered mathematics and the natural sciences. As these sciences defined what counts as knowledge in the Western world, the concept of method has deeply influenced policies and practices in industrial societies and managing technical or social change (Ellul 1964). It is therefore not surprising that the IS community in so far as it deals with changes in several object system domains have striven hard to develop methodologies. Information systems development methodologies can be defined as follows:

An *information systems development methodology* is an organized collection of concepts, methods, beliefs, values and normative principles supported by material resources.

Its purpose is to help a development group successfully change object systems, that is to perceive, generate, assess, control, and carry out the proposed system changes in them. Methodologies are normative in the sense that they organize sets of behavioral and technical rules into a coherent approach which prescribes how to address major development problems.

A few aspects beg for comment here. First, the idea of an organized collection implies that methodologies are not random sets of rules, but they imply instead some type of coherence and integration between their parts. Second, methodologies are not just rules, but they include concepts and beliefs that define the content and behavior of the object systems (and their possible change) as well as values which state what properties in object systems are good and desirable. In addition to rules, they also point to methods which specify procedures for accomplishing well-defined tasks, and normative principles (such as decision rules and organizing rules) which specify behavioral expectations. Finally, methodologies are closely connected to material resources such as instruments and tools which are drawn upon when the methodology is followed and enacted.

Methodologies currently in use are consistent with our definition. They include concepts and beliefs that enable developers to identify and order phenomena. They suggest a pool of methods, languages and techniques (i.e. normative principles) for representing, selecting and/or implementing the change. Finally, they all employ various resources: manpower, tools, technology, etc. for carrying out ISD.

Features of methodology use

Methodologies must meet several conditions to achieve their change mission. They must be written so that they can be taught, learned and transferred over a wide range of development situations. They must be understandable and socially acceptable. Often their use must be motivated by rewards and sanctions, because a methodology change requires people to change their working habits, thinking and language. Finally, methodologies must be legitimized. Reasons to use them must be accepted and justified by those who decide on their use.

Methodologies differ in many ways. For example, they can sustain alternative beliefs about the type of uncertainty involved in systems design. For this reason they can prefer distinct development strategies. For example, approaches founded on the systems life-cycle notion (Wasserman and Freeman 1983; Yourdon 1982; Cotterman *et al.* 1981) focus on reducing means uncertainty, and propose a linear, stepwise development process to structure the application of appropriate 'means' in the form of methods and tools. They fail to address other types of uncertainties, e.g. effect uncertainty and problem uncertainty noted above, and thus can lead to the error of the third kind. Other methodologies, such as Checkland's soft systems methodology (Checkland 1981), concentrate on problem uncertainty. As a result they think of the development process as a learning cycle.

A methodology's organizing principles prescribe how the development group is to be arranged. They can specify a complete autocracy where systems development is done by outside experts or they can promote genuine participation. A methodology's goals and values can be predetermined and fixed as in software engineering methodologies. However, other methodologies, like Checkland's, emphasize the fuzzy and emergent nature of human goals and values and the need for debate and reflection about them.

Object systems as defined in some methodologies have very little in common with those as defined in others. Methodologies thus act like perceptual filters which identify certain phenomena at the cost of neglecting others. For example, Mumford's ETHICS (1983) and structured analysis and design approaches (DeMarco 1978) have very dissimilar visions of the nature of ISD.

No single methodology covers all aspects of systems development, although some are clearly more comprehensive than others. Nor is there any accepted classification of methodologies that assures complete coverage of the systems life-cycle. However, the following categorization should prove helpful in that it identifies the major foci of some methodologies.

First, different methodologies prefer different object system classes:

(1) A very popular group of methodologies focuses on modeling organizational processes and data flows. These subscribe to a perception of the object system that has become known as process-oriented analysis and design. The best known of these are the family of structured analysis and design methodologies, *cf.* DeMarco (1978), Gane and Sarson (1979), and Yourdon (1989). See also Olle *et al.* (1982) where a broader spectrum of process-oriented methodologies is presented.

(2) Another important group of methodologies shifts the emphasis from processes to representing the organization and its environment as a structured collection of facts and associations among them. These are called data-oriented analysis and design approaches and typically model the organization in terms of entities and relationships. Many variations of these exist, but among the best known are Chen (1976) and Martin (1983). Some of these deal specifically with the question of how to convert one or several data models of user views to a database schema (*cf.* Batini *et al.* 1986).

3) Around 1990 there appeared methodologies which reject the process-data dichotomy. They propose modeling the world in terms of software units that encapsulate both methods and data and which communicate

with each other through messages. These are called object-oriented
analysis and design approaches (Coad and Yourdon 1990).

The distinction between process-, data- and object-oriented methodologies is important, because it reflects different ontologies, i.e. assumptions
about the basic building blocks which constitute the objects system. It
helps to project some order in the terminological Tower of Babel. Most conscious of their terminological base are data-oriented approaches. In the data
modeling literature there is explicit discussion of the concepts of universe
of discourse (data modelers' preferred term for the object system), entity,
attribute, relationship, object, message, method, etc. The most important
details of this terminology are introduced in chapter 7. In contrast to this,
the literature on process-oriented systems modeling approaches has been
much less conscious of their fundamental constructs than the data-oriented
approaches. The notions of process, business function, activity, task, etc.
tend to be very methodology specific or left almost entirely to the interpretation of the user of a methodology. A notable exception to this is the
literature on structured systems specification which gives explicit definitions of the semantics of the domain of change (the equivalent of the object
system), process, data flow, data store, events and terminator in DeMarco
(1979) and Yourdon (1989). Business Systems Planning, explicitly introduces the notion of a 'data class' which is quite different from the notion of
an entity. (A data class is a set of data which is under the control of some
organizational entity and may combine attributes from different entities.)
Also Checkland (1981) discusses the notion of a human activity system and
how to conceptually model it. But most process-oriented methodologies do
not carefully introduce the definitions of all of their basic constructs. To
some extent, the terminology base proposed in this chapter is a first step
to remedy this situation by cross-referencing some basic ontological notions
and concepts. However, when it comes to further details, we can only reflect
the terminological base of the data-oriented approaches in chapter 7. The
corresponding material on process-oriented systems modeling is missing in
chapter 5. We simply follow the terminology of the four methodologies which
are introduced in chapter 5.

Second, not all stages of the systems life-cycle are equally well covered by
methodologies. Therefore, it is helpful to classify methodologies by the stage
(or stages) of the life-cycle to which they specifically address themselves (*cf.*
Davis 1982).

(4) A small number of methodologies help to identify problematic situa-
    tions and object systems for change, i.e. they help sense-making and
    problem formulation (Mitroff 1983) as the front-end of the life-cycle.
    The most comprehensive of these is Checkland (1981) and Checkland
    and Scholes (1990), but Davis' (1982) framework for selecting an infor-
    mation requirements analysis approach is also in this category.

(5) The life-cycle differs as to whether it embraces organization-wide plan-

ning for information systems, or is limited to a single application focus. Only a handful of methodologies have addressed themselves to the organization-wide information systems planning phases. Among these are some primarily process-oriented approaches such as IBM's BSP and BIAIT (Burnstein 1980). Examples of data-oriented information systems planning methodologies are Finkelstein's (1989) Information Systems Engineering and Martin's (1983) Subject Data Base Design.

(6) Another category of methodologies draws on principles of accounting and economics to assess and evaluate the effectiveness and efficiency of system design proposals. They are called cost–benefit analysis and assessment methodologies (Kleijnen 1980; Bjorn-Andersen and Davis 1986). Depending on the organization's preference, these have been applied at the front-end of the life-cycle as part of the feasibility assessment, or at the back-end to evaluate the outcomes of systems development.

(7) The largest group of methodologies address themselves to the middle stages of the life-cycle covering analysis and design. The best known here are the family of process-oriented methodologies.

(8) Eventually system design proposals have to be implemented to obtain workable software and achieve real organizational change. Software engineering methodologies like structured programming help to carry out and implement the technical changes (e.g. Jackson 1975; Boehm 1981; Pressman 1987) and organizational implementation strategies achieve social acceptance (e.g. Keen and Scott-Morton 1978, Kolf and Oppelland 1980).

In chapter 5 we shall explore some of the details and methodologies associated with categories 1, 4, 5 and 7; and in chapters 6 and 7, categories 2 and 3 are explored.

In conclusion it can be said that a systems development methodology links directly to object systems. A methodology 'guides' the choice of object systems through its intrinsic assumptions about the nature of IS as a social or technical system. Methodologies are limited in the kinds of object systems which they address.

The definitions provided above reflect a set of beliefs about the nature of IS and ISD. The background to which developers adhere determines the way a problem is framed and approached. Developers adhering to the same set of beliefs share a certain view of the world which lead to specific ISD behaviors and practices. Hence, the meaning of each definition will change depending upon the background which one brings to bear in interpreting the definition. As will be observed later in the book, each set of beliefs directs attention to different sets of aspects of information systems development resulting from different interpretations of the definitions. When systems are developed, the developers cannot deal with the whole totality of an object system. In building a simplified abstraction of the real object system, they are heavily influenced by a set of beliefs which guide them to pay more attention to some aspects than others. In this sense, systems development methodologies capture a preferred way of developing the system and may reflect the practical progress or learning experience in developing systems which leads to emphasizing new organizational issues in ISD. Section 2.3 provides a guided tour through those aspects which have emerged as important during various stages of the evolution of methodologies. Before we turn to this, we need to round out our basic definitions with a brief review of data modeling concepts.

2.2.3 Definition of data modeling

Our discussion of methodologies has made several connections to data without providing any systematic treatment of data modeling. Such a treatment is important because data modeling occupies a prominent position in the ISD literature.* The term data model has two meanings in the field. Unfortunately, these two senses are quite often mixed which adds to the terminological confusion (Schmid 1983). In the first sense a data model is a set of conceptual and notational conventions which help to perceive, organize and specify some data. In this sense the term 'data model' is sometimes combined with the word 'language', as for example in data modeling language or data description language (DDL). In the second sense, a data model means the outcome of using a data modeling language in some specific situation. In this second sense, the term data model is often replaced by the term *schema*. To clarify the difference between the two meanings, consider the following example. In accounting, the data modeling language consists of the terms and principles of double-entry bookkeeping that guide our perception and arrangement of economic data. The schema is the chart of accounts for a specific company. The distinction between data model language and its use (in a schema) implies that the first must exist before the second can be created. Usually they are also developed by different people. Data modeling is the activity of creating a data model (in the sense of a schema). If the data model becomes accepted by the organization it will produce changes in the organizational knowledge base. We shall therefore define data modeling as a change process, similar in definition to that of information systems development as provided above:

---

* In the literature, it is not uncommon to see the term 'information modeling' used as well. Data modeling, however, deals not only with linguistic issues but also technical ones such as data structures and storage organization. Information modeling or conceptual modeling are often used to connote that part of data modeling which deals only with linguistic modeling. While this is indeed the focus of this book, we have decided to use the term 'data modeling' so as not to add to the already confusing terminological jungle of information systems development.

Data modeling is a *change process* taken with respect to *object systems* consisting of data and its uses in a set of *environments* by a *development group* using a *representational form* to achieve or maintain some *objectives*.

In other words data modeling produces changes in the representation form, structure, and use of linguistic constructs (language change) that form the environment for communications through information systems use. The *change process* relates to the changing of the form, content and use of the data. Data modeling can accordingly consist of several partially overlapping *object systems*. The target of the change process is data, i.e. all invariances that are stored and manipulated in the computer system and their potential meanings for different users of the IS. In the data modeling literature this change target is typically referred to as a 'universe of discourse' (UoD) or the representation of the UoD (van Griethuysen 1982). For example, the UoD for a payroll system would include employees, their names, ages, salaries, dependents, departments, and their former representations in the payroll data base. In this book the terms UoD and object system are used as synonyms in discussing the potential target of data modeling. There are many ways to classify object systems in data modeling. As noted above, it is possible to differentiate between three families of object system classes: static, dynamic and hybrid. Most well-known data modeling approaches such as entity-relationship modeling, cover only the static features of the target. The object system is perceived as static units (entities) connected through possibly changing relationships. Dynamic modeling approaches in data modeling are fewer in number. They conceive object systems as dynamic systems consisting of state representations which change over time (Jackson 1983). More recently hybrid data modeling approaches have started to emerge in the form of object-oriented data modeling. They combine dynamic and static features of object systems. In this approach, the methods (or processes) are specified along with the data through 'strong typing' (see chapter 7). Basically the data are encapsulated with the methods so that the data 'knows' which methods apply to achieve desired results. For example, account deposit data might evoke methods for updating accounts and printing receipts.

The *representation forms* applied in data modeling are typically semiformal graphical notations and formal languages such as first-order predicate logic. The set of *environments* for data modeling refers to 'the set of conditions and factors' which include different stakeholders involved in data modeling and the way they are organized, information systems strategy and policy statements, standards followed, tools used (e.g. data dictionaries, case tools), database administration principles, and application areas covered. Typical data modeling tools cover data dictionary generation, editing *entity-realtionship* (E-R) diagrams or structure charts, and so forth. The development group consists of the assembly of people who are involved in conducting the data modeling exercise. The *objectives* refer to goals of data modeling such as increasing the return on the data resource investment, control of data definition and conflicts, and minimization of errors through higher quality of data (accuracy, timeliness, etc.), business process reengineering, and so forth.

Data modeling focuses primarily on linguistic phenomena. This is not to deny that it also is concerned with finding efficient storage structures. This is still a significant design problem in data modeling. All data modeling, however, presumes either implicitly or explicitly some form of modeling of data meaning, because it is only through the knowledge of data meaning that an understanding of the design problem as stated above is possible. Thus, data modeling starts initially with modeling data meaning. Therefore, it is not surprising that several language theories and philisophies of language have been used as a source of inspiration for the development of data modeling approaches. Accordingly, with regard to the philosophical and conceptual foundations of data modeling, we shall distinguish between fact-based and rule-based data modeling which can be derived from the two main camps of linguistic philosophy: analytical and hermeneutic (continental) philosophy. The key ideas of data modeling will be taken up from a philosophical perspective in chapters 3, 6 and 7.

2.3 Seven Generations of ISD Methodologies

2.3.1 Background

The field of IS was created in response to certain business needs which the advent of computers created for users and corporate executives. Teaching IS was to provide the knowledge and training of professionals who could help organizations to capitalize on information technology. To a large extent the spectacular increase in IS professionals and research output (witness that approximately 20 new scientific journals have been created between 1989 and 1993) is prompted by the accelerated rate of change. Until the advent of computers, information technology evolved relatively slowly. For example, it took over two centuries until desk calculators were widely used in business after the first one was built by Pascal to aid his father with his administrative duties in the 1640s. Computer-based systems have leaped a generation roughly every five to seven years. With each successive generation, new application systems have to be created in much shorter time spans, often counted in months rather than years.

But it is not only the pace of change that creates a challenge. Much larger and much more complicated systems than ever before require a new profession dedicated to building computer-based information systems. In order to cope with the complexities of ISD, practitioners looked to science and its offspring, engineering, for inspiration. This gave birth to the notion of methodologies as preplanned procedures to streamline the building of systems. It is fruitful to conceive of the emergence of different ISD methodologies in evolutionary terms. Couger (1973) was perhaps the first to document the evolution of what he called 'systems analysis techniques'. He described their evolution in terms of four distinct generations. Nine years later, he expanded the evolution to include five generations (Couger 1982). Others have also tried to document the emergence of new methodologies but not so much from an historical perspective but rather as a comparative review or feature analysis (*cf.* Cotterman *et al.* 1981; Olle *et al.* 1982, 1983; Maddison *et al.* 1983; Avison and Fitzgerald 1988). In this section we explore the emergence of ISD methodologies in a fashion similar to that of Couger, but instead of focusing on 'techniques' we specifically look at 'methodologies', so it is not surprising that our categorization is quite different from his.

To meet the challenge of keeping the historical review concise, we use a broad brush to highlight the prominent features which characterize important directions among the hundreds of methodologies that have been proposed over the years. These are summarized in figures 2.3 and 2.4.

Briefly sketched, we see the evolution of ISD methodologies to have taken the form of eight overlapping stages or generations: The first stage is not really a generation of methodologies. It could be referred to as the era of the 'seat-of-the-pants approaches'. We consider this a pre-methodology era and reserve the term 'generation' for approaches that were actually codified. History is, of course, too complex for any single classification to do justice to its richness. As will be seen, the grouping of the methodologies into 'generations' is inspired by certain theoretical and philosophical principles discussed in later chapters of the book, particularly those associated with paradigmatic assumptions (see chapters 3, 4 and 6). The following discussion of the methodologies suggests a possible, but by no means absolute, ordering of methodologies and its validity is open to debate.

2.3.2 Pre-methodology era

First administrative information systems were built in the mid-1950s. At that time the only conceivable system design task was programming and specifying computer room operations (Somogyi and Galliers 1987). To accomplish these complex tasks system developers often followed a variety of systematic practices. New practices were invented as needed, and they were usually very technology oriented. Those practices which seemed to work in previous development projects were subsequently mobilized again. They became the developer's 'rules-of-thumb' and, in a sense, his/her 'methodology' (*cf.* Episkopou 1987). They were typically passed on to other system developers, often by word of mouth. These practices were typically not codified and sometimes not even written down, although diagramming techniques such a flow charting were fairly well-documented. Systems development was considered a technical process which was to be undertaken by technical people. Even though some large systems were implemented in the military (such as SAGE: Semi Automated Ground Environment) and industry (SABRE: the first on-line reservation system), many less ambitious projects failed due to the lack of methodical guidelines and theoretical conceptions of IS.

Generation	Principal Management or Organizational Issue
1. Formal Life-Cycle Approaches	Control of SDLC; guidance of analysts/programmers through standardization.
2. Structured Approaches	Productivity (information requirements quality assurance to meet '5Cs' – clear, concise, cost-effective, comprehensive and complete specifications); better maintainable systems; control of analysts/programmers (division of labor, e.g. Kraft 1977).
3. Prototyping and Evolutionary Approaches	Speed and flexibility of ISD (SDLC methodologies take too long and are too rigid); overcoming analysts/user communication gap with technical specifications; emphasis is on getting the right kind of system vs. getting the system right.
4. Socio-Technical, Participatory Approaches	Control of ISD by users through participation; conflict management in ISD; joint optimization: cost-effectiveness and better QWL through technology.
5. Sense-Making and Problem Formulation Approaches	Dealing with multiple perspectives in problem framing; software development as social reality construction.
6. Trade-Union Led Approaches	Labor/management conflict; workers' rights; industrial democracy.
7. Emancipatory Approaches	Overcoming barriers to effective communication due to power and social differentiation (e.g. blockage, bias, jargon, ambiguity); eliminating repression and furthering emancipatory effects of ISD (ISD as social learning and therapy, e.g. questioning dominant forms of thinking, improving access to facts and arguments, removing unwarranted uses of power, etc.).

Figure 2.3: Summary of seven generations of ISD methodologies with associated management or organizational issues

2.3.3 First generation: the emergence of formal life-cycle approaches

The end of the pre-methodology era can be roughly dated to the mid-1960s when several influential treatises on methods, tools and general principles of system development appeared. Before that time, Canning (1956) is likely to be the very first treatment on life-cycle methods to develop computer-based information systems (*cf.* Agresti 1986). Others refer to Rosove (1967) as the

Generations 1 through 3 generally imply external control of ISD and assume an organizational equilibrium model emphasizing regulation (top down or self-regulation in the case of 3).

Generation 3 need not be a stand-alone approach, but can be used to complement any of the other approaches and then takes on their values and ideological flavor.

Generations 4 and 5 acknowledge a conflict model of organization and favor conflict resolution by compromise through participation of all affected parties. Otherwise they are similar to 1 and 2.

Generation 6 presumes a class conflict model which affects organizational life. It attempts to place control of ISD in the hands of the working class, either through trade-union representation or direct participation.

Generation 7 presumes a social conflict model of organizations, but does not predefine any specific groupings which are intrinsically hostile (like social classes); it also favors conflict resolution through negotiation, but requires specific conditions to be met for consensus solutions to be valid or rational. These conditions are to assure equal chances for access to relevant knowledge, to be heard, to influence others (no power asymmetries) and to question proposals, claims, excuses, etc.

Figure 2.4: Comparative observations on the seven generations

first textbook source for the systems development process. The first higher level system specification methodology was proposed by Young and Kent in 1958 (Young and Kent 1958). Soon after that, the CODASYL committee proposed a formal specification language called information algebra (1961).

An important early contribution came from Langefors, the founder of the 'Scandinavian School' of systems design. In a number of articles and books of the early and mid-1960s, he presented the foundations for a theory of systemeering (as the higher level systems analysis and design which preceded programming was called by Scandinavian researchers). These were later organized into a major scholarly treatment of systems development called *Theoretical Analysis of Information Systems* (Langefors 1973). Langefors' work covered a wide range of areas in information systems development ranging from information requirements and organizational modeling, information analysis and logical systems design to algorithms for technical design. Some of his models resulted in high level formal specifications of the computer system which could be analyzed and later used for optimal computer system design (which was a major task in the days of magnetic tapes). The major contributions in Langefors' work were a theoretical distinction between logical and physical design called the 'infological and datalogical levels'. He also outlined foundations for data modeling (through his notion of object system models), logical program design (through his concepts of precendence and composition analysis), and an iterative, recursive approach to system design problems (through his notion of design methods for imperceivable systems). Langefors was also far-sighted enough to take into account problems of interpretation and user participation in stating information requirements through his notion of an infological equation. Many of these notions were taken up and operationalized by his students, especially Lundeberg, Bubenko, Solvberg and Goldkuhl. Each of them worked on the development of more refined and operational methodologies based on Langefors' ideas.

In 1969 another influential treatment of MIS development appeared (Blumenthal 1969). It focused on the front-end and higher level analysis of systems development and presented an information systems framework of generic information processing modules. In part these modules would be shared by major information subsystems and in part they were unique to a single information subsystem. Blumenthal also noted the importance of information systems planning for requirements determination and prioritization of projects. He suggested 'planned evolution' as a methodology for orderly, organization-wide IS development based on his experiences with the System Development Corporation (*cf.* Rosove 1967).

A third trigger for the development of methodologies came from software engineering. In 1968 the term 'software engineering' was coined by a NATO convened workshop to assess the state of software production and possible avenues for improvement (Shaw 1990). The use of this term gained popularity in the 1970s and is now often used to refer to the fairly well-structured methods and tools of program design, implementation and testing under the assumptions that systems requirements are given.

Overall it became quite clear that in order to grow and to be taken seriously, the IS profession needed to codify its techniques (Somogyi and Galliers 1987; Friedman and Cornford 1989). Especially in the late 1960s far too many development projects were failures and it became necessary to formalize practices of systems development so that the successful lessons of the past could be documented and passed on. Codified techniques proliferated and the beginnings of piecing them together into more formal 'methodologies' began. Organizations grew up to help in the codification process (for example the National Computing Centre in the United Kingdom, *cf.* Daniels and Yeates 1969, 1971). Courses in systems analysis and design became commonplace in both public and private institutions. More and more methodologies emerged (e.g. Glans *et al.* 1968; Burch and Strater 1974; Millington 1978; Lee 1978). Systems were built from the requirements elicited by the systems analyst from the users. User requirements elicitation was considered a difficult but largely noncontroversial exercise: users had to be asked what information they needed in their jobs. This formed the basis of user requirements. Additionally in this generation, a more comprehensive strategy was taken for the entire exercise of systems development, from the initial stage when a system was considered, through to its implementation and maintenance. This became known as the 'systems development life-cycle' (SLC). It divided systems development into distinct stages which allowed the development process to be better managed. It also gave rise to advancements in project management (Cleland and King 1975) and information systems planning (McLean and Soden 1977). The ISD methodologies or approaches of the first generation have been described as the 'traditional approaches' by Wood-Harper and Fitzgerald (1982), 'the classic approaches' by Hirschheim, Klein and Newman (1991), and 'second and third generation systems analysis techniques' by Couger (1982). Systems development continued to be viewed as a technical process to be undertaken by technical experts aimed at technical solutions. Hence the technological issues dominated the first generation methodologies.

With the increasing codification of a technical 'orthodoxy' of information systems development, there also appeared the first critical analyses. They either drew attention to the organizational problems causing many 'IS failures' (Argyris 1971; Lucas 1975) or called for consideration of fundamentals insisting that IS development and use must be seen in the broader context of human inquiry and its limits (Ulrich 1983; Kirsch and Klein 1977, Kent 1978). These critiques were informed by a different context, one that is informed by social analysis (Kling 1985) and provided the first window on the organizational context in ISD. Later generations would build on this.

2.3.4 Second generation: the emergence of the structured approaches

While the methodologies of the first generation helped the developer to build systems by offering a procedural structure for development, they failed to adequately deal with two perennial problems: changing user requirements and understandable system designs. From the developers' point of view, the users constantly changed their requirements which meant that it was difficult, if not impossible, to design the system. There was a need to freeze user requirements so the development could be undertaken. From the users' perspective, it was difficult to know in advance what the implemented system was going to look like. Analysts, it was claimed, failed to adequately describe what the system would embody in its finished form. Computer jargon was often viewed as the culprit. And users often felt the systems developers could not, or would not, speak in a way which was comprehensible to them.

These obstacles were felt to be overcome by the development of two methods associated with the so-called 'structured methodologies' of the second generation. These methodologies made in theory and practice a clear distinction between the logical and the physical design and also offered methods to speciy the system both on the logical and the physical levels. Moreover, they suggested means (albeit insufficient) to map logical design onto physical designs. Two major sources of structured methodologies can be found. In the Scandinavian tradition these methodologies emerged from attempts to codify and refine Langefors' ideas into a workable set of procedures and representation techniques. The most well-known representative of these attempts is the ISAC methodology (Lundeberg *et al.* 1981) which was fully operational in the mid 1970s. Another stream of structured methodologies originated in the U.S. as a logical extension to 'structured programming' (see Colter 1982 for an excellent overview of the evolution of these methodologies). Structured methodologies such as SADT, SSADM, and SA proliferated (*cf.* DeMarco 1978; Gane and Sarson 1979; Yourdon and Constantine 1979; Weinberg 1980). The methodologies of this generation are referred to by Couger (1982) as 'fourth generation techniques'. They also facilitate handling of other important design issues which had become critical such as user friendly interfaces, and ergonomically sound design. The latest enhancements to structured methodologies involve the use of automated tools to assist the analyst (i.e. CASE and integrated CASE tools); for an early discussion see Teichroew and Hershey (1977).

One goal of the structured methodologies was to permit more manageable systems development through 'sign off' and 'structured walk-through' procedures. The former permitted the analyst to work to an agreed logical specification with the users which was then signed off by the users. The latter, structured walk-throughs (at least in theory) permitted the users to better understand what the finished product would look like as they were systematically 'walked-through' the details of the system design during formal sessions.

With second generation methodologies, systems development was still perceived as a technical process but one which had social consequences to be considered. Systems development is seen as a form of engineering: from software engineering (Boehm 1976) to information engineering (Land 1989). The engineering metaphor reinforces the focus on the technological issues inherited from first generation methodologies, but the engineering metaphor also suggests more sophisticated ways to deal with the complexity of IS (as opposed to the technician view in the first generation methodologies).

2.3.5 Third generation: the emergence of prototyping and evolutionary approaches

Several thorny problems with systems development became more pressing in the late 1970s: as organizations' environments continued to change at an increasing pace due to increased competition, internationalization and the like, so too did user requirements. No longer could users wait two to three years for their systems to be developed, nor could they wait that long to find out that the system eventually delivered no longer met their needs. An equally serious problem was that the communication gap between professional analysts and users continued to grow as computer-based information systems addressed increasingly complicated applications. At the same time technical sophistication and platforms to design and implement systems improved at a fast pace which provided opportunities for faster and more productive systems implementation. Hence the idea emerged that users needed first-hand experience of the software they are going to use. With new technological tools this software could be delivered quickly and the users could experiment with it so as to 'get a better feeling' of what the final system would be like. This was the purpose behind evolutionary (Lucas 1978, p. 44) or adaptive (Keen 1980) systems development and prototyping (Earl 1978; Naumann and Jenkins 1982; Alavi 1984; Budde *et al.* 1984). Simply stated, a prototype is an experimental version of a system which is used to improve communication and user feedback (and sometimes to demonstrate technical feasibility or efficiency of new software designs; Floyd 1984, p. 3). A prototype is a scaled down variant of the final system which exhibits some of its salient features and thereby allows the users hands-on experimentation to understand the interfaces or computational power. When prototyping first emerged, no clear distinction was made to evolutionary systems development. Following Iivari (1982), we can speak of evolutionary systems development if the prototype continues to be improved until 'it becomes the system' (Lantz 1986; early examples *cf.* Keen and Scott-Morton 1978). Early prototyping was generally thought to contain five phases:

Identify the basic requirements; develop a design that meets these requirements;

implement the design;

experiment with the prototype noting good and bad features; and

revise and enhance the prototype accordingly.

Through prototyping, a number of the problems associated with linear 'life-cycle' methodologies could be overcome. Users could tell much earlier on if the system under development would meet their needs. If not, it could be modified now rather than waiting until it was finished. Additionally, prototyping allowed users who may have had difficulties in formulating and articulating their requirements to work with a prototype, thereby allowing them a much better chance to accurately specify their requirements. And all this without the delays typically associated with life-cycle methodologies. In this generation, prototyping and 'evolutionary development' are seen as an advancement over standard life-cycle approaches (Hawgood 1982). Systems development through prototyping, like the previous generation, was still perceived as a technical process but one which had social consequences which had to be considered. The flexibility of prototyping allows analysts and users to be more sensitive to other issues than just technological ones if they so choose (such as work design or ergonomic aspects). Experience and work pressures would naturally lead them to consider a broader range of aspects that affect 'usability', be they technical or organizational.

2.3.6 Fourth generation: the emergence of socio-technical, participative approaches

The methodologies of the second and third generations advanced the field greatly but they were still plagued by deficiencies with which a number of individuals in the IS community still felt uncomfortable. For one, the level of user involvement permitted in the structured approaches was not considered sufficient by researchers who also had practical experience such as Bostrom and Heinen (1977), Mumford (1981), DeMaio (1980), and Land and Hirschheim (1983). They felt that sign offs and structured walkthroughs were potentially helpful but were fundamentally misguided in their ability to elicit true user involvement. A second concern was with the focus of development. System development approaches had traditionally focused on the technical system rather than the social system. This led to information systems which might have been technically elegant, but were not ideal from a social or work standpoint. They produced work environments which were at best no worse than before the system was introduced but often decreased the quality of working life. This was perceived to be a missed opportunity by the socio-technical community which suggested ISD should lead to both an optimal social as well as technical system. In contrast then, the fourth generation approaches used systems development as a vehicle to rethink the social work environment in which the new system would be implemented. Issues such as job satisfaction, learning, opportunities for advancement with the development and use of new skills rose to the fore. In this generation we see the emergence of the participative systems development approaches, e.g. ETHICS (Mumford 1983); PORGI (Oppelland and Kolf 1980); and Pava's (1983) STS approach. These methodologies all focus on:

(1) having the users not only be involved in systems development but take control of the process; and

(2) redesigning the work situation leading to an optimal social and technical system through systems development.

The number of systems developed using participative approaches such as ETHICS is not very large so it is difficult to assess their success rate. However, research on the use of participative systems design methodologies has reported positive results (cf. Hirschheim 1983, 1985a). Clearly another difference with this generation of methodologies is the movement away from viewing systems development as a technical process. Instead, systems development is viewed jointly as a social and technical process; for example ETHICS through separate teams focuses equally on both the technical and the organizational issues.

2.3.7 Fifth generation: the emergence of sense-making and problem formulation approaches

At approximately the same time as participative methodologies were emerging, other approaches were being developed to overcome a number of shortcomings in the structured approaches. One significant concern surrounded the issue of problem formulation. Earlier generations adopted the position that while problem formulation might not have been easy, it could, nonetheless, be tackled in a relatively straightforward way by adapting the scientific approach to problem solving (*cf.* Newell and Simon's 1972 theory of problems solving). Not everyone agreed with this. Checkland (1981), for example, presented his Soft System Methodology (SSM) as an alternative which insisted upon a richer interpretation of the 'problems of problem formulation'. Checkland felt that prior methodologies conceived of the problem which the system was to overcome in too narrow a view. Problems, or perhaps more precisely user requirements, were not easily articulated, in fact it may be misleading to assume that a problem 'exists' rather that one is constructed between various 'stakeholders' adhering to differing perspectives. According to Checkland, SSM tools such as rich pictures and concepts like root definitions and description technique, what he calls conceptual modeling (this should not be confused with conceptual modeling in the conceptual schema development, see 2.4.2.2), allow for successful problem constructions more so than formal problem definitions as advocated in management science and kindred schools of thought (*cf.* Dumdum 1993 for a comparison of the different problem formulation support features of SSM, ETHICS and structured approaches).

Using SSM as a base, two additional methodologies emerged which attempted not only to apply SSM during ISD in a systematic manner, but to include insights from other methodologies: MULTIVIEW (Wood-Harper *et al.* 1985; Avison and Wood-Harper 1990) and FAOR (Schafer *et al.* 1988). Each of these embraced the need for 'multiple perspectives' and adopted vehicles for implementing it. Others in the IS community, arguing along similar lines, felt the need to develop approaches which would cater for a better mutual understanding to take place between the users and the developers. The term which was generally used to denote this was 'sense-making' (*cf.* Boland and Day 1982; Banbury 1987). More specifically, sense-making can be defined as 'the modes in which a group interacts to interpret their environment and arrive at socially shared meanings.' (*cf.* overview in Klein and Hirschheim 1987a, p. 288)

Capitalizing on these conceptual developments, a number of system development projects were initiated focusing specifically on vehicles and tools to facilitate sense-making; for example FLORENCE (Bjerknes and Bratteteig 1984, 1985) and MARS (Mathiassen and Andersen 1985). The latter in fact has grown into a systems development approach which could be termed 'the professional work practices-based approach' (Andersen *et al.*

1990) (see chapter 5). While these projects cannot be called methodologies in their own right, they have nevertheless produced a number of methods and tools which could be used in the development of a methodology for sense- making, e.g. diary keeping (Jepsen *et al.* 1989), mappings (Lanzara and Mathiassen 1984), and use of metaphors (Madsen 1989). As many of these methodologies are fairly new or currently being developed, we cannot say they are more effective in producing successful systems. Clearly another difference with this generation of methodologies is the movement away from viewing systems development as a purely technical process. It is conceived as mostly a social process, grounded on an explicit philosophical basis which is sensitive to the organizational and broader social context of ISD. The philosophical foundations for the fifth generation were based on the later Wittgenstein's *Philosophical Investigations*. They were then further developed by the revival of the phenomenological and hermeneutic tradition (*cf.* the review in Boland 1985, 1991).

2.3.8 Sixth generation: the emergence of the trade-union led approaches

Somewhat concurrent with the development of third generation methodologies and to a large extent as an antithetical reaction to the ideological underpinnings and negative social effects of the first and second generation approaches, a trade-union based strategy to ISD was proposed (Kubicek 1983). It focused on the interests of the work force, or more specifically on the trade union representatives of the work force, and how they could control systems development. One segment of the IS community, spearheaded by a group of Scandinavian researchers, saw the need to embark on system development projects which put control in the hands of the work force rather than management. They felt that socio-technical approaches were a form of manipulation to reduce worker resistance to systems which served mostly the interests of managers and owners and offered little to improve the position of the workers. Using action research (Sandberg 1985) they developed a set of guidelines, tools and techniques which would allow the trade unions to dictate the direction and outcome of the systems development exercise and escape entrapment in systems thinking and methodologies laden with managerial biases.

The four most prominent projects which implemented this strategy were: the Norwegian 'Iron and Metal Project' (Nygaard 1975); DEMOS (Carlson *et al.* 1978; Ehn and Sandberg 1983); DUE (Kyng and Ehn 1985) and UTOPIA (Ehn *et al.* 1983; Howard 1985; Bodker *et al.* 1987). The first three have been called 'first generation projects' and the lastr a 'second generation project' by Ehn and Kyng (1987) as a way of distinguishing their main thrusts: first generation projects focused on 'supporting democratic planning' while second generation projects added in the idea of 'designing tools for skilled workers'. As in the sense-making approaches, these projects have not produced a particular methodology, but rather a set of tools, techniques and principles which could form the basis of a methodology. Taken as a whole, the loose assembly of these tools, techniques and principles has been termed the 'collective resource approach' by Ehn and Kyng (1987).

Recently, the approach has evolved to include what is termed 'cooperative design' (Kyng 1991; Greenbaum and Kyng 1991). While this name is suggestive of a movement closer to the participative approaches, cooperative design also has the goal of keeping the control of systems development in the hands of the trade unions under the rubric of 'democratic planning'. Little research has been done to evaluate how effective this approach is in developing successful systems and safeguarding labor interests at the some time. Some proponents such as Ehn (1988) claim positive results, while others shed some doubt on its efficacy to represent genuine worker interests against management (Kraft and Bansler 1988, 1992). Systems development is fundamentally conceived as very much a social political process rather than a technical one.

2.3.9 Seventh generation: the emergence of emancipatory approaches

This latest generation is very much in the making with no examples or strict methodologies available. It focuses on emancipation and adopts features of the previous generations. It takes its motivation from the work of Habermas' (1984) *Theory of Communicative Action.* It too conceives of systems development as a social process and sees the need for sense-making (what is called mutual understanding), but where it differs is in its orientation toward emancipation which is striven for through the use of rational or emancipatory discourse. Communication comes to the fore in this approach and hence vehicles are developed to overcome obstacles to free and undistorted communication. The goal of systems development is a system which would not only support emancipatory discourse but also mutual understanding for all its users. Some progress has been made in this direction in the development of projects and tools to support the emancipatory ideal. The SAMPO project (Lehtinen and Lyytinen 1983, Auramaki *et al.* 1988, 1992a,b) provides an approach based on discourse analysis which is supportive of the emancipatory theme. Other work suggests how the emancipatory ideal might be applied in the context of ISD (e.g. Lyytinen and Klein 1985; Lyytinen 1986; Ngwenyama 1987; Lyytinen and Hirschheim 1988; Hirschheim and Klein 1989; Ngwenyama 1991; Klein and Hirschheim 1991; Hirschheim and Klein 1991; and Hirschheim, Klein and Lyytinen 1991). But as of yet, progress has been primarily on the conceptual front (*cf.* Lyytinen 1992, Hirschheim and Klein 1994) and there are no approaches which implement this emancipatory theme nor specific systems development projects which have adopted it.

The social and philosophical basis of the seventh generation methodologies suggests that systems development must rely on understanding the users' work language (Klein and Truex 1994) and other experiential knowledge that can only be acquired through participation in a community's forms of life. System development is science insofar as work practices can be 'rationally reconstructed' (Hirschheim and Klein 1994) which puts them on a clear conceptual foundations as a prerequisite for their 'rationalization'. However, as systems development means changing forms of life, it is invariably bound up with organizational politics that threaten its rationality. These approaches guide developers to focus more on the organizational and symbolic issues related to IS use rather than on thinking of technology alone.

2.4 Evolution of Data Modeling

Somewhat concomitant with the ending of the pre-methodology era and the arrival of the first generation of ISD methodologies, data modeling as an area of concern began to surface. Basically, data modeling grew out of the techniques of data organization and file design which led to the development of database technology around the mid-1960s (see e.g. Senko 1975). It should also be seen in connection with the need for data independence, data abstraction and the evolution of knowledge representation schemes. This, of course, was not apparent from the beginning. Furthermore, the natural connections between data modeling and requirements specification in the systems analysis phase were largely ignored in the beginning (*cf.* Kahn 1982, Sundgren 1973). In part this can be explained by specialization: there was insufficient communication between traditional systems analysts and the emergent database community.

In order to see how various themes emerged and are interrelated, we distinguish between two periods in this section. The first of these daringly collapses the evolution of record keeping techniques in all of the pre-database technology into a single era: about 5000 years in which human kind progressed from using simple written icons or hieroglyphics to extensive systems of automated record keeping. The only excuse for this extreme simplification is that we are not primarily concerned with the history of data organization, but with the evolutionary role of data modeling.

2.4.1 Pre-database architecture: from the Phoenicians to file organization

Modern civilization depends to a large extent on the possibility of keeping and retrieving written records. This is impossible without some form of record organization. Ever since the code of Hamurabi went into effect about 5000 years ago, the predominant form of record keeping was either in library scrolls (books) or formatted lists of alphabetical and numerical strings. The latter were used to describe Phoenician merchant records, army supplies, census data, etc. Even today the concept of text files is separate from formatted files. The basic unit of a formatted files is a record, i.e. a collection of predefined data items which are grouped together into one unit with a predefined format. Record organization improves the effectiveness of data storage and retrieval when compared to retrieving specific items from an unstructured text file.

Until the arrival of advanced file technology, the grouping of data items into records was determined by the purpose and the physical limitations of the storage medium. All data (and only those) which were perceived to belong together was to be combined into one record. But, no more than what could physically be inscribed could be stored together (e.g. a 19th century ledger card can hold more data than a 19th century B.C. clay tablet). Beginning with the U.S. census in 1890, ledger cards and paper records were converted to punch cards. The 'unit record' concept was born: a punch card is the physical medium not only for storing and retrieving one record, but also for performing all other 'data processing operations', such as sorting, merging, calculating, and extracting.

Early databases were, in essence, little more than direct extensions of the unit record concept to large file systems of the type described. They provided a single level of data description, making no distinction between logical and physical levels. Thus no separate views of data were possible; the data model embedded in the program was determined by the engineer who had decided the technical characteristics of the machine readable medium, in particular punch cards and magnetic tapes.

From the viewpoint of efficiency and ease of maintenance it is natural to store all records of a particular type physically together on one type of medium and call this collection of records a file. The set of all machine readable files is the first definition of a database. This definition carries over from punch cards to magnetic tapes to sequentially organized disk files.

The introduction of magnetic tapes and disks, however, brought one major technical advance in that it helped to separate logical and physical records. Under disk or tape organization it is no longer true that the unit of retrieval is the same as the unit of data processing operation. This was well-reflected already in the design of high level programming languages such as COBOL or RPG in the 1960s. In this architecture, a physical record is all the data recorded between two physical inter-block gaps or on one (hardware) part of the disk such as a track or sector. This may very well be more or less than one logical record. Hence, we have one unit for storing and retrieving — the physical record or block — and another for specifying logical operations such as sorting, merging, and formatting etc. The collection of data fields treated as a unit internally (as determined by program logic or software) is called a logical record or application record. But the separation of logical and physical levels to organize files was found to be insufficient because programs were not well-insulated from changes in logical data organization (such as sorting order) or in data representation. A striving for higher levels of data independence led gradually to an increase in the number of levels in the subsequent generations of database architecture.

2.4.2 The emergence and evolution of advanced database architectures

As noted above, most early file organizations provided a single level of description. No separate user views were possible. Later file organizations distinguished between two levels but were still insufficient in providing a necessary degree of data independence. Therefore more advanced database organizations started to emerge in the mid-1960s which first tried to address data independence by a more complete specification of two level architectures and later on by introducing three level architectures.

2.4.2.1 Two level database architectures

A major advancement in database architectures occurred in 1971 with the publishing of the CODASYL DBTG report. The report sought to develop a database architecture that would provide fuller data independence. It suggested a two level architecture, including as separate concepts 'database schemas' and 'user subschemas' on the logical level. This separation was shown to lead to higher data independence. Here the database schema provided a centralized logical description of the data whereas the user subschemas provided a view of data as seen by the user (through a query language) or a program. Changes in the data had to be reflected in the user view only if that part of the centralized data description was changed (and not necessarily even then). In addition the DBTG committee later outlined a device media control language to allocate, manage and monitor physical storage devices. The publication of the DBTG report initiated a heated debate on the desired properties of the two level architecture, and especially what should be the logical and computational properties of the data description language at the centralized level. Originally the DBTG report suggested a network model to model the logical organization of the data. The model had some clear deficiencies such as the ban on n:m relationships, and no recursive relationships which were later removed from the standard. However, the deficiencies in the network model led at the same time to suggest two alternative data models: the hierarchical model and another as a theoretically clean and more advanced concept — the relational model (Codd 1970). The network, hierarchical and relational models formed the basis for the structuring of database systems for the next two decades to come, and different database management systems founded on the alternative data models proliferated.

2.4.2.2 The ANSI/X3/SPARC three level architecture

Though the two level architecture with separate database schemas and user schemas was a major advancement in the field (especially how these were implemented in the relational model) the architecture was still insufficient. It was shown to have two major problems:

(1) it could not easily provide mappings between databases described using different data models, and

(2) several scholars showed that the data description languages were fraught with several deficiences in describing the logical properties of data that were due to their record orientation (see Kent 1978, Kent 1983a,b, Senko 1975, 1977).

Therefore a more advanced notion of database architecture started to emerge in the mid-1970s which was called the three level architecture (for the evolution see e.g. Senko 1975, Senko *et al.* 1973, Engles 1972).

The concept of a three layered architecture comprising a three level data description structure was officially proposed in the ANSI/X3/SPARC proposal in 1975 (hereafter referred to as ANSI/SPARC) as a foundation for the next generation database standard. The proposal specified the database management levels in terms of 'internal schema', 'conceptual schema', and 'external schemas'. Broadly speaking, the internal schema is the level in which the physical storage and organization of the data is managed. It is concerned with the way in which the data is actually stored, managed and monitored. The external schema is the level closest to the users, i.e. the one describing the data as seen by the individual users. The conceptual schema was referred to as a 'level of indirection' between the other two and was defined as a community user view. ANSI/SPARC felt that the conceptual view was concerned with the meaning of the data and the conceptual schema should capture this meaning.

Unfortunately, it was never entirely clear from the ANSI/SPARC proposal what the conceptual schema concept entailed. Referring to it as a community user view, a level of indirection between the internal and external views, the specification of the meaning of the data, or an enterprise view of data, captures the spirit of what is meant but still leaves a great deal unanswered. For example, external schemas map onto the conceptual schema, but yet are expected to have some degree of data definition independence from the conceptual schema. Moreover, the proposal allowed for a direct linking of external schemas to internal schemas if program efficiency rather than data independence was desired. For another, it is far from clear whether the conceptual schema should be a data model dependent or an independent view of data. And there was the problem of where and how to provide for privacy and security constraints. Deen (1980) makes the point that it would be difficult to get most experts to agree on a minimal subset of the contents of a conceptual schema, although he does propose one. (His subset contains four elements:

(1) logical data description,

(2) description of data relationships,

(3) description of integrity constraints, and

(4) description of privacy constraints.)

Yet, even with the potential difficulties cited above, a great deal of momentum was gathered behind the conceptual schema concept (and still is).

This is evident from the profileration of a large number of high level (semantic) data models suggested for the purpose of conceptual schema development (see chapters 6 and 7).

Overall three developments have strenghtened the conceptual schema movement:

(i) The concept of an enterprise schema was proposed to link the conceptual schema with the notion of organizational purpose or goals and thereby to the ideas of IS strategy and IS planning. This gave database modeling greater visibility and importance in organizational planning and this makes the conceptual schema quite different from the earlier concepts of subschema and schema which were largely technical notions relating to mundane issues of managing a complex database organization. Moreover, the concept of external schema is seen as subject to user bias, whereas the concept of internal schema is seen to be distorted by machine dependent efficiency considerations (*cf.* Chen 1977).

(ii) Data abstraction as a major concern in all computer science research was at the same time proposed to increase data independence in the conceptual schema formulation. The conceptual schema movement was linked with a major research area in computer science which gave it much more credibility. The idea to model the underlying, time invariant structure of reality which supposedly exists independent of current user views or technological constraints was thereby theoretically appealing and challenging.

(iii) A rich variety of data models and data modeling constructs emerged for conceptual schema development accompanied by an attempt to define a standard (see Nijssen 1976, 1977, Nijssen and Bracchi 1979, van Griethuysen 1982). This development was linked with the evolution in the ISD methodologies to derive higher level requirements specifications (see e.g. Bubenko 1980) and led to the profileration of data models and data modeling methodologies.

2.4.3 Proliferation of high level data models

The late 1970s and 1980s saw a dramatic growth in the number of data models. The literature abounds with attempts to improve the three classical models, particularly the relational model due to its inherent weaknesses in capturing the meaning of data (see e.g. Kent 1978, 1983a; Bubenko 1980). Alternative models and families of models started to proliferate. Examples are the semantic models, object-oriented models, interpretive predicate logic models, and the entity-based models (van Griethuysen 1982). Also dynamic modeling approaches were proposed (Jackson 1983, Durcholtz and Richter 1983). Nearly all of these repeat the same assumptions and principles but show astonishing variety in their visible data model constructs. A great variance can be found in the type of entities (simple, complex), in relationships (degree, constraints, unknown values), which object types can have 'attributes', in how entities are identified, and so forth (see for example Nijssen 1977; Nijssen and Brachhi 1979; van Griethuysen 1982). The growth of the number of different types of data models also led to the development of a number of data model taxonomies (Kerschberg *et al.* 1976; Bubenko 1978; Jardine and Reuber 1984; Klein and Hirschheim 1987b; Stachowitz 1985). At this point in time, data modeling had clearly intertwined itself with evolutions in ISD methodologies (see e.g. Sundgren 1973, Bubenko 1980), and also critical voices, in line with the rule-based approaches, started to be heard (Stamper 1979, Lyytinen 1981). The further clarification of these developments including a more detailed analysis of the conceptual and philosophical roots of data modeling will be taken up in chapters 6 and 7.

2.5 Summary and Conclusions

In this chapter we have articulated theoretical concepts and definitions that are necessary for successfully completing our journey through the philosophical and conceptual terrain which awaits us. We also offered a brief overview of the history of information systems development methodologies and data modeling that sets these concepts in a historical context. Even from this short review, it can be seen that the history of ISD and data modeling is not only a rich one, but one which has to a greater or lesser extent, been shaped by rival concerns and as will be demonstrated below, by philosophical principles. This historical fact, we believe, makes our path so winding and long.

3
Philosophical Foundations

3.1 Introduction

All systems developers approach the development task with a number of explicit and implicit assumptions about, for example, the nature of human organizations, the nature of the design task, the value of technology, and what is expected of them. As was noted in chapter 2, these assumptions play a central role in guiding the information systems development process. They guide not only the definition of object systems, but also the preferred approach to inquiry, i.e. how the developers improve their understanding and knowledge about them. The assumptions can either be held by the system developers or be embedded in their preferred development approach. In either case they affect the designed and implemented system.

But in order to understand the relationship between assumptions and development approaches we need to elaborate on the notion of 'paradigm' and how it applies to ISD. An exploration of the philosophical assumptions underlying different methodologies and their tools is a prerequisite for a better understanding of the influence of philosophical attitudes on the practice of ISD. Groups of related assumptions about reality and knowledge are at the core of research paradigms. By introducing a general classification of the assumptions that characterize alternative research paradigms, this chapter provides the philosophical basis for the analysis of ISD and data modeling in the subsequent chapters of this book.

The purpose of this chapter is to look at the nature and kinds of philosophical assumptions that are made in the literature on information systems development and data modeling. Insofar as professional analysts are influenced by the literature these assumptions also guide the practice of systems development. However, this relationship is mediated through the individual critical reflection and practice of analysts applying the literature. It is quite possible that a practitioner applies a method in a way which is different from its implied assumptions. This is clearly pointed out with the idea that practitioners have a large measure of 'autonomy' (*cf.* Baskerville 1991; Episkopou 1987) in applying different methods and tools.

3.2 Definition of Paradigms

The most fundamental set of assumptions adopted by a professional community which allow them to share similar perceptions and engage in commonly shared practices is called a 'paradigm'. Typically, a paradigm consists of assumptions about knowledge and how to acquire it, and about the physical and social world.* As ethnomethodological studies have shown (Garfinkel 1967), such assumptions not only are shared by scientific communities but also by all professionals. As developers must conduct inquiry as part of systems design and have to intervene into the social world as part of systems implementation, it is natural to distinguish two types of related assumptions: those associated with the way in which system developers acquire knowledge needed to design the system (epistemological assumptions), and those which relate to their view of the social and technical world (ontological assumptions).

3.2.1 Epistemological and ontological assumptions of paradigms

Following Burrell and Morgan (1979), we note the assumptions of paradigms can be classified along two dimensions: a 'subjectivist–objectivist' dimension, and an 'order–conflict' dimension. Of course, these labels are simplifications marking the extremes of philosophical positions. In the first dimension, the essence of the objectivist position is to 'apply models and methods derived from the natural sciences to the study of human affairs. It treats the social world as if it were the natural world.' (Burrell and Morgan 1979, p. 7). Objectivists adhere to the ideal of a universal method of science that applies equally to the natural and social universe. In contrast, the subjectivist position denies the appropriateness of natural science methods for studying the social world and seeks to understand the basis of human life by delving into the depths of subjective experience of individuals. 'The principal concern is with an understanding of the way in which the individual creates, modifies and interprets the world in which he or she finds himself'. (Burrell and Morgan 1979, p. 3). Consequently, Habermas (1967, p. 1) speaks of the 'dualism of the natural and cultural sciences'.

In the second dimension, the 'order–conflict' dimension, the 'order' or 'integrationist' view emphasizes a social world characterized by order, stability, integration, consensus and functional coordination. The 'conflict' or 'coercion' view stresses change, conflict, disintegration, and coercion. The dimensions when mapped on to one another yield four paradigms (see figure 3.1):

functionalism (objective-order);

social relativism (subjective-order);

radical structuralism (objective-conflict); and

neohumanism (subjective-conflict).

---

* Paradigms are defined by Burrell and Morgan (1979) as: 'meta-theoretical assumptions about the nature of the subject of study' (p. 35). This differs somewhat from Kuhn's (1970) classic conception of paradigms which were defined as: 'universally recognized scientific achievements that for a time provide model problems and solutions to a community of practitioners' (p.viii).

This particular framework has been chosen because it allows us to capture the distinguishing assumptions of alternative approaches to information systems development in a simplified yet philosophically grounded way.

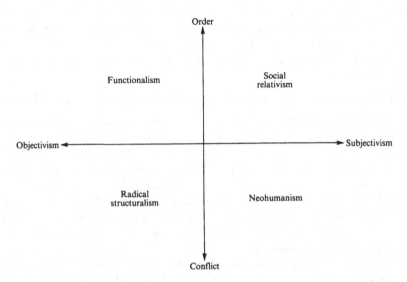

Figure 3.1: Information Systems Development Paradigms (adapted from Burrell and Morgan 1979)

3.2.2 Classification of four paradigms

The *functionalist* paradigm is concerned with providing explanations of the status quo, social order, social integration, consensus, need satisfaction, and rational choice. It seeks to explain how the individual elements of a social system interact together to form a working whole. The *social relativist* paradigm seeks explanation within the realm of individual consciousness and subjectivity, and within the frame of reference of the social actor as opposed to the observer of the action. From such a perspective: 'social roles and institutions exist as an expression of the meanings which men attach to their world' (Silverman 1970, p. 134). The *radical structuralist* paradigm has a view of society and organizations which emphasizes the need to overthrow or transcend the limitations placed on existing social and organizational arrangements. It focuses primarily on the structure and analysis of economic power relationships. The *neohumanist* paradigm seeks radical change, emancipation, and potentiality, and stresses the role that different social and organizational forces play in understanding change. It focuses on all forms of barriers to emancipation: in particular, ideology (distorted communication), power and psychological compulsions and social constraints.

It is our contention that these paradigms, initially identified by Burrell and Morgan (1979) in the context of organizational and social research, also manifest themselves in the domain of information systems development.* Yet to show how the paradigms are actually reflected in ISD is complicated. The paradigms are largely implicit and deeply rooted in the web of common-sense beliefs and background knowledge (Quine and Ullian 1970) which serve as implicit 'theories of action' (Argyris and Schon 1974).

3.3 Paradigms in ISD

In lieu of an elaborate philosophical discussion of the four paradigms link-ing them to the philosophical literature, the following relies on a series of tables to clarify their meanings and illustrate their connections to ISD as a process. Section 3.4 will build on this to discuss the role of paradigms in shaping data-oriented approaches to ISD. Chapter 4 takes up the connec-tions of the paradigms to principles of systems development in more detail in two ways. First it will give archetypical characterizations of how systems analysts might behave if they try to put the tenets of each paradigm into practice. This will expand in the terse entries in tables 3.2 and 3.3. Second, chapter 4 will link the evolution of methodologies as described in chapter 2 to different paradigms and chapter 5 will expand on this by discussing four methodologies in terms of the their underlying paradigmatic assump-tions. Chapter 4 and 5 focus on a process-oriented view of ISD. Chapters 6 and 7 will complement this with the data-oriented viewpoint. Of course, real methodologies do not fall neatly into ideal paradigmatic categories. Nevertheless, some major differences will come into focus through such a comparison of methodologies. With this in mind we now summarize some key points for each paradigm.

Table 3.1 provides an overview of the principal concepts and ideas associ-ated with each paradigm along with some representative references. These relate to the paradigms in general and are not specific to IS. The paradigms are contrasted in terms of their fundamental assumptions about ontology

---

* The view that these four paradigms capture the whole of sociological and organizational research is not without its critics. Numerous writers have criticized the Burrell and Morgan framework for being oversimplified (*cf.* Hopper and Powell 1985; Chua 1986). For example, many are unhappy with the way functionalism is portrayed, e.g. that it denies conflict and that functionalists always adopt positivism. Coser's (1956) treatment of functionalism does take into account conflict; and certain functionalists did not necessarily adopt positivism (*cf.* Talcott Parsons). Others argue that the dichotomies projected by Burrell and Morgan are artifical. Although there are other frameworks for categorizing social science research (*cf.* Gutting 1980; Reason and Rowan 1981), none is as representative of the IS development domain. We see the framework proposed by Burrell and Morgan — with some modification — as best depicting the different classes of ISD approaches, relatively speaking. This is not meant, however, to close the door on exploring other alternatives.

Paradigm	Ontological Assumptions	Epistemological Assumptions	Assumptions About Values	Representative References
Function-alism	System requirements and constraints exist independently of theories or perceptions. They can be described by an empirical base of observations formulated in a neutral language free of distortions. This is realism and it tends to reify system requirements by suppressing their human authorship.	Empirical-Analytical methods of observation, measurement and induction.	Value statements express intentions or emotions and cannot be falsified. Unity of scientific method: there is no separate mode of inquiry for the cultural sciences; social theory is concerned with the 'middle range'.	Russell (1929); Popper (1965, 1972); Nagel (1961); Alexander (1985). In IS: Minnesota School and their descendants; e.g. Dickson et al. (1977); Ives et al. (1980).
Social Relativism	System requirements and constraints are socially constructed; they change as perceptions change and perceptions change through continuous social learning and evolution of language and culture.	Interpretivist reflection and hermeneutic cycles; raising of consciousness and dissemination of ideas through social interaction.	Individual value judgments are determined by the social institutions and general conditions of human existence (e.g. agrarian versus post-industrial etc.). Locally, value judgments are rational if based on an interpretive understanding of the totality of these conditions, e.g. child labor was necessary in the early industrial phase in England, but it is unacceptable now.	Typical of interpretive sociology and theories of the social construction of reality [e.g. Berger and Luckmann (1967)]. In IS: Boland (1985); Andersen et al. (1990).
Radical Structuralism	Only the objective economic conditions of the social mode of production exist. These in turn determine the 'ideological super-structure'. System requirements and constraints exist independent of theories or perceptions. The existence of an independent social reality is denied.	Empirical-Analytical methods for physical reality. Physical reality is perceived to include the 'objective relations of ownership of the means of production'. One's vested interest in either maintaining the status quo or its revolutionary change, determines what one recognizes as truth in the social realm.	Those values are rational which lead to social progress. They can be studied as part of the dynamics of the social totality — the development goal of society. There is no other reality than matter; mind is a form of appearance of matter; hence if the material basis of society is changed, the collective consciousness will change with it. If the actual beliefs are different, they represent 'false consciousness' which is to be unmasked by studying the deterministic conditions of social evolution.	Marxist writers and many, but not all of their descendants, see Braverman (1974). In IS: The Marxist position on ISD is not well developed; but see Briefs (1983); Ehn and Sandberg (1983); Ehn and Kyng (1987); Sandberg (1985).
Neo-humanism	Differentiates physical from social reality; the former is similar to the ontology adopted in Functionalism; the latter to Social Relativism.	Postulates the need for multiple epistemologies. To gain knowledge about physical nature, approaches similar to those of Functionalism are adopted. The only difference is that the correspondence of truth claims is established through critical debate — truth is 'warranted assertability'. Extends this notion to knowledge acquisition about social reality where consensus is the key. Consensus may be fallacious, but is 'correctable' through critical debate. Through such critical debate, it is possible to escape the prison of our prejudices.	Principal value is the transformation of historically constituted social reality to allow for the maximal realization of human potentials. At any given time there are constraints on people. Some of these are natural, others are due to the current limits of technology or imperfections of social conditions. These only seem natural and hence are 'unwarranted'. Through social reorganization informed by rational discourse people can emancipate themselves from unwarranted constraints. A rational discourse is an undistorted debate among equally well informed peers.	Most of the writings of the Frankfurt School of Critical Social Theory; see McCarthy (1978) and Habermas (1984). In IS: not developed but see Lyytinen (1986); Ngwenyama (1987); Lyytinen and Hirschheim (1988); Hirschheim and Klein (1994).

Table 3.1: Summary of paradigm assumptions

(what is assumed to exist), epistemology (how we can know about the things assumed to exist) and values for systems development.

Table 3.2 is in two parts: I and II which are specific to IS. Part I compares the paradigms along three dimensions: the role of designer (what the IS developer's function should be); the nature of information systems application (what the purpose of the information system is); and objectives for design and use of information systems (what the goals of information systems development should be). Part II of table 3.2 presents an overview of the deficiencies (weaknesses of the paradigm) and the implications for legitimation of systems objectives (how system goals are legitimized).

Table 3.3 compares the four paradigms in terms of their implications for the various functions of systems development. More specifically, the comparison considers six (fairly standard) functions of systems development along with how each paradigm perceives information and information systems development. In the case of the latter, each paradigm is depicted in terms of its 'preferred metaphor for defining information' (its basic view of the concept of information), and 'preferred metaphor for defining information systems development' (its basic view of what ISD does). In the case of the former, the six functions explored are: problem finding and formulation, analysis, logical design, physical design and technical implementation, organizational implementation, and maintenance.

3.3.1 Differences relating to human interests

The paradigms also differ in terms of how they deal with human interests, i.e. what interests are sound and proper. In radical structuralism, for example, only the workers' interests are seen as legitimate. In social relativism all interests are seen as legitimate. In neohumanism all interests are considered legitimate as long as they are generalizable, i.e. arguable in a rational discourse, however no interest is privileged. Functionalism also has the potential for considering all interests. For example it could support the realization of workers interests. However in practice, it tends to favor the interests of the societal elites, and most of its methods and tools are biased towards these interests. It is therefore difficult to see functionalism supporting these other interests without a major effort requiring large resources which are unlikely to be granted by those in power (*cf.* Klein and Lyytinen 1985 and conclusion in Klein and Hirschheim 1987a).

In realizing human interests, functionalism can appeal to the common interests and common understandings by incremental, evolutionary reforms of the status quo. Social relativism appeals to all common interests through the search for consensual norms and common understandings. Radical structuralism denies the existence of a common interest between workers and the owners of capital. The appeal to common interests is seen as a strategic plot for controlling the workers by manipulating and distorting communication and not addressing the root cause of conflict, namely social injustice. Neohumanism appeals to the common interests but explicitly recognizes that

Paradigm	Role of IS Designer	Nature of Information System Application	Objectives for Design and Use of Information Systems
Functionalism	The EXPERT; similar to an engineer who masters the means for achieving given ends	IS is built around deterministic laws of human behavior and technology to gain optimal control of socioeconomic environment.	ISD is concerned with fitting technology, i.e. IS design is a means to better realize pre-defined objectives. IS use is aimed at overcoming computation limits of man and improving productivity.
Social Relativism	A CATALYST who smooths the transition between evolutionary stages for the social system for which he is a part.	IS is concerned with the creation and sharing of meaning to legitimate social action whatever it may be: overcoming of tension due to transition from one set of conditions to another.	To elicit the design objectives and modes of use which are consistent with the prevailing conditions; to help others to understand and accept them. To develop systems which implement 'the prevailing Zeitgeist' (spirit of the times).
Radical Structuralism	A WARRIOR on the side of the forces of social progress.	IS can contribute to the evolution of society by overcoming the inherent social contradictions; use of IS should be to achieve emancipation of working class. This involves aggressive application of the natural sciences which is a force of progress.	ISD must be a process of better understanding the requirements set by the current evolutionary stage of society and the place of the organization within it. IS designer must be on guard not to work in to the hand of vested interests, in particular the use of IS must further the class interest and not the exploitation of the common man.
Neo-humanism	An EMANCIPATOR from social and psychological barriers.	Understanding of the options of social action and free choice; IS is to create a better understanding of these by removing bias and distortions.	IS development must be concerned with removing bias and distortion due to seemingly natural constraints; external (power) and internal (psychopathological) barriers to rational discourse must be removed.

Table 3.2 (Part I): Implications for Information Systems Development

Paradigm	Implications for Legitimation of Systems Objectives	Deficiencies
Functionalism	Goals are dictated by a 'technological imperative', i.e. only those goals consistent with the ideal of technical/economic rationality are legitimate.	Cannot explain how users associate meanings with measurement, how goals are set; resistance is interpreted as failure to comprehend the systemic needs and is irrational. It cannot explain the origination of subjective meanings, conflicting goals, and the like.
Social Relativism	Any goals or values are legitimate which are consistent with social acceptance; but there is no way to critically validate the acceptance.	Unable to distinguish between justified, informed consensus from social conventions and cultural stereotypes; tendency toward relativism and anarchy.
Radical Structuralism	All objectives other than those which further the class interests of the workers are considered illegitimate and reactionary.	Cannot explain the notion of community of interests and social differentiation on the basis of criteria other than economic status; postulates that conflict will vanish if all become members of the working class.
Neohumanism	Extends notion of 'warranted assertability' to the establishment of norms and values: those system objectives are legitimate which survive maximal criticism and thus are shown to serve generalizeable human interests.	Fails to explain why a rational consensus by the mere 'force of the better argument' will occur. And if it does occur, how does one know that the consensus is 'authentic'; it might just be another social consensus — better informed perhaps, but still historically contingent.

Table 3.2 (Part II): Limitations of the Paradigms and their Implications for the Definition of System Goals

Activities in ISD	Functionalism	Social Relativism	Radical Structuralism	Neohumanism
Preferred Metaphor for Defining Information	Information as a product; it is produced, traded and made available at will, like a commodity	Information as a journey with a partner; information emerges from reflection, interaction and experience	Information as a means of manipulation and a weapon in ideological struggle	Information as means for control, sense-making and argumentation.
Preferred Metaphor for Framing ISD	ISD is like engineering with the systems developer being the expert of methods and tools	ISD is like a journey to an uncertain destination with the systems developer acting as the facilitator	Information systems development is like a form of rationalization directed against worker interests; or a counter-strategy by the workers to deflect exploitation	Information systems development is like an opportunity to improve the control over nature and to overcome unwarranted barriers to communication
Problem Finding and Formulation	Improved prediction and control of the various entities in the business functions through maintaining and analyzing data; identify misfits between organization mission and IS; align structure of IS with business strategy; seek opportunities for competitive advantage	Improved conditions for learning and cooperation; identify means to support the improvement of mutual understanding and the creation of new meanings; facilitate interaction and the exchange of information	Improved productivity of the workers; or improve the position and enhance the craftmanship and skills of the workers	Improve institutional tools and organizational arrangements for prediction and control, mutual understanding and discourse, and emancipation of all stakeholders
Analysis	Determine how the key processes of the organization contribute to the intended performance outcomes and which data they need for their effective functioning. For a good review of possible requirements determination strategies see Davis (1982)	Understand and investigate the existing basis of interaction and communication such as differing horizons of meanings of various stakeholders	Identify how IS can increase competitiveness and productivity by increasing work intensity, division of labor and control; or, identify alternative forms of IS that improve the wages and general conditions of work	Identify existing technical, social and linguistic barriers for optimal prediction and control, mutual understanding, and emancipation from unwarranted constraints
Logical Design	Model the portion of organizational reality which is relevant for the system using tools such as process modeling, object modeling and demonstrate functionality through prototyping	Reconstruct user language to support interaction to more effectively capture meanings as conveyed in ordinary speech (Boland and Day 1982)	Construct systems models that enhance productivity and competitiveness; or, use of prototypes or experiment with technology that will retain and enhance the skills and tradition of the craft	Reconstruct the technical, linguistic and organizational basis for improving prediction and control, mutual understanding and discourse, and learning and emancipation
Physical Design and Technical Implementation	Find cost-effective hardware and software solution to implement the logical design	Not discussed in the literature	Find cost-effective hardware and software; or, find alternative hardware and software solutions that will improve the workers' quality of work life	Realize changes in technology, language and organization to improve control, mutual understanding and discourse, and emancipation
Organizational Implementation	Develop strategies to seek compliance by the users to avoid resistance and implementation games (Keen 1981)	No implementation strategy needed since ISD supports the on-going evolutionary change	Develop strategies to seek compliance by the workers to avoid resistance so as to maximize productivity. Or, consider structural changes of control in work organization to enhance the position of the workers	Anticipate potential impacts of changes in organization, language and technology on each other; develop strategies to mitigate unwanted side-effects
Maintenance	Monitor environmental changes and continued functionality of IS	No difference between maintenance and continuing evolution of IS	Monitor the realization of the system objectives regarding productivity and competitiveness; or, monitor the continued use of IS to support the interests of the workers	Monitor the actual performance of IS with regard to control and prediction, mutual understanding, and emancipation and make adjustments accordingly in the domains of technology, language or organization

Table 3.3: Paradigmatic Implications for ISD Functions

distortions may prevent its realization. It therefore argues for removing the barriers to common understanding which would then allow the generalizable interests to be realized based on non-distorted communication.

3.3.2 Differences in ontology

In addition to the description of ontological differences offered in table 3.1, there are some additional differences worth noting. For example, both radical structuralism and functionalism postulate an independent reality and therefore favor development methods and tools that are similarly objectivist in nature, i.e. reflect a given reality. Radical structuralism postulates the existence of an inevitable conflict in the social domain which is unresolvable except by revolutionary change. Whereas functionalism denies radical conflict, it does however allow for conflict, but in a different sense from radical structuralism. Functionalism treats conflict as a phenomenon that does not challenge the fundamental basis of society, but is potentially productive because it contributes to innovation and change. The ontology of neohumanism and social relativism postulates the primacy of language as the only reality that we may have which leads to an epistemology which sees reality as socially constructed.

3.3.3 Differences related to user control and the kind of system produced

Differences in the kind of system produced relate to the differences arising from the application of the four paradigms, i.e. variations in terms of the systems that each produces; to put it differently, how the systems that each paradigm produces differ from the others. The differences in developed systems relate to the output and control of systems development and include the following eight features: technology architecture; kind of information flows, control of users, control of systems development, access to information, error handling, training, and raison d'etre. See table 3.4.

(1) Technology architecture refers to the way in which specific hardware and software components are configured and matched with the structural units of the organization. The structural differentiation supported by alternative technology architectures, for example, has a considerable impact on the opportunities and privileges afforded various user groups.

(2) Kind of information flows refers to the intended meanings of the information dealt with by the IS. For example, the meaning of the information of one system might be to formalize a particular user group's diagnostic skills so as to leave them out of the diagnostic loop, whereas in another, it might be used to improve the diagnostic capabilities of the users.

(3) Control of users refers to how the information system would contribute to or diminish opportunities for one group exercising power, authority or other forms of social influence over another.

(4) Control of systems development refers to the locus of influence over the systems development process. In principle this can lie with the people affected by the system or some external group or a mixture.

(5) Access to information refers to who would have access to the information provided by the IS and with it, who stands to benefit from improved information. Control of the access to information can dramatically alter the power structure of an organization.

(6) Error handling refers to the arrangement for detecting errors and who would deal with them. Depending on how errors are looked upon, they can be used as a basis for external sanctions and rewards, as a means of subjugation, or, more positively, as a challenge to creativity, source of learning and creation of new meanings.

(7) Training refers to the role that education plays as part of system change, who will be selected for training, whether it is seen as a means to enhance the individual and his or her social position, or whether it is confined to mechanical skills for operating the system.

(8) Raison d'etre refers to the primary reason for the existence of the information system. For example, is it seen as a means for overcoming social barriers, for improving policy formation and competitive advantage, for enhancing management control over workers, for achieving cost-savings by replacing labor, etc?

It should be noted that the eight features chosen for comparing systems differences were derived from an analysis of the systems development literature. They are by no means exhaustive as others could have been chosen nor are they necessarily mutually exclusive.

(1) Technology architecture was derived from Ciborra (1981) who notes the importance of technology architecture for lowering the costs of organizational transactions.

(2) Kind of information flow was derived from the language action view of information systems (Goldkuhl and Lyytinen 1982a) which focuses on the purposes of information flows.

(3) Control of users was derived from Kling (1980) who notes that it: 'is often assumed that when automated information systems become available, managers and line supervisors exploit them to enhance their own control over different resources, particularly the activities of their subordinates' (p. 77).

(4) Control of systems development was derived from Briefs *et al.* (1983) who note the importance of internal and external control of the actors who participate in systems development. (See also Mathiassen *et al.*'s (1983) critique of both traditional management strategies of ISD and trade union agreements at 'primarily aiming at controlling the development process from outside' (p. 262) either with the purpose of

	Functionalism	Social Relativism	Radical Structuralism	Neohumanism
Technology Architecture	Technology is fit to existing organizational structure respecting departmental boundaries and spheres of influence and authority; replacement of human input which is seen as error-prone and unreliable by automatic devices: sensors, scanners, etc. whenever possible.	Technology is distributed so as to facilitate free flow of information to all forms of symbolic interaction; taking care not to encroach on tasks which provide opportunities for exercising human judgements, sense-making, and interpretations.	Technology is used as a means to radically change the boundaries of control and spheres of influence, so as to enhance the power of the work force, and retain control of their work products.	Technology architectures are designed with several purposes: to serve the technical interest, as in Functionalism; to serve the interest in human understanding, as in Social Relativism; and to overcome unwarranted uses of power and vested interests of any privileged group. As these may be in conflict, technology architecture must be decided upon by free and open negotiation.
Kind of Information Flows	Emphasis on objectively measurable quantities and automatic sensoring, under the control of management favoring top-down instructions and bottom-up control flows.	Emphasis on judgmental quality of perceiving, and leaving the original data input to humans who are encouraged to bring to bear their 'lifeworld' experience to assure common sense and meaningful inputs.	Emphasis on objectively measurable quantities, but under the control of the worker force. Information is not seen as entirely neutral, but as carrying ideological bias to serve vested class interests.	Providing checks and balances on judgmental human input; integrity and consistency checks using multiple channels and dialectics for cross-checking.
Control of Users	Consistent with existing power structures; tends to be top-down.	Eliminate all controls except those implied by evolutionary and egalitarian checks and balances in social interaction	Reversing the direction of existing power structures.	Eliminate unwarranted controls; balances between necessary controls and freedom.
Control of Systems Development	Under the control and direction of management, but mediated by professional expert interest groups.	Emergent from internal group interaction and evolution of peer norms and values.	Under the control of the work force.	Rationally justified rules and norms; legitimized by open and free discourse.
Access to Information	Dictated by formal organizational hierarchy: the 'need to know' standard.	Open to all.	As dictated by the need to implement worker control over the productive forces.	Open to all with safeguards against self delusion and distorted communication (from bias or ideology).
Error Handling	Detection through the reification of statistical data; correction by procedures that can be followed either by the users themselves or consultants.	Errors are uninterpretable phenomena; they prompt the initiation of a hermeneutic cycle to improve the group understanding. An example is the reinterpretation of a program bug as a special feature (Markus 1984, p. 2).	Errors are an opportunity for the workers to reaffirm the need for their skills and thereby can provide a power base. This leads to the continuing attempt by management to wrestle error control away from users.	Errors in the technical domain are handled in a similar fashion to that of Functionalism; errors in the mutual understanding domain are handled by the initiation of a hermeneutic cycle accompanied by clarifications; errors in the emancipatory domain are challenges to the assumptions underlying the system design regarding power and capabilities and must be handled by opening a discourse about them.
Training	Determined by division of labor and productivity concerns; instrumental orientation dominates. Education is a source of power and control for management.	Emphasis is placed on creative sense making and oriented towards furthering shared human understanding.	Education is a source of destabilizing the authority and power of management. It is also used as a source of enhancing the position of the workers vis-à-vis management.	Education is a means of emancipation from self deception and ideology; it has an egalitarian orientation. It should be free and open to all. It also includes skills and creativity training as in Functionalism and Social Relativism.
Raison d'être	Maximizing savings, minimizing costs, and improving competitive advantage.	Improving creativity and shared sense making.	Placing in the hands of the work force, the control of the productive resources; reducing individual alienation by enhancing the craftsmanship of each worker, and reaffirming the control over the results of his/her labor.	Improved technical control, human understanding, and emancipation from unwarranted physical and social constraints.

Table 3.4: Differences in Devloped Systems Produced by the Four Paradigms

minimizing costs or predetermining fixed points for participative decisions.)

(5) Access to information was derived from Markus (1983) who vividly shows through her FIS case that the access to information could change the balance of power between different interest groups. A similar point is made in Newman and Rosenberg (1985).

(6) Error handling was derived from Markus' (1984) case where an error was treated as a feature.

(7) The importance of training was derived from Kubicek's (1983) observation that worker sponsored production and distribution of information technology related knowledge should involve learning activities that are based on previous experience of the workers (*cf.* Ehn *et al.* 1983).

(8) Raison d'etre was suggested by studying the goals of information systems in the four paradigms.

3.4 Data Modeling Paradigms

The preceding comparison of the paradigms discusses their implications primarily in terms of systems development as a process. Our analysis so far is incomplete as the paradigms have had a rather strong influence on tools and methods of data modeling and knowledge representation, because data modeling is a process of inquiry that has intrinsic similarities with classic scientific theory construction. It is therefore concluded that an analysis of these assumptions will provide a richer understanding of the strengths and weaknesses of the current paradigms and approaches to data modeling.

In the realm of data modeling only one of the two dimensions used to classify paradigms is prominent, namely objectivism and subjectivism, because the order vs. conflict dimension is not typically considered. All data models presume a regulation or order point of view of the system they model and most data modeling approaches focus on representing reality. Therefore the functionalist point of view in data modeling abounds. The role of data models in organizational conflict has received virtually no attention. Consequently, radical structuralist approaches to data modeling cannot be discerned. If they existed, they could be recognized by their focus on how data models can support the finding of truth through adversarial debate. On the other hand, there is a consideration of differing user views, differing semantics, synonyms, etc. in the data modeling literature, but none of this speaks to the question of how data modeling could be used for radical change. In contrast to radical structuralism, we can distinguish functionalist and social relativist paradigms of data modeling. The latter tend to focus on modeling the rules of different user languages as opposed to modeling reality. The distinction between modeling language rather than reality corresponds to the subjectivist–objectivist dimension which was used to classify paradigms.

As will be seen in chapter 6, some groundwork for a neohumanist view of data modeling has also been laid, but it would not be appropriate to think that there currently exists a neohumanist data modeling paradigm. At the core of such a paradigm would be the notion that data models can contribute to fundamental transformation of organizational reality by aiding emancipatory discourse.

3.4.1 Ontology and epistemology of data modeling

In the context of data modeling, ontological assumptions are concerned with the nature of the Universe of Discourse (UoD) — the 'slice' of reality to be modeled. Epistemological assumptions are concerned with the appropriate approach for inquiry regarding what one needs to know to create the data model and with the cognitive status of the result: is a data model 'true' or is it merely a convenient fiction, i.e. a simplifying design assumption presumed to be valid only for a particular system at a particular time?

Objectivism postulates that the universe of discourse is comprised of immutable objects and structures that exist as empirical entities. In principle, a model of the UoD ought to exist which is correct independently of the observers' appreciation of it. A data model is 'true' if it accurately depicts the underlying reality of the universe of discourse. Different opinions about the UoD must be a reflection of human error and in principle can be eliminated.

In distinction to this, subjectivism in data modeling holds that the UoD is a subjective construction of the mind. A data model can at best reflect peoples' conventions or perceptions that are subject to negotiated change. Basically, the immediate social milieu of users and society at large preorder what subjectively is experienced as reality by means of socialization in the home, the educational institutions and at work. Important mechanisms by which subjective experiences take on an objective quality in the minds of individuals are the rules surrounding institutions (i.e. institutional programming), tradition as transmitted through artifacts and changing use of language and sedimentation (cf. Berger and Luckmann 1967). (Sedimentation refers to the ordering of experiences which is transmitted subconsciously by virtue of growing up in one segment of society as opposed to another or in different societies altogether, e.g. doing trade under the Koran or doing trade under US business conventions). From this view a data model is correct if it is consistent with the perception of the UoD as constructed by institutional programming, sedimentation and tradition. In contrast, the objectivist view holds that language neutrally depicts reality which is the same for all regardless of culture and individual perception.

Under a more radical interpretation of the subjectivist approach, data modeling does not merely reflect social consensus perceptions, but it affects the very process of reality construction. This is so because socially transmitted concepts and names direct how reality is perceived and structured. The construction of reality varies with different languages and cultures. As data modeling typically introduces new concepts and ideas in the users world, it intervenes with the very definition of what counts as reality. It changes what is subjectively experienced as an objective reality and its appreciation (what may at one point have been accidental or not even noticed may become very important and recorded in detail). Data modeling is a form of institutional programming and once a data model has been in use for some time it may become part and parcel of sedimentation and tradition. In this sense, data modeling is never neutral, but rather a partisan negotiation of reality.

A second important implication of data modeling paradigms relates to understanding the role of data modeling in the situation of social conflict and the treatment of inconsistencies. As the objectivists presume that the reality to be modeled is empirically 'given', differing opinions about the UoD must be a reflection of human error. These errors can in principle be eliminated by treating differences as questions of fact to be answered by empirical inquiry. Therefore inconsistencies between different views are unwarranted. They are also unwanted because they are a threat to data integrity. This is really a rather limited view of the role of conflict that associates the objectivists with the functionalist paradigm.

In contrast, the subjectivist would expect that the social construction of reality would lead to substantial differences about the appropriate representation of the UoD. As the training, interests and experiences of different user groups vary, so must their scheme by which they order and represent the meanings associated with their perceptions of reality. There is no objective reality except through cultural sharing. With the exception noted below, differing opinions about the UoD must be expected and cannot be eliminated without alienating those who hold them. Inconsistencies between different view are not necessarily a sign of mistake. Rather they are a result of accurately representing the different views. An exception of this occurs if through interaction between different groups a genuine consensus among them emerges. But consensus is not guaranteed nor does consensus signal that it is necessarily more accurate than the prior views which were conflicting. The consensus view could simply be the result of 'group think'. Therefore conflict about the appropriate representation of the UoD is not only warranted, but also desirable, because it is the only safeguard against misunderstandings and other types of errors.

This is, of course, a somewhat functionalist interpretation of conflict in that it assigns conflict a role to system stabilization. If one adopts a neo-humanist perspective, conflict is not only a prerequisite for truth finding through discourse, but also challenges the status quo, helps to reveal distortions and unwarranted uses of power. Hence building conflicting data models (as suggested by alternative root definitions in soft systems modeling, *cf.* chapter 5) contributes to emancipation of suppressed interests. From a radical structuralist perspective, conflict is endemic to work life. To try to manage it or use it for finding generally warranted truths without taking clear sides is manipulative. The famous biblical aphorism 'He who is not with me is against me' is the likely motto of the radical structuralist.

In summary, in contrast to ISD where the four paradigms are at least somewhat represented in the literature, the same is not true for data modeling. There are virtually no methods which address the role of data in social conflict, assuming instead either the ideal of a given reality that can be captured in a globally consistent representation or a shared language in which some of its rules can be formalized. It should be noted that it is through the focusing on shared language that the research on subjectivist data modeling approaches has proceeded. It should also be noted that the functionalist tradition in data modeling is dominant because the approaches which focus on the modeling of a shared language comprise only a very small portion of the literature.

3.4.2 Philosophical origins of data modeling paradigms

In order to understand how the subjectivist and objectivist paradigms are reflected in current data modeling approaches, one must recall the sources of their modeling formalisms. Generally speaking, the formalisms for data modeling have been adapted from predicate logic and linguistics which in turn draw on theories of knowledge, in particular those that can be traced back to Aristotle and Leibniz.

In the *Organon*, Aristotle proposed a theory of categories and predication (*cf.* Kapp 1942). It suggests that knowledge is represented in terms of subjects and predicates. The subject–predicate dichotomy is fundamental for those data modeling approaches based on primitives such as entities, attributes and relationships. In *De Interpretatione* Aristotle was concerned with the nature of propositions and valid rules of inference, i.e. the famous syllogisms. The latter are incorporated in data models in the form of integrity constraints. The basic tenet of the objectivist data modeling paradigm is that a data model expresses a set of true propositions about reality — the UoD to be modeled. The data modeling approach provides the language means by which the essential features of reality can be represented. The propositions about the UoD must be faithful representations of that reality. Such requirements are expressed as integrity constraints. Hence the notion of a data model embraces the concept of validity checks which traditionally have been programmed into data editing routines. The basic logic of integrity constraints is an adaptation and generalization of the Aristotelian syllogism concept. An integrity clause imposes constraints on data in the form of logical tautologies. Data which violate the tautological rules are deemed to be invalid. The justification of this view of the nature of data modeling follows from the objectivist philosophical base first advocated by Aristotle and later refined by Tarski, namely the stipulation that truth is a matter of correspondence between what is described in terms of propositions and the actual state of affairs. In the *Tractatus Logico-Philospohicus* Wittgenstein (1922) in detail developed the theory that language is a picture or mirror of reality. There was supposed to be a unique and consistent decomposition of reality into elementary statements of fact (for more information see chapter 6). This idea is taken up by data models which propose methods and tools for modeling the facts (the so-called 'fact-based' school of data modeling, *cf.* chapters 6 and 7).

In contrast, Leibniz (1875, vol. 6, p. 612; 1890, p. 223) recognized that not all languages are equally well-suited to discovering the truth. He raised the question if there is any guarantee that the original propositions (the primitives and basic assumptions of the data model) are necessarily true and if not, how contingent propositions can be prevented from contaminating the 'truth'. Leibniz saw the need for a universal language to express the truth, the fact-based approaches believe to have found it in predicate logic. The choice of terms and logic seemed crucial to Leibniz for arriving at conclusions that are truly in 'harmony' with changing reality (*cf.* Leibniz 1890). The mirror of language might distort the truth. Critical examination of Leibnizian philosophy leads one to question if there is an objective meaning to language, and if we can be sure that our language is not too limited to express everything that needs to be known. This question was pursued further by Wittgenstein (1958) in the *Philosophical Investigations* where it is suggested that the meaning of language primitives depends primarily on how they are used in a social context. The latter determines which primitives are recognized and what sort of meanings they connote. This contrasts sharply with the above notion of the correspondence theory of truth. Integrity of data means consistency with (possibly varying) social uses and not a correspondence with an objectively given state of affairs. This provides the philosophical base of the subjectivist paradigm of data modeling: different approaches to data modeling will lead to different conceptions of reality. Therefore the ideal of a unique, consistent and objective model of the UoD has to be abandoned.

It is now widely recognized that classical logic is insufficient to model all meanings in human communication. New formalisms for data modeling which draw on recent advances in linguistics, in particular speech act theory (e.g. Searle 1979), have been proposed (*cf.* Lyytinen 1985; Lyytinen and Lehtinen 1984; Lehtinen and Lyytinen 1984) giving rise to the so-called 'rule-based' school of data modeling (*cf.* chapters 6 and 7).

3.4.3 Objectivism–subjectivism in data modeling

The fact-based approaches to data modeling tend to follow in the footsteps of the objectivist tradition. Under this interpretation, a data model is like a mirror or picture of reality. Reality is a given, 'out there' and made up of discrete chunks which are called entities. Entities have properties or attributes. Both entities and their properties have an objective existence. Entity-based approaches implement Wittgenstein's (1922) picture theory of meaning, i.e. data correspond to facts, and it is these that entity-based approaches seek to model. This is apparent when Kent (1983b, p. 3) notes that by 'focusing

on the facts . . ., we obtain a methodology for data analysis and design which
is at once simpler and more powerful than other methodologies' [for data
modeling].

The rule-based approaches to data modeling are heavily influenced by the
subjectivist tradition. Their proponents see the main task of data modeling
as formalizing the meaning of messages which are to be exchanged among a
professional community (e.g. accountants, managers, production engineers,
etc.). The expression of meanings must follow social determined rules which
facilitate the comprehension of what is communicated. They argue that
meaning is created within the human mind and related to human purpose
or intentions. The latter arise out of an understanding of reality which is
'socially constructed', i.e. it emerges from social interaction conditioned
by social conventions or rules. All computer data ultimately have to be
interpreted in terms of their natural language meaning(s). Hence data can
at best convey meaning from someone to someone, but they cannot 'have'
any objective meaning.

Is it possible to conceive of a third perspective on data modeling which
combines both objectivist and subjectivist principles of data modeling into
a synthesis? It could be argued that the object-based approach (also called
actor-based or frame-based in the literature) lends itself to such a synthesis. The basic modeling construct of an 'object' builds on the concept of
an imaginary actor as originally proposed by Alan Kay (1984). An actor in
Kay's sense is any software object that behaves in predefined ways. Actors
can be used to model 'real' objects, but they can also be used to model
imaginary objects that represent people's 'ideas' which exist only in their
minds and can then come to life on a computer screen as the figures in *Alice
in Wonderland*. Because ideas can be captured in mental frames, this approach to data modeling has also been referred to as frame-based. An actor
or frame view of data is based on the idea that a description of data with
its permissable operations should be combined into an 'actor' or 'knowledge
frame'. A frame or actor is a particular type of abstraction concept for arriving at a particular categorization of phenomena. Unlike entities, frames are
not necessarily assumed to exist 'out there' as real objects. Other names
which have been suggested for similar types of data modeling constructs
which are simmilar to objects, frames and actors are plans and scripts (*cf.*
Hewitt 1986). We shall continue to refer to it as object-based in this book.

The potential of objects to model imaginary, 'ideal' or socially constructed
worlds has not, unfortunately, been widely recognized in the data modeling literature. While object-based approaches can theoretically be used to
implement either subjectivist or objectivist interpretations of data, it is
possible to conceive of them as predisposed towards subjectivism. This is
because of the difficulty with defining the object contents which makes it
obvious that there are no objective rules for this. Surprisingly, the literature
has taken the opposite direction: objects (or actors) are conceived to be the

representation of real world objects. The discussion has focused on the kind of qualities with which objects need to be imbued as to most conveniently reflect the building blocks that supposedly make up application environments. In addition, there has been considerable discussion about what should be a basic stock of objects (or actors) in an initial library of objects from which one can easily build more complex objects in the context of a particular application. The basic library objects are theoretically reusable in many different applications and should therefore allow the building of software from standard components. Therefore object-based modeling in the current literature is best viewed as a variant of objectivism in data modeling. Some of its details are taken up in the first part of chapter 7.

3.5 Paradigmatic Implications for Object Systems Definition

As each paradigm projects a preferred ontology about the domain of change and thereby constitutes the development world differently, it is not surprising that each paradigm is likely to lead us to perceive the objects system for ISD differently. In other words there is a close linkage between the paradigmatic choices and the preferred concept structures used in framing and making sense of the design situations. The influences of the paradigms on the conceptualizations of object systems manifest themselves differently for approaches embracing process-oriented and data-oriented object system classes (*cf.* section 2.2.2). The key differences are summarized in table 3.5.

3.5.1 Object systems in functionalism

In the process-oriented approaches, the functionalist paradigm leads to perceiving the object system in terms of structured activities which sustain the organizational mission. Typically these are classified into procedures for transforming well-defined inputs into outputs. Processes interlink through well-defined inputs and outputs, each contributing a specialized service or product to the organizational mission as a whole. In this way, the complex mission is decomposed into simpler component processes which realize economic efficiencies through standardization and specialization. By studying the individual processes and their interfaces, the organization can be designed, as any machine-like system, for optimal functioning.

In applying the data-oriented perspective, the preferred object system in the functionalist paradigm is either depicted in terms of entity or object classes. The former follows the classical Aristotelian subject–predicate dichotomy in perceiving reality. The Aristotelian dichotomy still guides the predominate practice when organizing the data of one or several applications into entity classes. Each entity class corresponds to a set of subjects (people, events or things) in the object system.

More recently, the subjects constituting an object system are organized into hierachies of actors or 'object classes' where an actor or object encapsulates both attributes and methods (strong typing). In this way, the

Paradigm	Ontological Implications for Object Systems
Functionalism: focuses mostly on technical change	Object systems are artifacts designed to meet prespecified requirements. The requirements specification focuses on measurable attributes, controllable functions and desirable features as defined by physical characteristics. Data capture selected attributes of objects which are deemed to exist independently of the observer. Either data or processes may be the primary filter through which object systems are defined.
Social Relativism: focuses on language change and social interaction	Objects systems are autonomous, emergent, symbolic interaction systems. Requirements are defined by emergent properties, unpredictable interactions, are implicit, mainly contributing to 'natural' social equilibrium. The principal filter through which object systems are defined is the symbolic interaction perspective as mediated through language. There is no clear distinction between data- and process-oriented design; it is merely a question of language preference.
Neohumanism: focuses on control of nature as well as social change and emancipation	Object systems are either inanimate (parts of nature or humans treated as quasi-natural 'masses') or sentient beings. In the latter case, they are either viewed from the perspective of control or social interaction as being equal partners in human communication. Under the control perspective, object systems are defined in the same way as in functionalism and from the social interaction perspective in a similar way as Social Relativism. The difference is that language is viewed as potentially distorting and in need of critical reflection and improvement (cf. rational reconstruction). The overriding concern in rational language reconstruction is the improving of the conditions of human existence in the object system towards the ethical ideal of freedom, justice and good taste. [Strictly speaking the social interaction perspective has two different orientations which give rise to two different object system classes. In the first orientation, social interaction is oriented towards mutual understanding on the basis of agreed upon background assumptions and shared values. This perspective generates the kind of object system class described in social relativism. In the second orientation, the social interaction is oriented towards 'discourse' in the sense of checking on background assumptions when these are no longer taken for granted, asking for reasons and grounds to justify them. This generates object system classes which focus the designer on the structure of arguments and checks and balances facilitating the presentation of the best possible evidence through adversarial debate. Each of these object system classes emphasizes different outcomes for information systems design and calls for different design strategies. The details of this are beyond this introductory overview, but see Hirschheim, Klein and Lyytinen (1991) for a fuller treatment.]

Table 3.5: Paradigms and their Ontological Implications for Object Systems

Paradigm	Ontological Implications for Object Systems
Radical Structuralism: focuses on the need for radical change to overcome the class conflicts inherent in capitalist society	Object systems are concrete social systems organized around the physical means of production and their control as expressed in industrial labor relations. A critical property of the object systems is the power conflicts which govern the social relations between those in control and those subject to control and which manifest themselves in many contradictions at the language level, such as conflicting evaluations of the desirability of proposed object system changes and the equity of work arrangements. Object system change is seen as being propelled by the tensions which arise in the process of handling these conflicts. The distinction between data-oriented and process-oriented perspective of object systems is not developed, but the process-oriented perspective is implied.

Table 3.5: Paradigms and their Ontological Implications for Object Systems (cont.)

processes are organized by the objects which need to invoke them; they become subservient to the design of objects. The principal details of this are taken up in chapter 7. The object classes correspond to the common sense notion that we 'interact' with the objects in the real world: when going to a ticket counter we don't expect it to be passive, but respond to our service requests; when driving a car we expect it to respond to our control signals; and when entering a river we expect to experience buoyancy and currents. Moreover, when two object classes are similar, we expect the interactions to be similar in kind (e.g. if you know how to maneuver on ice skates you expect to be able to handle rollerblades as well). Inheritance of properties and dynamic behavior characteristics appears to be built into nature. Hence the advocates of object-oriented analysis claim with some justification that the separation of the world into program and data is 'unnatural', that the object is a more befitting ontological primitive to depict the world than the static entity–attribute categories. However, there is also some awareness that a good set of primitives for reconstructing the world is hard to find, that — philosophically speaking — a good theory of types or categories is as elusive as it was to Aristotle and Kant. However, the implications of this, i.e. that realism is untenable in software construction, are not typically realized in the mainstream literature (for an exception see Floyd *et al.* 1992).

3.5.2 Object systems in radical structuralism

From a proces-oriented perspective, the radical structuralist paradigm shares with functionalism the notion that reality can be depicted in terms of material processes and subjects, but denies that such a depiction is neutral or 'interest free'. However, the definition of processes does not reflect a decomposition of the organizational mission as dictated by efficiency imperatives (i.e. economic technical requirements) but rather the economic interests of some ruling elite. Therefore, the object system is either designed to serve the needs of the ruling elite or the needs of those exploited by the ruling elite, i.e. the workers. The conceptualization of the object system includes a value bias which goes beyond the neutrality assumed in the functionalist paradigm.*

3.5.3 Object systems in social relativism

The process-oriented view of the social relativist paradigm focuses on the symbolic interaction and sense-making processes. These are not definable by economic technical efficiency standards but emerge through shared creation of meanings. The object system therefore embraces the use of myths, metaphors, language and other forms of symbolism.

From a data-oriented perspective, the social relativist paradigm leads to two types of preferred object systems. One type views the object system as a socially constructed image. This image can also be modeled in terms of entities or objects and then in practice social relativist data modeling can apply the same methods and tools to object systems modeling as the functionalists. However, the interpretation of the result changes drastically. The description of the object system reflects a shifting group consensus rather then an unbiased picture of reality. A data model is like an agreed upon painting, the usefulness of which is in the eyes of its beholders, not a depiction of reality which can be made more or less accurate. However, in either case the notion of 'precision' applies in the sense of showing more or less detail.

The second type of object system to which the social relativist paradigm leads focuses on the importance of language as the principal vehicle through which the construction of reality is mediated. This viewpoint assigns a strong role to language analysis in data modeling. From the linguistic point of view the object system is not a perception of reality, but the rule system through which communities interact to make sense of and construct reality. These rules pertain to the ways in which language is used (semantics and syntax) and which govern the intentions and effects of language use (pragmatics, or performative meanings). The principal implications of this type of preferred object system for data modeling methodologies will be taken up in the second part of chapter 7.

3.5.4 Object systems in neohumanism

The neohumanist paradigm shares with social relativism the notion that the preferred object system is the rule system (language) which governs the symbolic interaction of the user community, but adds language critique and rational reconstruction of meanings as an additional important consideration. It thereby takes up some of the concerns of radical structuralism

---

* Since there is no example of radical structuralist data modeling, no discussion is provided on such a data-oriented perspective.

albeit on a different plane of thought. The processes of language use can be distored by threatening social influences such as authority relationships, asymmetry in education and access to information, unwarranted uses of power (e.g. control of hidden agendas), and other barriers to effective communication. Along with these process distorations, the language itself can produce miscommunication through unwanted connotations, loaded terms, euphemisms, misconceptions, jargon, etc. Therefore, the object system of the processes and rules of language use includes the requirement for rational reconstruction of the processes and rules of language use. Some of the basic principles implied by this type of object system are outlined at the end of chapter 6.

3.6 Summary and Conclusions

This chapter has sought to analyze a set of assumptions that developers and researchers alike must make about the domain of change in ISD. These assumptions were shown to form and establish a set of commonly shared practices called paradigms. We confined these assumptions to those concerning epistemology and ontology and the nature of social or human organization. We also clarified the strengths and weaknesses of each paradigmatic position by providing a high level overview of the paradigmatic influences on ISD by analyzing the role of the designer, the nature of IS and objectives of design. We deepened this understanding by examining further how paradigmatic assumptions have shaped conceptions of six functions of ISD. We also discussed what the different paradigmatic positions could mean within the context of data modeling and how each position would approach the data modeling task. Finally, we considered how paradigmatic assumptions affect concept formation and choice, i.e. how paradigmatic choices are likely to constrain choices of object system definition. Overall, our analysis has focused on generic and architectural features of different methodologies and data modeling approaches. Next, we shall explore how these features are reflected in methodologies in 'action'.

4
Conceptual and Paradigmatic Foundations of ISD

4.1 Introduction

In this chapter, the general philosophical basis laid down in chapter 3 will now be applied to provide a broad but more concrete perspective on systems development. Systems development will be explored in two steps: first, we focus on the underlying concepts; and second, we look at the application of the concepts in various methodologies. More specifically, chapter 4 elaborates on the theoretical concepts of ISD as introduced in chapter 2, and ties them into the paradigmatic notions as discussed in chapter 3. ISD tries to show how the conceptual foundations introduced thus far can actually help us to better understand, organize and analyze the rich variety of approaches which have been proposed in the literature. In chapter 5 we deepen this understanding by analyzing in detail four specific methodologies to ISD.

Our first task in this chapter is to convey a more vivid picture to the reader of how systems development might actually proceed in practice if it were to adhere to different paradigms. To this end we shall provide an ideal-type description of the 'scene' of systems analysis under the four paradigms identified in chapter 3, thereby illustrating their underlying fundamental concepts in a systems development context. In the last part of this chapter we relate the four paradigms to the evolution of approaches to ISD as introduced in chapter 2.

4.2 Paradigms of Information Systems Development

Each of the following four descriptions of systems development was derived from interpreting pools of systems development literature which share the assumptions of a particular paradigm. These pools have been identified by analyzing the specific core assumptions and beliefs which are revealed in the concepts and examples they employ. This allows us to explicitly compare sets of assumptions which typically have neither been widely articulated nor systematically confronted with one another.

First we give a brief general description of ISD in each paradigm. Next we provide a theoretical interpretation and discuss some of its potential consequences. The theoretic interpretation will take the form of discussing the:

(1) key actors in the systems development exercise (really the key roles played by various agents) — 'who' is in involved with ISD;

(2) narrative — 'what' occurs during systems development (what are the key features and activities);

(3) plot — 'why' the various activities occur; and

(4) assumptions — these are the fundamental beliefs held by the various actors during ISD, and are discussed in terms of epistemological and ontological assumptions in general and their implications for each paradigm's preferred object system.

The four paradigms are not as clear-cut nor as animated as they are made out to seem. There is overlap and their differences are overstated for the purpose of effect. They are, in fact, archetypes — highly simplified but powerful conceptions of an ideal or character type (Mitroff 1983). These ideal types do not exist as 'real' entities, rather it is their properties which are exhibited (to a greater or lesser degree) in existing entities which give the archetype meaning. The archetypes reflected in the paradigms play an important role in conveying the essential differences which exist in alternative conceptions of, and approaches to, systems development. It must be noted that the four paradigms are not equally well-developed nor known. The same is true of their consequences. For the first paradigm, there is a large experiential base on which to draw. It is the orthodox functional approach to systems development and has been used to develop information systems for decades. Its consequences, therefore, are reasonably clear-cut. The other three are more recent and have not been widely applied. Thus the practical knowledge on them is sparse and their consequences largely conjectural. They are presented in the rough chronological order in which they emerged and this order will be clarified further in section 4.3.

4.2.1 Paradigmatic assumptions of functionalist ISD

4.2.1.1 General description

The basic metaphor for the process of systems development in functionalism is to build systems which achieve given ends (systems development as instrumental reasoning) and the role of the analyst is that of a systems expert. The theory and practice of functionalism in ISD has progressed considerably over the years (*cf.* Olle *et al.* 1982, 1983, 1986, 1988; Couger *et al.* 1982; Teichroew and David 1985; Cotterman and Senn 1992), and has been practiced successfully while developing a large variety of systems. Functionalism suggests that all information systems are designed to contribute to specific and clear ends. The role of information systems is to provide timely information which is relevant to decision makers for organizational problem solving and control. The role of management is that of the leadership group in the organization who knows or develops the ends which are then translated and specified in terms of systems objectives. The usual assumption is that the specification is as objective as possible. The resolution of polemical issues associated with objectives is seen as the prerogative of management and not normally within the domain of the systems developer. As a result, the ends can be viewed as being well-articulated, explicitly agreed, and aconflictual. Of course, there are many kinds of conflicts with which the system developer does deal in achiving his ends, but the tools and methods used typically concern only the choice of means to prespecified ends, not the substance of the ultimate ends of a system.

The primary role of the analyst is to be the expert in technology, tools and methods of system design, and project management. Their application helps to make systems development more formal and rational, placing less reliance on human intuition, judgment, and politics. Politics is seen as irrational as it interferes with maximal efficiency or effectiveness. As noted by DeMarco (1978, p. 13): 'Political problems aren't going to go away and they won't be 'solved'. The most we can hope for is to limit the effect of disruption due to politics. Structured analysis approaches this objective by making analysis procedures more formal'.

Functionalist approaches to ISD presume that there exists one reality which is measurable and essentially the same for everyone. Otherwise it would not be possible to have what McMenamin and Palmer (1984) call the 'true requirements of the system'. The role of the developer is to design systems which model this reality (van Griethuysen 1982) in a way which will turn the system into a useful tool for management to achieve their ends (Bariff and Ginzberg 1982). In principle, these ends coincide with organizational goals.

Through the concept of economic requirements, economic reality becomes measurable taking on a nature-like, given quality. The economic reality (translated into quantitative, financial goals and systems performance characteristics) allows systems objectives to be derived in an objective, verifiable, and rational way. Systems design becomes primarily a technical process.* Therefore functional methodologies assume very little or no problem uncertainty, some effect uncertainty and considerable means uncertainty. Moreover the change process is an ideal situation expected to have deterministic features similar to a production process (Lyytinen and Lehtinen 1987).

4.2.1.2 Interpretation

Key Actors: management, the system developer and users. Management

---

* This is in part due to the reification of economic requirements which hides the human authorship of systems objectives, presenting them as mere technical objectives. Such a view has a rich historical backing. The belief that the economic laws are not of human authorship is very clearly portrayed in the writings of Adam Smith's *The Wealth of Nations* who speaks of an 'invisible hand' which directs management decisions to realize the economic interests of individual companies for the common good. From a social and economic policy perspective it is therefore unwise to question the legitimacy of management in deciding system objectives. This could only reduce the general welfare by leading to suboptimal allocation of economic resources. Furthermore this story adopts many features of the 'bureaucracy ideal type' of Weber (1947) such as instrumental rationality, formalization, and depersonalization.

are those organizational members who are responsible for providing the systems objectives. The systems developer is the 'expert' who takes the objectives and turns them into a constructed product: the system. Management dictates the ends, the developers use specific means to achieve the ends. The users operate or interact with the system to achieve organizational objectives.

Narrative: information systems are developed to support rational organizational operation which also applies to effective and efficient project management. Therefore rigid functional specialization and standardization of jobs and tasks is emphasized and monitoring and controlling the development through hierarchical and organizational arrangements is preferred. The effectiveness and efficiency of IS is tested by objective means tests, similar to the empirical tests used in engineering. Requirements specification builds on the notion of a manifest and rational organizational reality. Information systems development proceeds through the application of 'naive realism' — the notion that the validity of system specifications, data models, decision models and system output can be established by checking if they correspond to reality. Reality consists of objects, properties and processes which are directly observable.

Plot: the ideal of profit maximization. As an organization's primary goal is to maximize its shareholders' wealth, the developed information systems must contribute to its profitability. Management is seen as the most appropriate group to decide how profitability is to be attained and thus is empowered to specify what the systems objectives should be.

Assumptions: The epistemology is that of positivism in that the developer gains knowledge about the organization by searching for measurable cause effect relationships. The ontology is that of realism since there is believed to exist an empirical organizational reality which is independent of its perceiver or observer. Object systems are seen as a part of a larger organizational reality which together with organizational goals defines objective constraints and performance requirements for appropriate system functioning. The paradigm 'seeks to provide essentially rational explanations of social affairs' (Burrell and Morgan 1979 p. 26).

4.2.1.3 Analysis and discussion

The functionalist methods and tools of systems development through their emphasis on various forms of modeling, focus on grasping the underlying order of the domains in which organizational actors operate. In the process, functionalism assumes that there are general laws or regular patterns which help to explain, predict and control reality. It seeks to capture these by identifying key organizational relationships and aspects in IS which help the actors to orient themselves and to achieve their objectives. This has the effect of simplifying a complex reality, making organizational life more rational. Rationality, in this case, relates to choosing the best means for achieving given ends (i.e. maximize efficiency) by resolving primary problems related to means uncertainty. The systems development approach suggested by functionalism has a good basis in the 'scientific method'. This aids its clarity and comprehensibility, and makes it widely acceptable to the community at large. Moreover, it helps in the operationalization of fuzzy issues and directs efforts to finding productive technical solutions.

These features support a number of apparently appealing beliefs. First, it allows the developer to play a neutral and objective role during systems development which helps in clarifying the implications of alternative system design options. Second, many would claim it makes the issues of power, conflicting interests, and system goals appear to be largely outside the domain of the systems developer, i.e. masks out problem and effect uncertainty and problems associated with goal setting. Moreover, there are a large number of systems which have been successfully completed by following the tenets of this approach.

However, as Bostrom and Heinen (1977) have pointed out, the systems designers' assumptions associated with this kind of approach can lead to a number of conditions that contribute to system failure. The application of functionalism in ISD, therefore, has a number of potential dysfunctional consequences. For one, the primary emphasis is on investigating means rather than discussing ends. There is an implicit assumption that the ends are agreed, i.e. they are aconflictual, clear and serve only one purpose. But in reality, ends are always controversial, ambiguous and a subject of considerable disagreement and debate. By assuming the ends and thus system objectives are agreed, legitimation can become little more than a hollow force or thinly concealed use of power. The prespecified ends meet the needs of certain system stakeholders at the expense of others. There are also more fundamental problems with legitimacy. It is now widely doubted that economic laws govern social affairs in a similar way as natural laws govern the physical universe. Instead it is believed that economic laws are the product of social conventions and the decisions of a powerful socio-political elite. They are not some rational, deterministic force which emerges from an objective reality.

A reaction to the erosion of these legitimating beliefs is users' resistance. To overcome such resistance to change, system developers have relied on a series of approaches, games and strategies. These have taken the form of planned change models (e.g. the Lewin-Schein and Kolb-Frohman models), implementation strategies (Lucas 1981; Alter 1980), counterimplementation and counter-counterimplementation strategies (Bardach 1977; Keen 1981), and the like. These approaches, however, simply perpetuate the notion that systems development and implementation is a type of game; there are winners and losers. They continue to concentrate on means not ends. The assumption is still that the system objectives are legitimate and agreed. Failure to focus on the legitimation of the ends has led to an inappropriate conception about why users resist change.

The adoption of functionalism as the preferred paradigm for organizational knowledge acquisition also poses problems. As Burrell and Morgan (1979) point out, the assumptions intrinsic to functionalism have proved to be at odds with much of recent social science thinking. Functionalism's two essential assumptions:

(i) that there exists an objective empirical reality and positivistic methods are the best way to make sense of it, and

(ii) the nature of the social world is best conceived in terms of order rather than conflict;

are widely felt to be problematic. Many now argue that functionalism has not been a particularly successful paradigm for understanding organizational and societal life, as the subject of study — people — does not lend itself to study through positivistic means (*cf.* van Maanen 1979; Lessnoff 1974; Fay 1975; Klein and Lyytinen 1985; Hirschheim 1985b; Boland 1985). People have free will and there exists an asymmetry of observation. This latter point reflects the fact that people as objects of study always 'observe back'. They can perceive the observer's plan of study and counteract it. (It must be noted, however, that the more recent forms of functionalism (*cf.* Alexander 1985; Faia 1986) have recognized these problems and have proposed ways to overcome them.)

In some of the more advanced thinking in ISD, there is an awareness of the changing nature of organizational reality facing the developer. It is explicitly recognized that at any point in time a system can, at best, approximate the changing requirements emerging from the constantly shifting trends and policies of organizational life which can never fully be known to developers.* Such insight transcends the mental 'cage' of functionalist tenets in ISD. In so far as practitioners realize the consequences of this, they will see value in the other paradigms.

4.2.2 Paradigmatic assumptions of social relativist ISD

4.2.2.1 General description

The basic metaphor for the process of systems development in social relativism is to build systems which facilitate sense making and mutual understanding. The role of the analyst is that of a facilitator for social evolution and change. The second paradigm has emerged more recently in ISD (*cf.* Checkland 1981; Boland and Day 1982; Bjerknes and Bratteteig 1984,

---

* In particular, consider the case when users and management are identical, such as in executive support systems. In such cases, the goals of systems development cannot be treated as if they were predetermined by higher authority. Rather, the goals are derived from an analysis of the shifting forces from the environment that affect the continued viability of the organization. This is the responsibility of senior management. On the other hand, in the classical data processing era, it was easy to set the goals for systems development because the systems dealt with well-understood and structured tasks.

1985; Mathiassen and Andersen 1985; Banbury 1987; Checkland and Scholes 1990). It is partly a reaction to the shortcomings of functionalism and in many ways its opposite. It recognizes that knowledge about human means and ends is not easily obtained because reality is exceedingly complex and elusive. There is no single reality, only different perceptions about it. Business does not deal with an objective economic reality, but one that evolves through changing traditions — social laws, conventions, cultural norms and attitudes. Trying to discern economic laws is one way in which people try to make sense of their confusing experiences by imposing a possible order. No one has a privileged source of knowledge, all see different parts. Furthermore the role of people in shaping reality is very unclear. What they subjectively experience as a willful choice of action may simply be a reaction induced by enculturated habits or by circumstances.

Management, too, tries to make sense of the confusion and instill others with a commitment to the organizational mission. It is not given, but constantly evolving. IS are part of the continually changing social environment and somehow should help to identify which ends are desirable and feasible. The distinction between ends and means is fluid and reversible, i.e. goals are ambiguous, multi-functional and conflicting. System objectives emerge as part of the organizational construction of reality, the 'sense-making process' (Berger and Luckmann 1967). The role of the system developer is to interact with management to find out what type of system makes sense; but there is no objective criterion which distinguishes good from bad systems. It all depends on what the parties come to believe to be true. The developer should work from within the users' perspective and help them to find their preferred views. He should ease the transition from one viewpoint to another, thereby alleviating possible resistance to change. Ideally the developer — by virtue of prior experiences, wisdom or special insights — is able to reduce the pains of change. Hence social relativism emphasizes problem uncertainty and the process of negotiation and clarification to reduce it. Overall, the purpose and direction of change is hidden from all participants and the analyst's expertise is similar to that of the midwife who can ease the process of birth and make sure that the baby emerges safe and sound, but has no part in 'designing' its genetic characteristics.

Any system that meets with the approval of the affected parties is thought to be legitimate. To achieve consensus or acceptance, continuous interaction among all parties is critical. Through interaction, objectives emerge and become legitimized through continuous modification. Systems cannot be designed in the usual sense, but emerge through social interaction. The mechanism of prototyping or evolutionary learning from interaction with partial implementations is the way technology becomes embedded into the social perception and sense-making process.

4.2.2.2 Interpretation

Key Actors: users and the systems developer. The users are the organizational agents who interpret and make sense of their surroundings. The systems developer is the change agent who helps the users make sense of the new system and its environment.

Narrative: information systems development creates new meanings. The effectiveness of the information system rests on its ability to help users better understand the currently accepted conventions and meanings. Information systems development proceeds through the application of 'symbolic interactionism', which suggests that organizational actors interpret systems objectives and specifications and act according to the meaning provided by their interpretation. Mead (1934) captures the essence of symbolic interactionism when he writes: 'Language does not simply symbolize a situation or object which is already there in advance; it makes possible the existence or appearance of that situation or object, for it is part of the mechanism whereby that situation or object is created' (p. 78).

Plot: none manifest. As the social environment is under continuous evolution, no particular rational explanations can be provided to 'explain' organizational reality.

Assumptions: The epistemology is that of anti-positivism reflecting the belief that the search for causal, empirical explanations for social phenomena is misguided and should be replaced by the will and need to make sense of oneself and the situation. The ontology is that of nominalism (constructivism) in that reality is not a given, immutable 'out there' but is socially constructed. It is the product of the human mind. Object systems emerge as part of the ongoing reality construction and the act of bounding the scope of object systems and defining requirements contributes to the ongoing process of sense-making. The paradigm, social relativism, focuses on understanding social phenomena and is primarily involved in explaining the social world from the viewpoint of the organizational agents who directly take part in the social process of reality construction.

4.2.2.3 Analysis and discussion

The paradigm of social relativism focuses on the complexity of reality, which is by its very nature confusing. It does not try to conceal this complexity by pretending that there is an underlying order which can be captured in simplifying models. Reality is socially constructed and the product of continual social interaction, i.e. the change process is emergent and cyclical. Each person's involvement in the social interaction produces unique experiential knowledge. The emerging meanings are a function of experience which is always changing and never quite the same for two people. The uniqueness and idiosyncratic nature of each situation does not allow it to be handled by applying universal laws and principles. There is a shift from the rigorous scientific paradigm of prediction by explanatory laws to interpretative accounts based on a digest of experiences that have been articulated by leader figures or handed down through tradition. The concept of means-ends rationality does not play any significant role here. Instead, developers act rationally if they simply accept prevailing attitudes and values, remain consistent with general opinion, and implement changes in a way that does not threaten social harmony.

As this paradigm emphasizes the complexity of systems development, it doubts the efficacy of objective and rigorous methods and tools. Instead, it favors an approach to systems development which facilitates the learning of all who are concerned and affected. This implies a switch in role of the developer from one of system expert to facilitator who helps to stimulate reflection, cooperation and experiential learning. In practice, the social relativist approach seeks to provide specific tools which the facilitator at his discretion may use to support the project group interaction. Examples are diary keeping, various forms of mappings ('historical, diagnostic, ecological, and virtual', Lanzara and Mathiassen 1984), special group pedagogy, use of metaphors to stimulate mental shifts ('breakthrough by breakdown', Madsen 1989), etc. These tools can be used by the organizational actors toaddress and reduce problem-uncertainty and to clarify ambiguous goals, i.e. 'for exploring, for learning, for increasing awareness, for inventing solutions to problems, and for undertaking action' (Lanzara and Mathiassen 1984). This is accompanied by the belief that it is not so much the result of systems development that is important but the way it is achieved. Hence it intrinsically favors strong participation. Social relativism favors systems that stimulate creativity and induce change in systems of interpretation. Here, the use of creativity is not seen as a means to achieve any specific or wider benefits but to learn to see things differently. The local or global effects of ISD, good or bad, are not a conscious concern. The assumptions of this paradigm do not support the notion of a political center that attempts to strike a balance between individual and collective interests. Consequently, consensus is not viewed as a social means to maintain interest-based coalitions or for achieving an overall global optimum to which individuals interests are subordinate.

As the name of social 'relativism' suggests, the assumptions of this paradigm do support the attitude that all is relative; acceptance is the only thing that matters. Social interaction is crucial for acceptance but there is no way to distinguish between valid and fallacious (inauthentic, manipulative) consensus (what Habermas 1984 terms 'naive consensus'). Because of its relativist stance, social relativism is uncritical of the potential dysfunctional side-effects of using particular tools and techniques for ISD. Different products of systems development are simply viewed as the result of different socially constructed realities.

4.2.3 Paradigmatic assumptions of radical structuralist ISD

4.2.3.1 General description

The basic metaphor for the process of systems development in radical structuralism is to build systems which strengthen the position of the working class in their struggle against capitalist domination. The role of the analyst is that of a labor partisan to aid the common man to win his or her rightful share of rewards for the fruits of their labor.

The radical structuralist like the social relativist paradigm is also a fairly recent reaction to functionalism (*cf.* Briefs 1983; Ehn and Sandberg 1983; Howard 1985; Sandberg 1985; Kyng and Ehn 1985; Ehn and Kyng 1987). It differs from social relativism by postulating that a fundamental social conflict is endemic to society; yet it agrees with functionalism in that there is an objective economic reality. The conflict is alleged to exist between the interests of those who own the sources of production (shareholders of the organization) and labor (*cf.* Braverman 1974). Economic reality is explained in terms of the dialectic (interdependent) unfolding of the conflict between these two social classes. The conflict is a result of the objective condition of ownership. It contends that the invention of economic market laws is a ploy by the owners of the sources of production to make the working class believe that there is no alternative way to arrange working conditions. Management has sided with the owners and are mere agents of their interests.

Under the assumptions of this paradigm, the developer is faced with a choice: either he sides with management and becomes their agent, or he joins the interests of labor. In the first case, the systems he designs would rationalize the interests of management and the owners. In this case, the developer will direct systems rationalization against the workers' interests by affecting the intensity of work, changing the instruments of work, or re-placing the object of work altogether. Systems development in the interest of management increases intensity of work by using computers to direct the work flow or supervise workers, for instance by issuing detailed, optimally sequenced work schedules (as in the ISA-KLAR project, Ehn and Sandberg 1983), monitoring machine operations (keystroke counting, measuring idle time), etc. An example of changing the instruments or tools of work is the replacement of typewriters by word processors. An example of where the object of work has been replaced is in the watch industry where integrated circuits replaced mechanical watch movements. In all these cases worker interests are jeopardized because of loss of jobs, decreased dependence of management on labor, deskilling of jobs by increased specialization or stan-dardization, and so forth.

System developers can choose, however, to side with the workers, design-ing systems which help their interests. In this case, they should use tech-nology to enhance labor's traditional skills and craftsmanship, attempting to make work both more rewarding — economically and psychologically — and deliver a better product. There may also be productivity gains, but these must benefit the worker: by shorter work weeks, more time spent on planning and organizing the creative part of their work, time for continuing education, more autonomy, and better wages. The system developer needs to avoid replacing labor by capital through automation. Technology could also help workers to manage their own productive concerns — the interest of those who manage and those who do the productive work would then coincide.

At present, systems developers have chosen the former alternative to the virtual exclusion of the latter, i.e. they have acted as the agents of management. But trade union-led projects in Scandinavia such as DEMOS (Ehn and Sandberg 1983) and UTOPIA (Howard 1985) are instances where systems development was placed in the hands of the workers.* No matter which role the system developer chooses, the source of system objectives is the collective interest of the conflicting classes: profits for the owners or improvement of working conditions for labor. From a radical structuralist perspective, choosing the former leads to the exploitation of the common man. Thus, the legitimate system objectives are those which enhance the lot of the workers who must earn a living through their labor.

4.2.3.2 Interpretation

Key Actors: two classes (owners and labor), management, and the systems developer. The two antagonistic classes, the owners of the productive resources and labor, are engaged in a classic struggle. The owners become the beneficiaries of information systems while labor becomes the victim of system rationalization. Management acts as the agents of the owners. The system developer has a choice of either being an agent for management or labor.

Narrative: information systems are developed to support managerial control. Systems objectives reflect the desire to support the interests of the owners at the expense of the interests of labor. Information systems development is embedded in the historical unfolding of 'class struggle' — it either strengthens the side of the owners (ruling class) or their opponents: labor. In other words goals are clear and conflicting. The underlying hypothesis, that of 'dialectic materialism', suggests that the material economic conditions are fundamental for the shaping of class interests. The social conflict between the two classes follows the pattern of the dialectical triad: exploitation of one class by the other, revolt, and synthesis. The synthesis takes the form of a new political order and ideology. Information system development is part of the rationalizing forces by which the owner class exploits labor.

Plot: the ideal of evolution from slavery through feudalism and capitalist market economy to a collectively planned and managed economy. The purpose of systems development should be to help labor to overcome the constraints of capitalism by supporting labor activism.

Assumptions: The epistemology is dialectical inquiry in the specific form of a materialist view of history and society. The ontology is that of realism reflecting the belief in a pre-existing empirical reality. Object systems are

---

* Currently the approach does not make it clear how systems development could help those who are not employed at all or those who live in countries who have not developed along the lines of the Scandinavian democracies. (This point also applies to the other paradigms.)

those objectively given conditions of work which become the target of management initiatives to rationalize work processes by changing the means of production and the general organization of work. The paradigm, i.e. radical structuralism, reflects a critique of the status quo with the aim of providing the rationale for radical change.

4.2.3.3 Analysis and discussion

The assumptions of the radical structuralist paradigm focus on the fact that systems development intervenes in the conflict between social classes for prestige, power, and resources. Conflict is seen as endemic to society and generally follows a predictable pattern which can be discerned by analyzing vested social interests and the structures and relationships supporting them. An example of this is the effects of rationalization on workers. The principles of this paradigm deliberately exhort the developer to become an advocate of labor to redress the balance of power between management and labor as the only morally acceptable course of action. The paradigm promotes the insight that all knowledge relates to human interests and thus a neutral science is impossible (*cf.* Fay 1975). Culture, knowledge and human interests are seen as intimately related. Cultural norms and values are revealed to be subtle, but nevertheless effective mechanisms of behavior control. They are a ploy to legitimize managerial goals and turn workers into faithful servants of the ruling elite.

As a consequence, user resistance is seen as positive because it is a sign of labor becoming aware of their collective interest which in turn is a prerequisite for social progress. This should motivate the developer to seek cooperation with labor and their representatives. The paradigm advocates a participative approach but only with one party — labor. Only those ends (systems objectives) which evolve from the cooperation between labor and the developer are considered legitimate. This is thought to lead to systems which emphasize enhancement of craftsmanship and conditions, and a higher quality of products for the consumer although at a higher price. Rationality is tied to the interests of labor. Only those systems objectives, tools and methods which enhance the position of labor and thereby lead to social progress are considered rational.

The attitudes favored in this paradigm lead to a number of potentially dysfunctional consequences. In practice, radical structuralism embraces the notion of 'activism' (where it is believed it is more important to change the world than interpret it) which reduces the possibility of a justified consensus where cooperation instead of conflict is sought. It is uncritical of the effects of social differentiation introduced by organizing class interests into unions or other forms of worker organization (political parties and the like); for example, the manipulation of the constituency by their leaders, and the effects of 'co-optation' and relative isolation of the leaders who often become involved in different social spheres than their constituency.

Moreover, it has a tendency to oversimplify: for example, there exist only two parties, there is no conflict between workers and their representatives, there exists a homogeneous management class, and so on. It also sees the lack of conflict as undesirable in that it reinforces the status quo, except when the classless society is reached as the end product of the struggle. It assumes that there are immutable nature-like laws that determine the future of society. This leads to the so-called 'fallacy of historicism' where all events are seen in terms of an inevitable, evolutionary conflict.

4.2.4 Paradigmatic assumptions of neohumanist ISD

4.2.4.1 General description

The basic metaphor for the process of systems development in neohumanism is to build systems which permit emancipation through rational discourse. The role of the analyst is that of an emancipator or social therapist. While the other three paradigms can be observed in actual systems development cases, this one is somewhat hypothetical in that it has been constructed from theory (Lyytinen and Klein 1985; Lyytinen 1986; Ngwenyama 1987; Lyytinen and Hirschheim 1987; Hirschheim and Klein 1994). Current systems development approaches do not typically possess tools that are supportive of neohumanist goals, although in some approaches or projects there is some recognition of communication barriers and possible therapeutic measures, for example, ETHICS (Mumford 1983), PORGI (Oppelland and Kolf 1980), SSM (Checkland 1981; Checkland and Scholes 1990), MARS (Lanzara and Mathiassen 1984), FLORENCE (Bjerknes and Brattetieg 1985), UTOPIA (Bodker *et al.* 1987) and DEMOS (Ehn and Sandberg 1983). Furthermore, the SAMPO project (Lyytinen and Lehtinen 1987; Auramaki *et al.* 1992a,b) moves some way toward supporting the emancipatory goal by focusing on language modeling, and Kerola's (1985, 1987) reconceptualization of the systems development life-cycle addresses emancipatory concerns through emphasizing social learning during systems development. Thus, as the application of neohumanist principles in ISD is not yet well understood, the following has the character of a tentative sketch of a subject that is just emerging in the research literature.

The principal concern of neohumanism is with the transformation of the conditions of human existence to overcome injustice, social domination and other obstacles to human self-realization and freedom. The principal strategy for improving the conditions of human existence in this sense is through an emancipatory discourse which reveals and tests the constraints that limit the realization of justice, freedom and self-realization. The fundamental attitude of neohumanism is that through rational discourse the truth can be discovered and once discovered 'truth will make us free'. Constraints that limit the recognition of truth and justice may exist in three 'domains': first, they can be physical arrangements in the external world such as barriers of time and space. The physical barriers can be addressed through economic technical means (e.g. improved productivity, medical advances, transportation and communications technology). Second, they can be social conventions (such as laws and policies, stereotyping). Third, they can be internal psychological compulsions (such as defensive behaviors and self-delusions) which are often induced through distorted or manipulative communication such as in advertising and political propaganda or dysfunctional family histories (alcoholism, domestic violence, ghettoization).

In order to reveal claims and constraints in the physical, social or psychological domain and test their validity, the neohumanist paradigm recognizes an ontology consisting of three worlds, all of which are affected through systems development. The first world is the external world of physical objects, events, processes, etc. Systems development helps to predict and control this world. The second world is our world of shared meanings and language. Information systems affect this world by redefining the channels of social interaction and the modes of social communication (how people relate to one another). The third world consists of subjective meanings and emotional states which in principle are not directly accessible to anyone except to the individual in question. Information systems development affects the contents of this world in two ways:

(1) directly by giving easier access to some information and favoring the access to certain types of information (e.g. that which is stored in databases on CD-ROM which overcomes some of the barriers of time and space) and disfavoring others (e.g. those which require trips to the library which introduces new types of barriers to enlightenment); and

(2) more subtly, by changing the ways in which the world is experienced and subjective meanings are formed (e.g. by suggesting new ways of seeing and thinking, and imposing new concepts or mental frames upon our habitual modes of perception).

The neohumanist paradigm also distinguishes between two spheres of human activities, each of which calls for different types of IS support: work and social interaction. Work aims at achieving given purposes by exercising control over natural objects or people. Social interaction proceeds on the basis of assumed background assumptions and is oriented toward mutual understanding and agreement. If however understanding or agreement is in jeopardy, then social interaction proceeds on the basis of justifying arguments to restore the orientation of mutual understanding and agreement. In such a case, social interaction can lead to emancipation from unwarranted constraints such as social domination. Emancipation involves the testing of validity claims through socially appropriate arguments.

Work in neohumanism

Through work organization people participate in the struggle against nature to produce the material basis for their survival. More specifically, through technically organized work, the members of the organization reproduce their material basis for the particular way of life provided by 'their organization' (i.e. the organizational resources from which the participants draw wages and other benefits). In work, everyone and everything is seen as an 'object' to be manipulated, i.e. predicted and controlled. In this sense, work is strictly an instrumental activity. Objects, in this case, include people which are treated as production factors whose behavior is subject to measurement and control, just as inanimate objects. Conflict of interests are either denied or deemed to be dealt with by submission to organizational policies and work directives.

An essential feature of the evolutionary development of the human species is the emancipation of its members from those aspects of work which are unnecessarily burdensome. This involves overcoming natural constraints through technology. An example is flood control or replacing work in dangerous and physically unpleasant places by robots who can be maintained in the comfort of an air-conditioned workshop. Of course, true emancipation must be global. Elites, even if well-meaning, must not buy their relative comfort at the expense of misery or alienation of others (as in Huxley's *Brave New World* or Vonnegut's *Player Piano*, for example). True emancipation means that meaningful forms of life exist for all.

Social interaction in neohumanism

The other activity, social interaction, is quite different from the instrumental work concept. It deals with creating shared meanings and reaching 'mutual understanding' in a network of communicative relations. It is typically oriented towards agreement in that mutual understanding relates to the need of people to share their views and have others agree with them. The solidarity of our friends and associates comforts us all and in return we are willing to make adjustments to our own opinions until a common basis of agreement is reached. If the primary interest is one of achieving consensual mutual understanding and agreement, then one must acknowledge the other person as a partner for human interaction rather than an object of manipulation. This is not to say that manipulation does not occur, but that it alters the way in which participants relate to each other.

Mutual understanding may be realized through many forms of communication which create shared meanings which are then stored as the stock of knowledge as part of culture and a person's 'Weltanschauung'. Individuals engage in a process of sense-making aimed at understanding one's culture, one's own psyche and the psyche of those with whom one interacts — that is one's kin, friends, clients and even enemies. An essential insight is that all understanding depends on some preconceptions (Gadamer's 'preunderstanding' or 'prejudices') which are carried into interpretation and changed through it. Typically these prejudices come from one's background in a culture — the life world. Seeking understanding means to revise one's preunderstandings and these revised 'prejudices' then become the basis of the next round of interpretation (for a more detailed analysis see chapter 6).

In order to build shared understanding, some form of interaction is crucial. For example through participation in design, shared understandings are built that help overcome problems — this is the hermeneutic aspect of participation. The emphasis on mutual understanding also suggests the need to establish social conditions which are accepted as good and just and thereby the consensual commitments are maintained which are necessary to regulate all human affairs: from the family to government and international relations.

In order to maintain loyalty and commitment in the organization (as well as in other human dealings), social interaction is crucial. Hence both work (for material reproduction) and social interaction for socio-cultural reproduction of community feelings and beliefs (the interpretative basis for work) are key imperatives of organizational life. Through ordinary language communication the community bonds are reproduced (maintained) and mutual understandings are continually adjusted to keep pace with an always puzzling and at times threatening world.

Different types of knowledge are important for undertaking work and achieving mutual understanding. The engineering sciences, for example, improve our means of prediction and control and thereby 'emancipate' us from natural constraints by proposing and testing technical rules. Through applying these, we achieve greater freedom from external needs and are more efficient at work. The cultural sciences, on the other hand, assist in understanding ourselves and others: history, literature, philosophy, psychoanalysis, and sociology, serve to improve the understanding of ourselves and our fellow human beings and cultures. Their contribution is primarily to improve the chances of mutual understanding in all walks of life. The cultural sciences, through fundamental criticism, also may assist in revealing how we as human beings are governed and controlled, overtly and covertly.

Emancipation in neohumanism

While consensual interaction is the normal mode of operation in human affairs, not all consensus is desirable, because it can be based on fallacious assumptions (such as that slavery is a natural law) and ideological distortions as are maintained through limiting communication by the exercise of power. Both access to knowledge and the agenda of communication can be limited. The overcoming of such internal and external compulsions is called 'emancipatory'. This broadens the concept of emancipation from overcoming natural-physical constraints to include man-made (psychological and political) constraints. Henceforth we shall define emancipation as all conscious attempts of human reason to free us from pseudo-natural constraints. Pseudo-natural are constraints which operate by non-transparency or unrecognized 'error' and therefore appear as if they were a natural condition. Non-transparency often is the result of reification which suppresses (i.e. through social 'forgetting' or ideology) the human authorship of certain conditions or practices which then appear indistinguishable from natural law. Emancipation proceeds by revealing the sources and causes of the distorting influences which hide alternative ways of life from us. Emancipation through 'enlightenment' can also be achieved, for example, by following the Socratic ideal of 'know thyself' and 'truth can make us free'. The dominant orientation of emancipatory communication (or discourse) is the testing of validity claims of intelligibility, social appropriateness, correctness (truth), or justice. A historical example is science in the Age of Enlightenment: it was emancipatory in that it helped to free mankind from unwarranted dogmas and superstitions. It tested many of the validity claims inherited from the middle ages and found them wanting on many grounds.

The cultural sciences, key for improving the potential of consensual interaction, do not necessarily contribute to revealing all forms of domination and the emancipation from bias and self-delusion, unless they are critical. One key issue is that we are caught in the web of our own language and customs and it is difficult to escape the blind spot of our own tradition — the cultural biases that have been handed down to us 'in the way things are done'. How to overcome the mental and emotional prisons of our received culture and practices (including language) has been the key topic in the Gadamer-Habermas debate (*cf.* the summary in McCarthy 1982). Gadamer has argued that participation in some culture is a prerequisite for all thought including critical reflection.

In summary, whereas social interaction is concerned with interpretation and understanding ('sense-making') in the spirit of agreement, emancipation is concerned with 'correct' understanding in the spirit of veracity and critique. It is normative in that it proceeds by social criticism and aims at removing unwarranted constraints to social and personal growth. The cultural sciences facilitating mutual understanding (such as history or literature) are better developed than those that might help with social emancipation. Critical reflection, psycho-analysis, historical reflection, comparative critique of literature and analysis of ideology are prototypical of emancipatory or 'critical' sciences.

Implications for ISD

Information systems (and ISD) can support work, social interaction (mutual understanding) and emancipation. Information systems development which is consistent with the functionalist ideals (and embracing the engineering sciences) emphasizes how to rationalize and make work more efficient. However, information systems development can play an equally important role in the realization of mutual understanding and social emancipation.

In pursuing mutual understanding the system developer might elicit, through interaction, a shared understanding of the many obstacles to human communication. This implies that he must acquire an insider knowledge of the different viewpoints and existential situation of the different stakeholders. This can only be done by 'dialogical interaction' (Habermas 1984) and not just by external 'objective observation'. Genuine participation is crucial. Obstacles, however, abound both in weaknesses of human personality (internal compulsions) and imperfections in the social-institutional context that shape the work situation (external compulsions). We shall refer to these types of compulsions also as unwarranted constraints. Internal compulsions are induced by psychological forces internal to the individual personality. They can be addressed through psychological counseling and group therapy such as leadership programs, and employee assistance groups. More intractable are external compulsions which to some degree are beyond the control of system developers or even the organization.

External compulsions are unwarranted constraints imposed by forces from the surrounding society or the organization. They are external to the individual, although not necessarily beyond his or her control, but typically require social action, i.e. coordinated action of groups of people that change the institutional arrangements and climate. That such is possible without changing society is obvious from even casual organizational comparisons. There are striking differences in the degree to which different organizations in the same region put stress on their staff (including managers), encourage or inhibit personal growth and self-realization, give remuneration, and so forth (Hirschheim and Miller 1993).

Systems developers should be aware of external compulsions for two reasons. First, system development affects society in many ways and to this extent must be held accountable for perpetuating inequitable social conditions (*cf.* Bjorn-Andersen *et al.* 1982; Grewlich and Pedersen 1984, for example). There can be an accumulative effect if many small companies in an economic region change their ways, for example by turning to participatory approaches in educating their work force. Large organizations have a strong direct influence on the community in which they exist both through what they do and through their leadership role (by the way they affect the perception of others, e.g. by welfare capitalism or its opposite). Large corporations can sometimes create a societal island that is better or worse than the macro society. To the extent that this applies, large system development projects may change societal conditions.

Secondly, if societal conditions are beyond the reach of system development, the developers must be aware of these conditions and how they affect and limit the benefits of ISD. Project goals must then be formulated which are realistic with regard to the limiting factors. If major issues exist, they ought to be brought to the attention of the highest levels in the organization. Through ISD, organizational life is changed, but the rationality of this change is heavily constrained by social influences which channel the values, perceptions, work rules and other norms of all participants. Unwarranted distortions of communication and thinly disguised power structures may be effective which could be revealed and overcome through enlightened system change. If information technology could remove some of the obstacles to free and unrestrained inquiry, then systems development could contribute to human emancipation from the subserviency of organizational power.

In neohumanism, it is therefore paramount that system development gives careful attention to unwarranted constraints from within the organization. As these are external to individuals, organizational arrangements may need to be changed. Courses of action that focus on selected individuals, such as leadership programs or employing consultants on specific issues are likely to be ineffective. Often, organizational compulsions take the form of communication difficulties and typical examples of this are:

(a) Use of authority and illegitimate power that create anxieties and cause people to distort or withhold information in order to protect themselves;

(b) Presence of peer opinion pressure ('group think') which tends to create tunnel vision for the sake of protecting loyalties. This reduces the validity of judgments by suppressing possible validity checks through criticism;

(c) Misallocation of time and other resource that prevent adequate, democratic access to knowledge or information. This includes the common situation that knowledgeable people remain silent due to lack of motivation to participate because of work overload or the socially created need to withhold important information unless it is to one's advantage to engage in a debate;

(d) Social differentiation, in particular differences in the level of education and other forms of specialization which create difficulties in understanding the relevance and implications of organizational plans, memoranda and the like across hierarchical levels or departmental and professional boundaries;

(e) The influence of the prevailing organizational culture and incentive system.

In pursuing the ideal of emancipation, the systems developer seeks to develop information systems which lead to an emancipation from all unwarranted constraints and compulsions (e.g. psychological, physical and social) towards a state of justice, freedom and material well-being for all. Such information systems would need to facilitate the widest possible debate of organizational problems among the most knowledgeable actors to implement the best policies which establish truly shared objectives and an authentic consensus on how best to achieve them. Such a debate, free of all social pressure, which has the best chance to correct psychological distortions due to individual bias, is called a 'rational discourse' or 'ideal speech situation'. The goal of information systems is to help with the institutionalization of an ideal speech situation which in turn validates a consensus about system objectives and modes of design and implementation. The force of reason is the only force that operates under the conditions of a rational discourse.

The ideal speech situation would legitimate a moving balance between the fundamental three objectives of information systems development, namely improved technical control (i.e. work), better mutual understanding, and continued emancipation from unwarranted social constraints and psychological compulsions. Information systems should also seek to approximate a 'rational discourse' about valid organizational goals and their implementation with regard to all areas including information system planning, strategy, design, and implementation.

The neohumanist view of knowledge differs from its functionalist counterpart (*cf.* Popper 1972) in the emphasis it puts on socially shared and personal knowledge, and in the recognition of different methods of inquiry that are appropriate for the different types of knowledge. In particular, it abandons the correspondence theory of truth in favor of the following version of the coherence or consistency theory: true is what 'survives' (is least inconsistent with) maximal criticism and is comparatively best supported by (is maximally consistent with) all available evidence. The epistemology of neohumanism is therefore much more general than the empirical–analytical philosophy of science adhered to by functionalism.

Neohumanism assigns an equal role to the following three principal categories of knowledge. The first category is empirical–analytical knowledge which is the object of research in mathematics and the natural sciences. In this regard, there is no difference to functionalism. The second category of knowledge consists of shared beliefs about 'our' world: it includes knowledge about rules, customs, laws, values and systems of ethics, which is also called practical knowledge. The following three-fold, classical distinction from Kant helps to characterize this kind of knowledge: rules of skill are mostly comprised of technical knowledge on how to accomplish given ends: i.e. how to drive a car or how to maintain a home; rules of skill are prototypical of empirical–analytical knowledge and easily subjected to a means test. Rules of prudence are concerned with knowledge of good long term policies in the conduct of personal and community affairs. They require wisdom which is acquired through a life of trial, error and reflection with social institutions. Categorical rules require wisdom and knowledge about ultimate values and ethical principles. Both rules of prudence and categorical rules are prototypical of knowledge about our social world. The third category of knowledge consists of personal insights: only you can know how you feel, whether you meant what you said at the last party, what you thought before going to bed last night, and so forth.

In summary, systems development embracing neohumanism has both process and product implications. The process implications of ISD emphasize critical inquiry into the deficiencies of the conditions of human existence and suggest possible improvements at three levels: the institutional environment of the organization (local community and society), the organizational policy level, and the project level. Such emancipatory inquiry is nurtured in the arena of a rational discourse, where all three categories of knowledge can be brought to bear. Checks and balances on all three categories of knowledge are needed to guard against social biases which might create unwarranted constraints and to allow 'undistorted communication' to occur. This means that both the physical and social barriers to a rational discourse need to be identified and removed. A successful system, in this context, is one which permits a better approximation to an ideal speech situation than the status quo. Information systems development proceeds through the application of the principles of hermeneutics so that comprehensibility and mutual understanding are improved by removing misunderstandings and disagreements or other obstacles to human communication. Further, in neohumanism, legitimate system objectives emerge from a free and open discussion which leads to a shared understanding and does not suffer from the harmful effects of the barriers to social communication.

From a product perspective, neohumanism suggests that information systems would have features to support technical control and as such would be similar to those developed under the functionalist influence. Other features would support the creation of shared meanings and reflect the objective of mutual understanding. This is similar to systems inspired by social relativism. Finally, there would be a comprehensive set of features to support emancipatory discourse. This means that information systems are developed which facilitate the widest possible debate of organizational problems such that truly shared objectives could be agreed upon as well as policies for achieving them. The goal of information systems is to help with the institutionalization of an ideal speech situation which in turn validates a consensus about system objectives and modes of design and implementation. The ideal speech situation would legitimate a moving balance between the fundamental three objectives of information systems development, namely improved technical control, better mutual understanding and continued emancipation from unwarranted social constraints and psychological compulsions.

4.2.4.2 Interpretation

Key Actors: stakeholders and the systems developer. The stakeholders are a diverse group of individuals including customers, labor and their representatives, heterogeneous levels of management, and the owners of the productive resources. They exist within a complex, intertwined set of social relationships and interactions. The stakeholders take part in communicative action. The systems developer acts as a social therapist and emancipator in an attempt to draw together, in open discussion, the various stakeholders.

Narrative: information systems are developed so as to remove distorting influences and other barriers to rational discourse. Systems development is governed by three objectives. The first objective (technical control) directs the developer to be sensitive to issues associated with effective and efficient management of the systems project. The second objective (mutual understanding) directs the developer to apply the principles of hermeneutics, which according to Misgeld (1977, p. 331), examines the rules of language use and other practices by which we improve comprehensibility and mutual understanding, remove misunderstandings, and disagreements or other obstacles to human communication. The third objective (emancipation) directs the developer to structure systems development to reflect the principles of rational discourse.

Plot: the ideal of emancipation. Information systems should lead to an emancipation from all unwarranted constraints and compulsions (e.g. psychological, physical and social) towards a state of justice, freedom and material well-being for all.

Assumptions: The epistemology adopted in this paradigm is of two types: positivism for technical control (which includes both nature and man); and anti-positivism for mutual understanding and emancipation. The ontology adopted is also of two types: realism for technical control; and nominalism (socially constructed) for mutual understanding and emancipation. This ontology implies multiple object system classes, i.e. those relating to the symbolic world of language (similar to social relativism) and those relating to changes in the objective world (similar to functionalism). Hence, system change has to be analyzed with regard to more than one object system, e.g. a technical network change may not necessarily improve social networking. The adopted paradigm, i.e. neohumanism, reflects the desire to improve the conditions of human existence for organizational actors (through their emancipation) by the developing of information systems which support rational discourse.

4.2.4.3 Analysis and discussion

Neohumanism focuses on human potential and how it is threatened by ideology, power and other distorting and unwarranted constraints. In distinction to functionalism, it emphasizes what could be rather than what is. It adds to the notion of instrumental rationality (in affairs associated with technical control) and communicative rationality (in affairs governed by mutual understanding) the notion of discursive or emancipatory rationality. It emphasizes the use of human reason to both recognize deficiencies in the conditions of human existence and to suggest improvements. Such emancipation is nurtured in the arena of a rational discourse where the intelligibility, veracity, truthfulness and appropriateness of all arguments are checked through maximal criticism. Checks and balances on individual opinions are needed to guard against unwarranted constraints and biases to allow undistorted communication to occur, which means that both the physical and social barriers to a rational discourse need to be identified and removed for maximal criticism to occur. The concept of rational discourse applies both to the development and use of information systems (Lyytinen and Hirschheim 1988).

Rational discourse is an ideal which cannot be fully implemented. By the use or development of information systems some, but not all, of the barriers to a rational discourse could be mitigated. For example:

(a) data modeling would lead to reduce some of the bias and distortion by specifying stringent integrity checks;

(b) proper organization of the system development process could provide rational motivations to participate, share and elicit missing information;

(c) networks could help to overcome the limitations of time and space;

(d) conferencing systems could motivate people to contribute their expertise by advertising agendas and making it easy to append comments and suggestions;

(e) highly interactive, object-oriented designs could help to overcome educational differences; and

(f) proper security controls could protect individual rights through anonymity and motivate people to communicate criticisms and radical change proposals by shielding them from the threats of the powerful.

Neohumanism seems appealing because it captures many positive features of the previous paradigms and adds the important notion of emancipation. However, while theoretically strong, it is difficult to see how neohumanist ISD actually works in practice. The paradigm is normative without providing clear details on how it could be implemented. For example, it is not clear how notions like the systems development life-cycle should be modified to accommodate not only technical control but also mutual understanding and emancipation; what tools and techniques should be developed to apply the concept of rational discourse to systems development; how to broaden the methods for integrity checking to guard against the numerous forms of fallacious reasoning; and so forth. A more fundamental issue is whether people would be willing and able to radically change their behavior to fit the ideal of rational discourse. Nor is it clear that people would be motivated to participate in the debate or wish to take part if given the option. Moreover, one must question the implicit assumption that there are no natural limits to human potential, that through emancipation we can overcome the psychological and social constraints on human capabilities which have been inherited from the distorting influences of the past. It is difficult to see how the goal of a society free of ideology and domination can be realized. One must also question the assumption that technological progress will be sufficiently powerful to overcome the significant physical constraints confronting the emancipation of all.

Figure 4.1 summarizes and highlights the salient details of the paradigms.

Of course, the above analysis of how different paradigms relate to typical attitudes in systems development is largely hypothetical. In order to shed some further light on the relationship between philosophical concepts and approaches to ISD the last section of this chapter will examine how different paradigmatic assumptions received varying degrees of attention during the evolution of ISD methodologies. As a large variety of alternative methodologies exist which differ greatly in their perspectives and practical emphasis, it would not be very surprising if some of these differences could be explained by their authors being committed to different philosophical

Paradigm	Developer Archetype	Systems Development Proceeds	Elements used in Defining IS
Functionalism	Expert or Platonian 'Philosopher king'	From without, by application of formal concepts through planned intervention with rationalistic tools and methods	People, hardware, software, rules (organizational procedures) as physical or formal, objective entities
Examples: Structured Analysis, Information Engineering Approaches			
Social Relativism	Catalyst or 'Facilitator'	From within, by improving subjective understanding and cultural sensitivity through adapting to internal forces	Subjectivity of meanings, symbolic structures affecting evolution of sense-making and sharing of meanings of evolutionary social change
Examples: Ethnomethodological approaches, FLORENCE project			
Radical Structuralism	Warrior for social progress or 'partisan'	From without, by raising ideological conscience and consciousness through organized political action and adaptation of tools and methods to different social class interests	People, hardware, software, rules (organizational procedures) as physical or formal, objective entities put in the service of economic class interests
Examples: Trade-union led approaches, UTOPIA and DEMOS projects			
Neohumanism	Emancipator or social 'therapist'	From within, by improving human understanding and the rationality of human action through emancipation of suppressed interests and liberation from unwarranted natural and social constraints	People, hardware, software, rules (organizational procedures) as physical or formal objective entities for technical control; subjectivity of meanings and intersubjectivity of language use in human understanding and emancipation
Examples: Habermas' critical social theory, SAMPO Project			

Figure 4.1: Summary of the four paradigms

positions. This theme is further pursued through a more detailed analysis of four key methodologies in chapter 5.

4.3 Paradigms and the Evolution of Methodologies

Even our highly selective review of the evolution of information systems development methodologies in chapter 2 demonstrates that numerous methodologies exist. We cannot know how many methodologies exist, but most likely there are hundreds. A key contention underlying this book is that the bewildering array of methodologies can be reduced to a few major types by relating them to paradigms. This idea is not necessarily tied to the specific classification of paradigms that we have proposed (based on Burrell and Morgan 1979) and which has its own difficulties, but this classification could easily be replaced if a better one emerges.

4.3.1 An approach to paradigmatic placement of methodologies

Given some classification of paradigms, how does one detect the paradigmatic influences in existing methodologies? This is a particularly thorny problem if the authors of the methodology were not even aware of their being influenced by a paradigm. Sometimes it is possible to ask the author(s) (as has been done, for example, by Andersen *et al.* 1990, p. 302). Some authors have either by hindsight or in advance specified their paradigmatic connections. For example, Goldkuhl, one of the originators of the ISAC methodology, has critically evaluated its underlying paradigmatic assumptions and Checkland explicitly reveals the phenomenological foundation of SSM (in Checkland 1981, ch. 8, esp. p. 277). In some cases we have sought personal conversations with authors to clarify their paradigmatic position.

When classifying methodologies we assume that one can identify the key principles and building blocks for each methodology. It is then possible to associate each of these features with one particular paradigm. If a feature appears to have multiple paradigm connections it should be decomposed further into simpler components until it can be clearly related to a distinguishing paradigmatic assumption. Table 4.1 illustrates this kind of procedure. It summarizes six information systems development methodologies noting how their key building blocks (or features) relate to paradigmatic assumptions. Each of the six is then placed in its paradigmatic form, i.e. related to either functionalism, social relativism, radical structuralism or neohumanism. It should be noted that table 4.1 has been kept concise by singling out the most important features for each methodology, but it is not claimed to be complete. Further paradigmatic features are identified in chapter 5 where the respective methodologies are discussed in some detail.

When interpreting table 4.1, it may be helpful to keep in mind how we resolved the following two sources of disagreement about methodology placement. First there is the issue of multiple paradigmatic influences. As will be seen in chapter 5, some methodologies do not fit easily into a single paradigm. Soft Systems Methodology (Checkland 1981), for example, while

Methodology	Key Building Blocks or Features	Paradigmatic Representation	Resulting Paradigmatic Placement
Structured Methods	1) Functional decomposition	F	
	2) Physical vs. logical model	F	
	3) Self-defining primitives	F	Functionalism
	4) Consistency checking	F	(F)
	5) Validation and walk-throughs	F	
	6) Nominalism in data dictionary definitions [According to DeMarco (1979), this applies to data dictionary definitions. It is the Humpty Dumpty nominalism notion: "When I use a word" Humpty Dumpty said, "it means just what I choose it to mean — nothing more nor less." (p. 143).]	SR	
	7) Avoiding political conflicts	F	
Prototyping	1) Use of database languages, code generators and screen painters	F	
	2) Emphasis on measurable costs	F	Ambiguous,
	3) Link with data modeling, entity life-cycle analysis, etc.	F	Functionalism
	4) Complete and fully formalized specification	F	is dominant
	5) 'Cooperative design'	SR	but can support
	6) Facilitates learning and communication	SR/NH	Social Relativism
	7) Improves user understanding	SR	
SSM	1) Rich pictures	SR	
	2) Weltanschauung	SR	Social
	3) Conflicting root definitions	SR	Relativism
	4) Social community (ecology vs. human activity system)	SR	(SR)
	5) Linkages to phenomenology	SR	
	6) Functions of human activity system	F	
	7) Conceptual modeling	F	
Professional Work Practices	1) Emphasis on user learning and reflection	SR	
	2) Respect for significance of the actual work practices and seeking their understanding	SR	
	3) Change of working practices	F/NH	Social
	4) Disclosure and debate of project interests and values	NH	Relativism
	5) Democractic project organization	NH	
	6) Preference for field experiments with emerging methods and tools	SR	
	7) Learning through interaction with objects (concrete experiences)	SR	
	8) Little concern for resource constraints and organizational control	SR	

Table 4.1: Methodology Placement

largely influenced by the social relativist paradigm, also adopts features of functionalism. The same is true for the ETHICS methodology (Mumford 1983). It is largely functionalist but it does possess a number of characteristics of social relativism and neohumanism. Prototyping, too, seems

Methodology	Key Building Blocks or Features	Paradigmatic Representation	Resulting Paradigmatic Placement
Utopia	1) Focus on labor/management conflict	RS	
	2) Union leadership in SD	RS	Radical
	3) Recognition of economic necessities by the market	F	structuralism
	4) Focus on enhancing position of members of the craft	RS	(RS)
	5) Technology can lead to progress for workers	F/RS	
ETHICS	1) Job diagnosis	F	
	2) Social and technical objectives and alternatives have equal weight	SR	
	3) Ranking of alternatives by synthesis based on group consensus [Neohumanism requires a 'normative consensus' based on certain standards that serve as a safe-guard against bias, group-think, and other forms of distorted communication which cause a 'fallacious' consensus. ETHICS does not emphasize such safe-guards; it does not even recognize the issues of fallacious consensus.]	SR	Very ambiguous, functionalism (F) is dominant but with neohumanist (NH) and social relativist (SR) influences
	4) Emphasis on discussion between proponents of technical and social viewpoint	NH	
	5) Expansion of solution space by improved communication [Functionalism would emphasize empirical means-tests or fit to power structures. Opinion cannot decide on matters of truth by mere discussion, and value issues are decided by those who have the authority to do so., i.e. managerial fiat.]	NH/F	
	6) Emphasis on measurable cost, resources, constraints	F	
	7) Joint optimization/fit	F	

Table 4.1 (cont.): Methodology Placement

to adopt influences from more than one paradigm. Some of its features are clearly functionalist, while others are consistent with social relativism. (When a methodology is influenced by more than one paradigm, it can be applied in a spirit which is more or less consistent with a given paradigm and thereby grants a great deal of 'autonomy' to the practitioner to follow his own predilections; this point is taken up below.) On the other hand, some of the methodologies are very heavily influenced by a single paradigm. Structured methodologies, for example, are virtually totally informed by functionalism, while the UTOPIA project (Ehn and Kyng 1987) is strongly informed by the radical structuralist paradigm. In cases where methodologies are strongly influenced by more than one paradigm, one needs to be sensitive to one's biases and identify all significant influences by seeking out features belonging to different paradigms. Admittedly this does not totally eliminate subjectivity, but by consulting with knowledgeable colleagues we have attempted to minimize any oversights. The scoring of ETHICS and prototyping in table 4.1 illustrate how we attempted to cope with ambiguities. In principle it should be possible to relate key methodological principles and objectives to one paradigm. The overall allocation is then a matter of judgment on which features one should focus for a particular purpose.

A second type of ambiguity arises because to some extent the paradigmatic nature of a methodology's feature is in the eye of its beholder. Baskerville (1991) uses the term 'philosophical attribution' to call attention to the 'fact that a method or tool does not possess an independent philosophy.' (p. 678). It is either the originator, the researcher or the user who interprets a methodology by imposing his framework. To some extent, the practitioner is 'autonomous' and can make a methodology fit his own paradigmatic predilections by 'casting' it into some suitable framework that is based in his or her own preunderstanding of the design situation (p. 682). In fact this is the similar type of cycle which leads one to revise one's own understanding of what the methodology is all about and what the design situation is all about. If those applying a methodology find themselves uncomfortable with its underlying assumptions and concepts, they may bend them to better fit their own orientations and understanding. For example it is possible to give an interpretivistic meaning to some of the features of a functionalist methodology and vice versa (*cf.* the examples in Baskerville 1991).

Our approach to methodology placement attempts to score the philosophical foundation of methodologies as they are discernible from their *published* form or are known to us from personal conversations with their originators. Baskerville notes that 'the philosophical "tendencies" ' of a methodology could flex, if not entirely alter the set of knowledge assumptions ordinarily reflected by an investigator (unless the investigator carefully guards these assumptions)' (p. 678). Here we have tried to reveal these inherent 'philosophical tendencies' of methodologies by identifying the influences of alternative paradigms on their principal features. Baskerville (1991) pinpoints an interesting research issue arising from a paradigmatic assumption analysis, namely that one cannot simply assume that methodologies are applied as intended. Rather one needs to examine very carefully to what extent methodologies are applied concordant or discordant with their 'underlying tendencies'. This requires a careful study of the actual working practices of system developers and we shall return to this specific point in chapter 5 when we discuss the 'professional work practices approach'.

4.3.2 The relationship between paradigms and generations of ISD methodologies

We can now return to the question of how the chronological organization of the evolution of methodologies relates to a deeper, conceptual connection among the members of each generation. It is our contention that from the beginning, information systems development methodologies were primarily influenced by the paradigmatic assumptions of functionalism. This is not only true of the classical systems life-cycle and structured methods which copied the known methods of data collection from social science (observation, interviewing, questionnaires, etc.) into the tool kit for the system analyst, but also prototyping and the methodologies associated with sociotechnical system design. The functionalist nature of prototyping can be seen in its emphasis on cost-effective design while the structured methods retained from the classical systems life-cycle the orientation of finding the best means to achieve given ends through systems development. User communication is emphasized, but in a very limited way. Rather than engaging in joint sense-making and problem formulation, user communication is seen as the means to obtain specific information because it is realized that users hold the keys to some information or knowledge that is needed to define requirements.

This limited viewpoint of the many functions of social communication during systems development is also evident from the narrow way in which generation 1 and 2 methodologies conceive of object systems, i.e. technical phenomena. Because the methodologies in generation 2 do not emphasize the need for an open-ended dialogue for constructing a consensual world view and socially shared problem definition, the importance of language escapes them. We hasten to add that this only applies to the management of the system life cycle and not to technical systems implementation. Through programming languages and data base theory, especially through the concepts of codes, data structures and normalization in the relational data model, a great deal of effort has been extended on optimizing language constructs. Similar considerations apply to the area of human interface design and documentation guidelines. However, the fundamental point of a very limited notion of the 'function' of communication remains valid. Whereas, in interface and documentation design, language considerations are extended to the human domain, their treatment is limited to efficiency concerns of how to transmit the information for intended system usage (an exception is Grudin 1989). By and large the treatment of language issues has not been extended to coping with change, problem perception and problem formulating requirements. This is consistent with the earlier observation that these methodologies focus on means uncertainty and to a large extent ignore effect and problem uncertainty.

Socio-technical approaches, too, seem to borrow from functionalism. This is particularly evident from the emphasis on 'joint optimization', i.e. a synthesis between social and technical concerns of systems design. This presumes that order and regulation will prevail over fundamental change. However, they differ fundamentally in their approach to participation. The need for dialogue is explicitly recognized and this is seen as the only means to cope with effect and problem uncertainty. In ETHICS for example, this is achieved through forming separate teams: one to work out problem formulation and solution approaches from a social-organizational perspective, and the other from the more conventional technical perspective as in the generation 1 and 2 methodologies. Hence there is more explicit consideration of object systems embracing both organizational and technological phenomena. As the authors of the socio-technical approaches did not build upon the philosophical turn to language that was taken by the later Wittgenstein or the literature of hermeneutics and phenomenology, the importance of language in their original formulation has also escaped them. However, this is not entirely true for later work.

As the discussion progressed and the rigidity of the functionalist approaches to information systems development became more apparent, influences from other paradigms became more and more effective in interpreting the methodologies or modifying them. This includes an explicit recognition of linguistic phenomena as early as 1982 (Goldkuhl and Lyytinen 1982a). Subsequently, a language action model of systems development was proposed (Lehtinen and Lyytinen 1986).

In the most recent research literature on methodologies (e.g. Ehn 1988; Mathiassen and Nielsen 1989; Lyytinen and Hirschheim 1988; Hirschheim and Klein 1989; Greenbaum and Kyng 1991; Nissen *et al.* 1991; Floyd *et al.* 1992), criticisms of strictly functionalist approaches to systems development have become quite prominent in that their limitations have become much more widely recognized. For example, the communication gap between technical staff and users has become very visible (Bansler and Havn 1991), the emergent nature of system requirements is now obvious to almost anyone (*cf.* Kling and Scacchi 1980, 1982; Truex and Klein 1991) and the role of power in organizations has become more clearly understood and can no longer be denied (Pettigrew 1973; Pfeffer 1981; Markus 1983). This has produced important shifts in our thinking opening the minds of more and more systems developers to ideas from alternative paradigms. Power has become recognized as one of the principal obstacles to genuine participation (*cf.* Briefs *et al.* 1983; Mulder 1971). Wherever there is the use of power, conflicts are to be expected and the nature of conflict and its legitimacy have become serious research concerns (Keen 1981; Newman and Noble 1990) and emergent sense-making has been researched as an important theme in the institutionalization of computer-based packages (*cf.* the web model and interactionist theories in Kling 1987; Kling and Iacono 1984; Kling and Scacchi 1982). Shifts like these in current thinking are reflected in a number of research efforts into building upon socio-technical approaches (Whitaker *et al.* 1991) or the development of new, alternative ISD methodologies.

To summarize, it is our contention that the first two generations of information systems development methodologies (i.e. generations 1 and 2), mostly reflect the paradigm of functionalism. Generation 3 approaches, i.e. classical prototyping, are largely informed by functionalism, and to a lesser extent by the socio-technical approaches (generation 4).

Depending on where the emphasis is placed, generation 4 approaches with their heavy emphasis on genuine participation strongly encouraging a constructive dialogue about user worlds and systems building, do mark a turning point towards social relativism even though they did not go far enough by explicitly considering human interpretation in terms of their object system conception. Insofar as these approaches have also seen the need for mutual learning (for analysts and users), some emancipatory concerns are realized. This aspect was not well developed in their original form, but could be strengthened (*cf.* Hirschheim and Klein 1994).

Generation 5 methodologies associated with sense-making and problem formulation approaches reflect the social relativist paradigm, as to a large extent do the generation 4 methodologies (i.e. the socio-technical, participative approaches). Generation 6 methodologies associated with the trade-union led approaches reflect the radical structuralist paradigm. And the last generation, associated with emancipatory approaches, reflect a neohumanist paradigm.

4.4 Summary and Conclusions

In this chapter we have explored information systems development using our paradigmatic analysis. We examined the process of systems development by reconstructing a theoretical interpretation of the process by looking at key actors, the narrative, the plot and the belief system sustained. Our analysis points out that this kind of reconstruction through archetypes — though being largely conjectural — is a useful and rich vehicle for 'giving life' to the paradigms and to demonstrate how they can influence actors' behaviors in systems development. As a second step we analyzed how paradigmatic influences have shaped the evolution of systems development methodologies by placing and analyzing some methodologies and methodology generations into our paradigmatic map. This broad classification and placement is useful as an orientation to find one's way through the 'jungle' of methodologies. In particular, it is useful in demonstrating how our knowledge of, and for, systems development has changed over time and become more sensitive to social complexity and subtleties. Though our analysis is insightful in providing a coarse 'genealogy' of systems development knowledge and its underlying assumptioms, it is of limited value for suggesting concrete improvements for this knowledge. For this a much more detailed step by step analysis of specific methodologies is required. In chapter 5 we take up this task by selecting four specific methodologies as documented at a particular moment in time. The detailed analysis of chapter 5 is also helpful to further clarify the relationship between the paradigmatic shifts in our thinking about general social-organizational issues of ISD and the construction of methods and tools to address them.

5
Paradigmatic Analysis of ISD Methodologies

5.1 Introduction

This chapter explores, via a paradigmatic assumptions analysis, four theoretically appealing information systems development methodologies (i.e. process-oriented approaches to ISD). Such an analysis is prompted in part by a broadening of the conceptual base in the most recent literature on ISD. At present one can identify several systems development research communities that have coalesced around different paradigmatic beliefs (in the sense of Kuhn 1970) which inform their research efforts. Some researchers have been attracted by the emergence of alternative theoretical foundations and are using them to inspire new ways of thinking about ISD. Examples of such theoretical foundations for ISD are speech act theory, activity theory, critical social theory, self-referential systems theory, semiotics, structuration theory or, with a reactionary turn to the classics, Mao's theory 'On Contradiction'.

However, many of these new ways of thinking about ISD (some might refer to them as 'schools' of ISD) are not driven by an explicit reflection of the philosophical groundings upon which a new theoretical base could be formed. To help understand this issue more clearly, this chapter provides an ex post reconstruction of the philosophical grounding for four influential 'schools' of ISD. Our attempt parallels the paradigmatic analysis of contemporary schools of IS by Iivari (1991). However, our goals in selecting these schools were somewhat different.

5.2 Selection of Approaches and Plan of Analysis

Whereas Iivari's (1991) purpose was to cover all the major schools of thought in IS development, our initial goal was one of illustrating the influence of the four paradigms in current approaches to ISD. Consequently the original goal was not to describe all the schools that are currently well documented in textbooks or textbook-like material, but to choose four methodologies (or families of methodologies in the case of information systems planning/structured methodologies) each of which reflected the assumptions of one of the four paradigms. It was not expected that all of these methodologies would necessarily be well known. Moreover, we intended to go one step further than Iivari could in the space of a single paper by making constructive suggestions about how the methodologies could be improved by drawing on the results of a paradigmatic analysis.

But as was noted in chapter 4, there are no existing ISD methodologies for either the radical structuralist or neohumanist paradigm. Systems development projects like DEMOS, DUE and UTOPIA which reflect many of the ideas of radical structuralism have not transformed themselves into methodologies although they have led to the 'collective resource approach' (Ehn and Kyng 1987) that originally was motivated by radical structuralist principles. Even in its newest form the collective resource approach has managed to retain some of the radical structuralist political values albeit in a democratically refined (some would say 'revisionist') format that brings it closer to neohumanism. The practical lessons from these projects seem to have moved the researchers' philosophical thinking away from the strict radical structuralist notions more towards the position of 'cooperative design' (*cf.* Ehn 1988, Kyng 1991) which has emancipatory implications. Through cooperative design workers can continue to learn and this may help them to realize their talents and creative potential. The hope is that this would not only enhance their career prospects, but also meet 'the need for users to become full partners in a cooperative design process where the pursuit of users' interests is a legitimate element.' (Greenbaum and Kyng 1991, p. ix)

Because of the historical significance of these types of projects, an overview of the UTOPIA project is presented in section 4 of Appendix A as an illustration of how radical structuralist paradigmatic principles could influence ISD (for a recent guide to the literature see Whitaker *et al.* 1991). As a whole, the collective resource approach and its successor are too much in a state of flux and insufficiently settled in their directions to serve as a good example for a paradigmatic analysis. Moreover, such an analysis would be incomplete unless it is broadened to relate the collective resource approach to the 'labor process perspective' on the actual problems and practices of software development (*cf.* Kraft 1977; Bansler and Havn 1991, p. 146). The labor process perspective appears closer to radical structuralism as it focuses primarily on the issue of organizational control of systems design and views the distribution of control among various organizational groupings (e.g. labor and management) as a zero sum game. In distinction to this, the cooperative design approach appears to presume that giving workers control over their immediate tasks through better technical tools under participatory management arrangements is sufficient for realizing their legitimate interests. The labor process perspective is very critical of this because it neglects institutional disparities in policy formulation and reward allocation.

Thus, as there were no clear examples of neohumanist and radical structuralist methodologies, we could not choose any to specifically analyze in this section (but this has not stopped us from attempting to convey some key ideas on the significance of neohumanism for advancing the art of ISD; *cf.* Hirschheim and Klein 1994). Yet neohumanist and radical structuralist ideas have been influential, particularly in Scandinavia (as is also noted by Whitaker *et al.* 1991, p. 40), and we do consider their influences (actual and potential) on other methodologies. Indeed, much of the four chosen methodologies' weaknesses are based on the insights gleaned from neohumanism and radical structuralism.

Therefore we have chosen four methodologies (process-oriented approaches) which exhibit influences primarily from either functionalism or social relativism. The methodologies chosen for our analysis were done so with the desire to provide a broad overview of the domain of ISD approaches. The first one is information systems planning and reflects the principles of functionalism. It was chosen because of:

(1) its large literature base and available methodologies such as IBM's BSP;

(2) the importance attached to it by the IS community; and

(3) its broad focus, which from an information engineering perspective, includes structured methodologies, computer aided systems engineering (CASE), and object orientation.

The second one chosen is prototyping because of its potential as a stand-alone methodology. While prototyping may not currently be considered a formal methodology, but rather an approach to systems development, it has made an important historical contribution to broadening our understanding of the process of information systems development. Indeed, much of the current thinking on ISD embraces prototyping in one form or another. Moreover, it is unique in that it seems to change its essence depending upon the paradigm from which it is interpreted.

The third one chosen is Soft Systems Methodology. SSM was chosen for four reasons:

(1) It has been influential through contributing a number of general ideas to the advancement of ISD, especially in Britain; its influence may also have been aided by its own journal (*Journal of Applied Systems Analysis*) where the discussion about SSM and its foundations can be easily followed.

(2) While it has strong ties to social relativism, it embraces much which is consistent with other paradigms (*cf.* Mingers 1981).

(3) It has inspired the development of additional methodologies, e.g. MULTIVIEW and FAOR. It has also been applied to many information systems development projects (*cf.* Checkland and Scholes 1990).

(4) Moreover, the explicit philosophical grounding of its structure, tools and techniques in phenomenology makes it a methodology that is not only interesting, but also important to analyze.

The fourth one chosen, which originates from Scandinavia, is a relatively unknown one: the professional work practices approach. It is not a methodology per se, but an approach to systems development strongly based on social relativism. While it has a number of principles and tools, it is not nearly as structured as the other methodologies considered. It was chosen because of both its novelty and interesting notions, many of which may well find themselves in the toolkits of tomorrow's analysts.

Our investigation of the principles which drive current research on ISD methodologies will reveal significant cross-paradigmatic influences in a number of the chosen methodologies. Such influences manifest themselves in attempts to draw on ideas originating from different paradigms to overcome the limitations that became apparent as ISD methodologies evolved. We first elaborate on the methodologies by concentrating on four aspects of each. We start by providing an *overview* of the methodology concentrating on its problem focus and key features. Next we explore its *strengths*, and then its *weaknesses* from the perspective of different paradigms. Then we consider *possible directions for future improvements* in the methodology which emerge from our previous analysis. Finally, we provide a *comparative review* of the four approaches by relating them to the key concepts of ISD that were presented in chapter 3.

5.3 Information Systems Planning and Structured Approaches

Early methodologies were adaptations of engineering and scientific management approaches that emphasized preplanned and well-defined procedures. Based on the precedence with the engineering of complex electromechanical machines like tool production systems or airplanes, three approaches were adopted to information systems development. The first of these is IS planning (ISP) understood to mean the global planning of the complete IS application portfolio of an organization. The object systems of IS planning are the current and future IS applications of the enterprise as a whole, i.e. it has an organization-wide focus. Its result is not a working system, but an IS architecture that gives priorities and guidelines for creating individual applications. The architecture is the basis for an orderly information engineering approach to systems development.

The second approach is to ignore the complexities of organization-wide planning and treat each system request separately. This is called project-oriented systems development. In response to this, methodologies were developed with a single application focus. The family of life-cycle approaches using structured methods and tools are a case in point. (See section 1 of appendix A for a brief discussion of structured methodologies).

The third approach (which is discussed in more detail in section 5.4) involves evolutionary systems development and prototyping. In situations that are too complex to be handled by design calculations, engineers often build prototypes and this was also adapted to IS design. An important difference is that a physical prototype is often made from different material (e.g. a car body made of clay), and a different scale where it cannot really be used (a scale model of a building). Closest to IS prototypes are early complete versions of a product that are actually tested to make improvements for the production version. Note that the prototype is distinct and separate from the production version.

5.3.1 Problem focus and overview

Structured methods were proposed to overcome the following productivity problems with the early SLC approaches:

(1) The early development approaches had no standard format for researching and documenting system requirements. This made it simply impossible to create requirements specifications that were complete, comprehensible, consistent and cost-effective, because not even the criteria for consistency or completeness were defined. As there was no standard format with an agreed upon interpretation, the same specifications document was subject to multiple interpretations by different audiences: users, developers, programmers. This led to many specification errors that were extremely costly to correct, if they were detectable at all before the system was installed.

(2) It was impossible to obtain meaningful user input because both the analysts and users were overwhelmed by the sheer volume of unstructured specifications.

(3) The specifications were out of date as soon as they were created, because it was impossible to track down all the places in the documentation where a change in the specifications had to be reflected.

(4) It was difficult to train new analysts except through a long apprenticeship with many costly mistakes.

Much progress with these problems has been made by the well-defined format of structured business systems analysis and specifications. The historical evolution of structured methods indicates that their primary focus has been on standardizing the system development process in three ways: one, standardizing the type of data that are needed to define the logical functions of the system independent of their physical implementation (logical design); two, standardizing templates for system descriptions that supposedly result in consistent, concise, cost-effective, non-redundant yet comprehensive system specifications and documentation; three, standardizing the diagramming methods and tools supporting the systems development process. Further advances with the cost-effectiveness of structured methods can be expected by the computer-supported maintenance of the structured system descriptions in CASE tools. At its best, a CASE tool will check the consistency of different parts of a specification (as the definition of file contents with the contents of the inputs to a process; the latter must be a subset of all files accessed), alert the analysts to missing parts, maintain system descriptions both in graphical and other formats (tables, text) and generate code from the CASE data repository. The code can be used for generating prototypes and may also increase programmer productivity when implementing the final system by providing schemata, program module skeletons, or screen designs.

As a whole, however, structured methods have not been able to resolve the software crisis. One very intractable issue is continuing user communication problems. Many systems are developed that do not truly meet the business needs, and sometimes whole departments need 'to work around them' rather than with them. Two tangible symptoms of this crisis are that an ever larger portion of the information resource management budget has to be dedicated to maintenance and that there is a rising applications backlog. In part this backlog is invisible because many requests for computer support are not even made because users know they might have to wait for months (even years). The two principal causes of backlog are system incompatibilities (locking users out from retrieving data that are stored in diverse formats), and ripple effects of adaptive maintenance: the attempt to modify one major module of a system to meet a new need causes a multitude of secondary changes to keep the remainder of the system working. It is then very time consuming to test all these changes.

Table 5.1 lists a variety of approaches that have been proposed to deal with these issues. This table makes no attempt to identify the paradigmatic foundations of the various approaches; these will become apparent as some of the approaches are discussed in more detail in the subsequent sections of this chapter. After briefly introducing the key concepts of the table, we shall focus on what we consider the most critical advance in functionalist approaches: computer-aided information systems planning and information engineering (ISP/IE). From a functionalist perspective, an orderly development of the IS applications portfolio is paramount for addressing the software crisis and only the linking of structured systems development with an ISP/IE approach, provides a hope of getting the growing anarchy of IS under control. The issue whether the apparent 'anarchy' is required to maintain flexibility (Hedberg *et al.* 1976), 'healthy confusion' and organizational checks and balances against 'intelligence failures' (Wilensky 1967) has received comparatively little consideration in the information systems literature (*cf.* Hedberg and Jonsson 1978 for a notable exception).

The rows of table 5.1 divide the approaches to ISD into two categories depending on whether they rely on the preplanned stages of a formal life-cycle with milestones and sign-offs after each stage or not. Approaches that handle systems development in an emergent rather than preplanned fashion by improving a given system incrementally through experimental changes in response to user feedback, are called prototyping in the broadest sense. The columns divide known approaches into two extremes depending on where they place the principal authority and responsibility for information systems development. If the 'users are in the driver seat' so to speak, then we have end-user computing or methodologies in which the role of analysts is that of advisors or assistants. Control is internal to the user community or the eventual owners of the system. Alternatively, control may be external if it rests with the systems developers.

It should be noted that not all known approaches can easily be placed

PRINCIPAL LOCUS OF CONTROL OF ISD:		
Approach	Internal Control (Users are in control)	External Control (Systems experts are in control)
Iterative/ Evolutionary Approaches	End-user developed systems Cooperative prototyping Professional work practices prefers 'experimental' approaches, but is also compatible with SLC	Evolutionary systems development Most forms of prototyping Executable specifications
Approaches with a preplanned life-cycle	ETHICS Information Systems Analysis and Construction (ISAC) PORGI (Planning ORGanizational Implementation)	Classical system life-cycle (SLC) Structured analysis, specification and design (SASD) approaches Information systems planning and information engineering (ISP/IE)

Table 5.1: Partial Classification of System Development Methodologies

in the table above. For example, while SSM certainly favors genuine participation, in practice it gives the analyst and the systems sponsor much opportunity to be in control of the development effort. Checkland (1972) himself has noticed this, hence SSM's locus of control is ambiguous.

One widely discussed approach to the applications backlog is end-user computing (EUC). EUC, or more appropriately, end-user developed systems, is implemented by providing easy to use programming tools that allow users to do some of the applications development themselves. Examples are spreadsheets or high level database languages like SQL or QBE. Effective EUC depends, however, on a well organized company-wide IS architecture (ISA) such as could be defined by an enterprise schema (more on ISA definition below). Without such an ISA and some general guidance and support, EUC will likely further add to existing incompatibilities and ultimately increase the maintenance burden. The reason for this is that EUC cannot remove system incompatibilities, hence data already stored will simply be reentered when inaccessible, proliferating redundancies and inconsistencies. If allowed to grow unchecked, EUC could ultimately result in total anarchy of stand-alone systems. Hence we believe that the most critical advances in functionalist approaches will come from integrating information system planning, conceptual schema development and structured methods, in a unified methodological framework. To put this framework into practice it will need to be well supported in its principal activities of ISD by powerful CASE tools that allow a fair amount of experimentation with various types of prototyping in order to overcome the rigidities and bureaucratic tendencies of any planning approach. Within a well-planned information systems architecture, EUC can thrive and will make an important contribution to reduce the backlog and reduce the cost of ISD.

The idea of orderly developing individual information systems applications by matching them against a global ISA (information systems architecture) may be called 'information engineering' (IE). An ISA is a high level map of the information needs of an organization relating them to the principal business functions and components of the organizational structure.

Various formats have been proposed for describing such a map that can serve as an ISA (*cf.* the literature survey in Grant 1991), but the key components are always a model of business functions and their data needs as describable in a data model (*cf.* Martin 1983; Finkelstein 1989; Brancheau *et al.* 1989). We think that a more refined version of an ISA needs multiple models. This is a crucial frontier for the future of functionalism (see section 5.3.4).

ISP (IS Planning) is the effort of developing and maintaining an ISA (*cf.* King and Srinivasan 1987 for a possible SLC approach to ISP). Output of ISP is not a working system, but a broad statement as to what extent the current or future portfolio of IS applications meets the needs of the organization and its individual participants. Because of the complexities involved, ISP usually first needs to document the existing applications portfolio. IBM's Business Systems Planning (BSP) is a possible approach to derive the current ISA by an organizational self-study. From the current ISA one can glean an understanding of the current IS application portfolio, its principal applications, their strategic interconnections, its strengths (if any) and weaknesses (usually many). A small ISA may have 20 to 30 principal entity classes. A large one might consist of 20 to 30 subject databases each comprising several dozens major data classes (or entity groupings). In very large organizations, ISP may be limited to the divisional level leading to a hierarchy of interlinked object systems: one for each division plus one focusing on the corporate headquarters and the interdivisional connections.

Based on an understanding of the current applications portfolio, ISP derives an improved ISA and thereby defines priorities for developing the next state of the applications portfolio over a horizon of 2 to 4 years. This includes major modifications and new developments. The new (normative) ISA usually requires major restructuring of processes and data classes. A current influential school of thought holds that data are more stable than processes and at the core of the ISA therefore is a stable data model. An approach to structure the data classes is to use subject database classifications each of which is documented in a canonical (third normal form) conceptual schema (*cf.* Martin 1983; Brancheau *et al.* 1989; Finkelstein 1989). (See also chapter 7.)

The preceding characterization of ISP/IE presumed that IS will be divided into data definitions and programs as has conventionally been the case. At the frontier is the question whether this is, indeed, the best representational format and which alternative software architectures should be considered for defining and documenting an ISA. Two alternatives come to mind: object-oriented organizational ISA and rule-based systems as have been widely applied in knowledge-based systems (also called expert systems). A proposal to use a knowledge representation based, modular, open systems ISA has been made by Kaula (1990). Its review is beyond the scope of this chapter. The assumptions of object-oriented thinking are briefly discussed in chapter 7.

5.3.2 Paradigmatic analysis of strengths

The principal strength of functionalism is that it has greatly refined its concepts and instruments to predict and control complex technical systems. No other approach can currently match it in this regard and it is therefore not surprising that all large projects relied on functionalist approaches (even though some participants voiced significant concern afterwards: *cf.* Brooks 1975 for a classic). Examples are airline reservations systems, the Apollo space missions, or large operating systems. When it comes to developing large scale systems, there is little alternative.

Because of its Cartesian vision of clear, concise and well-formulated methods, functionalism has greatly succeeded in rationalizing its foundations into a well-articulated body of concepts. It therefore ranks high in understandability and lends itself well to teaching and knowledge transfer. The functionalist assumptions about the nature of reality and the appropriate ways to test human knowledge through means-tests are consistent with widely held beliefs as taught throughout educational institutions. This further helps to communicate the approach and motivate newcomers to believe in it and 'make it work'.

Functionalism is naturally oriented towards efficiency and effectiveness and this seeks to conserve valuable resources. Because of the relative rigor and internal coherence of its conceptual basis, functionalist system development methodologies lend themselves more easily to computer support with CASE tools. This promises to further strengthen its cost-effectiveness. To the best of our knowledge all commercial CASE tools embrace mostly functionalist methods. A final strength of functionalism is that it has shown itself to be rather flexible: to learn from its critics and absorb some of the key insights from other paradigms. Hence it may overcome some of the weaknesses which are discussed in the next section.

5.3.3 Paradigmatic analysis of weaknesses

Whereas functionalism emphasizes efficiency and effectiveness it is very poor in helping to formulate and legitimize the ultimate goals which system development should serve. In this context we need to mention both an unwarranted and valid criticism of functionalism. Under the label of 'positivist research', functionalists have often been accused of contributing to an exploitative ideology of capitalist entrepreneurs. This argument has taken a moderate and more radical form (for summary and references to the key ideas, *cf.* Bleicher 1982):

(1) Functionalist theories contribute to stabilizing the status quo thereby perpetuating possibly inequitable unjust social conditions.

(2) Functionalism has developed theories which make exploitation more effective.

From this perspective the ideas of science which in the Age of Enlightenment were a liberating force from religious doctrine and absolutist forms of government, have been pressed into the service of a rationalist economic elite that applies natural and social scientific theories to control nature and people, respectively.

While this analysis may have some historical merit, it need not carry forward to the future. There is no reason why functionalist research cannot be put in the service of the justifiable interests. There is no reason why the obstacles to this which are both financial and social (*cf.* Wilensky 1967) could not be overcome. To put it more simply: functionalism may serve managerial interests just as well as those of disadvantaged groups. A worker perspective need not necessarily only be informed by radical structuralist ideas and neither must a managerial perspective be limited to functionalism. This issue leads into an explicit discussion of ultimate goals for systems development. Functionalism does not have difficulty with admitting conflicting alternative values in its discourse, but is deficient in dealing with the meanings of any value statements regardless of whose interests they serve.

Historically, functionalism recognized only those statements in the domain of science which either have direct empirical content or which can be related to a base of observational knowledge through predictions: any speculative concepts are admitted provided they have predictive power. Even though values could be used in predicting people's behavior, in the past functionalism espoused an ideal of value neutrality and considered value statements devoid of empirical content. Discussing the pros and cons of morals and values was unscientific. It is therefore not surprising that functionalism up to now has failed to develop an adequate approach to deal with value issues (*cf.* Klein and Hirschheim 1993.) Consequently, by following a functionalist approach, developers may subtly be steered away from carefully evaluating system goals which tend to be stated poorly under the best of circumstances. This may lead a development team to efficiently spend resources on a project that should not be conducted in the first place or effectively design a system that fails to meet the real needs of the work environment. For the same reason, they could easily fail to consider ethical and social implications of a system development project. The always dominant efficiency value (in terms of keeping within budget) often further reinforces this tendency.

In order to improve the functionalist approach to value issues, one needs to understand what is most likely the central flaw of the approach: an inadequate concept of meaning and human language. Functionalism insufficiently realized the nature and active role of language in the social construction of reality (for a good theoretical treatment see Berger and Luckmann 1967). Practical applications of functionalism do not deal well with the ways in which humans create, negotiate and understand 'meaning', because functionalist approaches tend to adhere to some version of a denotational theory of meaning. Typically they tend to define meaning as a correspondence relationship between real world objects and their representations. This relationship is called reference and defines the propositional content of a statement. In another version, the meaning of some linguistic expression (like an utterance, a program or some program output) is identified with the behavioral reactions that it produces or is intended to produce (*cf.* Bariff and Ginzberg 1982). This version appears particularly appealing for the meaning for rules, but both versions confuse meaning with naming: this is so, because one can name meaningful objects (such a Pegasus or mermaids) that need not exist (and hence have no reference), but are still meaningful (*cf.* Quine 1963, p. 9). Making matters worse, functionalism treats correspondence relationships as being relatively fixed assuming that the objects referred to exist *a priori* and independently of their representations. In contrast to this, humans treat meanings as context dependent, negotiable and emergent (*cf.* Truex and Klein 1991 for the system development implications). The same sentence, word or rule can mean different things depending on who uses it in what context. Hence wit, irony, or metaphor become meaningful. Humans have intentions and will fix the meanings of the words so that they serve to realize their intentions. On the spur of the moment they can say we will interpret this letter in such and such a way or in this meeting we shall treat *x* as if it was *y* and everybody knows. *A functionalist approach that assumes that meanings are fixed by correspondence rules tends to create systems that would work if the past were to repeat itself.*

The denotational theory of meaning leads to inadequate analysis and hence numerous problems. First it leads to misinterpreting the use of IS as being mere repositories or processors of given meanings (*cf.* Boland 1987). Secondly, it not only prevents a deeper understanding of the formulation of system goals and requirements or the evaluation of the likely effects of system changes, but also of the problems with systems descriptions in general as used in maintaining documentation of past and present systems. Functionalists will study how people have reacted to certain design options in the past and then conclude that the same designs or system descriptions will create similar effects in the future. They forget that the link between designs and the effects they produce is the meaning attributed to them and this can change from one day to the next. Winograd and Flores (1986) have pointed out that the whole notion of an internal representation may not be appropriate for capturing meaning and that descriptions can never be complete.

The denotational theory of meaning also fails to account adequately for the active role of language in creating shared meanings. This is of particular importance for understanding why the best plans will have little meaning if they are not created by common sense-making through some form of interaction. From the denotational viewpoint, language is seen as a neutral medium of description. As long as one understands the syntactic and semantic rules of the language, any description can be meaningfully transferred. Contrary to this, language has a constructive role, because it shapes our thoughts. The terms that we use create the reality that we see (see chapters 6 and 7 for further elaboration of ideas.) The Sapir–Whorf hypothesis states this succinctly. It holds:

> that all observers are not led by the same physical evidence to the same picture of the universe, unless their linguistic backgrounds are similar, or can in some way be calibrated. (Chase 1956, p. v).

If planners, developers and users do not interact and find ways of sharing their concerns and conceptions, the discourse at the planning level creates meanings and interpretations that are felt to be of little relevance and meaning at the implementation level.

Another weakness of functionalist approaches is their lack of a critical perspective on the connections between control of data, the definition of data meanings by controlling the language and politics. It is not true that data exist in some neutral forms of descriptions that support or contradict some organizational policy, rather it is the policy that defines which kind of data are meaningful in the first place (*cf.* chapter 6 for a more detailed analysis). The lack of insight into this prevents functionalism from adequately addressing the close linkages between system development and policy issues. Most functionalist methodologies aim at avoiding politics. Thereby they either define irrelevant IS or unwittingly become the political instrument of some prominent interest faction and then are bewildered if the results of their efforts are strongly resisted or 'sabotaged' by the opposing political faction (Hirschheim and Newman 1988).

Functionalist approaches are, however, quickly changing. In the past, when faced with a choice between rigor and relevance, functionalists have tended to pursue rigor at the expense of relevance. This could easily change if the key points discussed here become widely believed. In the future it might be easier for functionalism to relax its standards of rigor in order to become more relevant than for other approaches to support their richer theoretical frame of reference with clearly defined work practices in order to become more efficient and effective.

5.3.4 Suggested directions for future improvements

Progress with ISP/IE is currently hindered by some common misconceptions lingering from earlier eras of DP. Contrary to some claims (i.e. Brancheau *et al.* 1989, p. 9) an ISA to a large degree is personnel, organization and technology *dependent*. Unless the architecture matches the organizational culture in general and the personal needs of executives in particular, it will have little effect. Moreover, the ISA needs to be in a representational medium and format that is easily accessible to key persons. An ISA can cause the organizational structure and shared views to change of what information technology can do for career aspirations and the organization. In that sense, ISP should contribute significantly to 'double loop' organizational learning (Argyris 1982). Contrary to overly optimistic viewpoints (i.e. Finkelstein 1989), comprehensive computer-aided IE is at this point more a concept than a practicable approach. However, it is a concept with a history of at least 25 years and progress will be made if some of the pitfalls of ISP are remembered.

Besides overcoming past misconceptions, ISP/IE needs to meet the following challenges through future research: flexibility and constructive representation, accommodating a social constructivist concept of meaning and language, and addressing communicative rationality issues in organizational discourse. Besides prototyping, alternative software architectures, multi-perspective modeling methods and tools could help to address these issues.

In order to retain flexibility in an ISA, ISP must be merged with prototyping. The fundamental idea of combining both global planning with limited prototyping experimentation to improve the knowledge base for planning was suggested by Sackman's (1967) concept of evolutionary planning. Essential progress can be expected if the challenge on how to accomplish this in practice is met either by alternative forms of software design or by taking advantage of the many refinements of prototyping (*cf.* section 5.4 in this chapter). Two alternatives that promise greater flexibility than the conventional process–data software architecture are object-oriented modeling and knowledge representation (*cf.* Bubenko 1986, for example). Kaula (1990) has shown how a knowledge-based architecture could be modularized. These are technical approaches that could help to implement flexibility in an ISA. They are not replacements for prototyping, but different software support environments for them.

Prototyping is essential as, together with a multi-perspective modeling approach, it could redress some of the sense-making and communicative rationality deficiencies of functionalism. If functionalism is to overcome the weaknesses that follow from the reliance on denotative concepts of meaning, it needs to implement representations that allow the construction of new meanings through computer-mediated social interaction. We propose the label constructive representation for this and believe that prototyping in an appropriate software support environment and multi-perspective rapid systems modeling are possible avenues to realize this concept. Instead of prototypes, mock-up simulations could also be used*.

Prototyping together with Chaffee's (1985) notion of an 'interpretive strategy'** points to a promising research avenue for improving the sense-making aspect of functionalist system development approaches because it allows different communities to interact in 'experimental futures of the organization', i.e. those described in the ISA. For example, constructive ISA representations could help to overcome the difficulties of linking ISP/IE to the other principal sense-making processes at all levels of the organization: if this does not happen the horizon of meaning of the planners will not overlap with the horizons of the various 'work language communities' that carry on the day to day business of the organization. If that happens, the notion of a 'work language' explains why ISP will have no real effect. A work language differs both from a professional language in that it is more task and organization specific. Typically the functions of a work language are (*cf.* Holmqvist and Andersen 1987, p. 328 and 348) to negotiate the organization of work and establish specific types of cooperation, address the work tasks proper and to maintain social relations, shared knowledge and a supportive climate (work solidarity and collegiality). A work language is different from a sociolect (the language of a socio-economic class such as that of a blue-collar neighborhood) and it typically overlaps with several professional vocabularies (as taught in higher education) or national languages (*cf.* Holmqvist and Andersen 1987, p. 348). If the work language of the planners remains distinct from the remainder of the organization, ISP/IE will not affect the organization of work and forms of cooperation and contribute to the other functions as stated. This is like saying ISP/IE will have no influence on the organization.

Multi-perspective modeling (MPM) is a possible analysis approach to overcome the language barriers of communicating with different work language communities. At present the principal focus of MPM is on realist aspects of information systems modeling. A brief outline of these may provide some hints on how this approach could be expanded to capture the key aspects of different work languages and thereby address semantic–linguistic barriers of organizational communication. From a realist perspective, a multiple model or multi-perspective approach to IE needs to capture the following aspects (these are in addition to the activities and data structure descriptions of structured methods (data flow diagramming models) and entity–relationship models which are now widely used):

---

* See the discussion of mock-ups in Ehn and Kyng (1991).

** The following ideas on the interpretive model of strategy, also appear applicable to interpretive ISP. "The interpretive model of strategy ... assumes that reality is socially constructed ... reality is defined through a process of social interchange ... Strategy in the interpretive model might be defined as orienting metaphors or frames of reference that allow the organization and its environment to be understood by organizational stakeholders." (Chaffee 1985, p. 93).

(1) the environment of the business or business unit for which the ISA is developed (called a high level context model);

(2) a documentation of the organizational structure and the key responsibilities of the positions and how they relate to the overall business strategy (functional–structural model of the organization);

(3) the principal resources consumed by each business unit (entity life-cycle models).

Grant (1991) and Grant *et al.* (1991) focused on exploring a multi-perspective approach for ISP/IE. Avison and Wood-Harper (1990) through their action research have developed a phase-structure for a multi-view approach to ISD that is based on SSM. While their approach is single-application oriented, it gives considerable food for thought for expanding it to a multi-perspective approach to ISP/IE. The same is also true for another multi-perspective approach, FAOR (Schafer *et al.* 1988).

Presently the vocabulary of ISP appears to be shaped by the work language of the planners. This creates numerous communication problems. A critical issue is how to link the results of ISP to subsequent application oriented systems development. The transformation of an ISA to well-defined, structured specifications of an applications system is ill-defined and requires a great deal of creative imagination. As it is to be expected that the team creating the ISA is different from those in charge of fitting applications to the ISA, a serious communication gap can be expected between the planners and the application developers. There is a good chance that the application developers simply ignore the ISA plan because they have not sufficiently participated in the discourse that made it meaningful and prefer to start from scratch*. In light of the previous discussion it is unrealistic to expect that the plan's descriptions as such can carry all the meaning necessary for its proper interpretation let alone to persuade others of its validity and usefulness for future application development.

Progress with this can be made if the planning is highly participatory so that the ISA enters the organizational discourse. Furthermore, the planners themselves need to provide some prototypes that support key ideas of the ISA. The application developers and users can then get some hands-on experience with the kind of systems that the ISA inspires. If the prototypes

---

* This in fact happened in a pilot ISP/IE project. Under guidance of one of the authors, the analysis class in one semester was charged with developing an ISA for a small organization involving 12 departments. Another class was given the ISA and then charged with providing prototypes to illustrate the feasibility and implications of the ISA. In spite of some briefing by the instructor who helped with formulating the ISA in the first case and some subtle pressure to use the ISA architecture, the prototype developers preferred to do their own analysis and barely considered the documentation of the ISA that had been created. Hence, it is mandatory that the ISA team is also involved with some prototyping or that there is overlapping team membership.

produce promising results, this will carry a great deal more weight than thick manuals. Finally, the ISA with its supporting prototypes should be documented in a format that is easily accessible to all, such as in a central project data repository of an IE work bench — a CASE environment for ISP. Developers should be able to call up pertinent descriptions and work with them rather than study them and re-enter them.

Through a semiotic approach to work language analysis, rapid systems modeling and prototyping could be extended to multi-perspective modeling and prototyping so that the ISA can speak to different user groups in their work language about the topics of interest to them just as now IS models and descriptions speak to IS planners and developers (at best). This is because the ISA enters the planning discourse by primarily relying on derivatives of planners' and developers' work languages. Some progress has been made in this direction by designing interfaces that are directly derived from a work language analysis (*cf.* Andersen *et al.* 1990).

The above presumes that all want to communicate if they could only overcome the 'Tower of Babel' of organizational work languages. But this assumption is unrealistic. Improving communicative rationality requires addressing both the improvement of sense-making and the improvement of the conditions which shape the general arena of communication. Consider an analogy with transportation. Comparing communication with the business of getting products and services to people, then the former is like improving the transportation vehicles' speed, capacity and riding comfort (so that people want to travel and the vehicles reach their destination quickly and comfortably); while the improvement of the arena of communication is the analog of improving roads and waterways so that everyone can be reached and people can get to where they really want to be and not where the roads happen to take them (*cf.* Klein and Hirschheim 1991 for an in-depth analysis on how different methodologies currently realize communicative rationality; see also Hirschheim and Klein 1994).

In order for ISP/IE to improve communicative rationality effectively it needs to explicitly address the typical organizational barriers to communication. While these are case specific, Wilensky's (1967) classification of communication barriers may give some initial pointers. He discusses the effects of hierarchy, power and secrecy, 'officialdom', prevailing myths, taboos and other biases. Wilensky's analysis can be complemented with ideas from critical social theory (see chapter 4). For example, planners need to understand how their planning process is put at risk by existing distortions in organizational communication (*cf.* Albrecht and Lim 1986, p. 126 and Forester 1989). By the same token, those responsible for creating an ISA need to understand how communication barriers and biases affect the ISP process and whether the resulting ISA will contribute to mitigating existing communication barriers or possibly introduce new ones.

The above discussion has illustrated that substantial efforts are needed to make ISP/IE workable, but the theoretical, cultural sciences based knowledge and technology to implement it already exists to some extent.

5.4 Prototyping and Evolutionary Systems Development

The ideas inspiring prototyping in the broadest sense (including rapid, evolutionary systems development) can be traced back to optimistic speculations about man–machine communication or man–computer symbiosis and cooperation (see for example Licklider 1960, 1968 or Carroll 1965, 1967). Since real prototyping applications were first described and tested with interesting results (e.g. Scott-Morton 1967, 1971; Earl 1978; Keen and Scott-Morton 1978; Courbon and Bourgois 1980), a rich variety of differing concepts and interpretations of prototyping has been proposed in recent years. Because of the confusion surrounding the meaning of prototyping, we shall build on Iivari (1982, 1984), Davis (1982), Floyd (1984) and Groenbaek (1989) to review the principal types of prototyping and evolutionary systems development.

5.4.1 Problem focus and overview

Early evolutionary systems development was seen as competing with 'linear' SLC approaches and therefore incompatible with information systems planning (*cf.* Courbon and Bourgois 1980; Naumann and Jenkins 1982). Evolutionary systems development is described in section 2 of Appendix A and could be considered as the first version of prototyping in a very broad sense. However, in the following we shall make some finer distinctions. We shall look upon prototyping in a more narrow sense primarily as a strategy to collect information for system development through a form of experimentation (Iivari 1984 speaks of prototypes as 'means of producing information' for the decision makers in systems development which includes the users) and to facilitate communication and learning by interacting with a real system which cannot be as effectively achieved by using abstract system descriptions (this differs from Iivari 1984). Following Iivari (1982, 1984) we assume that a prototype implements an abstract, simplified model of a future, more comprehensive system. The prototype implementation consists of hardware and software, its operation and use requires people, and the prototype is able to exhibit essential features of the future, final system. The use of a prototype is intended primarily for experimentation and gaining feedback through hands-on experience. Hence with prototyping there is no commitment that the 'prototype becomes the system' even though nothing precludes reusing all or parts of the prototype in the implementation of the final system. The strategy to develop a final system through a series of experimental changes will be called evolutionary systems development (Hawgood 1982) rather then prototyping. (Floyd 1984, p. 10 proposes the terms 'evolutionary prototyping' or 'versioning'.)

The narrower sense of prototyping just defined is consistent with the use of the term in a very influential research article by Davis (1982). It describes prototyping as a 'strategy' for 'discovering requirements through experimentation' in situations of high uncertainty. Based on this, many authors have suggested using prototyping as a means of reducing uncertainty during the requirements determination stage (*cf.* Senn 1989; Kendall and Kendall 1988; Yourdon 1989). From this vantage point, prototyping is restricted to the elicitation and validation of requirements specifications that are then frozen for the remainder of the SLC. Prototyping is one of several methods in the analyst's tool kit for quality assurance of systems requirements. This second version of prototyping might be called specifications prototyping. It should be noted that our first definition of prototyping (following Iivari 1984) is broader in that nothing prevents us from using a prototype to collect information about other important concerns of systems development, not just requirements testing. For example prototypes can be used to demonstrate the technical feasibility or efficiency of a software design concept, or the workability of a new kind of technology (like object-oriented design and programming). Floyd (1984, p. 8) calls this experimental prototyping (which is a pleonasm if one accepts the narrow definition of prototyping as stated above).

Others have reversed the relationship between the SLC and prototyping by suggesting that prototyping should be improved by incorporating some steps of the SLC. In particular, the formulation of the initial problem should be done more carefully by using some semiformal requirements determination method before building the first prototype. This is seen as cutting out some unnecessary iterations. Almost any of the requirements specification approaches introduced elsewhere could be used for this purpose as long as they do not unduly stretch out the process of problem analysis: rich pictures, root definition analysis, data modeling, sketches of entity life-cycle analysis, data flow diagrams and so forth. This third version of prototyping is really a variant of evolutionary systems development and illustrates that there need not necessarily be a sharp boundary between conventional system development and evolutionary approaches. Developing systems with the SLC is simply evolutionary systems development in slow motion (with maintenance providing the different versions). This is not to deny that the speed-up of the SLC in evolutionary systems development produces very significant effects. In this version, the notion that the preliminary system eventually becomes 'the system' is retained and we shall refer to this third version as evolutionary systems development with explicit problem formulation.

Executable specification languages have been proposed as a kind of accelerator for the SLC (analogous to elapsed time photography on a motion camera). If the specification can be used to generate a working system, it is possible to experiment with alternative, formal specifications. We shall refer to this fourth approach as formal specifications based prototyping. It should be noted that in this version the users need not be involved in the writing of the specifications. Rather they can evaluate the specification by working with its result: the automatically generated system. This approach ultimately aims at a complete and fully formalized specification which classical prototyping tried to avoid altogether. As there is no commitment to reuse any of the experimental versions of the formal specifications, the label 'prototyping' rather than evolutionary systems development appears appropriate.

A fifth view of prototyping emphasizes its learning and communication capabilities. We shall refer to this as rapid and expansive prototyping. Rapid prototyping attempts to overcome the limitations of horizontal prototypes where most of the user interfaces are implemented, but very little of the computation. Horizontal prototypes can easily be generated with screen editors and linked with a state-transition diagram editor so that the users can get a feel of the interaction with the system. This inhibits the user from having any real 'man–machine communication' by which new insights can be gained. Consequently with horizontal prototypes there is no great motivation for users to explore the prototype in depth, because it fails to produce meaningful responses that give proper feedback. In applications which involve more than fact retrieval, prototypes without computations fail to provide a sound basis for judgments on whether the prototyped application will really be useful. Vertical prototypes, on the other hand, implementing a few critical functions in depth may be too expensive to develop. These difficulties are overcome by rapid prototyping which combines some of the capabilities of both horizontal and vertical prototypes. This is achieved through the use of tools with screen and code generation capabilities such as fourth generation languages.

In spirit, this approach is not different from classical evolutionary systems development only more effective tools are used to save time and effort in generating more comprehensive preliminary systems. If this fifth strategy gradually turns preliminary versions of a system into a final one no new work is needed. One may simply speak of computer-aided rapid (evolutionary) systems development or computer-aided rapid prototyping depending on whether the code is primarily experimental or not.

Computer-aided, rapid evolutionary systems development can also address the following problem. Some business situations are changing so quickly (or at least the human perceptions and understanding of them are) that any formal system life-cycle effort would hopelessly lag behind the quickly evolving user demands (Truex and Klein 1991). Formal specifications based approaches might be applicable, but their goal of finding a valid and complete specification is defeated. In this kind of situation, each version of the 'emergent' system is no longer seen as a preliminary, experimental version of a better system to be delivered later, but rather each version 'is the system'. It is immediately put to use with the understanding that it is a 'quick and dirty solution' to the current state of the problem (a spreadsheet for grading a course that changes each semester is a simple example). If the solution is found wanting, it is upgraded or changed (but not necessarily upgraded and better documented) as the situation evolves. This approach emphasizes that through evolutionary systems development users may learn more about some important aspect of the total situation which then changes their comprehension of their roles and tasks. This is a revival of the old idea of problem solving synergy through man–machine communication. Computational cycles and knowledgeable, human judgments interact to produce results that could not be achieved without interactive computational power.

The notion that prototyping should primarily be a learning experience is at the core of the sixth and seventh approach called expansive prototyping and cooperative prototyping, respectively (*cf.* Groenbaek 1989; Greenbaum and Kyng 1991). As the emphasis here is on experimentation and learning feedback rather than use as a workable system, the label prototyping is in order. Expansive prototyping adopts the idea that by experimenting with evolving software, users can 'expand' their capabilities and learn new ways of seeing themselves and their work situation. This should ultimately lead to 'working smarter'. Expansive prototyping activates and enhances the users' tacit expert knowledge. This occurs not only through using the prototype (which was seen much earlier in classical prototyping), but also by intimately participating in building the prototype. Hence expansive prototyping adds to rapid prototyping the idea that users either develop the prototype themselves or at least are deeply involved in defining the prototype changes. In this way users can acquire a deeper understanding of their work situation and based on this they can better tell what kind of system support they really need. Based on the information gained in this way a good system can then be implemented. We may suspect that many first time spreadsheet users used them as expansive prototypes (that were never effectively implemented due to the backlog of user requests with data processing or information centers), but note that spreadsheets are a very limited type of software and expansive prototyping should not be limited by the simplicity of software. The focus of expansive prototyping is on the user or user group and the work situation for which the prototype is being developed.

If expansive prototyping is extended to a broader range of software that is too sophisticated to be run by non-computer professionals, it requires cooperation with professional system builders. This seventh version is called cooperative prototyping — a term suggested by Bodker and Groenbaek (1989). Cooperative prototyping attempts to implement the idea that users can take a proactive role in prototype design such as when a future house owner builds a model of his dream home and brings it to the architect. The home-owner is sufficiently handy to directly manipulate the model, but he cannot finalize the plans for the end product. In a similar fashion, cooperative prototyping depends on 'direct manipulation tools' (Schneidermann 1987; Groenbaek 1989), but should not be limited to prototyping tools that are sufficiently simple to be easily mastered by end users. Users still participate in actually building the prototype but have computer experts on their side to help with the implementation using sophisticated software or other approaches:

> Cooperative prototyping is meant to combine the ideas of using computer-based tools for exploratory prototyping with approaches to design that allow users to participate in the modification of wood and paper mock-ups as described in Bodker *et al.* (1987). (Groenbaek 1989, p. 228)

Bodker *et al.* (1987) discuss a set of requirements for tools to support cooperative design. In addition, Groenbaek (1989, p. 230) emphasizes the requirement for direct manipulation support. He suggests that animation, simulation, design by example and related approaches could be used to supply some of the functionality needed in cooperative prototyping when generating the computational model is too time consuming. In this case prototyping merely serves creative learning purposes and the prototype does not become the system which is quite different from neoclassical rapid prototyping.

5.4.2 Paradigmatic analysis of strengths

The rich variety of purposes and orientations associated with prototyping begs for clarification. We suggest that it can be explained by the observation that some forms of prototyping are informed by different paradigms. This is easily checked by studying the terms and reference literature that researchers use to describe their prototyping concept. If we assume that prototyping spans at least two paradigms and allow for some evolution of the prototyping concept within each paradigm, then we can easily expect numerous forms of prototyping.

From the functionalist perspective prototyping's principal strengths are that it:

(1) sustains the motivation of users to participate in system development thereby providing the most reliable information on requirements;

(2) overcomes some of the rigidity of the system life-cycle

(3) allows the determining and validating of system specifications by conducting experiments with a system to decrease and control problem uncertainty or effect uncertainty.

Functionalists will therefore tend to view prototyping either as a step in a system life-cycle or as an approach in situations which puts a premium on speedy and flexible system development. Prototyping versions two, three and to some extent four and five (insofar as the emphasis is on cost-effectively matching systems to changing requirements) appear to address these issues. The functionalist underpinning of executable specifications prototyping is particularly apparent in the assumptions that a full specification is possible and that through iterations the correct specification can be found in that successive attempts at specification will converge on a correct solution.

Consistent with functionalism is the use of prototyping as a means to predict user reactions by providing a quick and dirty version of the system and thereby control the total cost of systems development. So, too, is its heavy use of productivity tools such as database languages, code generators, screen painters and the like.

From the perspective of social relativism, the principal strength of prototyping is its concrete support of human interaction, sense-making and the creation of new meanings. Prototyping provides not only for intense interaction between users and designers through 'cooperative design' (Greenbaum and Kyng 1991), but also a concrete object to which both users and developers can relate. It is not an exaggeration to say that common meaning is created through manipulation of a shared work 'cult' object — the prototype. From a phenomenological perspective, it is only through direct manipulation of 'things' in the shared life world that the common situation of 'being in the world' (in the prototyping literature called the 'work situation') can be experientially understood and with this the needs that arise from 'being' in the work situation. To the extent that all prototyping forms support more interaction than the SLC, they contribute to better communication based on close interaction.

Classical prototyping was formulated sufficiently flexibly to allow easy association with an extremely broad range of theoretical ideas (see for example Courbon and Bourgeois 1980 who associate the principal steps of prototyping with the Kolb model of the learning process)*. Neoclassical rapid prototyping has retained some of the emphasis on user understanding and

---

* Kolb's learning theory introduces feedback between four interrelated learning stages which he depicts in the shape of a circle. In clockwise order beginning at noon these are: Concrete Experience, Reflexive Observation, Conceptual Abstraction, and Active Experimentation. The individual moves thought these four stages and at each revolution reaches a higher level of personality development. Courbon and Bourgeois (1980) suggest that prototyping (which they call 'the evolutionary approach') can be given an interpretation in which implementation corresponds to experience, consciousness (the design stage in which people become conscious of change and relate it to developing new norms of behavior for dealing with the outcome of design) with reflexive observation, analysis with conceptual abstraction and norms (as explained in the previous parentheses) with active experimentation. This makes clear that prototyping can be interpreted as a social learning model. This view has also been developed by Kerola (1985, 1987).

learning. It focuses, however, more narrowly on the technical and cognitive feedback aspects than on a deeper theoretical foundation of human communication and understanding. These foundations come most clearly into focus with expansive and cooperative prototyping. Their paradigmatic strengths derive from their explicit foundation on hermeneutic and phenomenological principles regarding human understanding, forms of expert knowledge (*cf.* Dreyfus and Dreyfus 1986) and learning through the creation of shared meanings. Their theoretical grounding is obvious from some of their terminology. For example, they explicitly refer to system descriptions as social constructions that fail to support genuine participation because they 'only made sense to us the systems designers . . .' and 'to the users they were literally nonsense' (Ehn and Sjogren 1991, p. 248). Cooperative and other forms of prototyping can help to overcome the 'meaninglessness' of system descriptions by producing 'breakdowns' (which means that some unexpected event in using a prototype in the real work situation forces a reflection such as may be caused by 'a bad or incomplete design solution', *cf.* Bodker and Groenbaek 1991, p. 200), so that a situation 'ready to hand' (one that is handled smoothly and routinely) is transformed into one that is 'present at hand' (consciously experienced and reflected, *cf.* fuller treatment in Winograd and Flores 1986; see also Madsen 1989). The paradigmatic connections of the latest forms of prototyping is also apparent from the extensive discussion of a new philosophical basis for system design (see for example Ehn 1988, 1990).

The sense in which a neohumanist perspective on prototyping reaches beyond what already has been said, can be summed up in one key word: emancipation. At this point we can only speculate in what way prototyping might be emancipatory in that this is unexplored territory. Emancipatory prototyping would have to open up new opportunities to overcome either:

(1) personality deficiencies or

(2) organizational deficiencies while

(3) at the same time implementing some checks and balances against introducing new kinds of obstacles and biases to rational communication.

Regarding (1), prototyping could be introduced in such a way that it provides a non-threatening, supportive environment encouraging learning and growth of employees with low status and self-esteem. It could do so by tying new ideas and abstract concepts to concrete circumstances in the work place. This should help to overcome anxieties and defensive reactions thereby aiding the learning process of users with little formal education. To the same end, prototyping can also be used to encourage serious exploration in a 'playful manner'* thereby further encouraging self-confidence and creativity. These ideas find some theoretical support in Freire (1971).

---

* The importance of play to improve participation in design is recognized in Ehn and Sjorgen (1991). In their paper the authors use situation cards and icons for work related artifacts like

Prototyping is probably not very well suited to addressing the second kind of deficiency or barriers to emancipation which are rooted in the organization or institutional environment. As will become apparent in the analysis of paradigm weaknesses, prototyping has a bias towards individuals or face to face groups and appears to assume rather idealistic organizational conditions.

5.4.3 Paradigmatic analysis of weaknesses

From a functional perspective, prototyping lacks controls for project management and reliable outcome measures. Because of the emergent nature of prototyping solutions it is difficult to plan milestones, delivery dates and clear budget figures and in many situations it is unsatisfactory that no reliable milestones and budget figures can be given. (Proponents of prototyping will no doubt counter that the milestones and budget figures of system life-cycle approaches are notoriously unreliable and prototyping can work with upper budget limits.) In addition, there is a lack of clear rules when the prototyping process has reached its goals. To put it simply: the users' appetite for changes could continuously grow and there is no guarantee that the changes made are worth their expenditures. Particularly in the literature on rapid and cooperative prototyping available, there appears to be little or no concern for cost control and means tests of the effectiveness of the approach except for user enthusiasm (Bodker and Groenbaeck 1989, p. 22).

From a social relativist perspective, the 'high tech' nature of prototyping is of concern for two reasons. First, there is the danger that communication and learning is biased by the ideas and values underlying the latest technological fashion and not by genuine social concerns. Also technical glitches and other frustrations common in a high tech environment could interfere with the essential aspects of sense-making and the sharing of meanings. Second, and more fundamentally, an inescapable limitation of prototyping is that it treats information systems as technical systems which can be discontinued without further consequence if deemed deficient. This is fallacious. Social relativism suggests that IS are symbolic interaction systems and any intervention in the living organization produces irreversible effects in the minds of the affected people. In that sense, there can be no prototyping because prototyping is a form of social intervention whose effects are irreversible.

From a neohumanist point of view, prototyping fails to take note of institutional barriers to the rationality of communication. Discussion of the possibilities and effects of prototyping reach at best up to the group level. The

---

notice boards to organize a scenario play. In this play, the participants design new professional roles and a new work organization to cope with changes induced by desktop publishing technology. It is easy to see how prototypes could be used in circumstances where the new technology is still under development or to make the simulation more realistic.

organization as the sponsoring environment is presumed to supply limitless resources. There are no vested interests, hidden agendas, ideological biases, interdepartmental warfare and the like. Moreover, one stern institutional lesson from the UTOPIA project has been forgotten in the enthusiasm for the high tech gadgetry in most if not all of the prototyping literature: that all technology is developed with clear interests in mind and hence reflects values and trade-offs which limit the degrees of freedom to design the content and organization of work (*cf.* Ehn, Kyng and Sundblad 1983 as quoted in Ehn 1988, p. 328). As an alternative to prototyping, Kyng (1989) examines several tools and approaches, most notably mock-ups, simulations, workshops and work-place visits. This is important so that resource weak groups gain access to adequate means to support their design and evaluation of information systems. The ideal is to arrive at good support environments that facilitate high quality 'designing for a dollar a day' (Kyng 1989; *cf.* Ehn and Kyng 1991 for a fuller discussion of various generations of mock-ups and their comparison to prototypes).

5.4.4 Suggested directions for future improvements

The review of current approaches to prototyping shows prolific conceptual growth. This growth is highly desirable, but it lacks clear direction and order so that different research groups can build on kindred results. We shall briefly raise four points: the first item high on the research agenda for the further development of prototyping is more conceptual clarification. Second, this should be followed by more extensive field tests. Third, the results of these field tests need to be critically reflected in cross-paradigm analysis to gain better insights into the potential significance of different research strategies. Fourth, the advantages of prototyping should be incorporated into ISP/IE.

Conceptual clarification should aim at formulating the theoretical foundations and implications of different versions of prototyping more clearly. Having reviewed earlier attempts at conceptual clarification, we reach the conclusion that the nature and significance of prototyping can only be adequately assessed if the assumptions made about the nature of systems development are clearly stated. Essentially this requires an explicit framework or meta-theory about systems development. An interesting proposal in this direction has been made by Iivari (1982). A clear statement of the paradigmatic foundations on which different research approaches build, could significantly contribute to conceptual clarification.

In addition to conceptual development, we need more field work with prototyping. This field work should also be inspired by different paradigms so that the strengths and limits of different approaches become more clearly visible. Among the different research methodologies that should be considered for this are both action research and more observationally oriented approaches of real world implementations: grounded theory, cognitive mapping, content analysis of design records, case studies and exploratory laboratory experiments all have their place. The danger exists that this may simply add more details to the confusion. Therefore, the careful cross-relating of results is necessary to achieve any real progress. An interesting and unresolved theoretical question is whether the paradigm underlying the research methodology should be consistent with the paradigm underlying the prototyping approach that is being investigated. Here, too, there is much room for new kinds of research. For example, very interesting insights could be revealed by studying a functionalist prototyping approach with an interpretive research methodology such as cognitive mapping (cf. Banville 1990).

Prototyping played a prominent role in the examination of possible future directions for functionalism. The proposals made in the context of functionalism need to be interpreted in light of the cross-paradigmatic connections of prototyping. As functionalism has shown great flexibility in absorbing insights from different paradigms, significant advances could be expected if ISP/IE methodologies and structured methods are enlarged by experimenting with different versions of prototyping. The high tech nature of all prototyping approaches should make it relatively easy to integrate them into a functionalist frame of reference.

5.5 Soft Systems Methodology

Soft System Methodology (SSM) (Checkland 1981; Checkland and Scholes 1990) is not a methodology limited to information systems development, but a very general approach to address many different kinds of political, social and organizational problems. However, SSM has served as the basis for at least two methodologies specific to information systems development, MULTIVIEW (Wood-Harper et al. 1985; Avison and Wood-Harper 1990) and FAOR (Schafer et al. 1988). As we are concerned here with the fundamental principles underlying different methodologies, it is appropriate to deal directly with SSM rather than with its derivatives.

5.5.1 Problem focus and overview

SSM may perhaps be more aptly termed a meta-methodology in that it is more concrete than a general philosophy for analyzing the world, but broader and more flexible than a specific professional method that is usually limited to a predefined problem domain. SSM focuses on broad problem-solving situations, involving what Checkland calls 'human activity systems'. In human activity systems, problems are manifestations of mis-matches between the perceived reality and that which is perceived might become actuality. SSM is different from the traditional systems development approaches in that it does not prescribe tools and methods that are specific to information systems, but only general problem formulating principles and methods.

The classical version of the methodology (Checkland 1981) as described in section 3 of appendix A distinguished seven steps within the methodology which were categorized as 'real world' activities and 'systems thinking' activities. The steps in the former may involve the people in two ways, one is 'express the problem situation' through 'rich pictures' and the other, implementing 'feasible and desirable changes'; the steps in the latter attempt to provide conceptual models of the denoted problem situation which are then brought back into the real world for comparison. In the newer version of the methodology (Checkland and Scholes 1990) this distinction is replaced by 'two interacting streams of structured inquiry which together lead to an implementation of changes to improve a situation' (p. 28). These two streams are termed 'cultural analysis' and 'logic-based analysis'. The stream of cultural analysis involves three analysis phases: analysis of the intervention; social system analysis; and political system analysis. The stream of logic-based inquiry involves four phases: selecting relevant systems; naming relevant systems; modeling relevant systems; and comparing models with perceived reality.

An interesting aspect of this is that SSM incorporates an explicit inquiry model from which other methodologies could also benefit substantially. All system development methodologies pay attention to appropriate approaches for collecting the information and data which provide the knowledge basis needed for analysis and design. Whereas the seat of the pants approaches relied mostly on user interviews and the analysts' common sense investigation skills, modern methodologies have become much more sophisticated in their approach to inquiry. Inquiry includes system modeling (deriving requirements from an existing system, *cf.* Davis 1982 for a survey of alternative approaches to requirements determination), walkthroughs, discussion of system specifications in personal meetings, counseling with users by demonstrating prototypes and a myriad of other ways to collect needed information. We can analyze any system from the perspective of inquiry (*cf.* Churchman 1971) and this applies to methodologies as well. This viewpoint suggests the need to define the inquiry model as the range of procedures recommended by a methodology to collect data, and create the knowledge which becomes the basis of analysis and design. The assumptions made about what type of knowledge is important for system development and how it could be obtained is referred to as the epistemology of a methodology or inquiry model.

Among existing methodologies SSM has the most explicit inquiry model with ETHICS closely following (see section 5 of appendix A for a brief description of ETHICS). Through the division of inquiry into cultural analysis and logic-based analysis, SSM hints at the possibility of dialectic inquiry, but does not fully implement this idea.

5.5.2 Paradigmatic analysis of strengths

SSM embraces much which is consistent with the assumptions intrinsic to social relativism. In fact, it appears to be primarily informed by the social relativist paradigm (*cf.* table 4.1 in chapter 4). For example, the use of 'rich pictures' for describing the problem situation in an imaginative and creative fashion is an interesting vehicle for supporting sense-making. Similarly, the ability to construct alternative 'root definitions' which are sensible descriptors of the problem situation, offers another vehicle to encourage the creation of new meanings. A key component of the root definition is the philosophical notion of 'Weltanschauung' which allows multiple perspectives to be recognized in the development process. Lastly, Checkland's adoption of Vickers' 'social community' concept is consistent with Checkland's call for SSM to embrace phenomenology because the social community is essentially seen as emergent and unpredictable. Social community is contrasted with human activity systems which abstract the purposeful, predictable and hence designable aspects of social systems.

The methodology is also somewhat informed by the functionalist paradigm, but to a much lesser extent. Clearly the notion of a human activity system itself is functionalist (Checkland himself notes the engineering connection of this term). Furthermore, the attempt to determine the functions of human activity systems and its conceptual modeling step is clearly consistent with the tenets of functionalism. So too is its emphasis on improving the goal achievement of human activity systems. Usually this is done by improving the human activity systems' ability to predict and control its environment.

5.5.3 Paradigmatic analysis of weaknesses

In terms of paradigmatic assumptions, SSM is mostly closely aligned with the 'integrationist' dimension in viewing social order (see chapters 3 and 4): it favors stability, coordination and integration. Its seeking a consensus during problem formulation involving multiple perspectives through the use of a variety of sense-making techniques is clearly integrationist. Thus, the radical structuralist and neohumanist paradigms appear the most in opposition to SSM. Both radical structuralists and neohumanists will be critical of SSM's failure to reflect on whether it can be misused in realizing the goals of one group in the organization at the expense of another. Neohumanists would also be critical of SSM on the grounds that it does not attempt to analyze and mitigate potential distortions and communication barriers while seeking a consensus (or at least accommodation) on root definitions. Hence the cognitive basis of the conclusions may be flawed by undetected bias. This also leads to ignoring the nature and influence of organizational power and it fails to be sensitive to the issue of whether the new system will strengthen emancipation of all organizational participants or continued domination. An emancipatory system design would lead to a more equitable distribution of rights and duties (potentially shifting unwarranted use of power away from those in possession of it already). A system contributes to existing forms of domination and social control if it continues the inequities of the status quo. For this reason SSM has been criticized along similar lines as functionalist approaches in that it is likely to do little to alter the plight of the workers.

An important advance of SSM is the recognition of alternative perspectives in the inquiry process by which it collects information for analysis and design through building root definitions and conceptual models. This focuses on improving the collective understanding of the problem situation. Yet here is also an essential weakness. In the classical version of SSM, the inquiry process was seen to involve two 'domains' or 'worlds': a conceptual domain, the world of systems concepts, and the real world. It failed to address the issue of how one can be independent of the other. A reasonable amount of independence was assumed, because a crucial step was to validate the models by comparing them with the actual situation.

If one takes the position that concepts shape the world that we experience (i.e. interpretivism), then no real comparison is possible. If concepts come first, a comparison of the conceptual models with the real world is self-confirming: 'experience only confirms what the concept teaches' is a well-known dictum from Hegel that sums up an essential insight of the interpretivist position. Radical structuralists will insist that systems thinking is the ideological vehicle by which the dominant elite will seek to rationalize and legitimize primarily those designs that do not threaten their privileges and vested interests. The comparisons are phony, because no attempt is made to broaden the discourse and use elaborate checks and balances against self-delusion or 'cooking the data'. The emancipatory potential of SSM is lost for want of critical reflections of the connection between social-institutional boundary conditions of systems development and epistemology — the validity of the premises and ideas on which design solutions are based.

Emancipatory systems can only be designed through genuine democratic participation. Neither in the classical nor in the recent version of SSM is there an explicit discussion of the meaning and significance of participation let alone of the difficulties of implementing a participatory design approach. The failure to address participation is perhaps surprising yet indicative of the direction of how to improve SSM. It is surprising because social relativism strongly reminds us through the concept of the hermeneutic cycle that interaction is the very basis of human understanding and sense-making. Given that SSM is heavily influenced by social relativist ideas, one wonders why it failed to consider the implications for participation.

5.5.4 Suggested directions for future improvements

The previous paradigmatic assumption analysis reveals several directions in which SSM could be improved. Because of the ambiguities in the paradigmatic foundations of SSM (which adds to its richness), several lines of improvement are possible, although not necessarily totally consistent with each other.

First, SSM needs better modeling methods and support tools. Its conceptual modeling method is too simplistic even when compared to standard structured process modeling (i.e. leveled data flow diagramming), let alone when compared to object-oriented organizational modeling. Its communication with users could also benefit from incorporating prototyping features.

Second, SSM should incorporate principles to check on social conditions that may bias the cultural stream of inquiry and thereby invalidate the consensus. Through insisting on a cultural and a logic-based stream of inquiry, SSM opens itself up to critical discourse and it should explicitly realize this potential. But in its current form SSM lacks, perhaps purposefully, a clear focus on the possibilities of realizing the emancipatory responsibilities of systems design. To accomplish this it needs to reconstruct its inquiry model in a way so that it more directly aims at approximating a rational discourse. The replacement of the distinction between systems thinking and real world thinking by a logic-based and cultural stream of analysis cannot accomplish this. It is no substitute for an approach to cross check and validate assumptions and intermediate results. Without a critical component, SSM is subject to the same kind of weaknesses as were hinted at earlier in the discussion of the paradigmatic weaknesses of prototyping (section 5.4.3).

Currently, SSM appears to be content with harnessing the intepretive (communicative) potential of participation. From a neohumanist perspective it could be strengthened by also recognizing the important emancipatory roles of participation.

In summary, if 'improvement' of SSM means the realization of neohumanist, emancipatory concerns, it could substantially benefit from the same kind of suggestions as proposed for ETHICS in Hirschheim and Klein (1994). This implies:

(1) giving careful attention to the larger institutional context of systems development, i.e. setting the stage. Setting the stage involves considering the impact of the organizational culture and policies on the outcomes of systems development;

(2) recognizing the various roles of participation for symbolic interaction and assisting people to develop active, non-servile and democratic personality structures, and overcoming the alienation caused by the rigid division of labor;

(3) implementing a critical model of inquiry approximating a rational discourse.

5.6 Professional Work Practices Approach

In the early 1980s many researchers thought that significant practical improvements in ISD could be achieved by providing new methods and tools for practical development. The term methodology came to mean an assembly of tools and methods into a systematic approach covering the complete life-cycle from problem formulation to implementation, evaluation and maintenance. Lars Mathiassen, the chief architect of this approach, defined a methodology as consisting of the definition of an application domain which is approached with a certain perspective and preferred principles of organization and cooperation (a preferred structure of division of labor and coordination) which guide the application of specific design principles, methods and tools (Mathiassen 1981). A common belief was that better methodologies would improve the effectiveness of practitioners by displacing poor approaches to ISD and shorten their learning cycle by transferring the knowledge that supposedly is encoded in advanced methods and tools.

A small research group in Denmark challenged these popular assumptions by studying the actual working habits of system development practitioners. This research grouped originated from the trade unions projects that were conducted in Scandinavia during the 1970s and early 1980s (as reported in Nygaard and Haandlykken 1981, Kyng and Mathiassen 1982, Ehn and Kyng 1987 and Bansler 1989). They found that the more experienced analysts were, the less they followed documented methodologies. This applied even if the organization had introduced a specific method of its own as a development standard. Methods were at best crutches for beginners to be tossed aside after a period of apprenticeship. More important for understanding how systems are developed are the actual working practices in the organization which the beginners joined. The implication of this is that the usual academic training of software professionals with a heavy emphasis in computer science and software engineering needs to be complemented with practical experience and knowledge from actual development projects if the goal is to train effective system development professionals.

5.6.1 Problem focus and overview

The professional work practices approach builds on these early insights of the MARS project. In Danish, MARS stands for 'Methodical work habits (the 'AR' in Danish comes from ARbejdsformer) in System development'. The systems development approach which grew out of MARS is described in Andersen *et al.* (1990). This project shared with mainstream research on methodologies the commitment to improve the processes by which systems are developed. This is, however, interpreted in a somewhat broader sense than the rational design perspective of functionalism suggests. Building on Floyd (1987), a process view of ISD means that software is seen in its connection with human learning and communication as an emergent phenomenon:

> taking place in an evolving world with ever changing needs. Processes of work, learning and communication occur both in software development and use. During development, we find software to be the object of such processes. In use, software acts both as their support and their constraint. (Floyd 1987, p. 194).

In contrast to this:

> the product oriented perspective abstracts from the characteristics of the given base machine and considers the usage context of the product to be fixed and well understood, thus allowing software requirements to be determined in advance. (ibid)

The professional work practices approach to software development draws from this the conclusion that system development research must be anchored in a thorough understanding of the actual work habits of practicing system developers. Hence research on ISD must investigate the ways in which actual projects have been conducted including the institutional constraints surrounding them. One important component of this is organizational culture which may encourage or hinder a change of existing work practices in information systems development through prevailing attitudes to change (i.e. the 'not invented here' syndrome), incentive systems, peer pressures, and the like. The focus of the professional work practices approach is on the work practices of information system developers (including the aspect of project management and better management of developers' group work practices) rather than users. Because of this priority the approach has so far failed to adequately consider user relations and participation (cf. section 5.6.3).

The term 'professional work practices' is intended to refer both to the unsystematic, evolutionary connotation of work habits and to the methodical connotation of systematically designed work standards and procedures. In this sense, working practices can be learned by a combination of study (i.e. documentation of new methods and tools) and experience (i.e. by working with accomplished masters of the art; cf. Andersen et al. 1990, p. 60). Moreover, the principal aim of ISD research is to help practitioners improve their professional learning skills and their ability to manage their learning processes. A catch phrase for this is 'being a professional'. Several avenues are proposed for its achievement:

(1) The emphasis is on helping practitioners to design and maintain their own ways of learning. This also includes trying new methodologies or frameworks of analysis. For example, the approach experimented with structured analysis and design, Boehm's spiral model of system development and risk management and more recently with SSM and object-oriented analysis (Coad and Yourdon 1990).

(2) A second important avenue to achieve professionalism is to help practitioners improve their capabilities to reflect upon their experiences and then change their behaviors accordingly. In this way both successes and failures become important assets for improving the practice. A special tool proposed to support this is diary keeping (cf. Lanzara and Mathiassen 1984; Jepsen et al. 1989).

(3) A third avenue to improving learning is building open-minded professional attitudes which encourages practitioners to actively seek out pertinent information by interacting with the professional community and through the study of the literature. Andersen et al. (1990, p. 9) state that an environment and tradition for professional systems development should contain elements such as the following: active system

developers, sufficient resources, exchange and evaluation of experience and study of literature.

Following these basic ideas, in 1983 Andersen *et al.* began studying the working practices in eight development projects that took place in four large organizations (two projects in each) for one year. In the next phase, they attempted to influence the working practices by introducing new methods and tools. One of these organizations withdrew after the first year. Hence in the second year, six projects from three of the four organizations experimented with new work practices as suggested by the researchers. The solutions that resulted from this were carefully evaluated (references to the detailed Danish reports can be found in Andersen *et al.* 1990 under MARS 2 to MARS 10). In the third year the researchers reported their experiences and disseminated what was learned in three ways:

(1) in book form (written in Danish in 1986 and translated into English: Andersen *et al.* 1990),

(2) through University courses, and

(3) through professional courses for practitioners.

The experiences from these projects confirmed the following five maxims (or basic principles) that characterize the professional work practices approach in its present form (as well as many other Scandinavian research projects):

(i) Research on ISD must be committed to achieve and facilitate change at the work place. Abstract theories or experiments reported in scientific journals read by a small elite are insufficient to accomplish this. Instead a change of working practices through better learning must take place.

(ii) Each research project in ISD should consciously select and define the interests that it is to serve through the knowledge change it produces. This is a generalization of the principle in the MARS project that stated improvement in ISD must serve the professional interests of the participating practitioners.

(iii) The research project organization should be democratic so that practitioners and researchers form a communication and cooperation community of peers. Researchers possess general theories and methods. Often they are more articulate than practitioners in analyzing problems with abstract ideas on how to approach a solution. But theories are empty unless they are appropriately applied to the specific setting. For this, the researchers depend on the experience of the practical system developers. Only the latter are familiar with the details of system development and the use of the methods that are specific to their organization.

(iv) The preferred research approach is experimental, because theories and methods are subject to ambiguous interpretation and their true consequences cannot be understood from logical deduction, but only by experimenting with them in concrete working situations. For example, cognitive maps were used to better understand the problems of a specific project and to analyze their causes and consequences (Lanzara and Mathiassen 1984).

(v) Each research project must plan for the collection, reporting and dissemination of its results. The dissemination must take more than one form to be effective in practice, i.e. academic publication outlets are one important form but insufficient by themselves. They must be accompanied by professional presentations, courses or other forms of disseminating professional knowledge.

5.6.2 Paradigmatic analysis of strengths

This approach has been able to operationalize many of the important insights of social relativism especially those that were borrowed from hermeneutics (see chapter 6) and phenomenology. Clearly the emphasis on reflection is an application of the basic concept of an interpretive cycle. The approach recognizes the importance of metaphors as an interpretative vehicle for understanding design situations and identifying design options building on Lakoff and Johnson (1980) and Schon (1983).

Because of the theoretical connection to the 'reflective practitioner', the approach could potentially build on a deep understanding of the problematical relationship between human action and thought (Argyris and Schon 1978; Argyris 1982). In its current practice this is partly realized by its insistence on learning through self-reflection and partly through the emphasis on interaction as a basis for dialogue (below we shall note that much of this is implicit in the research practice and the theoretical connections need to be formulated more clearly along with their implications). Moreover the approach also recognizes that dialogue must be informed by experiential feedback from shared practice. The theoretical rationale for this comes from the phenomenology of life-worlds (Schutz 1967; Schutz and Luckmann 1974; Madsen 1989). All this adds up to a sound theoretical basis for reaching a deeper understanding of the problematical nature of human communication and of the significance of genuine participation as a basis for symbolic interaction. As system development is an interpretive process that tries to 'read' the organizational text in requirements definition and create new meanings in the design of a solution, it follows that developers cannot and should not impose these new meanings 'from the outside'. Consequently, the professional work practices based approach gives analysts primarily a facilitator role in the users' sense-making and learning processes (cf. Hirschheim and Klein 1989, p. 1205).

Another strength is that the hermeneutic tradition checks 'blind action' by assigning reflection a proper role. The professional work practices based approach takes note of this by seeking various means to encourage and support it (e.g. systematic diary keeping; Lanzara and Mathiassen 1984). All of these points are consistent with the recent philosophical ideas on human understanding and the outlines of a general theory of communicative action (*cf.* Apel 1980; Habermas 1984).

An approach purely based on theories of understanding runs the risk of withdrawing into contemplation and reflection. To counteract this, the professional work practices approach appears to be influenced by paradigmatic principles that favor human action. This is evident from at least four of the five maxims stated above (the possible exception being (v)). In addition to its social relativist influences, there are both functionalist tendencies in its emphasis on experimental prototyping and neohumanist tendencies in its commitment to reveal the interests and values of applying knowledge. It also draws on the ideas of neohumanism in its democratic project organization for facilitating the sharing of ideas. (Of course, functionalists might be inclined to argue that one cannot 'vote on what is correct'.) The democratic project organization can be seen as an approximation of the rational discourse model and the focus on pertinent interests as an attempt to realize what Habermas calls the 'generalizable interest' (*cf.* Habermas 1973). The two are not unconnected. Generalizable are those interests that emerge as legitimate from a maximal critique of all needs that should be served by a project. Insisting that the interests are made explicit and chosen consciously in a democratically organized group will most likely force a critical debate of these interests. Other devices to bring about critical discussion are also considered. For example, Mathiassen and Nielsen (1989, 1990) suggest that a consultant report on the key problem aspects can be written to initiate a debate about conflicting interests in a development project. However, the actual supporting of rational communication in system development needs to be better developed (as is noted in our critique below).

The approach balances the emphasis on communicative aspects with the need for direct action through the emphasis on practical experimentation and the commitment to achieve real change in the practice of system development. From a phenomenological perspective, the emphasis on experimentation is important for three reasons. First, it strengthens the basis of shared meanings. The results of the experiments equally inform the users (subjects) and the developers (scientists). This is different from the functionalist concept of experiment where an experimenter controls the conditions for the subjects that in turn do not benefit from the results. Second and equally important, shared experiments help to acquire the tacit knowledge basis which is the sign of true professionalism (*cf.* the analysis of expert knowledge by Dreyfus 1982). Third, the experimental component of the approach is also a vehicle to deal with the problem of unanticipated consequences of ISD which is consistent with the literature on the subject (Klein and Hirschheim 1983). Here the literature points out that ISD means a change of organizational life forms and the totality of such changes cannot be predicted by theory but at best partially anticipated and felt by experience.

A further connection to both neohumanist and social relativist ideas is the process orientation of the approach. If requirements are seen as emerging from the interaction between users and developers as both try to 'read' the organizational situation and make sense of it, then the process view is more appropriate then the product view.

A process approach to systems development is also suggested by the neo-humanist paradigm because neohumanism focuses us on improving the rationality of communication and discourse so that the participants themselves can determine what is appropriate, just and correct in a given situation. This advocates process characteristics not specific outcomes. In line with such philosophical principles a process-oriented approach to ISD should seek to improve the processes by which an organization 'reads' problematic situations, for example by improving cooperation, communication and knowledge bases. This is exactly what the professional work practices approach does. In line with this it also suggests that system developers should act as facilitators which is consistent with the tenets of the social relativist paradigm. This facilitator principle is implemented in the professional work practices based approach through the idea that system developers should help the organization to better manage its learning processes so as to better understand itself, the problems, and general situation which together determine together how IS are used. This is similar to the double loop learning concept of Argyris (1982).

5.6.3 Paradigmatic analysis of weaknesses

When viewed from a functionalist or neohumanist perspective several weaknesses of the professional work practices based approach stand out. From a functionalist perspective, the approach lacks clarity and structure. There is no explicit overall theory, only fragments of theories and singular experiences. This is by no means a necessary consequence of the interpretivist leanings of the approach. On the contrary, the recognition of the importance of clear communication should be an incentive to document itself systematically such as has been done with the project management aspects of the approach (*cf.* Andersen *et al.* 1990). Both the theoretical foundations and experience exist that are necessary for doing this. The project diaries record much experience. They could provide valuable information on what to emphasize in making the approach more accessible and thereby also 'teachable'. Regarding structure, one would not necessarily expect the procedural type of documentation in terms of methods, tools and life-cycle structure that is so effective for functionalist methodologies. Instead, a systematic discussion and enumeration of fundamental theoretical principles and how they have been realized in different cases might be more appropriate. The previous discussion has provided numerous pointers to this. Other possible starting points to review the theoretical foundations exist as well (e.g. Boland 1985; Winograd and Flores 1986; Lyytinen 1986; Ngwenyama 1987; Oliga 1988 and Ulrich 1988). The description of the theoretical basis should then be followed by examination of a list of common mistakes or misunderstandings with some friendly advice on the do's and don'ts. Again, the extensive project work and the documentation of participants' behaviors and thoughts in the diaries should provide valuable hints for this. The documentation structure chosen by the PORGI project (*cf.* Kolf and Oppelland 1980, p. 68) could point the way to an appropriate, yet clearly organized format. PORGI documented itself through five aspects:

(i)   the terminological basis (in PORGI called the descriptional framework);

(ii) a discussion of general design principles and the interventions to which they typically lead (called the pool of design concepts);

(iii) typical sequences of well-known design activities (procedural scheme);

(iv) a pool of recommended methods and tools; and

(v)   a pool of informative problems or case vignettes.

Both functionalists and neohumanists will also be critical of the lack of attention given to the cost and effectiveness of the approach. Clearly it is very cost and labor intensive and both neohumanists and functionalists will insist that cost be justified by results. Hence one misses a discussion of potential positive and negative outcomes of the approach and how they can be understood (functionalists would likely call for 'measures', but a broader concept of keeping score is applicable) and how it compares with other approaches to ISD.

From a neohumanist point of view, the approach is weak in recognizing the theoretical and practical difficulties of improving established working practices primarily through communication. It gives little consideration to the role of authority and power in organizational change which is rather unrealistic. This is somewhat surprising, because the need for a change strategy is recognized in Andersen *et al.* (1990, p. 238). Among the pertinent issues recognized under the heading of 'strategies for changing working practices' are the following:

(i)   who should take responsibility for change,

(ii) whether corporate culture impedes or encourages change,

(iii) the need for determining qualification requirements and appropriate ways to meet them, and

(iv) the need to foster learning and initiative.

For the most part the professional work practices approach appears to draw on a functionalist perspective of 'planned organizational change'. In so doing, it fails to explicitly analyze the multiple personal, cultural and linguistic barriers to learning and communication that may exist both within and beyond the immediate work situation. Of particular concern is the failure to recognize that work practices are connected to different work languages and to change either one means a change in 'forms of life'. For example the examination of the relationship between language and phenomenon as well as between system description and reality (*cf.* Andersen *et al.* 1990, pp. 209, 212) misses some of the most fundamental insights of social relativism.

From a social relativist perspective, the professional work practices approach fails to address the fundamental role that bias and 'prejudice' play in all human understanding (*cf.* chapter 6). In particular 'preunderstandings' in the form precedence and tradition would seem to apply to the analysis of work practices. Each 'work practice' entails a bias, a limited 'horizon' into which we are bound by various forms of tradition and domination. The concept of change strategy needs to be broadened to encompass the issue of how the participants can possibly escape the 'prison' of their own tradition. To say that 'the participants together should build up words and concepts increasing their understanding of similar phenomena' and 'the objective may be that this understanding should be a shared platform improving the quality of the design process' (Andersen *et al.* 1990, pp. 209, 210) fails to recognize how communities get entangled in the illusions and misconceptions of their own languages and how certain language patterns are stabilized by subtle forms of social control and domination.

A more penetrating analysis of the issues at stake would require an explicit discussion not only on how work languages could be changed (some of this is provided), but also how it could be changed for the better (i.e. in what sense improved). This would have to explain how different work practices can be fused in a new work practice both overcoming the limitations of the old (any language use implies a practice according to the later Wittgenstein *cf.* chapter 6). Some of the key issues with this surfaced in the Gadamer-Habermas debate on the limits of human understanding (*cf.* the review in McCarthy 1982, p. 162, esp. p. 171; and Held 1980). Habermas makes the point that communicative distortions are not the exception (as in propaganda, advertising or adversarial situations), but the rule in everyday life. One misses a clear recognition of how change of working practices can truly be changed for the better, i.e. be more than conforming to social norms that happen to prevail at a certain time in a certain place. Secondly one misses a clarifying word of what 'improvement' of working practices really means in practice (for example by interpreting a good case example). Typically, one will interpret 'improvement' as a synonym for 'progress' (the irreversible change of working practices for the better) and there are some difficulties with this notion (*cf.* the analysis in Alvarez and Klein 1989) which the literature on the professional work practices approach so far has failed to address. If this was done by way of a theoretical foundation of the approach, it would be possible to give a more penetrating analysis of the improvement of work practices (and work languages) with the difficulties to be expected in such an enterprise.

In our opinion the fundamental issues are the same as were noted in the section on information systems planning: there are different levels and communities of discourse and it is not clear how the meanings of different languages can be become shared and in what sense of the word this constitutes improvement. Addressing this issue squarely will amount to a research program on the 'rational reconstruction of the conditions of speech and action' (*cf.* summary in McCarthy 1982, p. 272) in the context of systems development. Implicitly the professional work practices approach has dealt with this through its emphasis on interaction and experience.

From a practical perspective, explicit, theoretically well-founded principles of participation and project organization will be critical for rational change of working practices and the treatment of this (*cf.* Andersen *et al.* 1990, pp. 171, 239 and 250) falls behind Mumford's analysis of participation and the extensive empirical work on principles of participation in the PORGI project (*cf.* summary in Oppelland 1984): who should participate?, under which conditions?, with which qualifications?, for which purposes? what are the barriers for effective participation (e.g. Mulder 1971)?, etc. Given the general strong emphasis on interaction, one cannot help but be surprised by the neglect of the pertinent literature.

5.6.4 Suggested directions for future improvements

We noted above the need for better documentation. The analysis of weaknesses points to two further fruitful avenues of research that could considerably strengthen the approach. One has to do with language and the other with the effects of power and distortions. Given the emphasis on understanding in the approach, it is surprising that no attention is paid to the role of language, in particular work language, in professional work practices. By incorporating some of the principles and methods of a semiotic approach to IS design (*cf.* Andersen 1991), some of the vagueness and lack of structure of the professional work practices approach could be addressed.

The second issue concerns the interrelationships between power, communication and language. One misses a clear discussion of a situation and interest analysis as is, for example, proposed in Iivari (1989). This should include the institutional context with a focus on goals, hidden agendas and overt and covert uses of unwarranted power. A first approach to this can be found in Mathiassen and Nielsen (1990). In general, however, the primary focus of the professional work practice approach is on change of working practices through creative learning and well-intended cooperation. This overlooks the following causes of development problems with users which are very difficult to deal with: perceived inequities of proposed changes, or lingering issues of frustration and social injustice that are imported in the organization from the surrounding society (*cf.* Newman and Rosenberg 1985, Braverman 1974, Bjorn-Andersen *et al.* 1982). Perceived inequities of organizational change tend to arise from shifts in the distribution of duties and rewards at the work place. These types of problems are more easily addressed in a project than the second problem type: frustration. General frustration among users is often revealed by examining the social contract between different socio-

economic groupings in a region or society from which the organization draws
its employees. Major imbalances in social justice cause large numbers of
people to feel that they 'never get a square deal' and the resulting latent
frustration surfaces when things change in the organization. If a change of
professional work practices is to be successful across a large number of different organizations, it must incorporate principles which allow the detection
of such issues.

In order to address this, classical functionalist theories of the nature of organizational incentives and power (e.g. Harsanyi, 1962) could be combined
with the neohumanist analysis of distorted communication. Neohumanism
emphasizes the connection of communication problems to macro societal
issues. The synthesis of such a conceptual base drawn from functionalism,
hermeneutics and neohumanism combined with the emphasis on working
practices might be helpful for two purposes: First, to address participation and project organization as was already noted. Second, to place the
professional work practices on a realistic socio-theoretic foundation so that
organizations and analysts can more clearly understand in which kinds of
situations it might produce promising results and in which it is unlikely to
be applicable.

5.7 Summary of Methodology Analysis

5.7.1 Methodology summary

In the previous characterization several references were made to emancipatory features. Yet, a fully developed emancipatory approach to ISD does
not exist in any concrete form. Such an approach could be constructed on
the grounds of the neohumanist paradigm. Although there are no methodologies which yet implement this neohumanist view, there is a literature
base coalescing around the theme of applying critical social theory to the
development of information systems (cf. Lyytinen and Klein 1985; Lyytinen
1986; Lyytinen and Hirschheim 1988, Ngwenyama 1987, 1991). The ideas
are still somewhat embryonic but there is enough substantive material available to suggest the nature and direction of an emancipatory approach to
information systems development. Elsewhere (Hirschheim and Klein 1994)
we take up this theme and sketch in some detail how emancipatory concerns could be realized in a methodology that originally did not focus on
emancipatory concerns. We believe that the ETHICS methodology* could
be developed further from a critical social theory perspective to incorporate
not only emancipatory but also communicative aspects. There are good
reasons why we chose ETHICS as an example (e.g. its dialectical, nominal
group formation principles to provide a rational discourse on design options), but this is not to prevent the application of neohumanist principles

---

* Because the ETHICS methodology has been referenced so often in this book, suggesting its
importance to the field of information systems development, we felt it necessary to provide an
overview of the methodology. It can be found in section 5 of the Appendix.

to other methodologies. There is room for many opinions on which methodologies could most easily be modified to serve emancipatory interests. It is tempting to consider neohumanism as providing an 'upgrade path' for all existing methodologies.

5.7.2 Comparative methodology review

Having presented a paradigmatic analysis of the four methodologies in the past sections of this chapter, we now offer a comparative review of them. It is our contention that if the four methodologies are compared in terms of their ideas, concepts and definitions as introduced in chapter 2, commonalities and differences become apparent that are often overlooked. Their commonalties are summarized in table 5.2, and their differences in table 5.3. Although we treated ISP and structured analysis as one methodology in this chapter, in this comparative review we divide them into two approaches since they are typically considered as two stages in a comprehensive SLC.

Common Aspect	Explanation
Definitional perspective of IS	All define IS more structural than functional: The product of designing an IS is seen as a collection of people, procedures, models with data, and technical devices
Intentionality of ISD	ISD is seen as a deliberate change process; cf. table 5.3 regarding the uncertainties which are recognized in this process.
IS development group	All favor an institutionalized, professional development group, but the nature of professionality is seen differently
Preferred object system classes	ISP, SAD and SSM tend to lean towards process-orientation; prototyping can begin with process or data orientation; there are no preferred object system classes for the professional work practices approach.
Consideration of object systems as linguistic phenomena	None gives adequate consideration to conceiving of object system as linguistic phenomena; to the extent that language is considered, formalisms derived from the applying of formal logic to modeling natural language are preferred. SSM gives informal recognition to the importance of professional speaking through the 'rich picture' modeling idea, and prototyping implicitly is very skeptical of linguistic specifications of object systems because of its distrust of all representations

Table 5.2 Common Aspects of the Selected Methodologies

Beginning with the rows on 'object system' of table 5.3, we note that all five approaches focus on the organization as a target of change, but there are substantial differences in the way they interpret the organization.

ISP sees the organization in terms of the principal business processes with associated formal procedures and data classes, and as carried out in organizational units like divisions and departments. Different ISP methodologies tabulate business processes and their data in varying formats (such as different types of matrices) to derive an architecture for the current and future IS application portfolio. The scope of ISP (and hence its conception of object system) is the whole organization and its comprehensive mission.

Aspect	ISP	SAD	Prototyping	SSM	Professional Work Practices
Object System	entire organization	functions of an existing IS	part of an existing organization and its IS	organization or IS	working practices of ISD
SLC stages	IS architecture definition	technical problem formulation to logical design	design to implementation	emergent problem formulation to logical design	n/a
ISD uncertainty	problem uncertainty	means uncertainty	means and effect uncertainty	means, effects, problem uncertainty	potentially all
Environment	resources & formal organization	resources and technology	user task complex	ideas, values resources	state of art
Objectives	given by strategic plan	by management	emergent	emergent	n/a
Data modeling epistemology	fact-based	fact-based	unspecified; user dependent	implicitly rule-based	n/a

Table 5.3: Differing Aspects of the Selected Methodologies

In distinction to this, Soft Systems Methodology focuses not on formal procedures, but on the different images which are held by users or other stakeholders. Through a flexible, pictorial representation called 'rich pictures', SSM attempts to document alternative visions of the organizational mission, its clients, principal actors, major processes (transformations), desired outcomes, etc. and arrive at the underlying 'root definitions'. SSM can be applied to a specific project or to enterprise planning. Unlike ISP approaches, it possesses no special methods to cope with the complexity of an enterprise wide study.

Both Structured Analysis and Design (SAD) and prototyping are concerned with one specific application at a time. SAD models the essentials of application domains in terms of four constructs: data flows, processes, data stores and interfaces which provide or receive data flows. SAD represents organizational units in terms of the processes they perform and the data stores they maintain. Prototyping, on the other hand, does not analyze the organization with simplifying constructs, but deals with the full complexity of organizational reality by directly introducing new technology at the work place in cooperation with the responsible users. It copes with this complexity by beginning with a highly simplified problem definition (agreed upon with users) and then through a series of iterations broadens the definition and improves the proposed solution.

The professional work practices approach deals with the organization in terms of the professional habits, customs, attitudes and work procedures that make up the 'culture' of a particular systems development department or group. It attempts to help practitioners reflect on their practices so that they can systematically learn from their successes and mishaps. Strictly speaking, it is not a specific methodology of ISD and therefore the concept of an SLC does not apply to it.

None of the other approaches covers all of the stages of the SLC. Prototyping aims at a working system, albeit one whose implementation is not necessarily refined. The streamlining and documentation of the prototype is left to conventional methods. Furthermore, prototyping does not have an explicit analysis and problem formulation stage. Rather problem formulation is handled emergently through interaction with the user(s).

In contrast, ISP and SSM provide explicit problem formulation. In the case of ISP this is a formal statement of the architecture of IS identifying both current and future IS needs. ISP defines problems deductively by going from the overall organizational mission and existing support systems to the single project. The IS architecture derived through ISP defines a connected set of ISD problems in terms of a systematic long-term agenda for ISD projects. It also helps to set priorities and constraints for the various projects. SSM focuses on the ill-defined perceptions and ambiguities surrounding a single application. It attempts to engage the various stakeholders in a dialogue about their perceptions and seeks a consensus view of the preferred problem formulation. It tries to avoid the imposition of rigid solution templates and encourages the handling of problem formulation in an emergent fashion. It is therefore particularly suited to tackle ill-defined application problems. On the other hand, SSM does not consider technical implementation and leaves this to some conventional approach.

SAD's approach to problem formulation is system modeling either by analyzing the existing system or event modeling. In the former, case requirements are derived from a model of the existing system. In event modeling the events (outside stimuli) are captured to which a system must respond.

Requirements are defined by the 'essential' processes that are needed to deal with these events. From this a refined model is derived that specifies an improved logical design. From this we conclude that SAD favors a technical perspective of problem formulation with the aim of finding effective and efficient technical design alternatives, but it does not prevent the analysts from exploring organizational improvements if the system model is interpreted from an organizational perspective. There are no specific features that allow the exploration of differing perceptions of organizational issues. Physical design and implementation is left to structured programming methodologies.

All methodologies recognize that ISD is fraught with great uncertainties, but only SSM attempts to give equal weight to all three types of uncertainties:

(i)   are we tackling the right problem? (problem uncertainty);

(ii) are we considering the right approach and means to achieve the desired outcomes? (means uncertainty);

(iii) will the outcomes produce the desired effects and only the desired effects? (outcome or effect uncertainty).

SSM is weakest in finding the best technical means but strongest in addressing the first and last issue (where other methodologies are weakest). It addresses the first issue by carefully selecting alternatives of relevant systems, for example based on different views of the issue at stake (Checkland and Scholes 1990, p. 32). It tackles the last issue by insisting on a comparison between the proposed conceptual model solution (the models of purposeful activity systems) and the real world through 'formal questioning': 'how is each activity proposed in the model judged?' 'Does it exist now?' 'How can it be done?' (Checkland and Scholes 1990, pp. 43, 53; cf. Mathiassen and Nielsen 1990 for an illustrative case).

SAD is strongest in handling means uncertainty. The professional work practices approach can potentially contribute to better handling all types of uncertainty because it can draw on any methodology to help professionals to consider more carefully the potential positive and negative effects of their interventions. (Potentially the same point could be made with regard to 'objectives' and 'data modeling epistemology', but to the best of our knowledge with the exception of the hints in Mathiassen and Nielsen 1989, 1990, these aspects have not received much attention by the advocates of this approach. On the other hand the uncertainty problem has explicitly been considered based on Boehm's concept of managing risk and uncertainty in ISD.)

For all methodologies, the resources given to ISD, the structure, climate and culture of the organization form the environment. In addition, the professional work practices approach is highly sensitive to the larger professional culture. SSM more than other methodologies is sensitive to the organizational culture and climate (note that it features a separate 'cultural stream of enquiry'). Prototyping is least affected by the overall culture and most by the immediate task environment that it tries to tackle.

ISP attempts to derive IS objectives from strategic organizational objectives which it largely presumes as given by the so-called 'strategy transformation' or 'strategic alignment'. Similarly SAD presumes objectives as given along with the management mandate for ISD. Prototyping has no explicit objective formulation stage, but is highly responsive to user reactions and thereby co-defines objectives with the emergent solution. From what was said earlier it is clear that SSM has the most systematic way of clarifying objectives.

Finally, both ISP and SAD conceive data as objectively recorded facts. This is also true of prototyping, but in fact, views of data are co-defined between users and analysts who construct a shared reality in the course of their interaction. SSM favors dialogically constructed shared views of reality, but lacks specific linguistic methods and tools to capture the emergent meanings in something like a grammar or dictionary of meanings and language use. Nevertheless it clearly views data structures which express the information categories embodied in information flow models as ultimately anchored in 'meanings attributed to the perceived world,. (Checkland and Scholes 1990, p. 57) and the perceived world is documented through 'rich pictures'.

But how can thinking of data as 'facts' or 'meaning attributions' be conceived in more concrete terms, and what types of conceptual structures and representation forms are needed to address these questions in different methodologies? To provide a more detailed answer to this question we shall turn our attention to theories of data modeling and meaning which will be our topic for the next two chapters. In chapter 6 we shall analyze the paradigmatic and conceptual foundations of modeling linguistic phenomena in IS. Chapter 7 continues this by conducting a paradigmatic analysis of two key data modeling approaches.

6
Conceptual and Paradigmatic Foundations of Data Modeling

6.1 Introduction

This chapter will show that the issues arising in data modeling have close connections to core issues as discussed in the theory of knowledge, epistemology and philosophy of language. The purpose of this chapter is to characterize data modeling in terms of the philosophical debate in these areas and connect it to the four paradigms to the extent as is appropriate. Whilst all of the paradigmatic assumptions have important implications for data modeling, neither the neohumanist nor the radical structuralist paradigm are specifically reflected in the literature on data modeling. Nevertheless, we believe that a neohumanist paradigm could be applied to data modeling. In the following we shall articulate some of its principal implications for data modeling. In addition, while no work has been published on a radical structuralist approach to data modeling (i.e. the equivalent of the UTOPIA project in the process-oriented approaches), we believe that its most important aspect, the articulation of the workers' perspective, could be accomplished within a neohumanist approach.

In order to provide a concrete focus for the philosophical treatment of data modeling in terms of the paradigms, we shall organize the discussion in section 6.3 around the following four questions:

(1) The ontological question (what is being modeled?)

(2) The epistemological question (why is the result valid?)

(3) The social context question (what is the relationship between the social world and data modeling?)

(4) The representation question (how well is the result represented?)

These four questions are introduced in section 6.3.1. and answered for functionalist, social relativist and neohumanist data modeling approaches in sections 6.3.2, 6.3.3 and 6.3.4 respectively. In section 6.2 we precede these four questions with a general introduction to the philosophical debate on which we drew to frame and answer the four question for each of the paradigms of data modeling, i.e. functionalism, social relativism and neohumanism. Section 6.2 also provides an overview of the philosophical roots which are specific to each of the two principal schools of data modeling discussed in chapter 7 (i.e. the fact-based and rule-based schools).

144

6.2 Philosophical Background

The basic view adopted in this chapter is not new: namely that data modeling is concerned with the representation of knowledge. Therefore, a philosophical background on human inquiry and the nature of knowledge is pertinent for understanding the problems of data modeling. In this section we provide this philosophical background.

6.2.1 Positivism and analytical philosophy

Historically, the efforts to employ a formal language to express facts in the world in an exact way are very old. The origins of such attempts can be dated back to Aristotle and to the Aristotelean syllogisms outlined in *De Interpretatione*. Aristotle was also the first to make observations about referential and intensional (semantic) meaning.* In the *Organon* he proposed a theory of categories and predication. It suggests that all knowledge is represented in terms of subjects and predicates a distinction which continues to be fundamental for data modeling approaches found in the fact-based school.

In the Modern Age the next advances of the fact-based theory were made by Leibniz. He presented the idea of a universal calculus (a new kind of symbolic logic) in which all truths could be derived. However, Leibniz was never able to devise any model for that language (even though it led him to discover calculus and the binary number system). Major advances in formalizing the meaning of language were made one hundred years later by Frege. Frege's ideas continue still to be influential in applied fields such as knowledge-based systems and database theory (Dummett 1981).

Frege in his theory of logic introduced a sufficiently detailed formal notation to describe first-order predicate logic (see Dummett 1981 for an excellent discussion). With this he paved the way to formally represent natural language sentences involving assertions. Frege's decisive invention was the principle of compositionality: the meaning of complex expressions is derived recursively from more basic ones until we have reached those terms that have a direct interpretation in reality.

Frege's impact has also been prominent in the development of theories of language. Frege was the first one who clearly distinguished between the concept of a reference ('Begriff'), and the concept of a meaning ('Bedeutung') a distinction which was later popularized in Ogden and Richards' (1949) triangle. The third penetrating insight of the Fregean program was to treat the meaning of a sentence as an objective fact that was independent of the

---

* In *De Interpretatione*, Aristotle makes the point that there is no objective experience for all speakers even though he admits that experiences can be understood by others. He states that: 'Spoken words are symbols of experiences in the psyche; written words are symbols of the spoken. As writing, so is speech not the same for all people. But the experiences themselves, of which these words are primarily signs, are the same for everyone, and so are the objects of which those experiences are likeness.'

users' subjective comprehension and could thereby be formally described. The meaning of the sentence was defined solely by its truth conditions, i.e. by knowing what the world would have to be like for a sentence to be true.

The Fregean program was further developed by several famous logicians during the 20th century. Wittgenstein (1922) in his *Tractatus LogicoPhilosophicus* developed a theory of how language can be seen as a picture of reality i.e. as a mosaic of fact descriptions. Russell and Whitehead's (1950) theory of types and Carnap's (1956) theory of intension attempted to define more exactly the syntactic and semantic principles of formal languages. Tarski (1956) added the insight that it is important to distinguish between the meanings in a language and a meta-language. A meta-language describes another language. With this distinction he was able to resolve many classical, puzzling semantic paradoxes (such as the liar's paradox). Tarski's theory led to a hierarchy of object-language and meta-language levels. Finally, the works of Montague (1974) introduced possible world semantics where several temporal, modal and deontic aspects of sentences could be handled formally. In possible world semantics the meaning of a sentence is defined by a set of possible worlds where the sentence is true (Dowty *et al.* 1981).*

Another stream of philosophical thought which joined forces with the developments in analytical linguistic philosophy was that of neopositivism (logical positivism). Logical positivism has its main roots with a group of philosophers called the Vienna Circle. The scholars in the circle tried to develop new foundations for science during the 1920s and the 1930s. The most famous participants in the Vienna Circle were Neurath, Schlick and Carnap, and later on, Popper. Positivist thinking has exercised much influence on the development of science during the 20th century. Because positivism proposed that there is only one model of science for both the natural and cultural sciences ('Geisteswissenschaften'), its influence has been especially dramatic on the development of the social and human sciences (see e.g. Kolakowski 1972; Bleicher 1982).

However, during the post World War II era, the positivist program has encountered growing difficulties in realizing its goals, and many of its basic presuppositions have become suspect. In response they have been greatly modified (see Bleicher 1982; Ulrich 1983) into concepts such as falsificationism (Popper 1972) or 'scientific programs' (Lakatos and Musgrave 1970) due to constant attacks from within (Feyerabend 1975) and outside (Habermas 1971). Yet, the positivists' image of science still forms the modus operandi of

---

* Although the importance of the Montague grammar cannot be underestimated in the development of analytic linguistic philosophy, it is odd his works have not been been widely applied and discussed in the database community despite their direct usefulness to data modeling problems. Only Stamper (1985a, 1987), Lee (1983), and Sowa (1984) have discussed Montague semantics in some depth.

many practicing scientists (see e.g. Morgan 1983; Reason and Rowan 1981) and also in information systems (Klein and Lyytinen 1985; Orlikowski and Baroudi 1991).

The neopositivist view of science was based on the following four presuppositions:

(1) scientific knowledge consists of 'facts' given independently of the researcher;

(2) the empirical–analytic method is the only mode of knowledge acquisition;

(3) scientific inquiry guided by the empirical–analytic method applies to all spheres of cognitive activity (e.g. construction of data models); and

(4) results of scientific inquiry are the only true form of knowledge (see e.g. Kolakowski 1972; Bleicher 1982).

Consequently, the program has investigated two aspects of knowledge acquisition: how knowledge can be strictly founded on empirical observations (data); and how the unity of scientific inquiry can be achieved by applying logical (mathematical) analysis. The ideas by which the positivists addressed these issues are highly visible in the functionalist schools of data modeling. For example, in the ANSI/SPARC report the conceptual schema is viewed as a formal 'scientific theory' which is derived following the empirical canons of logical positivism (see ANSI/SPARC 1975, pp. 130–140 and especially figure 5.1).

6.2.2 The later Wittgenstein and the concept of the language game

Of specific importance for the philosophical basis of social relativism and neohumanism are the contributions from two prominent anti-positivist philosophical schools: hermeneutics and the later Wittgenstein's philosophy of language (Wittgenstein 1958; for short representations see e.g. von Kutchera 1975; Blair 1990, Boland 1991. For hermeneutics see e.g. Palmer 1969; Bleicher 1980; for a short introduction to hermeneutics see Winograd and Flores 1986, Capurro 1992, Boland 1985). Both philosophical schools have attacked the premises of analytical philosophy and positivism, especially how they pose the question of meaning in language, i.e. the 'language–reality' dichotomy (Klein and Lyytinen 1985). Though both hermeneutics and the later Wittgenstein recognize analytical philosophy as a common 'enemy' and both share ontological presuppositions about the nature of meaning and language, the two antipositivist schools are quite different in their vocabulary and in the way they solve the question of meaning in the language–reality dichotomy. Separate treatment of the two philosophical schools is necessary in order to explain what each can add to our understanding of data modeling. In this section we shall discuss late Wittgenstein and the next section will provide a short introduction to hermeneutics. The focus in these analyses will be on how data models can and should be conceived as prescriptions and as enactments of rule-based social behavior which conveys meaning.

Wittgenstein's later philosophy grew out of his own disappointments with the *Tractatus* world. These led him to prepare a series of lectures which were published under the title *Philosophical Investigations* (1958). This book is a rich collection of thoughts and ideas scarcely connected with each other in any systematic way. The reason for this is that Wittgenstein did not want to develop a new semantic theory (i.e. a new ontology of language that would replace his *Tractatus* ontology), but only to free us from 'the bewitchment of our intelligence by our language'. In other words he aimed to fight false conceptions of the function of language suggested by analytical philosophy. The very same concerns are also at the center of criticisms directed against the functionalist approaches to data modeling. Wittgenstein approached these problems in a novel way.

In the *Tractatus*, Wittgenstein laid down the ontological presuppositions that are central to an analytical approach which we shall apply below to data modeling: correspondence between language constructs and reality, objectivity and neutrality of language, the ideals of exactness and excluded middle. According to this view, philosophical analysis (and data modeling activity in the same vein) aims to provide an ideal language that is a 'true' picture of reality; in such a language simple terms stand for simple objects, and sentences reproduce the structure of facts pictured. In accordance with this, the task of philosophical analysis and data modeling is to reconstruct the meaning of sentences in ordinary language which do not satisfy the ideal of the scientific exactitude to the extent necessary that a powerful and exact object system representation can be derived (and meaningless sentences can be discarded).

The major thrust in *Philosophical Investigations* is to turn this whole relation between language and reality upside down: it is through the description in language that the world is revealed to us. The world (reality) is never given to us in and of itself, but only through interpretation in some language. This insight was later formulated concisely in the Sapir–Whorff thesis: two observers when confronted with identical observations will not draw the same conclusions unless their languages can somehow be calibrated. There are as many worlds as there are different languages! The denial of the ontological picture theory of language with the associated objectivist epistemology has several fundamental consequences for data modeling theory:

(1) Abandonment of the realist theory of linguistic meaning

If the objects, attributes and facts of the object system are not given independently of language, then the meaning of linguistic expressions used to describe the objects system cannot be explained by saying that such entities are conventionally assigned to them as meanings. This applies to both the intensional and extensional theories of linguistic meaning. Instead, ontological structures in the object system need to be regarded as projections of the linguistic structures by which we speak about the world.

(2) Denial of semantic reductionism and absolutism

If the object system cannot be built up in an unambiguous (absolutism) and definite manner (reductionism), then how it is articulated depends on the linguistic forms available for describing it (*cf.* Sapir–Whorf thesis). This claim runs against the idea that an ontologically 'complete' ideal language can be devised which can picture the structure of reality in and of itself.

(3) Focus on how ordinary language works

If 'reality' is provided to us within ordinary language and if ordinary language is the major medium in which meaning is revealed, then the focus of data modeling must be in understanding how well ordinary language does its current job and what functions it serves in social activity. This may, or may not, require formal analysis; yet the ultimate 'guarantor' of the data modeling activity is not some 'objective' reality or 'formal verification', but how well the analysis serves the purpose of understanding the various uses of language in supporting organizational action.

(4) Collapse of the myth of linguistic precision

The demand for a complete picture of reality in some formal ideal language arises from the idea of linguistic exactness: well-defined objects and attributes depend on exact meanings of linguistic expressions. For the later Wittgenstein the concept of exactness is a delusion because it exists only in a relative way: there is no absolute measure of exactness in general; rather something is more or less exact within a specific context (e.g. for a given purpose). In a similar vein, the meaning of any sentence is defined only within certain limits and it remains open how these limits are to be drawn (see also Searle 1979) through language use. Therefore the ideal of an exact language arises from a mythological interpretation of the role of science as providing eternal truths. It therefore cannot be used as a rational basis for deciding how well any data modeling effort has fared.

For Wittgenstein the escape from the analytic straitjacket of the *Tractatus* world comes from the pragmatic criticism of the fact-based semantic theory. Its basic tenet is that language use is fundamentally a human activity like cutting wood, gymnastics or chess. He writes 'we don't start from certain words, but from certain occasions and activities' (Wittgenstein 1972, p. 3). Activities take place in diverse contexts and must therefore be analyzed against the backdrop of these contexts. These contexts Wittgenstein calls *forms of life*. Hence in later Wittgensteinian theory, language is part of forms of life and its function has to be defined anew for each new form of life: 'An expression has meaning only in the stream of life' (Blair 1990, p. 145). Moreover, as we conduct our lives in quite different ways and participate in diverse life forms, our ways of using language must also differ. These different templates of language use Wittgenstein calls *language games*.

We learn new words and linguistic expressions by means of language games. The games suggest schemes or grammars in which the examples of how a linguistic expression is used make sense. An individual who does not know the relevant language game will not learn from the language examples of how a word is used. The language games are not hidden or mysterious processes — instead they are right before us all the time, which makes them so difficult to grasp. Hence, in Wittgensteinian theory we engage ourselves in countless kinds of language games in which words acquire 'meaning'. These include telling jokes, giving thanks, greeting, describing objects, making financial statements or describing our data in the IS.

Wittgenstein wished to study the uses of language in their pragmatic contexts and to relate all analyses of meaning to the contexts of use. The concept of 'language games' places special emphasis on those aspects of language use which are represented in specific rules as followed in various forms of life. In other words, different systems of rules hold for different language games. Indeed, for Wittgenstein the rule-governed character of language use is the basis for having any language at all: without rules for using a word it has no meaning. Hence the 'meaning' can only be derived from studying typical uses of linguistic expressions and the meaning can only be as exact and stable as the rules which prescribe its use. This means that for an expression to be meaningful there does not need to be something 'behind' it such as a fact or an entity which is its meaning. In this vein Wittgenstein says: 'Don't look for the meaning, look for the use'. Beyond the use there is nothing else that constitutes the meaning of the words. It should be noted, however, that by 'use' Wittgenstein does here not mean 'instances of use' but 'patterns of use'. The latter are general templates for use, i.e. rules.

The importance of the later Wittgenstein's language theory for thinking about data modeling is dramatic and substantial: First, it denies the possibility of designing a universal, general 'business language' for defining the conceptual enterprise schema because different language games (uses of language) are tied to different forms of life. Second, it leads us to think carefully about how organizational activity (life forms) and language are tied together. Data modeling cannot proceed in an organizational vacuum — instead it must be grounded on an understanding of the organizational domain in which the data originates and is being used. Moreover, the existence of the organizational domain depends on the existence of the language games in which the organizational reality is articulated and made significant. Finally, it denies the possibility of specifying in any formal way the exact meaning of sentences included in the object system representation.

6.2.3 Philosophical hermeneutics

While Wittgenstein approached the issue of meaning from the viewpoint of demystifying it, hermeneutics has taken quite a different road. It has placed special attention on the means, theories and methods by which to interpret the meaning(s) of a text. Hence the basic focus is on understanding the social and linguistic processes in which meaning is created and through which it can be examined. Understanding meaning is seen as a fundamental problem for any study of language and language use. The original goal of hermeneutic study was to analyze how scholars can faithfully interpret texts — particularly ancient and sacred texts in order to reveal the original meaning of alien texts to the contemporary reader. Such a process is called exegesis.

During this century the original problem of hermeneutic understanding posed by the first generation of hermeneutic scholars (for a history see Bleicher 1980; Habermas 1972; Palmer 1969) has been generalized: the new key concern of hermeneutics is how to achieve an understanding of the meaning of any human expression which sets a challenge of interpretation. Examples of human expressions are written texts, oral chats, gestures and figures — in principle any expression which needs to be accounted for by its meaning. This naturally also applies to all elements of data modeling such as data schemas, data in the information system, computer output, or how user's apply the data in business contexts (i.e. user behavior is a 'text'). In accordance with this, students of hermeneutics will argue that data modeling cannot evade the challenges of interpretation.

The original program of hermeneutics dealt primarily with reliable methods of exegesis to reveal the 'objective' meaning of sacred texts. Later on this goal has been to a large extent abandoned, though the methods of literary interpretation are still found to be very useful. Instead, philosophical hermeneutics seeks to develop theories of meaning and interpretation, and philosophical analyses of social existence and meaning (Palmer 1969; Bleicher 1980). Because the theories of meaning are also the primary target of data modeling, philosophical hermeneutics will also be discussed in the following. Such theories have been developed for example by Heidegger in his phenomenology (Heidegger 1962), and especially by Heidegger's student Gadamer in his explication of philosophical hermeneutics (1975; 1976).

The basic idea in Gadamer's theory is to make explicit possible ways of appreciating different life-worlds (a set of phenomena that wait for our meaning projections). This distinguishes a hermeneutic study from a positivistic and analytical case study. In Gadamer's theory, modern science conceives of the world in similar ways as the object system is conceived in the fact-based school: a ready-made universe of objects to be observed and manipulated. This universe is simply 'out there' and our cause–effect knowledge allows us to operate on it. Language is conceived in a similar manner as in our discussion of the principles of the object system representation: a tool for conceptualizing and communicating the objects of interest (and manipulation). In philosophical hermeneutics this is contrasted with conceiving use of language and symbols as constitutive for the social world. As Gadamer puts it:

'Language is the fundamental mode of operation of our being in the world and the all-embracing form of the constitution of the world' (Gadamer 1976, p. 3).

Gadamer argues that the process of interpretation is not an esoteric problem which is only relevant to the translator of ancient texts, but a basic problem of how we 'exist' in a social space. The world must be interpreted by us in order for our intentional action to become possible. Hence the problem of interpretation is fundamental to our everyday activity — also in the business world.

To summarize these philosophical ideas and point to their implications for data modelling we may say that hermeneutics is concerned with the problem of interpreting and understanding the meaning of 'texts'. Anything that potentially has meaning can be considered as a text including 'the book of nature'. Hence the scientist reading the traces in a cloud chamber is involved as much in a hermeneutic (interpretive) task as the archeologist trying to decipher the famous rosetta stone. The complex issues raised by the interpretation of natural data are well illustrated by the historical example of Tycho Brahe who was unable to make sense of his own observations on planetary positions. Keppler approached the same data with a different preunderstanding and was able to support his heliocentric theory of the solar system with them (cf. Kuhn 1970).

Of particular interest for data modeling are socially created texts. These include 'reading' user activities and utterances. Hermeneutics considers the philosophical issues of text interpretation when these are difficult to 'read', i.e. opaque or 'alien'. Organizations and life-forms are such texts (as is well illustrated by the phenomenon of culture shock). Specifically reading (understanding) an application problem is like reading an alien text, because the analyst has to make sense of things with which he is more or less unfamiliar.

But how is the interpretation possible if it is so fundamental to human action? What are the basic elements of any act of interpretation? Gadamer argues that any act of interpretation is possible only within a horizon given by the preunderstanding of the interpreter. The 'horizon' is a metaphor that connotes on the one hand openness such as one may gain new horizons by travel and on the other hand structure such as when we look towards the horizon, things that are close are clearer than those that are further away. Interpretation is based on prejudice that 'narrows' and gives structure to our horizon. It includes assumptions implicit in the interpreter's language uses. Understanding is possible only if something has been understood already through language. The preunderstanding suggests a way to approach a text (note text means here any human expression), which, in hermeneutic theory, is seen as a projection of the horizon possessed by the originator of the text. Using his or her preunderstanding the interpreter approaches the text with a set of questions, which direct his or her reading and apprehension of the text. Hence, understanding is created through an interaction between the interpreter's and the creator's horizons.

While reading the text the interpreter will form some responses to his or her initial questions thus leading to an understanding of the text. This reading, in turn, will lead them to ask a new set of questions which arise from the first interpretation of the text. This, in turn will change the interpreter's preunderstanding (because new possible questions are added to his or her horizon). The circular movement from preunderstanding through the fusion of horizons to understanding which forms a new preunderstanding is called a hermeneutic cycle or circle.

The process of reaching understanding has several implications for a hermeneutic theory of meaning. First, meaning is never an observed relation (between a sign and a thing or a concept) or a psychological experience. Instead, it is a historic process which grows from the collision of horizons, and it involves an intersubjective dialogue between the interpreter and the creator of the text. Thus for Gadamer understanding (and meaning) is a never-ending intersubjective linguistic process which leads to an effective constitution and change of our horizons through which we appreciate the social world. Second, the meaning cannot be defined by any closure or limit of exactness. The meaning progresses as we become more aware of the prejudice we bring with us in our encounters with the social world. In this way we can become aware of our prejudices and emancipate ourselves from the limits the current language places on our thinking and become open to new meaning (with its own inherent limitations). Gadamer says that complete clarification is an illusion (*cf.* Gadamer 1980, p. 78). Third, meaning is always contextualized into some horizon. We cannot free ourselves from prejudice, because we cannot get away from preunderstanding as a condition to understand at all. Hence, the world of meaning is never given to us, it is constituted for us through our horizon.

From a hermeneutic perspective, there is no difference between preunderstanding, bias or prejudice — all understanding is biased by being based on preunderstanding that is composed of prejudice. Consequently, whilst there is no way to formally assess the quality of preunderstanding, because there is no anchoring point (all of them are biased), we can nevertheless elicit some of the presuppositions upon which the preunderstanding rests. This is called bracketing which may lead to a richer understanding and critique of the presuppositions upon which the preunderstanding rests (*cf.* Capurro 1986).

An example will help to clarify the idea of bracketing. Assume you are reading a map and have difficulty matching the landmarks that you see to the map. You may say to yourself, well maybe I am not here, but have already overshot my destination. You have now 'bracketed' a fundamental assumption. This means you have identified a fundamental presupposition on which your map reading up to this point rested, put it aside 'into brackets' and 'peeled it away' so to speak. By attempting to do this systematically, particularly in social communication where different minds look at the same 'text' from slightly different viewpoints, several layers of presuppositions may be revealed and bracketed. Again there is no guarantee that this converges or any implication that this leads to an 'approximation of reality'. The quality improvement of the preunderstanding is in the eyes of its beholders, i.e. the linguistic community which is engaged in the bracketing process.

The importance of philosophical hermeneutics involving the ideas of hermeneutic cycle, horizon, and bracketing for rule-based data modeling is far reaching. First of all, the hermeneutic approach links the meaning of any object system description to the historic process in which users read and interpret these expressions. There is no 'universal' meaning which can be associated with the object system representation that goes beyond the processes of creating and reading these representations in different contexts. The context-free semantics of the fact-based school, in fact, (not a pun here!) is a misguided perception of data modeling as it ignores the important role of prejudice in creating meaning. Second, the hermeneutic approach stresses the dialogical and intersubjective nature of any data modeling enterprise and the idea of 'bracketing' in improving the quality of data models. Meaning arises only in conversations in which significant horizons relevant to data use (or life forms in Wittgensteinian terms) interact, evolve and are peeled off layer by layer. In other words, data modeling forms a continuous conversation in which its stakeholders build up horizons through which models of data become significant and become questioned. Finally, philosophical hermeneutics reveals that meaning creation is an on-going historic process, and any data modeling process is only one step in a continuous hermeneutic cycle. These hermeneutic insights are of importance for characterizing the epistemological limitations of data modeling which are discussed in the course of this chapter.

6.3 Paradigms of Data Modeling

6.3.1 Philosophical perspective on data modeling

We now turn to the linkages between the concerns of data modeling and philosophy. One result of the philosophical debate on the meaning of language and hermeneutics is that it is impossible to capture knowledge simply in terms of articulable facts as the positivists had claimed. A broader concept of knowledge is relevant for understanding practical difficulties with determining the system (or formalization) boundary in specifying computer applications. This is addressed next.

It is widely recognized that data modeling should include the meanings and relationships among data which may be hidden from the users. It is for this reason that concern for the adequate recognition of the importance of tacit knowledge arises. Hidden meanings and knowledge can, at best, be only imperfectly specified as it falls within the domain of tacit knowledge. Moreover, just because users may know how to do their work, it does not follow that it is possible to capture their knowledge in explicit rules and descriptions (*cf.* Ryle's 1949 distinction between 'knowing that' and 'knowing how'). This remains true even if some of the users are asked to participate in IS design teams. In this sense it may be said that data modeling involves the design of a knowledge representation schema.* In so doing, it will inevitably try to penetrate some of the domains of tacit knowledge; that is, the data model will incorporate explicit descriptions of innate and learned abilities which the users are unable or unwilling to articulate.

Often the difficulties with this do not surface until the IS is in use. By this time it is extremely expensive to make the necessary corrections. Typically this kind of problem is called a 'specification error', but this is misleading. The term specification error suggests some kind of oversight or misunderstanding rather than a fundamental issue which is connected to the failure to understand the important role of tacit knowledge.

The classic response to the problem of hidden and tacit knowledge is the belief that, in practice, the designers' purpose in applying a data model is to construct a formal representation of some subset of the knowledge which the organization needs to carry out its business. Unfortunately, there are currently no good techniques to decide what to include and what not to include in this subset. In order to gain a deeper understanding of what is at stake here, we need to come back to the concept of a 'paradigm' which can shed light on the concept of knowledge itself.

In chapter 3 we identified four paradigms which underlie systems development. In chapter 4, we depicted each of the four paradigms as they relate to ISD. The addition of data modeling to these descriptions does not require any changes to their interpretation in terms of key actors, narrative, and plot because data modeling is simply one aspect of the general process of systems development. However, the short discussion of the assumptions is insufficient and needs some elaboration to address the specifics of data modeling. In addition, the general description of the paradigms incorporated the characterization of the social world by the order–conflict dichotomy. This also needs to be expanded to discuss the role of data modeling under the social world assumptions of not only order but conflict as well.

In order to identify how the alternative approaches to data modeling differ in terms of their paradigmatic assumptions about the nature of knowledge,

---

* It has been recognized for some time in the literature that data modeling and knowledge representation are essentially similar. They share the same fundamental assumptions and the following analysis is of equal importance to both data modelers who build databases and knowledge engineers who build expert systems. But for the sake of simplicity, the following will speak only of data modeling.

we compare the construction of a data model to the building of a limited theory of its application domain. This point of view is not new (*cf.* Kent 1978; Naur 1985) and a number of people have noted that there are important relationships between perception, data, reality, knowledge and representation (Churchman 1971; Checkland 1981; Stamper 1987; Goldkuhl and Lyytinen 1982a; Lyytinen 1987). Based on this prior work, it is natural to examine the existing approaches of data modeling with regard to the assumptions they make about:

(a) the nature of reality (ontology) , and the nature of the knowledge captured in a data model including the ways and means of how it is collected (epistemology), i.e. the paradigmatic dimension of 'objectivism-subjectivism';

(b) the nature of the social world, what can be termed the 'social context', i.e. the paradigmatic dimension of 'order-conflict'; and

(c) the representation of linguistic elements. We address these three philosophical issues in terms of four basic questions, each of which is explored below.

In exploring each question, the paradigmatic assumptions become visible.

(a) The objectivist–subjectivist dimension of a paradigm raises two questions: one dealing with ontology, the other with epistemology of data modeling.

(b) The order–conflict dimension of a paradigm raises the question, what influence does the social context exert on data modeling?

(c) As data modeling fundamentally is concerned with representation (of object systems), there is a fourth question dealing with the representation side of data modeling as part and parcel of software development.

(1) The ontological question (what is being modeled?) points to the fundamental assumptions of data modeling approaches about the environment or modeling domain, i.e. about the nature of the universe of discourse. Currently, there is no accepted terminology for talking about the ontology of data modeling. Examples of terms used to describe ontologies in data modeling are entities, relationships, messages, actors, inference rules, facts, speech acts, affordances, etc. The most important of these will be discussed in chapter 7. The ontology of data modeling also includes some fundamental assumptions about the nature of the application domain, i.e. whether there is a single or several user systems or no 'system' at all, whether the primary constituents of each user system are operations, roles, decisions, social action, or speech acts or something else.

(2) The epistemological question (why is the result valid?) points to the fundamental assumptions that are made on how one can obtain valid interpretations and knowledge about the UoD. Experimental modes

of schema construction (like prototyping) can be compared with the 'blue-print' specification approach as is associated with many versions of the so-called waterfall model of schema development (Kahn 1982, Bubenko 1980). The question of how to cope with different types of uncertainty (problem, effect) during data modeling is, of course, not the only consideration that is important in comparing experimental or specification approaches, but it is a good example to demonstrate that different methods imply different assumptions about knowledge and inquiry (*cf.* Churchman 1971, Goguen 1992).

(3) The social context question (what is the relationship between the social world and data modeling?) points to assumptions about the relation- ship between data and action. First, data are related to action because they are used to achieve purposes which in turn are shaped by the context of the social community in which data modeling takes place. Purposes can be latent which is seen when data are used to supply ra- tionalizations for decisions taken on ulterior motives (*cf.* Kling 1980). Second, the relation of data to action is revealed if we interpret the use of data analogous to the use of language.

The efficiency of language requires that utterances always be anchored to the unique and particular occasion of their use. In this respect, lan- guage is indexical: that is, dependent for its significance on connections to specific occasions, and to the concrete circumstances in which an utterance is spoken. (Suchman 1987, p. 184)

The same socio-linguistic assumption holds for the efficiency of data which is not made explicit in the classical approaches to data modeling.

(4) The representation question (how well is the result represented?) points to the assumptions that are made about the nature of the representa- tion forms that are most appropriate and effective to represent the linguistic object system. For example, the relational data model rec- ommends normalized tables over record types or sets.

Sections 6.3.2 and 6.3.3 take up these four questions, articulating the paradigmatic assumptions of the prevailing, functionalist approaches to data modeling and the possible alternative approaches as developed in the re- cent research. The alternatives include social relativist or constructivist data modeling approaches. We shall also consider how neohumanist con- cerns might be incorporated into data modeling.

6.3.2 Paradigmatic assumptions of functionalist data modeling

Functionalist data modeling approaches answer the ontological question by presuming that the world is given and made up of concrete objects which have natural properties and are associated with other objects. 'Given' means that the world is prior to the existence or appreciation of humans, it is not something which is created through social interaction. Therefore, this kind of world exists beyond beliefs and social practices of users. The object system is that part of the real world with which the data model is concerned. The data model is a simplified 'picture' of the object system because it is supposed to reflect all the pertinent 'facts' about it. A good classical definition of a data model from the functionalist perspective is the following:

> A data model is a specification language for representations of the real world. (Mylopoulos 1981)

Similar views about data modeling as factual specifications have been expressed in the notion of an enterprise model free of bias (Chen 1977), the van Griethuysen report on *Concepts and Terminology for the Conceptual Schema and the Information Base* (van Griethuysen 1982) and in most contributions to the so-called *CRIS proceedings* (Olle *et al.*, 1982; 1983; 1986). It should be recalled that functionalism is associated with realism through Tarski's correspondence theory of truth. This is explicitly recognized in van Griethuysen (1982) p. 37. Whenever the word realism is used without qualification in the following, we mean it in this sense. Otherwise it will be qualified.

The epistemology of current functionalist approaches assumes that valid data models can be built by applying proper observation and data collection methods to an object system, i.e. the application domain. The data model is like a picture of the object system. It may have more or less granularity to allow for selection, but its accuracy can be determined by checking how well it corresponds to the reality of the object system. By observing the deficiency of the application, one can infer the likely cause in the specification and correct it. In this way the data model can be tuned over time to improve its correspondence with reality. The same procedure can also be used to adjust it to changing requirements. Whereas data modeling does embrace user participation in this process of continuing correction and adjustment, the user's role is seen to be limited to two contributions:

(i)   providing input to the data modelers in the form of 'raw' data and definitions;

(ii) validating the formal specification in the sense of assuring that it corresponds to the true state of affairs.

Various devices have been proposed to improve the efficacy of user participation in this sense, for example graphical representation aids and walk-throughs. But the application of such tools does not change the fundamental assumption that validation is an accuracy test in line with the correspondence theory of truth.

The social context of functionalist data modeling emphasizes regulation to achieve order and stability. Organizational processes are primarily oriented to maintaining organizational stability and order, and data models are designed to provide the information on which these processes depend. Data models contribute to organizational goals through helping with purposeful interventions which serve organizational efficiency and effectiveness. Data models are not designed to contribute to a debate on fundamental organizational goals and policies in that organizational policy can be treated as consistent and well-defined. Policy makers know what they want and how to communicate it well so that policies establish rational preference orderings. Under these assumptions it is reasonable to believe that if data models consistently represent the organization and its environment, this will improve the information that can be used for organizational control. In spite of the emphasis on control, data models are deemed to be politically neutral. If there are conflicts, then it is assumed that they will be resolved by the powers that be. The analyst has no mandate for policy definition.

The representation question of functionalist data modeling focuses on the quality of data models which has been analyzed from two competing angles: formal rigor and ease of use. Formal rigor emphasizes that data models should be complete, consistent and fully formalized to eliminate ambiguity and allow rigorous inference. From this perspective the ideal data model provides a formal calculus to answer all questions about the object system. Answers should follow from the axioms and inference rules (Bubenko 1986). To a limited extent this has been achieved for example, by the studies on relational completeness (Codd 1972). Based on the work of Russell and Whitehead in *Principia Mathematica*, predicate calculus-based formalisms appear very promising to achieve this. It therefore is not surprising that many data modeling formalisms were proposed which provided constructs for directly representing the objects, properties and associations of the object system. One widely used representation form depicts the object system in terms of entity, attribute and relationship instances (Chen 1976; Teichroew *et al.* 1980), but similar ideas exist in the relational model. Data modeling languages also include a simple theory of types in which each instance belongs to exactly one type. The difficulties with this have recently become more widely realized and type theory has been expanded to include 'categories' (*cf.* Elmasri and Wiederhold 1985). However, the semantics of orthodox data modeling approaches are still limited to denotational theory in which the meaning of each term corresponds to the set of objects for which it stands (van Griethuysen 1982). Consequently, attempts to include more meaning into data models focus on defining constraints that are supposed to reflect real world structures such as temporal order of events, existence dependencies, object identity, and the like (for details see Codd 1979).

The second quality criterion of data models – ease of use – has been applied to explain the popularity of certain types of formalisms such as the ER model. The ease of use issue has been investigated empirically in a number of studies (see for example Batra and Davis 1989; Batra *et al.* 1988). However, the criterion has been recognized as difficult to apply in that no clear procedure for choosing among different data modeling languages appears effective (*cf.* Tsichritzis and Lochovsky 1982).

In summary, an analysis of the methods and tools of data modeling reveals the heavy influence of functionalism, similar to that described in chapter 4 for ISD. There are two principal sets of assumptions in which this is revealed: a realist ontology coupled with a positivist epistemology and an order or regulation view of human organizations. However, from the beginnings of data modeling, these assumptions have not been universally shared (Kent 1978). In particular, if we turn to the literature on information systems development in general (see chapter 5), we note a lively debate on the dangers of these assumptions (Capurro 1986; Winograd and Flores 1986; Blair 1990).

6.3.3 Paradigmatic assumptions of social relativist data modeling

We now return to the four basic questions noted above and explore the issues they raise as they relate to social relativist data modeling.

The ontological question is addressed in social relativist data modeling on the basis of symbolic interactionism which suggests that the object system is socially constructed through processes of communication in which individuals define their situations. This is related to both the language game notion of the later Wittgenstein and the principles of hermeneutic interpretation which were discussed above. The basic premise is that regardless of whether there are real things out there, they only become accessible through interpretive processes which deploy an emergent set of language games (*cf.* Truex 1993). Often users and analysts may subjectively believe that organizational reality exists, because they have forgotten its human authorship. The processes by which this objectivation comes about is called 'reification' (Berger and Luckmann 1967, p. 106). Habituation, language, tradition and institutionalization through roles and norms play a key role in this.

Building on these ideas, Boland (1979) drew a distinction between the decision model and action-based approach to systems design. The former relies heavily on objective representations and algorithmic manipulations. In the action-based approach:

> the design of an information system is not a question of fitness for an organizational reality that can be modeled beforehand, but a question of fitness for use in the construction of an organizational reality through the symbolic interaction of its participants. In essence, the information system is an environment of symbols within which a sense making process will be carried out. (Boland 1979, p. 262)

Applying this basic idea to data modeling suggests that data models should try to model the language by which users communicate in the application domain. This may be called 'the formal language development view' (*cf.* chapter 7) which contrasts with the 'reality mapping view' of the functional approaches. Language is used for several purposes such as reaching agreement, clarification, concealing or misleading, etc. Much of language use is concerned with interpretation and making sense of one's environment to understand what is happening.

From the formal language development perspective, data models are models of user languages rather than models of reality. User languages are languages:

> used in a work situation, with the purpose of supporting or changing the working process, the organization of work, the shared knowledge and values, and the social relations constituting the situation. (Holmqvist and Andersen 1987, p. 348)

The notion of a user language coincides neither with a language with special purposes nor with a sociolect (Holmqvist and Andersen 1987) but may include elements of both. An example of user language terms are the many acronyms coined by large corporations but also words borrowed from natural language and given special meanings.

User languages are complex rule systems, many of which are implicit to the speakers. This directs attention to modeling rules that define the syntax, semantics, and, to a certain extent, pragmatics (intentions and use situations) rather than given objects, and properties. Several attempts have been documented in the literature to develop rule-based data modeling methods and tools. The most important of these will be reviewed in chapter 7. However, it would be unrealistic to expect that complete models of language can be developed, because user languages evolve from the ordinary speaking practices which evade complete specification. The special nature of an information system is that it is built around a language which is more structured and formalized than user languages. Typically this implies restrictions for the functionality of the information system. Taking this into account, data models partially reconstruct the language by which users understand each other and make sense of their environment.

A fundamental issue for language modeling is to decide upon the basic building blocks constituting the object system which is the users' language.* Two obvious choices for the building blocks are sentences (like assigning an attribute to a noun) or speech acts. The former is in line with Frege's view of language who proposed that human language can be modeled with predicate logic. If one uses sentences as the basic ontology of language, one could use an entity-attribute notation to model user languages.

If language is seen to consist of speech acts rather than sentences, then the focus of data modeling is broadened. A speech act is a basic unit of communication by which a speaker accomplishes some extralinguistic purpose

---

* The idea of fundamental linguistic structures has been subjected to serious criticism within the recent poststructuralist debate (see e.g. Hopper 1987; Tagg 1989; Macksey and Donato 1972). However, this issue is beyond the scope of this book.

such as obtaining a piece of information (using the speech act of a question) or signalling a commitment (using the speech act of a promise). This admits human intentions into the realm of meaning. Searle has hypothesized that there are five basic types of speech acts (*cf.* Searle 1979) which convey basic human intentions: *questions, promises, assertions* (claiming something to be true), *declarations* creating new states of affairs (example: giving notice), and *expressives* (to communicate feelings of the speaker). Modeling a speech act requires representing three aspects: what is referred to (predication and reference), intent (illocutionary point), and likely consequences or behavioral outcomes (perlocutionary effects). Entity and relationship models capture at best predication and reference.

From the speech act perspective, data models are models of linguistic discourses that are made up of basic 'moves' which correspond to speech acts (Auramaki *et al.* 1988). Some formalisms for data modeling have been proposed to capture the semantics of simple speech act sequences (Lehtinen and Lyytinen 1986). An important research issue is how to extend this into more complicated domains, such as policy debates. An example of a system designed around the speech act of making commitments can be found in the last chapter of (Winograd and Flores 1986).

The epistemological question concerns the question in what sense a data model can be more or less accurate or more or less appropriate. Social relativist data modeling addresses this question from the perspective of hermeneutics (*cf.* Langefors 1977; Capurro 1986). Hermeneutics suggest that data models are limited in the following three fundamental ways. The first is that all data models are inescapably biased even though the understanding of bias can be improved through 'bracketing'. The second is that data modeling involves a meeting of at least two horizons of meaning: it always involves a double hermeneutic. Third, the number of horizons of meaning in complex organizations cannot be predetermined. Hence data modeling has to remain open-ended and critical to its own limitations.

These ideas suggest the following principles that should guide practice, research and methods of data modeling from a social relativist perspective (*cf.* Capurro 1986 for a set of similar ideas in the area of information retrieval).

(a) All data models have a fundamental bias that can be traced to the contingent preunderstandings with which they were built.

(b) To some extent, the bias can be made transparent through bracketing, a form of self-critical, reflective dialogue.

(c) Bracketing must not be seen as a procedure to decide between fundamentally conflicting preconceptions. Therefore a hermeneutic approach to data modeling is very skeptical of the idea that bias can eventually be substantially reduced or even be eliminated by a process of evaluative error elimination.

In applying these principles the practice of data modeling must take into account the fundamental differences between the separate and unique horizons of meaning between different communities like analysts and users. Different communities have unique horizons in the sense that when they meet each faces the problem of interpreting the other in terms of their own horizon and therefore mutual understanding is at risk. However, there exists the possibility of fusing the two horizons and thereby overcoming some of the likely misunderstandings because both horizons are open; i.e. each community, through symbolic interaction, ('being with each other' and 'orienting towards their shared problems'), can broaden their horizons and 'fuse' them to some degree. Applying the notion of horizon of meaning to data modeling, leads to two further conclusions.*

For one thing, each data model merges or 'fuses' at least two horizons. Even if users are excluded from the process of analysis, the developers will have to bridge two understanding contexts or 'horizon of meanings', i.e. meanings that are shared by two distinct communities, such as users and developers. Both groups have internalized different language games. The situation is symmetrical for the users. If they undertake the development themselves, they must cope with the fixed horizon of meaning that is embedded in the specification language and modelling tools that they use.

The fusion of horizons in data modeling involves three steps. In step one, the developers must try to capture some of the meanings that are shared by the users and which, initially at least, are 'alien' to the developers. In step two, they must translate their understanding into appropriate formalisms. These formalisms carry the implicit claim that, at least in part, they are valid substitutes for the user's existing language games. In step three the formalizations must be retranslated into the users' horizons of meaning and thereby become part of their everyday practices (that is if the fused horizon is accepted as appropriate, otherwise the cycle must repeat itself based on the new preunderstanding). Each step is fraught with many risks that need careful attention and are insufficiently addressed by the usual concepts of walkthroughs, documentation and user 'training'.

For a second thing the fusion of horizons can be facilitated through systematic 'bracketing'. The reason for this is that bracketing can be expected to be more effective if it is based on a dialogue between users and developers rather than on internal discussion within each group. This has been realized in particular by Checkland (1981) with the concept of constructing alternative 'root definitions' that must precede any conceptual modeling. It appears then that the double hermeneutic of users and developers is both

---

* The horizon concept bears some similarity to the term 'context of meaning' which is more commonly used, but there are some important differences. Context does not connote the increasing diffuseness of our understanding that becomes vague as we move more away from the gravity center of our life. Nor does context connote the openness of horizon.

a threat of creating rigidities and misunderstanding, but also a chance for improving mutual understanding through dialogue.

There are as many horizons of meaning in an organization as there are distinct user groups. Distinct in this context means that the users have distinct education and professional training and therefore share different kinds of expertise with their own specialized languages and practices. In other words: the center of their life interests must be sufficiently different. A good example is doctors and nurses in hospitals. Hence the double hermeneutic must be expanded to include multiple hermeneutics. The risks of misunderstandings exists not only between analysts and users, but between different user communities.

One conclusion of this is that there cannot be an overall consistency in an enterprise-wide data model. Of course, there can be a strategic data model of the organization and its horizon can include all of the organization. This simply provides another horizon of meanings, typically that of the high level planning staff. As such, it can provide a basis for a dialogue with other user groups and lead to a fusion of horizons and thereby to organizational learning. In practice, enterprise models may have always been intended to be used in this way. We note this because some of the data modeling literature suggests otherwise. There have been proposals to construct a consistent enterprise schema whose conventions are to be enforced. In a similar spirit, unambiguous definitions of an enterprise vocabulary and global validity tests of local databases have been proposed. None of this appears appropriate from a hermeneutic perspective. Similar conclusions follow from the sociology of data use.

The social context question is concerned with how data models can help understanding and facilitate learning of the organizational actors. Data modeling in this context presumes coexistence or benign neglect of multiple groups ('cultures') with independent viewpoints. Conflict is not seen as an issue and therefore willful distortion of data to influence others for the sake of advancing one's personal or one's own group's advantage is not recognized as a problem deserving special attention. Neither does the problem of weighing the evidence supporting alternative viewpoints arise: all are just prejudices and in time each will change through a series of hermeneutic cycles.

The representation question is concerned with the quality of data models (in the sense of representation languages and conceptual schemas). It interacts with the presumed ontology in the following way. If realism is assumed then data models are a means of representing reality. Under this assumption, different data models can be evaluated by applying such criteria as accuracy and completeness. This becomes impossible if the data model codetermines what will count as reality and what is legitimate evidence (Boland 1979). This is the case, because from the constructivist perspective data models are one of the means by which a social community makes sense of the environment. It is used to filter the meaningful and important from the unintelligible or insignificant. By helping to maintain a socially constructed reality, a data model guides action through constraining and channeling perceptions, influencing the availability of evidence, suggesting preferred types of evidence, alerting, masking, etc. This would also apply to actions aimed at validation of the data model which thereby becomes circular. Therefore validation can no longer be phrased in terms of finding representations that minimize distortions of true situations or that filter too much or too little of an underlying given reality.

The implications of this for data modeling or choosing appropriate data models have not been discussed in the literature. The suggestion that comes to our mind is that the role of data models should be seen in a similar light as the role of a theory for a scientific community — a rather controversial subject. Tentatively one might suggest that data models should be formulated in such a way that they help social communication. Ideally, good data models should facilitate communication that is sincere, relevant, clear and well-informed, i.e. it should encourage people to say what they mean, pertinent to the situation at hand, expressed in a way that is congenial to the listeners frame of mind and based on good, defendable reasons. However, such a view is rather idealistic and misses a number of important points previously discussed.

6.3.4 Paradigmatic assumptions of neohumanist data modeling

While there is no data modeling literature which directly uses neohumanism as a source of inspiration, the neohumanist paradigm as presented in chapters 3 and 4 suggests that a neohumanist data modeling approach could be developed. Indeed, in the following we wish to give an indication of what such a data modeling approach might look like. As we cannot draw on an existing research literature detailing a neohumanist approach to data modeling, we resort to an analogy to communicate some of its essential issues. This will illustrate that a neohumanist approach to data modeling would not only change many of the current assumptions of data modeling, but also broaden its scope considerably. We resort to a metaphor to communicate some of the key principles of a neohumanist data modeling approach.

If we look for a metaphor for a functionalist data modeling approach it is that of creating a picture, i.e. a formal representation corresponding to reality. In contrast, a neohumanist metaphor would view data models as a set of laws, and data modeling as the activity by which laws are designed and enacted.

There is a rational side to law making. They should be clear and consistent. They are not necessarily bound by current practices or state of affairs but can be inspired by emancipatory visions. Based on this they can create a new order and establish new domains of jurisdiction. Laws may define what counts as preferred evidence. In practice laws are difficult to interpret, always changing, limited to a certain domain of applications which in turn is never fixed and as a whole certainly not consistent. Hence laws pose serious hermeneutic issues and their validity is difficult to establish. Therefore law making is subject to much politicking. Laws are, of course, one specific type of social reality. In fact, the first data modeling project that attempted to formalize the computer representation of a specific object system which was seen by the researchers as a social reality construction concerned the programming a body of law (British family law, *cf.* Stamper 1983, for more details see chapter 7).

Just as laws led people to filter information and put their best foot forward, so do the rules of data models. Just as laws are formulated ambiguously to be acceptable to a mixed coalition of supporters, so are data models. Just as laws need to be approved by some sort of due process, so need data models. Just as laws constrain policy making and at the same time are the result of policy, so do data models. Just as laws should be supported by a democratic majority, so should data models (and this may only be possible at the expense of consistency or incompleteness). Just as the interpretation of laws changes with shifting policy orientations, so do data models. As information systems move closer to the centers of power and political will formation, data model development and interpretation grows inextricably entangled with policy formation and implementation.

If one looks at the rational side of law making, ignoring for a moment its many deficiencies as implemented in contemporary society, a number of principles suggest themselves that could serve as requirements for developing a neohumanist data modeling approach (based on Grice's maxims of conversation, *cf.* Levinson 1983, p. 101):

(1) Data models should facilitate cooperation for accepted purposes.

(2) They should help people to express what they believe to be the case and make them skeptical of beliefs for which they lack evidence.

(3) They should provide guidance to formulate reports and arguments which are to the point and available when required (such as is suggested in the model of argumentation for information systems use by Nissen 1989).

(4) They should support a format of communication which is unambiguous, concise and well-organized.

Ideally these principles define good laws and good data models. However, in practice, often the opposite can be observed. The reason for this apparent contradiction is that language and epistemology provide little focus on human interest and power. There is much talk of knowledge-based systems and strategic information system. It is surprising that there appears to be little inclination to investigate how the design of these systems can be made responsive to the political structures with which they are to interact. The consideration of such issues produces the following responses to the four questions regarding ontology, epistemology, social context and linguistic representation.

Ontological issues. Neohumanist data modeling needs to recognize multiple ontologies. For achieving instrumental prediction and control it will treat the object system just like functionalism. For supporting sense-making it will incorporate the insights of the previous section on social relativism. These will be responsive to the different world-views and horizons associated with the diverse power centers in the organization. However, a neohumanist approach will not stop there. While giving each view a fair shake, a neohumanist approach will seek to build informed preferences for the most appropriate data model. Such a preference will build on the epistemological premise of informed inquiry.

Epistemological issues. In contrast to social relativism, neohumanism does not give up the idea of truth. To be true, the implications of a data model must be 'warranted', that is to say that the fundamental perspective and simplifying assumptions which are inescapably built into any model must be legitimized through an informed consensus. From this it follows that the most appropriate data modeling must be informed by the widest possible participation. Only through equal and undistorted participation can informed inquiry be achieved. The functionalist approaches do not seem to have any way to incorporate the insights from the participation debate and if they did, they would move closer to the ideal outlined here.

Social context issues. From the perspective of neohumanism, data modeling should contribute to emancipation. Emancipation is a state of maximum freedom from unwarranted social domination, economic deprivation, and other compulsions. Emancipation requires understanding of social conditions and critical reflection of one's own personality needs and potentials. Data modeling could contribute primarily to a better understanding of the social conditions at the micro-level, in particular the work environment: the intraorganizational environment would embrace social relations and exchanges within and between departments. The extraorganizational environment would deal with data modeling for external intelligence about customers, suppliers, competitors, and other constituencies which are critical for the organization. All critical constituencies, i.e. those which affect the interests of the organization or are somehow impacted by organizational activities, contribute to the organizational situation which needs to be constantly assessed and reinterpreted in defining meaningful courses of action and the knowledge coded into data models can have a significant role in this. Insofar as the discussion of social issues invariably leads to reflection on one's own self, data modeling can also have a secondary effect on critical knowledge of one's self (identity).

To contribute to emancipation neohumanist data modeling needs to make a distinction between the role of data in two types of social situations at work: consensual action and discourse. This distinction applies to both the internal and external environment. The role of data in consensual action relates to the creation of shared meanings and fusion of horizons as has already been discussed in the previous section. By discourse we mean a form of communication that is aimed at seeking, providing and weighing of evidence without the use of threats or force. Discourse helps in overcoming the biases or unwarranted constraints of consensual action and contributes to emancipation from social and psychological compulsions. The roles of data in discourse have neither been addressed by the functionalist nor by the social relativist paradigm. We therefore expand on them here.

In praxis, data are not collected to establish truth or do justice to a preferred mode of communication. Data are collected to design action, to give meaning to action and to politically support action taken. Data modeling does not proceed in a social vacuum. In order to structure the discussion we might loosely distinguish between action to design policy (including critique of policy) and action to execute policy which is often called policy implementation. By policy design we mean the origination of long term goals, general directives and programs such as are typically on the agendas of boards, legislators and chief executive officers.

It is often assumed that policy making sets the preunderstanding of policy execution. This is inherent both in the models of administrative decision making of Simon and Anthony. This, however, overlooks the autonomy of complex bureaucracies which exists for several reasons (*cf.* Baier and March 1986):

(1) Ambiguous policies facilitate consensus formation to pass policy. It allows different constituencies to support the same policy for different reasons.

(2) Organizations often do not have the resources and skills to implement the wishes of policy makers even if they wanted to.

(3) Lower level officials have their own interests and constituents. They view new policies as an opportunity to pursue their own agendas.

(4) Policy makers are often unable to specify policies clearly. This overlooks that policy makers do not always know what they want and that conflicting policies are issued.

(5) Policy makers often make unrealistic assumptions about the possibility of following the directives which then leaves organizations to their own devices to implement them.

In light of this, data modeling, even in support of policy implementation, cannot count on predefined horizons of meaning. It defines and redefines the institutional frame of reference in which policy making takes place. Therefore data modeling is a political activity which affects the interest of various policy making groups.

But why is it not possible to separate data collection from policy making by assigning these tasks to different groups? In fact, this is often attempted. For example the U.S. census bureau has historically been perceived to be nonpolitical. However, its data often turn out to be politically biased. An example of this is given by Mitroff *et al.* (1982) noting that the methods of the bureau lead to a systematic undercount of minorities. This has many political implications and leads to calls to adjust the numbers. But there is no unique method and hence the decision on which methods to use and which numbers to get is ultimately intertwined with policy formation.

This point is more generally established by Tenenbaum and Wildavsky (1984) with a study on the role of energy data in policy formation. As we see it, data, far from preceding policy, are inextricably intertwined with politics; ... it is the policy that one has in mind that determines which data, accurate to what degree, are relevant. ... our conclusions about the relationship between data and policy may apply to any field of government or company policy. (Tenenbaum and Wildavsky 1984, pp. 83–84).

The basic reason for this conclusion is that both data and policies are needed in the hermeneutic (sense-making) tasks of policy formation. Data in a very broad sense constrain policy, but only at the extremes. On the other hand, data collected without paying attention to policy are irrelevant, even meaningless. In light of the earlier discussion, it should be of no surprise that there is an analogy between policies and scientific theories:

> Without considering the political preferences and relationships among people who would make decisions, no intelligent thought, including the selection of data, is possible. Just as philosophers tell us that all facts involved in testing hypotheses are theory laden, so too all data used in analyses are suffused with policy. (Tenenbaum and Wildavsky 1984, p. 100.)

Policy formation and implementation is primarily a process carried on by organizational insiders. But the previous analysis applies also to the management of external relations. Recently there has been increasing interest in building IS which can deal with external intelligence, e.g. about potential customers and their life styles, suppliers, competitors, etc. Data models can also help with organizing data for IS that are to support one's position in actual or future external relationships be they of a conflictual or supportive nature. For example, various data collection strategies have been explored by universities to obtain estimates of alumni income and wealth and to compare these data with their actual financial pledges to identify those which should be approached with worthwhile projects requiring greater donations. Cost data to be used in collective bargaining might be kept in a different format than those used for tax reporting or internal accounting. A marketing manager might want to project a competitive threat when seeking funds to mount a marketing campaign and then obtain the right metrics to demonstrate to management that the monies were spent successfully in the campaign. Some of these issues are discussed in designing IS for strategic advantage. However, the full implications of the use of data models to support various kinds of distorted communications has only been explored on a case by case basis (*cf.* Kling 1980; 1987). There is no systematic treatment or well-recognized theoretical base in the literature.

Representation issues. The representation forms for a neohumanist data model would be rich enough to capture intentions and beliefs that help to interpret the information captured in data models. Current data models do not allow the capturing of the following kinds of information: 'Based on data x the marketing manager strongly believes that demand will rise, but based on data y the production control manager has some doubts.' The representational forms of data modeling need to be considerably enriched to capture such strength of belief indices and in the section on rule-based data modeling some further details of this will be introduced (in chapter 7).

In sum, a theory of data modeling will remain incomplete unless it covers some fundamental principles that govern how data are used in social environments. The development of the ontological, epistemological and linguistic bases of data modeling, no matter how thorough, emphasizes only its rational side. It thereby paints an ideal. In order to complete the picture, the entanglement of data and policy must also be confronted, which implies the need for some type of neohumanist data modeling.

6.4 Summary and Conclusions

This chapter has provided a broad analysis of data modeling by analyzing how each paradigmatic camp would respond to four major questions that have to be addressed in any data modeling effort. These questions are: what is being modeled; why is the result valid; what is the relationship between the social world and the data modeling process and results; and how is the result represented? As our analysis demonstrates there are very different answers with very different languages and theory bases depending on which of the four paradigmatic camps we choose. Our analysis also points out that no radical structuralist alternative to data modeling has yet to emerge, and that the neohumanist approach is still in its infancy. There is, however, enough research literature to take a closer look at the functionalist and social relativist data modeling approaches (especially their modeling constructs and concept structures). This will be our focus in the next chapter.

7
Paradigmatic Analysis of Data Modeling Approaches

7.1 Introduction

The purpose of this chapter is to explore in some detail the different schools of data modeling which were introduced in chapter 6. The first school embraces objectivism in data modeling. It follows the footsteps of the empirical-analytical scientific method. It assumes that reality can be described by independent facts (which corresponds to the empirical base of observational statements in objectivist philosophy). The database captures these facts and data models provide the structure for organizing all the facts into a consistent picture of reality. In accordance with this, objectivist data modeling approaches were called fact-based or fact-oriented in chapter 6. The prominent features of the fact-based school will be discussed in section 7.2.

The second school of data modeling follows the social relativist tradition in the philosophy of science. It assumes that the domain of inquiry is not independent of the observer, and therefore reality cannot be described in terms of independent hard facts. Rather, what counts as reality are socially constructed images which emerge in social interaction, in particular through communication in some language. The details of these images are not completely arbitrary, but depend on the 'grammar' (the rules and 'meanings') which governs social communication. A data model attempts to formalize some of the informal social rules and meanings into a formalized grammar and hence a data model is a social construction par excellence. In accordance with this insight, subjectivist data modeling approaches were called rule-based in chapter 6. Rule-based approaches view data modeling as a reconstructive activity in which subjects codify linguistic rules which are enacted through the use of IS. These approaches will be explored in more detail in section 7.3.

Whereas ISD in general was divided into four paradigmatic schools (*cf.* chapter 4), data modeling approaches are divided only into two schools, i.e. fact-based and rule-based. This is because in the data modeling literature paradigmatic differences related to human interest and conflict resolution are not as visible and decisive as in other areas of ISD.* We shall, how-

---

* This may be surprising to some readers because language uses and communications in organizations closely relate to interest formation and ideology maintenance. However, these kind of power issues are not very visible unless we focus on certain types of organizational action, such as competition over resources or the nature of authority and social control. Because of its formalistic stance, these aspects are ignored in most of the data modeling literature. The

ever, see how issues related to interest formation and power are reflected in
different data modeling approaches whenever possible.

It should also be noted that the bipolar distinction between fact-based
and rule-based data modeling approaches is not necessarily as sharp as
we present it here. Many data modeling approaches incorporate some of
both and thereby occupy some 'middle ground' between the extremes of
fact- and rule-based. This, of course, may lead to some inconsistencies in
their conceptual base. Such inconsistencies are often not reflected, because
technical work in the area of data modeling is often unaware of the deeper
stipulations and assumptions on which newly proposed methods and tools
rest.

7.2 Fact-based School

The conceptual base of the fact-based approaches is grounded on concepts
which are related to given 'facts' (in the sense of existing state of affairs).
Typical examples for such concepts are entity, property and relationship. A
fact is typically defined by associating a specific attribute or relationship
(or its denial) to a given entity.

The fact-based school represents the mainstream of the data modeling
field. It has the longest history, and it has been intensively researched over
the last two decades (Chen 1981; van Griethuysen 1982). The approaches
suggested within this school have been widely applied, and there exists a
considerable amount of application experience. Therefore, the strengths and
limitations of this school are better understood than those of the rule-based
school.

The theoretical foundations and the evolution of the fact-based school
have been extensively discussed in several papers and books (Kent 1983a,
1986; Jardine and Reuber 1984; Sundgren 1973; Abrial 1974; Nijssen 1976,
1977; Senko 1977; Bubenko 1983). There exists great variety in the vocabulary and aspects of data modeling that are highlighted. Though we
treat the fact-based school as a unified approach (based on its ontological
and epistemological assumptions), the reader should bear in mind that the
school is by no means monolithic. Students of the fact-based school disagree
about many important aspects such as the number of basic categories and
constructs (Nijssen 1976, 1977; Jardine and Reuber 1984; van Griethuysen
1982; Bubenko 1979), the role of time (Bolour and Dekeyser 1983; Bubenko
1977b), and the appropriate design approach (Bubenko 1980; 1983).

Our discussion of the school will proceed as follows. In section 7.2.1 we
trace the historical origins of the school and identify some landmarks in
its evolution. Section 7.2.2. discusses the theoretical base of the fact-based

---

principal focus of data modeling research has been on modeling methods and tools to guarantee
'semantically' correct data models. In fact, power aspects become visible only when we examine
organizational impacts and social conditions in which certain data modeling methods and tools
are applied. This is often seen as being outside the research interests of data modeling experts.

school. Section 7.2.3 clarifies the basic view of data modeling adopted in the fact-based school. Section 7.2.4 clarifies three beliefs of the nature of object systems derived in the fact-based school. Section 7.2.5 classifies fact-based data modeling approaches into several streams including entity-based and object-based. Section 7.2.6 summarizes the principal strengths and weaknesses of the fact-based school and offers some suggestions for its improvement.

7.2.1 Historical roots

7.2.1.1 Database management

As previously noted in section 2.4 of chapter 2, before the advent of database management systems (DBMS) there was little consideration of the contents of data: data meanings and formats were determined by program design. Early database architectures were, in essence, slight extensions to the file management systems provided by operating systems as they provided only a single level of data description. Therefore, the syntactic structure and semantic content of data could not be easily separated from its physical implementation.

A major advancement took place in the late 1960s and early 1970s when the three classical data models — hierarchic, network, relational — were developed. These models offered two improvements. First, the models observed, and also implemented, a two level architecture that provided some independence between the logical and the physical description. Thus, the road was open to advance those data description techniques that did not focus on the physical aspects. Second, the existence of three models raised much debate about which of the three models was the best (Date 1975), and also how they could coexist under the roof of one database management system. Although the original goal of merging the three models soon turned out to be impractical, the idea of such a unified database management architecture led to the development of more advanced DBMS architectures such as the three level schema architecture suggested in the ANSI/X3/SPARC (1975) report. The major change here was the separation of internal, conceptual and external views (or schemata).

Although it was never entirely clear what the ANSI/SPARC report meant by the 'unified' conceptual level, and by the conceptual schema (see e.g. Deen 1980), the report created a great deal of momentum behind the development of data models that were in nature 'conceptual' or 'semantic'. It was one of several research activities in data modeling and DBMS research which were pursued in the early 1970s (see e.g. Abrial 1974; Engles 1972; Senko *et al.* 1973). The research activities achieved two results: formulating the fundamentals of the fact-based school; and proposing standardization for conceptual schema languages (Steel 1975; van Griethuysen 1982). The goal of standardization turned out to be unworkable. The fundamentals of the fact-based school of data modeling were formulated during the 1970s in a number of conferences* and widely read journal articles (Senko 1975; Biller and Neuhold 1978; Chen 1976).

Another outcome of the increased research activity on data modeling was the proliferation of data models. Since the late 1970s, literally hundreds of data models have been proposed. Nearly all of them repeat the same basic assumptions and construction principles (theory), but differ in detailed data modeling concepts such as: the type of entities (simple, complex), relationships (degree, constraints, unknown values), which object types can have 'attributes', how entities are identified, and so forth (see e.g. Nijssen 1976, 1977; Nijssen and Bracchi 1979; van Griethuysen 1982). This has also resulted in several data model taxonomies (Kerschberg *et al.* 1976; Bubenko 1978; Jardine and Reuber 1984; Klein and Hirschheim 1987b; Stachowitz 1985).

7.2.1.2 *Systems design methods*

Several researchers observed as early as the late 1950s and early 1960s (Young and Kent 1958; CODASYL 1961) that system requirements should be stated without considering the physical system implementation. To this end there is a need for concepts and language to capture functional and structural system requirements on a more abstract level. For an overview in the area see Kahn (1982).

One prominent representative of the early efforts was Langefors' (1963) seminal work. He suggested that IS design problems should be viewed on two levels: the infological and the datalogical level. The latter relates how the information is represented and processed efficiently. The former considers those information needs that must be served by the data system and the content of these information needs.

On the infological level the information needs and their contents are specified by representing the structure of information messages conveyed by the system. According to Langefors the analysis of the information messages is carried out by studying how information messages are composed of elementary messages and what precedence relations exist between them. Langefors proposed an elementary message concept consisting of three parts:

(1) the object about which some fact is stated. This is represented by an identifier — later in the relational model this was called the primary key of a relation;

(2) the property or the relation that holds for the object (its predicate) — the non-key domains in the relational model;

---

* There has been an endless series of conferences beginning with 'classical' conferences in the mid-1970s (Nijssen 1976, 1977; Nijssen and Bracchi 1979) and continuing with conferences in ER-modeling (Chen 1981) and data semantics (Meersman 1986). Also conferences dealing with information systems design (Olle *et al.* 1982, 1983, 1986, 1988) have added to the field. Good surveys of the development can be found in Senko (1977), Jardine and Reuber (1984). Also the journal *Data and Knowledge Engineering* focuses on the topic.

(3) and the time point of the observation (time stamp or time-reference); the importance of this was not originally recognized in the relational model.

In addition to stating facts in this way, Langefors proposed the notion of inference rules which connected a sequence of elementary situations through precedence relations. The inference rules correspond to computation procedures in everyday terminology or data manipulation language constructs in DB terminology. The precedence relation expresses a logical order between elementary or compound messages through computations or other forms of data manipulation (including updates). For example, given the elementary facts of salary and tax tables, the facts tax-withheld and salary-to-be-paid can be derived from them.

Langefors' influence on the development of systems design methods has been considerable. The concept of an elementary message was soon adopted widely to denote an elementary or an irreducible fact (ANSI/SPARC 1975; Falkenberg 1976; Biller 1979; van Griethuysen 1982), and it laid the foundation for several data models (Sundgren 1973; Bubenko 1980). The theory of information analysis was developed further by several scholars into derivation analysis (Solvberg and Kung 1984, Sernadas 1982). The concept of precedence relation has also been applied in several functional systems design methods such as ISAC (Lundeberg *et al.* 1981), and a structured analysis (DeMarco 1978; Gane and Sarson 1981).

Another area where researchers and practitioners early on recognized the need for more abstract data descriptions was database design. In the mid 1970s commercial database management systems (network and hierarchical) became widely used. However, these products were not compatible with each other. From the data processing departments' point of view it was desirable to have a database design method which was independent of a particular DBMS and its particular data model. The only way this could be achieved was to develop higher level data models. Another problem encountered was how to manage data descriptions centrally and thereby resolve inconsistencies and redundancies in the data. To address these problems many researchers suggested database design methods that relied on higher level concepts of data abstraction (Bubenko 1977a,b 1979; Yao *et al.* 1982; Solvberg 1977; Olle *et al.* 1982; Rocfeldt and Tardieu 1983). Similar research issues surfaced around the problems of database conversion and restructuring (Navathe 1980).

7.2.2 Theoretical roots

The above attempts established the need for appropriate theories of meaning. As many of these lie outside the core concerns of computer science (Denning *et al.* 1989), the theoretical and intellectual origins of the fact-based school must be traced to a wide range of reference disciplines including: philosophy (see chapter 6), linguistics, artificial intelligence and programming languages. Each of these is briefly discussed below.

7.2.2.1 Linguistics

Linguistics, by necessity, deals with similar issues to data modeling. Accordingly, there are several parallels between linguistics and data modeling theory (Lyytinen 1981). For example, models of linguistic competence (Chomsky 1966) form one sort of data model distinguished only by wider scope and different application purpose. Therefore, the linguistic debate on how to model language meanings has a close affinity to the debate on how to capture meaning in data models.

In linguistics the work of Chomsky have had the most direct impact on data modeling theory. Chomsky's goal was to develop a formal and unambiguous description of the syntax and semantics of language. To achieve this goal, Chomsky suggested powerful and general concepts to think about language (or data) (see e.g. Lyons 1977). These included the notion of a generative grammar; the distinction between deep structure and surface structure of a sentence; and the idea of a transformation grammar. All these notions have influenced the fact-based data modeling approaches. The idea of the data model as a generative abstract grammar was addressed by Smith and Smith (1982), Nijssen (1980), and also by Wand and Weber (1990). The distinction between surface structure and deep structure was proposed by Falkenberg (1977) as a foundation to develop external and conceptual data models. Finally, the idea of a transformation grammar is visible in the idea of a mapping between conceptual and external levels.

Another school in linguistics initiated by Chomsky's students was the generative semantics school (Fodor and Katz 1964; Fodor 1977; Lyons 1977). Proponents in this school focused on abstract semantic structures, in contrast to syntactic ones favored by Chomsky. The idea was to derive the meaning of a sentence by translating it into a system of semantic markers. In data modeling this corresponds to the idea that the meaning of data can be derived by translating a data structure into a set of conceptual structures (Falkenberg 1977; Kangassalo 1982).

7.2.2.2 Artificial intelligence

From the very beginning of computing, philosophers and scientists have tried to make machines (computers) understand natural language, or to translate from one language to another. Since the 1950s, this research has been carried out under the roof of a research tradition called artificial intelligence (AI) (McCorduck 1979). In all such attempts the researcher has to render a semantic and syntactic model of the sentences by which the 'understanding' is possible. Thus, the research into language understanding provides many useful insights for data modeling. The early efforts in the late 1950s on 'fully automated, high quality language translation' used direct dictionaries and parsed syntactic structures of sentences to understand language. Despite huge funding and high expectations these attempts were doomed to fail. Therefore, the AI researchers tried to develop a new approach that went beyond the dominant syntactic approach. Foundations for this new approach were developed in several papers in the mid-1960s (see Minsky 1968). The fundamental goal was to set up a formal representation that corresponds to the underlying meaning of sentences.* This representation could then be used in a systematic reasoning process as a part of a language comprehension system. The underlying view of meaning, as crisply illustrated by Winograd (1980), was strikingly similar to that advocated in the fact-based school. The focus was on the 'formal representation' and its correspondence to 'facts' constituting the world.

The influence of AI does not, however, stop here. As noted by Senko (1975), several principles of how to build formal representations in modeling data have been borrowed from early AI works (see e.g. Rovner and Feldman 1969). These include for example the use of associative binaries, or triples, to represent semantic connections between words and sentences.

7.2.2.3 Programming languages

Two research issues in programming languages have had a considerable impact on the development of the fact-based school. First, simulation languages such as SIMULA have tried to represent the abstract behavior of 'entities' in the simulated system by embedded data structures. Simulation also introduced the idea of entity life-cycle histories - a feature followed in many data modeling approaches (Davenport 1979).

Second, the notion of abstract data typing and 'strong' typing coincide with the evolution of similar ideas in the fact-based school (Brodie 1978; 1979). As Brodie observes, the data (base) models correspond to type systems in programming languages. Thus, the specification of a data model must follow principles that are similar to the principles of defining an abstract data type. Here we note two similarities (Brodie 1979). First, the idea of a 'strong' data type that can only be manipulated through a set of well-defined operations suggests that there must be some formal basis to verify that the data is correctly 'typed', i.e. that the operations are 'valid'. This amounts to finding out those laws and states in reality that can be used to determine that the data model is valid. Second, abstract typing implies that types are specified formally so that their consistency can be formally tested (Brodie 1979, 1980). The same principles are suggested in the fact-based school (Jardine and Reuber 1984).

7.2.3 Basic view of IS and data modeling

In this section we outline the fundamental concepts of data modeling as they are typically represented in the fact-based school. The conceptual base of the fact-based school has been mainly derived from the denotational or referential theory of meaning (Quine 1960). The basic belief in this theory is that the meaning of language is determined by the way in which the

---

* As can be seen from our discussion, and has been pointed out by many others (e.g. Winograd 1980; Fodor 1977), this insight by itself contains nothing new. However, some members of the AI community at that time claimed the superiority of the AI paradigm to language understanding.

elements of language strictly correspond to some extra-linguistic elements (entities, facts, etc.) in the world. Thus the fact-based school restricts the data modeling efforts to the syntactic and propositional aspects of language (and the technical concerns). In accordance with this, the goal of machine independent data modeling efforts is to model the syntactic structure of the data so that the constructed syntactic structures can be mapped directly onto structures in the world (semantics).

In what follows we shall mainly examine how this kind of denotational theory of data meaning is clarified in van Griethuysen (1982). The reasons for choosing this work as our primary focus are twofold. First, this work is one of the most profound and most systematic treatments of the subject in the field. Second, because the work summarizes the results of several years of standardization efforts, it can be regarded as conveying a minimal consensus about the foundations of data modeling in the fact-based school.

We shall first explore the fundamental concepts through a quick tour around the following key issues: definition of information system (7.2.3.1). This is followed by an analysis of underlying concepts of the definition including Universe of Discourse (7.2.3.2), entities (7.2.3.3), nature and type of entities (7.2.3.4-5), facts (7.2.3.6), conceptual schema (7.2.3.7), information base (7.2.3.8), and IS operations (7.2.3.9).

7.2.3.1   Definition of information system

The fundamental elements of the fact-based school are clearly expressed in the definition of an information system (IS) in the van Griethuysen (1982) report. It treats an information system as a fully predictable, formal system that mirrors the states of the Universe of Discourse (UoD). The idea of the 'mirror' nature of the IS is also crisply expressed by Wand and Weber (1990 p. 65) as follows:

> A one-to-many mapping must exist from the set of real world states into the set of information system states.

The real-world states which form the facts are similar to Wittgenstein's famous statement:

> 2. What is the case — a fact — is the existence of states of affairs. (Wittgenstein 1922)

In order to clarify further the notion of an IS as a state-tracking mechanism we need to build a model of an IS. Elements of such a model and their interrelationships are depicted in figure 7.1 (see also van Griethuysen 1982). As we can seen the IS consists of two parts (figure 7.1): an Information Processor (IP), and a UoD description (UoDD).

The operations of the IS as a state-tracking mechanism can now be briefly described as follows. The IS behaves deterministically upon receipt of a message from an IS environment by either changing the UoDD or retrieving some parts of it. The message is issued by an agent who is called the IS user. The message contains information about changes that have occurred in the UoD, or a command to retrieve and display parts of the UoDD. In the first situation, changes are observed in the UoD from the environment by the IS user and they are 'made known' to the IS. In the latter case no change is reported by the user. Instead, the IS user is interested in inquiring about current, past, or future states (by computation) in the UoD.

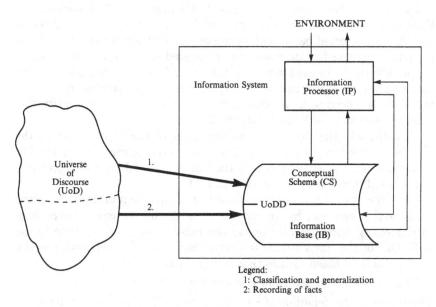

Legend:
1: Classification and generalization
2: Recording of facts

Figure 7.1: An information system in the fact-based view

In the following each of the basic elements of the definition are discussed.

7.2.3.2 Universe of discourse

A UoD is a selected portion of a world and it constitutes the universe made known to the IS and thus to the IS users by the IS. The UoD may be concrete, like an inventory, or abstract like the organizational structure of an enterprise. It may even be a result of abstract reasoning like some mathematical structure, or a hypothetical world like the Wonderland visited by Alice. Often the UoD contains parts of all three of these different worlds (see van Griethuysen p. F-10). Although not necessarily clearly formulated, the UoD is assumed to consist of concrete, 'hard' facts and to behave as prescribed by general causal laws that can be discovered. Thus the ontological stance adopted in this school is naive realism.*

7.2.3.3   Entities

In the fact-based school the UoD consists of discrete phenomena called
entities.** Sometimes these are also called things (Wand and Weber 1990),
and now fashionably objects (Shlaer and Mellor 1992, van Assche *et al.*
1991). The entities make up the facts reported by the IS. As Wittgenstein
(1922) writes:

> 2.01. A state of affairs (a state of things) is a combination of objects
> (things).

The entities (the basic units of the UoD) have several characteristics.
First, they can be separately distinguished, they have independent existence,
and they are selected based on how interesting they are for IS users. Thus,
prominent criteria for something to be counted as an entity are: it has a
unique identifier, its existence does not depend on the existence of other
entities (its existence is caused by a specific event that creates the entity),
and there is a need to know what facts are associated with the entity (i.e.
what IS users want to know about the UoD).

All entities in the UoD exist independently of the IS users. Thus, the
entities are not seen as creations of intersubjective agreements or the fiat
of an elite. Instead, they show how the world 'is' and how it is objectively
'constructed' (van Griethuysen 1982 p. 1–2).

Thus, the UoD can be seen to consist of independent entities that have
been, are, or ever can be. In accordance with this we can also speak of
various entity worlds formed by entities existing at the same time in the
UoD. One of the entity worlds is always the current (actual) entity world,
i.e. it consists of those entities that now populate the UoD.

7.2.3.4   Problems in distinguishing entities in the UoD

Unfortunately the definition of a UoD is not as straightforward as the above
principles suggest. Most important, the identity rules for entities do not suggest any unambiguous, formal criteria which can guide model builders and
IS users to decide upon the entities which are supposed to make up the UoD
and how to group them into mutually exclusive and collectively exhaustive

---

* How this assumption can be consistent with the claim that the UoD may also be a hypothetical or an imagined world has not been clearly resolved in the data modeling literature.
Clearly, these two claims are contradictory and the conflict must be solved either by an escape
to Platonic idealism (imagined worlds are also 'real'), or just by simply ignoring it (as is done
in the mainstream literature).

** Though the concept of entity is far from clear, as noted by Kent (1978), Lindgren (1984),
and Stamper (1987), the concept is so central in all fact-based approaches (including Kent's
own approach (1983b)) that we want to include it into the necessary conceptual base of the
fact-based school.

classes or types.* Whereas sometimes phenomena can be easily recognized as entities, often situations do arise in which the choice is ambiguous.** Some entities may not have unique identifiers, and some entities can be existentially dependent on other entities. Secondly, whether or not to include an entity in the UoD, to a large extent, is a subjective decision dependent on vaguely defined global system purposes and their interpretation by many stakeholders. Quite often different model builders find different phenomena important due to variance in their working environment and cultural background. Thus, how the UoD's boundaries are drawn and how it is divided into entities is far from obvious and rife with subtle social, linguistic and political problems which are by and large ignored in the fact-based data modeling literature.

A third problem is the circular nature of the entity definition: on the one hand entities form discrete chunks of facts (such as an entity's identifier, its time of birth, etc.) which are bundled together. On the other hand, facts are combinations of entities. Thus, an entity cannot be defined without the concept of the fact and vice versa (see van Griethuysen 1982 p. 2).

7.2.3.5 Nature and type of entities

The definition of an entity is highly abstract and does not help much in analyzing the entities in the UoD. Therefore, it is helpful to examine in more detail the types of entities that populate the UoDs.

Because the UoD can be concrete or abstract, also the entities can also be either concrete or abstract. Concrete entities are physical phenomena like 'this car', or 'a boy named Charlie'.*** Concrete entities usually have well-established names, they are operands of widely known operations or decisions, and they play obvious roles with each other (when forming facts).

Abstract entities are entities without a visible physical appearance. Yet, they exist and persist, depend on each other in playing various roles and are thus of interest. An example of an abstract entity is 'a train service', i.e. a train schedule consisting of an ordered sequence of planned departures and arrivals through several stations along a route. Another example of an abstract entity is 'a car-ownership' by a particular person. Abstract entities are often more difficult to identify, as they may have several different names and their boundaries are much fuzzier. Abstract entities often are results of some functions or formed by a relationship. An example of the former is

---

* For an excellent discussion see Kent (1978), and Stamper (1987).

** We use the term 'phenomena' to denote here an unstructured view of how the UoD is to be perceived.

*** We shall ignore for a moment the problem of ambiguous and shifting boundaries that are also typical for concrete entities. For example, 'the boy named Charlie' may turn out to be 'a girl named Rita' after an operation. There may also be considerable ambiguity when 'the boy named Charlie' ceases to exist and changes to 'a poor soul Charlie' or a pile of earth depending on one's religious view.

a function 'train-scheduling' which produces a list of 'train-services' for a particular environment. An example of the latter is 'car-ownership', which denotes a particular relationship instance between two concrete entities like between 'person John Doe' and 'car XKJ 110'.

Entities in the UoD are not interesting in themselves. We usually gain little, if anything just by enumerating all possible or existing entities in the UoD. Instead, what the IS users are interested in is to identify the entities as something (Israel 1979). Thus, we always identify an entity such as 'XKJ 110' as a car, i.e. as a member of a class or an entity-type 'cars'. Being a member of an entity-class, such as cars, the identified entity, in this case 'XKJ 110' has several states of affairs which make it a member of that class. These include class qualities, like in the case of cars, the model (Sierra 2.0i), the year of production (1989), manufacturer (Ford), number of seats (5), and so on. Moreover, entities in a class can form states of affairs that show their relationships with entities in some other or in the same class. In our case the entity 'XJJ 110' has relationships to its owner (John Doe), its driver (Lily Doe), its registration country (Finland), and so on.

7.2.3.6 Facts

All states of affairs associated with the entities are called facts or propositions. Facts are conceivable states of affairs concerning entities about which it is possible to assert or deny that such a state of affairs holds for those entities. Facts can concern one entity (such as the name of the current Pope), several entities (current players of The Houston Oilers), groups of entities (all motor-vehicles), entity-types (car manufacturers) and so on. Usually the fact-based school denotes prevailing (contingent) facts as 'information', and general facts that hold in several worlds that describe what is permissible or necessary as 'constraints'. All facts that are true in a given entity world are denoted as a fact world.

Defined in this way the facts form 'abstract' conceptual phenomena. In order to discuss and exchange information about which entities can exist and which facts hold for them, one has to describe them by some linguistic means. These representations of facts are called sentences.* Thus, sentences are linguistic objects (entities) which represent facts.

Sentences are defined as grammatically correct constructs in some formal language. Like other objects sentences also can be considered as entities. Sentences are composed of other linguistic constructs which are called terms and predicates. Each sentence includes both terms and predicates: terms

---

* The term sentence is ambiguous because there can be sentences that are not statements or assertions as is assumed in van Griethuysen (1982). Therefore the terms statement or declarative sentence could be used for linguistic objects which represent a proposition (i.e. 'represent' a proposition, rather than 'assert' a proposition as sentences assert nothing, their users use them to assert something). Commands which query the state of the UoDD should be classified as interrogative sentences.

show what entities the sentence refers to, and predicates represent the facts ascribed to them. Thus, terms are linguistic objects which represent (denote) entities, and predicates are linguistic objects, which represent properties (one place predicates), or relationships (many placed predicates).*

A necessary requirement for a language to represent the UoD correctly is that it must be formal. This implies two things:

(1) the syntactic structure of the language must be formally specified. The formal specification of a sentence explains how terms and predicates must be syntactically connected to form correct sentences; and

(2) the formal semantics of the sentence is specified.

This is done by showing how the truth or the falsehood of a sentence is derived by mapping terms onto facts in the UoD, and by comparing the resulting fact to existing states of affairs in the UoD. In addition, one can derive the truth value of the whole UoDD by using the truth-tables of predicate calculus showing how truthful sentences can be combined by logical operators (conjunction, disjunction, etc.) to yield new truthful sentences.

7.2.3.7 Conceptual schema

The UoDD is a formal representation of the UoD in the sense defined above. It is divided into the conceptual schema and the information base (data) as shown in figure 7.1. This partition is based on the nature of facts represented in the corresponding parts of the UoDD. The conceptual schema (CS) is a conceptual data model because it represents an abstraction of the UoD. Abstraction means that a CS includes sentences representing general facts, i.e. facts that hold for several entity worlds in the UoD. It thereby conveys modal knowledge, i.e. what states of affairs hold necessarily in these entity worlds. In analytical philosophy such sentences are called analytical sentences. In other words, the CS represents facts which hold for all entities that belong to any UoD. These facts define for example which entities can exist in all entity worlds, and in relevant cases, which entities must occur in each entity world — the necessary entities. Examples of such facts are:

'A car is of a particular model'

'A car is owned by a person, a manufacturer, or a dealer'.

The first sentence describes that in every entity world, if an entity belongs to a class of cars it must be of a particular model (it cannot be of 'no-model'). The second sentence specifies that only those entities that belong to classes of persons, manufacturers or dealers can have a relationship 'own' to an entity in the class of cars.

Usually the necessary facts included in a CS are further divided into two categories:

---

* We shall for the moment ignore the question of how many different sorts of ontological categories one needs to use to describe different 'types' of facts.

(1) class descriptions which are defined by facts that hold only for the members of that class, and

(2) rules or constraints, which define the behavior of the UoD.

The general facts in the UoD represented in the CS are called the abstraction system (see figure 7.1).

7.2.3.8 Information base

Those facts which are true in some entity worlds, but not necessarily in all entity worlds are called contingent. An example of a contingent fact is:

'A car XKJ 110 is owned by a person John Doe'

In some other entity world the car 'XKJ 110' may be owned by a person 'Ronald Reagan', or a dealer 'Rent a Wreck'.

Any collection of sentences representing contingent facts is called an information base (IB). Among all possible sets of contingent facts one can identify the actual information base which describes those contingent facts that hold for the actual entity world (an actual state space).

There are two important restrictions which determine which sentences can be included into the information base. First, all sets of contingent sentences must be consistent, i.e. the information base must not include sentences that assert both P and ¬P. Second, the information base must be consistent with the facts stated in the CS.* Thus, the IB together with the CS describe all facts in the actual entity world that have been found to hold, and which the IS users consider relevant for a specific entity world. They thereby describe a fact world for that entity world. For these reasons, the collection of sentences included in the UoDD must be necessarily consistent, if it purports to be a truthful description of the UoD.

Two clarifying remarks need to be made about this interpretation of the UoDD and the nature of IS. First, the fact-based school often sees that the UoDD 'establishes' a specific entity world. Only those entities are 'real' and 'exist' which are referred to by terms in the UoDD. Second, the fact-based school does not deny that there may be several UoDDs for a particular UoD. Yet, due to the nature of semantic rules for constructing the UoDD, only one UoDD can be at any time a part of the IS.

7.2.3.9 Changes in the UoDD — the IS operations

The IP has specific roles in maintaining the UoDD. Its task is to change the UoDD upon the receipt of a message from the environment. These changes can thus concern either the IB or the CS. Usually (in normal cases) they concern the IB and signal that new entities have appeared in the UoD (the actual entity world has changed), or some old ones have disappeared, or that

---

* This requirement provides a means by which the IP can act as a checking mechanism upon the receipt of a message or a command from the environment which verifies the correctness (consistency) of the IB using the sentences in the CS.

entities' states of affairs change. In this case, the IP either inserts or deletes sentences in the IB and using the CS checks that none of these operations lead the UoDD into an inconsistent state.*

When the CS is changed this means that new classifications and constraints are added to the CS, or existing ones removed. In these cases the new CS must be checked for consistency and validity. It may also imply that the scope of interest (UoD) is changing in the CS so that it expands or shrinks. In this case, the CS is changed and only syntactic checks need to be accomplished, i.e. that it is syntactically correct.** Finally, one must ensure that the new CS does not contradict the actual IB (which again can be an undecidable problem).***

The IP is also needed to gain access to the data in the IB in response to (inquiring) sentences from the environment. In this case, the operation of retrieval 'makes known' to the IS user sentences belonging to the UoDD which have been inserted into it earlier (in most cases the IB), or which can be deduced from it (using inference rules, the CS and the sentences in the IB).

7.2.3.10 Summary

We can now clarify why the definition of the IS defines an IS as constituting a fully predictable deterministic formal system that mirrors (tracks the states of) the UoD. It is formal because all parts included in it are formal (language) systems. It is predictable because its behavior must satisfy the sentences stated in the CS. It is deterministic because it obeys the laws found in the UoD, and its next state can be computed by knowing its current state and the content of the sentence added into the system. It mirrors the UoD because the semantics of the terms and sentences are defined through their mappings onto facts. In this capacity the IS acts like an informer in the Lockean inquiring system (Churchman 1971): the states of affairs in the actual, past, or future entity worlds can be made known by retrieving parts of the UoDD instead of directly perceiving or manipulating the UoD.

---

* For efficiency reasons this is rarely done 'on time' if ever, in actual database applications.

** This is called validation of the CS. As the relationship between the CS and reality (abstraction system in the UoD) cannot be formally specified (Bubenko 1977b) the suggested procedures are informal reasoning, negotiations, and experiments (e.g. prototyping) (Kyng 1989).

*** Although these operations are implied by the definitions of the IB and CS, there is lack of serious research into how these operations could be done. There are immense decidability problems, as well as problems with the required time to execute these operations. One of the few research efforts in this direction is Lundberg's thesis (1982) which discusses to some extent how the consistency is verified during the design phase. However, he neglects how the consistency is verified when the CS changes during the IS use. He also neglects how the CS can be changed to remove the inconsistency if it is found inconsistent (see also Tsichritzis and Lochovsky 1982).

7.2.4 Three beliefs underlying the fact-based approaches

The fact-based school assumes that developers and users of the IS can construct an unequivocal mapping from a UoD to a UoDD (arrows 1 and 2 in figure 7.1).* There are three beliefs which form the cornerstone of such an assumption:

(1) the belief in the objective nature of the UoD — that it can be perceived impartially,

(2) the belief in the factual, descriptive nature of information (sentences) contained in the UoDD, and

(3) the belief in the consensual role of the UoDD.

Clearly the first two deal with data modeling ontology and epistemology. The third belief states the implications of the first two for the role of IS and data modeling in organizational decision-making and interest formation. In the following we shall discuss each of these beliefs by relating them to philosophical arguments concerning the nature of language and reality and their relationships (ontology and epistemology). These have largely centered around disputes about the early Wittgenstein's seminal treatment of language philosophy (Wittgenstein 1922). Our analysis here is not in any sense unique. Stamper (1987), in the IS literature, and Winograd and Flores (1986) in AI, have done similar analyses. Moreover, an excellent critical examination of denotational semantics from a philosophical point of view can be found in von Kutchera (1975) and Apel (1980). Finally, an extensive evaluation of the denotational semantics from the viewpoint of linguistics is presented in Lyons (1977).

7.2.4.1   The objective belief

The objective belief suggests four principles for the construction of the UoDD:

(1) correspondence,

(2) objectivity,

(3) the excluded middle, and

(4) language neutrality.

The principle of correspondence states that every sentence in the UoDD corresponds to IS users' direct observations. In this view the UoDD faithfully represents users' perceptions of entities and facts, and there is a one-to-one (or one-to-many) correspondence between facts in the UoD and linguistic constructs in the UoDD (sentences and terms in IS). For example, Chen (1977, 1983) speaks of a UoDD as 'a 'pure' representation of reality' in the sense that the CS does not refer to anything else than the objects in the

---

* Here we bypass a related but different question: how the boundaries of the UoD are drawn. Clearly, one cannot include the whole universe into one conceptual data model.

UoD. In Wittgensteinian terms (Wittgenstein 1922), all that can be said, can be said clearly (by pointing to the 'pictured' objects) and we must remain silent about all that cannot be said.

The principle of objectivity presumes two things. First, it assumes that the UoD divides into entities and that all entities fall easily into different entity-classes. In other words, the fact-based school assumes some fixed, immutable entity-structure: entities are objective concrete structures, their boundaries are sharp and clear, and their definition is independent of any practical problems of human activity. Basically this is an ontological claim of the nature of the UoD. In Wittgensteinian terms this ontological claim of the UoD reads: the world is composed of existing states of affairs which are given to us and which are independent of one another. Not surprisingly, this view of the nature of the modeled reality has been influential in such fields as mathematics and logic where the abstract nature of phenomena studied makes it easy to establish such Platonistic immutable 'idea-worlds' (see Stamper 1987; Dummett 1981). In practice, this assumption is operationalized in the rule of individuation in logic.

Second, the principle assumes that all facts pertaining to identified entities can be observed without any great difficulty. Basically, this expresses an epistemological claim of how the knowledge about the UoD is acquired and justified. In this view, if problems should arise, they are caused by insufficient education of IS users, inadequate and poor measurement, or plain mistakes.* In addition, the principle assumes that the reality (UoD) is observed by an individual, not a group, and moreover there are no principal differences in different individuals' perceptions. Therefore, the complex and delicate social mechanisms are left out which support, enable, or constrain the identification of entities and recording of the facts about them (see Stamper 1985b, 1987). The principle of objectivity postulates the following requirement: all sentences in the UoDD can and must be formulated in the form:

$$\text{'It is true that } p\text{'}. \qquad (7.1)$$

In this form sentences do not reveal who knows p, and in what way. Hence all doubts about the grounding of the truth of p, or configuring those entity worlds in which p can hold vanish. In general, languages permitting only such expressions are called extensional languages, since the meaning of language is reduced to the extensions of sentences: truth-values. Accordingly, the principle of objectivity entails the principle of correspondence: the epistemology and ontology of the UoD must be matched perfectly with the ontology of the language.

Von Wright (1971) calls a logical world of the UoD and its representation constructed in this way a Tractatus world. In any Tractatus world

---

* The issue of deliberate errors is always ignored, though according to some studies these may have significant bearing on the use of the IS (Feldman and March 1981; Brinkmann 1986).

we can distinguish insignificant sentences from significant ones by examining whether they represent facts in the form stated in (7.1). Therefore, so–called intentional sentences are excluded which express propositional attitudes such as 'A thinks that it is true that p', i.e. relationships between subjects and propositions (Apel 1980). The truth-values of intentional sentences are opaque, i.e. they cannot be composed from the truth-values (or denotations) of their components. Accordingly, they cannot mean anything, as there is no meaningful semantic assignment. An example of such a sentence is:

'The marketing director believes that the sales have dropped by 10%'.
$$(7.2)$$
This sentence does not have a truth-value, because it may be true that the marketing director believes so, but the object of belief, i.e. a fact that the sales have dropped may not hold.

A consequence of applying these two principles to data modeling is that the modeled aspects of data are radically reduced. All data (sentences) which convey epistemic (believing or knowing), or modal aspects (possible, necessity) of social knowledge are excluded. Accordingly, data models do not include IS users as parts of the necessary knowledge to correctly interpret the data.* In the same vein they do not record any aspects of personal knowledge.**

The third principle, the excluded middle, forms a basis for forbidding to have both P and $\neg P$ in the UoDD. Fundamentally, this is an ontological stipulation about the UoD. It is usually shared by all adherents of the fact-based school. Bubenko (1983) states it crisply:

an information base contains a set of facts (sentences in our terminology) observed in, or asserted true of the UoD.

This principle entails that the UoDD describes what is the case or what isn't, there is no way that in can do both. If the excluded middle is not sustained there is no way to derive a logical contradiction — a basis to demonstrate the consistency of the UoDD. The principle basically claims that reality can allow only one case at a time: some state of affairs either exists or it does not exist, but excludes a third, 'middle' case.

---

* The impact of different user communities is only recognized during the early specification of the data model through so-called local views or 'user views'. However, all user views later on are merged into a global conceptual data model (or conceptual schema) in which differences between user views have been resolved. Even in the local views the originator of the data is formally not recorded (Lehtinen and Lyytinen 1986), at best the designer of the schema can choose a name for the user view which points to the originator.

** See for example how the car registration example is expressed in van Griethuysen (1982).

The fourth principle, language neutrality, insists that the UoD is independent of the language employed in representing it. This also is an ontological assumption about the language. According to this principle, an IS user 'stands on the limit of the world' (Wittgenstein 1922) by observing and recording facts in the UoD. The language she employs serves only as a technical means to represent observed facts, and it has no bearing upon what the user perceives in the UoD and how. Thus, language has no active role in shaping users' conceptions of the world. In consequence, the data modeling activity does not principally affect how the IS users view their organizational surroundings: it strives only to develop a more effective language to record facts that are known outside the language. For example, Wand and Weber (1990) make a supplementary requirement that the language must be ontologically complete, i.e. it must represent faithfully all states in the UoD.

7.2.4.2 The descriptive belief

The fact-based school assumes that a UoDD represents only factual information. All sentences in the UoDD codify facts or invariances, laws, represented as general, necessary facts. From a linguistic point of view this position limits the functions of language to just one: to describe reality in a way that can be asserted or denied. All other functions of language: to express personal attitudes, wishes and evaluations, to establish and maintain social relationships, and to regulate human behaviors are neglected.

In the same vein, the fact-based school does not always make a distinction between referential and intentional meaning* which was observed by Frege (1952). In Frege's theory, the intentional meaning expressed the meaning of the word, which was different from its reference. Consider for example the terms 'the evening star', and 'the morning star', where the former refers to the planet Venus in the morning, the latter, Venus in the evening. Both term refer to the same object — but yet do not have the same meaning. The discovery that both terms refer to the same thing, despite their different meaning, was in its time revolutionary. Therefore, to define meaning solely in terms of reference may be inadequate.

7.2.4.3 The consensus belief

According to the fact-based school the UoDD expresses an agreement or a theory on how the UoD is structured and behaves. A CS is a formal

---

* This is not true for all works inspired by fact-based theory. Lee (1983) and Stachowitz (1985) are notable exceptions as they draw heavily on possible world semantics and Montague grammars, which make the distinction between intentions and extensions. However, the ISO report (van Griethuysen 1982) blurs this distinction even though it refers to the notion of a (possible) entity world, fact world, and actual (current) world. Sentence meaning is ambiguously discussed and equated with knowledge (about things, facts, concepts, etc. of a UoD which is exchangeable among users). Eventually, sentence meaning is reduced to its truth value extension.

expression of a view of an enterprise and it describes the classifications and the laws of the UoD. It is also a valid model of the enterprise, namely the one which defines a:

long term unrestricted model (or view) of the enterprise (ANSI/SPARC 1975).

This model has been called an enterprise description (Senko 1977), and it is claimed to model all relevant aspects of an enterprise into a single consistent 'theory of enterprise'. Thus the fact-based school assumes that the abstraction system can be 'perceived' in a manner similar to the other parts of the UoD and its content can be validated by agreement without much dissent. Moreover, the existence of this agreement is emphasized as a necessary condition for the successful use of the IS: the fact-based school states that any meaningful exchange of utterances depends upon the prior existence of an agreed set of formal semantic and syntactic rules. The recipient of the utterances must use only the agreed upon rules to interpret the received utterances, if it is to mean the same as that which was meant by the utterer. In van Griethuysen (1982) this is called the 'Helsinki principle'.

On the one hand, the fact-based school assumes that the content of the abstraction system expresses a consensus (agreement) among the IS users, and, on the other hand, that IS users can provide good reasons which support this consensus. Both of these assumptions must clearly hold if the CS is to represent such an agreement. However, the fact-based school does not provide any detailed analysis about how these goals can be met in any practical situation. Neither empirical studies are provided which demonstrate that these conditions do hold in practice nor theoretical arguments why the consensual conditions should be expected to be true in practice. The problematic nature of these assumptions should be evident from the social context issues discussed in section 6.3. It has been known for a long time in the literature on the social impact of IS, e.g. Kling 1980, Hirschheim 1986, Wagner (1993).

7.2.5 Classification of fact-based approaches

In this section we shall classify fact-based approaches. Our starting point for the classification is to examine how many basic categories (primitives) are needed in alternative fact-based approaches to represent facts in the UoD. In this regard, we can find a great deal of variation between data models. Consequently, there seems to be no consensus among the experts of data modeling on how to model the UoD and what are its basic, fundamental constituents over the general definitions of entity and fact discussed above.

Data models differ by the number and types of primitives which they employ to model the phenomena in the UoD. Data modeling primitives are the particular constructs which a data model suggests for faithfully representing the meanings in the application domain, i.e. the semantics of the UoD. By looking at the number and types of these primitives of different data models, we can distinguish the following five, rough classes of fact-based data modeling approaches:

- interpreted logic-based approaches,
- entity-based approaches,
- binary and elementary *n*-ary relationships approaches,
- entity–relationship–attribute approaches, and
- approaches deploying higher level models.

These approaches are depicted in more detail in table 7.1. The last row of this table also includes examples of data models in the different approaches. The sample models have been selected from the vast literature (van Griethuysen 1982; Tsichritzis and Lochovsky 1982; Peckham and Maryanski 1988). The number of data models in different classes does not, however, reflect the popularity of alternative data model classes in the fact-based school. In principle, those approaches applying two or three basic primitives seem to be the most popular. The historical evolution also seems to move from the approaches at the center to those at the borders of the table; the current interest in the fact-based school is in higher level models and in the applications of logic (see e.g. Meersman and Steel 1985).

Class	Interpreted predicate logic	Entity-based approaches	Binary and elementary relationships	Entity-attribute relationships	Higher-level models
Central primitive	atomic fact	entity (function)	entity relationship	entity attribute relationship	entity attribute relationship specialization generalization inheritance complex objects methods polymorphism
Data Model	Interpreted predicate logic	Semantic hierarchic model, Single-name category model	Data semantics, object-role DIAM, semantic data model, semantic association model	EAR, Info-logical model, Grammatical database model	Object schema model TAXIS, CIAM, Set-function methodology semantic data model object-oriented, entity-relationship model NIAM, semantic hierarchic model, functional data model

Table 7.1: Classification of fact-based approaches

The rationale for distinguishing between alternative approaches is the following. In the interpreted logic-based approaches the only prominent concept is the notion of the fact, i.e. the internal structure of facts remains largely uninterpreted. This gives a greater degree of freedom to the designer on how to compose facts in the UoD (Lyytinen 1982; Schmid 1983).

The entity-based approaches directly support one primitive, i.e. that of an entity. Other primitives are supported only indirectly by seeing them as subsetting and ordering mechanisms for the modeled entities. The facts thus describe that an entity exists, or that it belongs to a set or to a particular place in an ordered sequence.

The entity–relationship approaches use two main primitives: an entity, and a relationship. With these you describe the following situations: an entity exists, or it participates in relationships with some other entities. Two decisions in the design of the entity–relationship data models influence the structuring of facts in these approaches:

(1) what is the allowed degree of relationships, and

(2) how the relationships are formed.

The first decision leads to distinguishing between binary and n-ary data models. The second decision leads to forming three general classes of entity–relationship models: entity–relationship, entity–attribute, and entity–function approaches. These models differ in their view of the relationship: in the first one the fact is seen as a relationship between entities, in the second the fact is defined as a predicate that holds between the entities, and in the third it is a mapping (function) where some entities belong to the domain of the function and the others to its range.

In the entity–attribute–relationship models three fundamental primitives are applied: entity, attribute and relationship. Here each entity may possess zero, one or more attributes, and it can participate in zero, one or more relationships. Facts are created when an entity exists, when it has attributes, or when it participates in a relationship. In addition, some approaches allow the relationships to posses their own attributes. This occurs when a relationship has an attribute and records a fact.

The higher level models usually augment the entity, entity–relationship, or entity–relationship–attribute models with some richer semantic primitives. These are currently known as semantic data models and provide additional primitives to represent necessary facts. The advocates of such models argue that the application of more powerful semantic modeling primitives leads to a more 'structured' interpretation of the UoD. Examples of such higher level structuring mechanisms are: generalization hierarchies (a part-time employee is a person), attributes applicable for a set of entities (the average salary of employees in a department), time and events (hiring and firing of an employee),complex objects (such as hierarchical decomposition of a project organization), and so forth. In other models, these structural facts can only be described with an additional effort, for example, by using predicate logic as a mechanism to extend the basic model (for fuller accounts see e.g. Teorey *et al.* 1986; Batini *et al.* 1986; Hull and King 1987; Peckham and Maryanski 1988).

The most recent addition to fact-oriented data modeling is the object orientation. It can be seen as a natural evolutionary extension to semantic data models (Mattos *et al.* 1992, Kim and Lochovsky 1990). Though object orientation is difficult to characterize concisely, one of its goals is to further increase the semantic modeling power of the data model. This is achieved by extending the static view of the entity-based modeling, i.e. declarative and structural properties of objects with procedural properties. This leads to an integrated modeling approach that captures the static declarative data model (as done in E-R models), the static structural data model (as done in semantic models with generalization, classification, and aggregation) and the dynamic behavior model (with procedural properties called methods). Therefore it is currently customary to say that an object orientation is an evolutionary extension to entity-based modeling approaches (Gorman and Choobineh 1991).

The aim to model entities and their behaviors together in an integrated manner is accomplished in object-oriented models through methods specification which are specifically defined for individual entity classes. This mechanism makes computer operations in object-oriented models entity-type specific. Object orientation aims at placing specific information about entities at the most appropriate level through the application of generalization and inheritance principles. This is accomplished by allocating information in the model only to those objects in which it most naturally occurs. For example, a student-id is only applicable to a student and not to a person in general. Therefore, it should only occur as a property of a student which is a sub-class of persons.

Object orientation also supports complex objects (which have their own properties and can participate in relationships). An example of a complex object is a car engine which is made of several parts (entities) such as a carburetor, pistons, or valves. The introduction of complex objects makes the representation of complex real world structures more natural such as those found in engineering disciplines or geographical applications (Maier 1989).

Through these extensions object-oriented data models can more easily enforce several important modeling principles in addition to generalization and inheritance. Such modeling principles are 'information hiding', abstract data type encapsulation and polymorphic types. Information hiding means that for each model component only those parts of the system are specified which are needed to understand that part of the system. By using method specifications object-oriented models also support abstract data type encapsulation. This implies that the data in each object type can be operated only through a well-defined (object) interface which provides a set of generic operations which preserve the consistency of the data. No other mechanisms to change the state of the object are available. Generalization and inheritance provide an efficient mechanism to master the model's complexity and to economize the specification of the data (Gorman and Choobineh 1991). Finally, the object-oriented data models provide polymorphic types, i.e. they can represent the same property in different ways. From different contexts, one can even view a relationship as an entity, or a property as an entity (i.e. red may be a property of a car, or an entity of the class 'paint').

Adopting object orientation in data modeling seems to somewhat relax the strict ontological assumptions of the fact-based school. Especially the support for polymorphism implies that an entity can be seen both as an entity and a relationship. The motivation to support this principle shows that the researchers in object-oriented data modeling do not necessarily argue which semantic primitive is best for a given context, and therefore leave the decision to the user. At the same time, object-oriented modeling approaches have relaxed some epistemological assumptions such as the independence of the knowledge of the inquirer, i.e. that a data modeler can know the reality with certainty. This implies that some objects are based on the designer's choice (see e.g. Martin and Odell 1992 p. 234). In the same vein some advocates of object-oriented modeling state that reality is composed of concepts and objects to which the concepts apply — hence admitting that reality is partly 'determined' by those concepts which the modelers possess.

Yet, it is obvious that the main stipulations of object-oriented modelers reiterate the fundamental assumptions of the fact-based school. This becomes evident if we examine some of the widely used text books and reviews of object-oriented modeling (see e.g. Martin and Odell 1991; Rumbaugh *et al.* 1991; Jacobson 1992; Mattos *et al.* 1992). Some quotations suffice to make our point: Martin and Odell (1992 p. 67) argue that 'OO analysis reflects reality more naturally than the more traditional systems analysis', Gorman and Choobineh (1991) write that object-oriented data models represent 'relevant abstractions' in a particular application environment; finally Rumbaugh *et al.* (1991 p. 4) tersely state that 'object-oriented modeling and design is a new way of thinking about software based on abstractions that exist in the real world'. Overall, it is easy to support the claim that object-oriented data models draw upon the four principles of the fact-based school: correspondence, objectivity, excluded middle and language neutrality. For this reason we have treated them here as the most encompassing and complex representatives of the fact-based school.

7.2.6 Possible directions for improvements

Data modeling theory in the fact-based school emanates from the assumption that data models and information systems reflect states and laws of some external objective reality. This assumption is further refined by formal models which represent the world in some rigorous language. In this sense the fact-based school is but one proponent of the rationalistic and empiricist tradition of science. Its strength is the emphasis on formal rigor and objectivity. These are used to achieve the goals of reproducability and reliability in scientific research which assumes that all trained observers at all times should be able to reach the same conclusions. It also leads one to focus on systematic methods and tools which safeguard against the fallibility of the human mind in coping with the complexities of IS development. Therefore, the school, in general, has focused largely on developing formal methods to help in designing and implementing information systems. It has filled the field with methods, tools, phase structures and more or less well-defined data modeling methodologies. In particular, it has strived to ease the formalization of the object systems (when conceived in terms of linguistic phenomena), and thereby to manage efficiently the mapping of the language into some technical implementation. In this task it has been quite successful and the art of managing and formalizing large portions of business languages has made large advances.

No wonder then, that the school has been quite naive about whether its goals and ideals are applicable in describing uses of symbols in business organizations. Moreover, even if they are, will their achievement lead to desirable results from the viewpoint of the whole social organization? This has led the fact-based school to largely ignore the study of social processes which surround design, maintenance and implementation of large scale business data models. Similarly, it has ignored the fact that data modeling is first and foremost a social and organizational activity and very little, if anything (excluding consulting folklore), is known how data modeling is exercised in practice and what its impacts are on organizations, their information systems management, and business operations. The espoused view of data modeling is that of an engineering discipline: data modelers come armed with good tools and methods when problems arise, they diagnose the situation with clarity and ease, they build formal representations which solve the identified problems, and thereafter they leave the organizational terrain to work in some other field. Clearly, this is a fairytale, told to retain the rationalistic image of the fact-based school.

Progress in the fact-based school is hindered by the misconceptions concerning the nature of reality and modeling and the nature of language which make it naive in relation to how symbols make-up and enter the domain of business. It is, however, conceivable that improvements in the fact-based school can be made by relaxing some of its philosophical beliefs and principles yet retaining the basic desire for a formalistic and analytic approach to language. Moreover, several improvements in fact-based modeling formalisms and tools can be made which make them more handy for real life situations. On the theory plane these improvements would lead to applying richer and more realistic theories of language which have been developed in analytic philosophy over the past twenty years. Though none of these approaches have been really tried out and suffer from complex and often times cumbersome formalisms so that such improvements in the practice will be

difficult to realize they provide ample potential for further improvements.
There are additionally often possible areas of theoretical improvements.

We can relax the principles of the objective belief by making adjustments
to them. This can be achieved in several ways. First, by making a clearer
distinction between 'sense' and 'reference' and by arguing that there is only
a 'correspondence' between signs and mental constructs (ideas, concepts)
through which the access to 'reality' is achieved we can free the school from
the naive version of the 'picture' theory of meaning. This idea is in line with
Frege's original program, as he never accepted a naive one-level description
of the relationship between language and reality (Dummett 1981). This idea
has been further refined by possible world semantics and intensional logics
(Montague 1974, Dowty et al. 1981) which help to formally capture propositions which can possibly be true in some world. Second, the principle of
objectivity can also be changed into a more evolutionary one by accepting
that concepts are not fixed and their construction and evolution can be
supported using mechanisms of formal concept refinement and analysis (see
Kangassalo 1982). This idea still retains the goal of formalistic tractability
and 'objectivity'. In this way concepts are 'objective' to the extent they can
be shown to be derived using some systematic and clearly defined principles.
Accordingly, there is no requirement to assume a Platonistic idea world, or
to subsume a realistic position in relation to reality. Giving up the principles
of excluded middle and language neutrality are more difficult in the fact-
based school, and there are no good examples of well-behaving formalistic
systems that would do this well. With respect to language neutrality Barwise's theory of 'situation semantics' (Barwise 1983) can offer some help, but
its problem is an excess and overload of mathematical formalism by which
the notion of 'context' is brought in. In relation to the excluded middle the
most promising alternative is to base the formal calculus of facts on fuzzy
logic which allows different levels of 'truth' to be formally manipulated.

Giving up the idea of a descriptive belief would lead to extensions of
original model theory and semantics of predicate logic (or tense logics). For
example adding deontic or epistemic operators to facts allows one to include
in modeling, notions of belief, i.e. distinctions between that something is
the case and what is one's certainty of this, or expressing the idea that
something must be the case. Such extensions have been worked out and tried
out in areas like truth-maintenance in databases (Dhar and Jarke 1988),
or the use of deontic operators to express obligations and commitments
in information systems (Lee 1988). If such extensions are made available
in modeling formalisms (for possible candidates see Dietz 1994, Lee and
Donaldson-Dewitz 1990) this easily leads beyond the basic postulates of the
fact-based school and will change the perspective on focusing on social rules
that make creation of commitments and obligations possible, or justify the
maintenance of some beliefs. Finally, the consensus belief can also be relaxed
by giving up the idea of global consistency of the schema and information

base that is enforced centrally. Instead a conceptual schema can be seen as a federation of conceptual schemata where each local subschema is only locally consistent, but the global level does not assume any consistency or consensus. Instead, different local schemata define which of their parts are seen globally. This approach also suggests negotiations as a means to resolve possible conflicts between different local views (such as naming conflicts, semantic inconsistencies, etc.). This approach is known as the theory of federated databases (Sheth and Larson 1990).

Though the above has dealt with possible improvements on a theoretical level, there is also the need to improve the art and practice of fact-based data modeling. Much of these stem from the simple and not yet developed body of tools and principles of fact-based data modeling. Here, the following four seem to be the most urgent needs:

(1) integration of static and dynamic modeling,

(2) management of incomplete specifications,

(3) modularization and management of large data models, and

(4) improving the semantic richness of data models.

Each of these addresses a specific and important practical problem.

Most of our discussion above dealt with the static aspects of data modeling. Yet, one vital aspect of representing the semantics of data is how it behaves over time as a 'reflection' of real world changes. So far the most prominent way of dealing with the dynamics has been by way of 'negative modeling', i.e. by specifying how data is not allowed to change. This is done through integrity constraints that are enforced at all times (van Griethuysen 1982). The other route, by defining what are admitted changes and how these changes can be realized, has been a much less explored area. In this sense, the emergence of object-oriented modeling is a truly remarkable improvement, as it tries to capture both the negative and positive mechanisms of modeling dynamics.

Most data modeling literature assumes that the modelers can arrive almost immediately at a complete and consistent data model. Nothing, however, can be further from the truth. Therefore, the theory and practice of data modeling must improve mechanisms by which incomplete and inconsistent data models can be managed, and develop theories as to what extent and how different types of incompleteness and inconsistency can be tolerated during design and how they can be resolved incrementally. This topic is addressed in research areas such as schema integration, integrity enforcement, requirements capture, and information and enterprise architectures.

Many times the UoDD description becomes extensively large and therefore difficult to manage. The idea of one flat description of the UoDD has been dominant in the research and it is also pervasive in many of the axioms in the area. However, fact-based modeling could and should be extended with mechanisms and principles by which the management of data and their specifications could be modularized. Some mechanisms of object-oriented data modeling such as inheritance and aggregation principles are first steps in the right direction but clearly are not sufficient. More powerful mechanisms are needed to cluster, integrate and hierarchically organize large real life conceptual schemata. Here we need improvement both in the theory and the tools of data modeling.

The evolution of fact-based data modeling has involved a continuous growth and invention of new semantic structuring mechanisms which have continually increased the complexity of the conceptual modeling languages. There is no reason to believe that this road to improvement has been totally exhausted though the pace of change is currently much slower and new principles have not been promulgated with the same vigor as in the early 1980s.

7.3 Rule-based School

If rationalistic assumptions in the fact-based school are relaxed so that standards of objectivity, correspondence, and language neutrality become empty words, and the goals of data modeling are conceived in a less rationalistic light, a different view of data modeling activity emerges. This is called the rule-based approach and is examined next.

In the rule-based approaches a data model describes rules which govern the uses of signs and symbols in organizational behaviors and thereby attach specific meanings to the organizational vocabulary. Therefore these approaches are largely derived from the concept of a rule. In general, a rule is regarded as a general prescription that governs the generation, meaning and use of linguistic expressions both informal and formal as are included in the information system.

It is important to note that in social theory a rule has a different ontological status than a fact, because it is the outcome of social habitualization, negotiation and other types of social interaction. Rules are socially produced and maintained by being continuously applied and instantiated. Thus, we can see this school to be a 'constructivist' one. This school presumes that by constructing and sharing linguistic and other rules, the participants (from within and without the organization) construct a social reality at the same time when they share it. Social reality in the rule-based approaches is not 'objectively' given and 'out there', but rather constructed and enacted. The IS intervenes directly in this process and hence does not merely mirror a given reality. Rules are also different in another way. They do not describe linguistic reality as such. Instead, they describe (and prescribe) general capabilities to generate and understand instances of linguistic expressions. In this sense, by describing rules, rule-based approaches aim at revealing and developing social knowledge and competence to produce and interpret linguistic expressions. In brief, they describe normative patterns of linguistic behaviors.

Rule-based approaches form a minority position in the data modeling field. It has been pursued by few researchers and its history can be dated back to the late 1970s and early 1980s (Goldkuhl and Lyytinen 1982a,b; Stamper 1979). Therefore, it should not be surprising that rule-based data modeling methods are much less developed than their fact-based counterparts. Moreover, these approaches have not been widely applied in their full form outside academia and experience of their usefulness is limited. One reason for this is their inner complexity and highly developed theoretical vocabulary which is difficult to adopt for practicing IS professionals. Some experience of the practical applicability of these approaches, however, does exist from Sweden (Goldkuhl and Rostlinger 1987), and the U.K. (Dobson *et al.* 1991). Some ideas from the rule-based approaches have also been adopted in the development and analysis of EDI applications (Donaldson-Dewitz 1991, Lee and Donaldson-Dewitz 1990), and in designing new CSCW applications (Flores *et al.* 1988; Malone *et al.* 1988). Finally, several practicing data modeling consultants have in recent years adopted ideas and assumptions that are similar to the basic beliefs underlying the rule-based approaches. Their reason for adopting these ideas and assumptions are the surprisingly poor results of applying fact-based approaches in large IS development projects (*cf.* Goodhue *et al.* 1992a,b).

So far there have been no extensive studies of the theoretical foundations and evolution of the rule-based approaches. Therefore what follows in this section is a modest attempt to gather and summarize some of the foundations for the rule-based approaches (see however Stamper 1987). This attempt is handicapped by the fact that rule-based approaches are less developed and their terminology is still under constant change. Though rule-based approaches have been developed largely independently from one another, there are a number of general ideas upon which all draw. These are discussed in the next subsections. We examine in more detail two prominent research projects pursuing rule-based data modeling: LEGOL/NORMA (LEGally Oriented Language) (*cf.* Stamper 1973, 1979; Stamper *et al.* 1988, 1991, Backhouse 1991), and the Language Action (LA) view and its associated SAMPO method (*cf.* Goldkuhl and Lyytinen 1982b, Auramaki *et al.* 1988, 1992a,b). Our discussion will proceed as follows. In section 7.3.1 we describe the historical origins of the school. Section 7.3.2 discusses its theoretical roots. Section 7.3.3 examines the conceptual base of the rule-based school. Section 7.3.4 discusses the theoretical foundations of the rule-based approaches. In 7.3.5 we analyze one major representative of the rule-based school the LEGOL/NORMA approach. In section 7.3.6 we illustrate another representative of the rule-based school — the language action view. The section concludes with a discussion of the nature of the modeling activity as conceived in the rule-based approaches and provides some examples of data modeling in the rule-based school. Section 7.4 summarizes the principal differences between fact- and rule-based approaches to data modeling.

7.3.1 Historical roots

The historical roots of the rule-based approaches are less connected to the evolution of IS development methods and technologies than was the case with the fact-based school. Some historical predecessors can, however, be traced. These are:

(1) concept of information in IS and its impact on information requirements specification,

(2) evolution of high level organizational specification methods and their interpretation in communication-oriented terms, and

(3) studies in legal informatics and their application to ISD problems.

7.3.1.1 Concept of information

One of the major conceptual landmarks in the evolution of the rule-based school was Stamper's book on information (Stamper 1973). For the first time this book provided a systematic treatment of the nature of information in business organizations. It applied a theory of signs to classify different conceptions of information and demonstrated how these could be applied in the IS field. Stamper also made clear that the nature of data (information) is much more elusive, complex and variable, than has ever been accepted by the fact-based school. This revelation also led Stamper to criticize the 'received' notions of information and their applicability in IS. In particular, he pointed out the need to develop socially sensitive pragmatic and semantic concepts of information. Such concepts could help in information requirements specification, i.e. in determining the business meaning and impact of the data supplied by the information system. This observation further led to the establishment of the LEGOL-project and the design of the LEGOL/NORMA language.

7.3.1.2 High level organization models

The early works of Langefors (1963) inspired the development of several functional system design methods, most prominently ISAC (Lundeberg *et al.* 1981). Among the features of ISAC which directly applied Langefors ideas were change analysis and precedence analysis (Lundeberg *et al.* 1981). Change analysis attempted to identify and describe a set of desirable and acceptable organizational changes which could provide a basis for developing an IS that is organizationally acceptable and desirable. Currently the ideas of change analysis have been revitalized under the term business re-engineering (approximately 15 years after its invention!). A method to support change analysis was also provided in the form of a graphical language called 'Activity graphs'. These graphs were primarily used to analyze interactions between organizational activities and to assess an IS's role in these interactions. These interactions were modeled by illustrating material and information flows between material and information sets and activities. The graphs also provided symbols to represent material and information stores, and to depict precedence relations between activities, flows and stores. Precedence analysis diagrammed the inputs and intermediate information states that were needed to achieve a desired outcome. For the purpose of IS analysis it considered the documentation of intermediate states (by data structures) more important than the inference processes by which one information state could be derived from one or more previous states.

Originally, the activity graphs were interpreted functionally. Moreover, they were composed in a hierarchical fashion starting from a high-level functional description of the organizational domain. Based on several field studies and experiences from a large body of application projects (where these graphs were not used as intended) the interpretation of the graphs, however, was gradually changed. This led to a number of criticisms against the first generation *A*-graphs (*cf.* Goldkuhl 1984). These criticisms prompted researchers to seek new interpretations of the activity graphs. Goldkuhl and Lyytinen (1984) suggested that they represented reconstructions of rules that govern organizational behaviors (both physical and symbolic) in some organizational domain. In particular, the graphs model organizations in terms of their authority and command structures, and how these structures allocate lines of responsibility over actions to different organizational actors. At the same time it was realized that the division of labor and areas of responsibility represented in these graphs also were the social structures which enabled various organizational actions. This changed the interpretation of the flows to became more active and constructive: they were seen to represent rule governed interactions between multiple organizational actors. These interactions would not just represent existing organizational structures but also point to their continuous remaking (emergence). All this led to the development of speech act based models of IS specification (see e.g. Goldkuhl 1984, Goldkuhl and Lyytinen 1984) such as SAMPO (Auramaki *et al.* 1988, 1992a,b; Lyytinen and Lehtinen 1984), and SIM (Goldkuhl and Rostlinger 1987).

7.3.1.3 Legal informatics

The third leg of the evolution of the rule-based school was legal informatics which can be seen as the application of computers in jurisdiction (Stamper 1979). Legal informatics is interesting in this connection because it deals with the problem of how the abstract rules of the law can be related to the real world of business. Usually human administrators have to make judgements regarding which of the myriad of case details count as the legally significant facts to which the abstract rules apply. When we try to automate this, the semantic issues of what counts as 'legally significant' facts and how these facts are to be interpreted become a major challenge. In legal cases it is not sufficient to know how a series of arguments can be logically strung together to resolve the case. In brief, the main question of legal informatics is the problem of resolving conflicting meanings about the interpretation of which facts are legally significant and which of several rules apply to them. This observation has a close affinity to a key task in

ISD, viz. resolving and defining meanings of linguistic expressions that are
used in communications through the IS to propose new ideas, arguments
or situational interpretations. In particular, ISD deals with automating the
bureaucratic rules that define appropriate and generalized behavioral patterns within the organization. These form the interactions through which
the relevant meanings emerge in the organizational discourse (Lee 1984).

7.3.2 Theoretical roots

The concepts underlying the rule-based school have been widely discussed in
several disciplines. The philosophical origins were discussed in the previous
chapter. Here we shall only briefly summarize the theoretical origins of the
rule-based school in the following fields of study: linguistics, organizational
and sociological theory, and law.

7.3.2.1 Linguistics

In the rule-based approaches the focus is on modeling linguistic activities
which will surround and make possible the use of the information system.
Therefore scholars in the rule-based school have eagerly applied theories
of signs and languages in developing appropriate means to describe data.
These theories have ranged from theories of syntax to semantic theories of
languages (see e.g. Lyons 1977; Stamper 1987; Lyytinen 1985). Of special
importance has been to propose categories and constructs for analyzing linguistic structures with the goal of more precise and systematic descriptions
of the underlying linguistic rules. Many of these attempts have followed functional schools of linguistics such as Leech's (1974), or Lyons's (1977) functional grammar. For examples, see Goldkuhl and Lyytinen (1982b; 1984),
Weigand (1991) and Stamper (1987).

Though important insights have been obtained from applying linguistic
theories of syntax and semantics to data modeling (see e.g. Lyytinen 1985;
Weigand 1991) the major focus in the rule-based school has been on the
study and application of pragmatics to data modeling. The area of pragmatics aims to understand uses and impacts of language in the context of
organizational action. In more concrete terms the interest has been on modeling communications between users of the IS. Usually such analyses have
been conducted using constructs from speech act theory (Austin 1962; Searle
1969, 1979; Searle and Vanderveken 1985), and from theories in discourse
analysis and pragmatics (Lyons 1977; Brown and Yule 1984; Levinson 1983;
Grice 1975).

7.3.2.2 Organizational and sociological theory

While the influence of the hermeneutic and late Wittgensteinian linguistic theory gained ground in the data modeling literature, several scholars also looked for inspiration from organizational and sociological theories which view organizations as negotiated orders, cultures and the like
(Morgan 1986). Proponents of the rule-based school have applied theories
of organizational learning (Argyris and Schon 1978), ethnography and an-
thropology (Schutz 1967; Garfinkel 1967; van Maanen 1979), interpretive

sociology (Winch 1958), and sociology of knowledge (Berger and Luckmann 1967). A prominent source of theoretical inspiration has also been Habermas' theory of communicative action and universal pragmatics (Habermas 1979, 1984, 1987).

7.3.2.3 Law

It is no accident that proponents of the rule-based approach have also been interested in the theory of law. First of all, understanding of the nature of rules and norms comes mainly from studies in legal theory (see e.g. Twining and Miers 1976). Another area of interest are formal theories of commitment and obligation more often called deontic logics (see e.g. von Wright 1963, 1968). Finally, several scholars have studied the parallels between how the domain of legal discourse (called jurisdiction) and the UoD are established and structured. In particular, research has focused on how the evidence for legal argument is established and what similarities this has with the process of how the UoDD is structured. This leads to seeking criteria which are used in social practices to classify and count some phenomena as instances of particular social facts (see e.g. Stamper 1987, 1990). A classical analysis of semantic disputes in legal activity is Murphy and Rawlings (1981).

7.3.3 Basic view of IS and data modeling

As noted above the conceptual base of the rule-based school has mainly been derived from hermeneutics, late Wittgensteinian theory of language and pragmatics. In line with these theories the fundamental postulate in the rule-based school is that the interpretation of computer-based data must be consistent with the meanings conveyed by the users when they follow rules which they find applicable to a given situation. The rule-based school therefore focuses on the modeling of meaning as it is captured in some domain of natural language discourse. In general the strategy is to study how the meaning is conveyed by natural language, and what aspects of language have to be captured by a machine readable representation of data so that computer-based information systems can function as an effective substitute or improvement for free-form natural language communication. This leads one to consider the regularities (and idiosyncracies) of language which enable a community of people to communicate with each other. Therefore the rule-based school focuses on the semantic and pragmatic subdomains in their modeling efforts. Moreover, it denies that semantics can be understood without considering the pragmatic and contextual aspects of language simultaneously.

In this section we outline the fundamentals of data modeling as it is typically represented in the rule-based school. We shall explore the definition of the IS in rule-based models and what implications it has on data modeling activity.

7.3.3.1 Definition of information system

The conceptual base of the rule-based school is derived from its definition of an IS. In the rule-based approaches an information system is seen primarily as a linguistic communication medium between different groups of people (see figure 7.2). In brief, an information system consists of different groups of people communicating in a formal language (Goldkuhl and Lyytinen 1982a; Nissen 1980) which is stored, manipulated and transmitted with the help of information technology.

The language includes formal messages that are meant to be exchanged between members of an organization. Thus, the definition poses the following question when developing an IS: who is communicating with whom and on which topic. The communications through an IS create, set up, control, and maintain social interactions in an organizational context. The special characteristics of an IS as a communication tool derive from the formal nature of its language, and the prespecified ways of its use as determined by the information technology and organizational rules and habits which surround the uses of the IS. From this perspective, a formal language is at the very core of any IS.

The formal nature of the language means that the syntax, semantics and parts of pragmatics (Lyytinen 1985) of the messages are closed. In other words, the structure, the content, and uses (intentions) of messages are systematically and rigorously formulated. Correspondingly, the IS should include messages with a correct syntactic structure, a meaningful semantic content, and an acceptable and significant pragmatic use. Because the language is formal, it precludes certain topics of communication via an IS (and facilitates others). The advantage of the formalization is that it makes it possible to draw formal inferences using inference rules represented in programs, and axioms stored in a database.

The communicated messages have effects on work duties. They concern important topics that are at the core of organizational action such as accepting orders, sending bills, planning of a new production line, etc. Much (but not all) communication is also aimed at achieving a common understanding of the communicated issue among the organization's members, or those interacting with it (customers, suppliers, etc).

The prespecified ways in which the IS may be used entails that the IS follows a systematic, prespecified pattern. Usually IS use assumes fixed and differentiated user roles (clerk, manager, etc.), and well-defined usage principles in terms of timing and interaction with the system, organizational procedures associated with the IS use, etc. All this amounts to a decrease in effort in repetitive and common communication tasks (Berger and Luckmann 1967).

7.3.3.2 *Implications*

In the formal language view of an IS, the communications take place by storing, retrieving, inferring and transmitting messages according to certain rules. The key idea is to see language as a rule-based system. The formal language is based on intersubjective rules shared between communicators; these define which message exchanges are significant through an IS, and

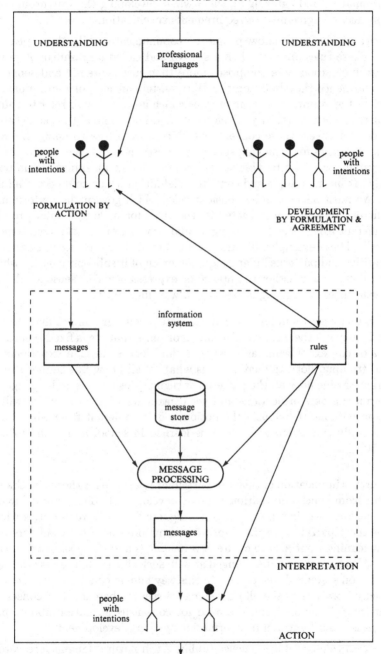

Figure 7.2: Information system in the rule-based approach

how and when they should take place. These rules are defined beforehand
by formulating and agreeing on them when developing the IS (through development and agreement of requirements specifications).

Basically, the rules allow people to communicate while they speak or
write. These rules are viewed as a system and called a grammar. A grammar as understood here comprises more than just syntactic and semantic
rules and hence they build on the Wittgensteinian idea of a grammar. In
addition, the grammar consists of rules which govern how to refer to things
in different contexts (theory of reference) and how the reality is structured.
Moreover, it covers those conventions which govern how to apply different
words or phrases for achieving specific purposes. For instance, in social welfare systems we must be able to deal with different meanings of the term
'family'. It has no unique and consistent definition which could cover all the
laws. We must also carefully consider rules which govern the performance
of different types of speech acts, i.e. the rules for making a valid promise
are different from those for making a valid proposition (truthful 'statement
of fact'). These examples illustrate that there exists a complex system of
regularities and patterns in language use, much of it subconscious, by which
people determine whether a sentence or expression makes sense at all and
if so what it might be (e.g. a promise, a warning, etc.):

> These regularities in language Wittgenstein calls 'grammar', and they
> go far beyond the element of meaning or sense that stays fixed regard-
> less of context. Grammar is what a child learns through experience
> and training, not explanation; it is what we all know but cannot say.
> Grammar includes all the patterns or regularities or rules in language,
> permitting new projections and yet controlling what projections will
> be acceptable. (Obviously the notion is quite different from what we
> ordinarily call 'grammar', which is learned in school.). (Pitkin 1973,
> p. 80)

A further implication of this is of particular relevance for the social change
which accompanies information systems development. Linguistic behavior,
(e.g. speaking, writing, pointing, gesturing, etc.) exhibits regularities which
enable those partaking in the respective community not only to understand
given meanings, but also to create new meanings and share these with each
other. Also the rules can be changed at will, such as is often the case through
information systems development. In this way human communication differs
markedly from animal signalling systems. However, there must be consensus
about the rule changes and the need for consensus formation about rules
changes is often forgotten in information systems development.

Whereas rule-based approaches (unlike AI in natural language research)
do not aim at duplicating all of the features and capabilities of communication in natural language, their central thesis is — following their basic

view of the IS — that if computer-systems are to improve communication at all, then they must be built around an explicit understanding of certain essential aspects of the language of user communities. Otherwise the computer-based system is isolated from the way in which users communicate and looses touch with their forms of life and thereby their information needs. There are as many user communities as there are languages spoken. The term language is used here in a fairly broad sense. It covers not only languages of different countries, but also the technical vocabularies of different professions and organizational specializations which are superimposed on the 'natural' grammar of the 'common', everyday language. The rules by which lawyers, accountants, engineers, etc. express themselves may be more similar between professionals of different natural language communities (say English vs. German) than between members of the different professions in the same natural language community (e.g. engineers and lawyers of one country).

From a rule-based perspective, the designer of an information system is faced with a 'Tower of Babel problem'. He has to deal with a plurality of views (horizons) and meanings. There is no objectively correct view, rather the organization is made up of several professional language communities (forms of life) none of which have a monopoly on the correct use of language (including criteria of truth). Meanings are not only influenced by conflict of interest and the functional definition of labor, but also by the social stratification of organizational participants: the influence on language from socio-economic status, union or party ties, regional and ethnic origins, etc.

From the rule-based perspective data modeling has a dual function: to improve the communication within each language community, yet also to improve the cross linkages between different language communities. There is the potential risk that by striving to gain acceptance of an information system from adherents of one view of the firm, e.g. the users' vs. top managements', the design looses its grip on the overall communication problem.

7.3.4 Three beliefs underlying the rule-based approaches

The previous, general comments reveal that rule-based approaches focus on a number of issues which the fact-based approaches so far have by and large ignored. Because the IS definition is based on understanding language as a social phenomenon (Lewis 1969), information systems are primarily 'social systems' which have been 'only technically implemented' (Goldkuhl and Lyytinen 1982a). The following three beliefs characterize rule-based approaches in more detail:

(1) an information system is tied to action, that is action which is oriented towards other people or their community institutions.

(2) an information system is a contextualized, institutionalized phenomenon (it is an institution which is itself surrounded with expectations and social rules), and

(3) an information system is purposefully developed and developing or changing.

7.3.4.1 The action belief

The action belief refers to the observation that the formulation and use of formal messages in the IS is a form of human, rule governed behavior (Goldkuhl and Lyytinen 1984). Uses of IS constitute actions which count as doing something significant for the IS users (Lehtinen and Lyytinen 1986). The meaning of messages produced in the IS cannot be separated from the human action associated with producing these messages (Searle 1969). The study of the meaning of a sentence implies that we must probe whether it expresses the human behavior of making statements, say the marketing director's stating his other beliefs, or whether it has some more subtle meaning (e.g. irony where the opposite is meant of what is said). In any case, rule-based modeling suggests that we must study the formal conditions which make significant human behavior possible: viz. make a sentence a meaningful utterance in a social context and lead to an understanding of the typical implications and effects of significant human behaviors.

It follows that the rule-based approaches are interested in all kinds of significant human behavior not only in making statements (descriptive fallacy), but also in giving orders, making promises, classifying things, etc. (Lyytinen and Lehtinen 1984; Kimbrough and Lee 1986; Lee 1984; Searle 1969). Given the wide range of possible language uses, information systems are designed for a limited set of linguistic human behaviors to be mediated by information technology. It follows that an IS supports a specific class of linguistic discourse (Lyytinen and Lehtinen 1984) and that information modeling should be seen as a study of message meaning (expressed in speech acts). This includes the study of the formal properties of speech acts and their possible combinations in discourses (Flores and Ludlow 1980; Lyytinen and Lehtinen 1984; Winograd and Flores 1986).

7.3.4.2 The institutional belief

The institutional belief emphasizes that an IS is a social institution. Like an institution it creates classifications of types of acts and actors that are reciprocally recognized and maintained. Only agreed on forms of IS use are enforced. The institutionalization can only proceed in an interpretation and action field (which is essentially the same as what Wittgenstein called 'forms of life'). A field is formed by a set of related social practices such as producing and dispatching things, selling airline seats, taking courses, etc. Understanding message meaning cannot be separated from those social practices from which the message exchange arises. Therefore, the drive towards an all-embracing consensus on language meaning probably is a useless effort.

All this suggests that information modeling forms an activity by which a communication institution is created and maintained (Lyytinen 1986).

Therefore, the success of information modeling depends on available mechanisms that safeguard the acceptance of the institution and on the extent to which this institution is in harmony with the forms of life in which it is to be embedded.

7.3.4.3 The change belief

The change belief captures the insight that the meaning of messages changes with the historical evolution of the language and the social practices in which an IS is embedded. This expresses the historical nature of message meaning. Every linguistic system is a cultural, historical phenomenon that serves specific forms of life. As organizations and their parts change (Pettigrew 1985), so too does the language. Information systems development is one mechanism to trigger a language change. It adjusts and constructs an understanding of a social world and defines rules for communication about that world. In accordance with this, the rule-based school sees data modeling as a question of language change with predefined language rules. The basic goal in rule-based approaches is to achieve intersubjective agreement on the formal language rules. A data model is seen as a means to understand communication in an IS and to reconstruct rules that underlie it. During data modeling the IS users formulate, develop, and agree on these rules. From this it follows that data modeling methods and techniques should support the IS users in actively changing their own professional languages. Any attempts to achieve a 'long term, unrestricted model of the enterprise' are doomed to fail. Instead, data modeling should emphasize adaptability, flexibility, and contextuality of developed conceptual schemas.

The study of message meaning involves at least three aspects: classifications, intentions and assumptions. First is the elicitation of the socially shared classifications. Defining 'entity-types' in the fact-based school, requires finding out what people mean by 'customers', 'accounts', etc. and what criteria they use to classify real objects into these classes. In distinction to the fact-based ontology, the rule-based approaches treat these entity-types as dependent on the form of life and thus subject to negotiation. They can be redefined, and their definitions can vary over organizational functions and areas. Hence there is no a priori, normative principle to aim at a globally consistent definition of terms. Consistency is only preferred if it serves some acceptable social goals such as improved organizational coordination, fewer misunderstandings and so on. Second, the rule-based approaches aim at uncovering intentions of language use by the study of linguistic functions and the type of commitments which the linguistic performances establish. This involves an understanding of common terms and of the activities to which they commit the organization. In other words, the study of the message meaning in the rule-based school includes the description of the linguistic behaviors associated with the use of the message. In brief, this amounts to describing the formal properties of speech acts; i.e. what are necessary and sufficient conditions to perform the acts in different contexts (Lehtinen and

Lyytinen 1986).

Third, the study of message meaning involves the study of background assumptions and presuppositions that are necessary to assess the meaning of sentences in a particular context. These include, among others, socially shared assumptions, presuppositions, implications and other constraints which affect how the message is composed and its meaning interpreted.

Unfortunately, these three aspects together make rule-based data modeling quite complicated and demanding (Lyytinen and Lehtinen 1984; Stamper 1987). In the rule-based school, data modeling is an important vehicle for organizations to learn about their communication practices: how actors make sense of their environments and communicate in them. The approach also emphasizes the study of mechanisms by which language use initiates, enforces, and controls organizational behavior. This also extends to the more 'political aspects' of data modeling (as were discussed in chapter 6).

In the rule-based school, data modeling is mostly concerned with translating meanings from users' professional languages into a formal language. Data modeling can help to detect distortions and inconsistencies in communication. This covers e.g. the identification of incompatible language meanings which are dysfunctional for an organization's activities (Lyytinen 1986, Backhouse 1991). In this sense, language modeling is a creative, interpretive task that is based on the understanding of ordinary language communication. This does not, however, preclude the application of formalisms. One approach to improve language is through formal methods, but it is not the only one. Formal methods can help to uncover constructs for correct language use and possible inconsistencies in them.

To shed more light on the technicalities of the rule-based approaches we will review in more detail two research projects. The first is the LEGOL/NORMA project, which can be viewed as the originator of the rule-based school of data modeling. LEGOL stands for LEGal Oriented Language and NORMA, the successor of LEGOL, for NORMs and Affordances. Our treatment of the LEGOL/NORMA project is based on several reports which have been published since its inception in the early 1970s. We shall in particular draw upon Backhouse's doctoral thesis (1991) which includes a brief but systematic treatment of the evolution of the LEGOL/NORMA approach.

7.3.5 The LEGOL/NORMA approach

7.3.5.1 Background and basic goals

The LEGOL/NORMA project has produced a series of dialects which support the elicitation and specification of information system requirements. It was started in 1973 at the London School of Economics (since 1988 the project has been primarily based at the University of Twente, Netherlands) with the expressed aim of tackling issues related to the thorny problem of meaning in defining IS requirements. Three fundamental problems were on the agenda of the project (Stamper 1989):

(1) How to describe a social system as an information system with the maximum formal precision compatible with the intrinsically informal nature of social interactions?

(2) How to deal analytically with the semantic problems of meaning of terms in the application domain that must be resolved by the system designers with the users whenever a computer-based system is developed?

(3) How to improve the methodologies for analyzing and specifying business requirements before the software engineering task is undertaken?

This agenda led to a series of languages (LEGOL 1, 2.0, 2.1, 2.2, NORMA) to represent norms and norm systems. They were created as research tools (prototypes) to investigate how to model systems of legal and social norms as well as business norms. These prototypes revealed the inadequacy of classical logics built upon predicate logic to analyze and represent norms (Stamper 1987). The reasons for this is that classical logics do well when there is already a good deal of agreement about what constitutes the structure and nature of reality. In the field of IS, as in the fields of law, business or social science, such agreements cannot be assumed. Indeed, much of the work in these fields tries to determine the individuality and identity of various legal, social and business entities, through articulating and comparing different 'world views' which 'promulgate' such entity worlds.

Prominent among the goals of the LEGOL/NORMA project is the notion that information requirements analysis involves the formalization of socially determined rule systems which deal with problems of identity and individuation. The language developed in the LEGOL/NORMA project has consequently focused on representing the logic of norms and affordances through which such acts of individuation and identification become possible. This language is called NORMA (Stamper 1985a).

Clearly, such a focus is fundamentally different from the static paradigm of the fact-based school. It foreshadows the idea that IS design is really concerned with the rational reconstruction of a subset of the intuitive (implicit) users' rule knowledge which they need to make sense of data (and reality). In particular, NORMA

> is based upon two simple philosophical assumptions: there is no knowledge without a knower, and his knowledge depends upon what he does (Stamper 1985a).

An immediate consequence of these assumptions is that NORMA represents an attempt to develop a concise formalism to elicit and describe social and business norms in which an active agent is included into the syntax (and semantics) of the language. Therefore all formulas in NORMA always have the structure of:

'AGENTbehavior or AGENTaction'

The effect of this is to require from the IS designer to specify who it is who is responsible for the knowledge. Hence, in place of an 'absolute' notion of truth, there is the notion of responsibility of a knowing subject. Another implication is that all behaviors in such constructs refer to here-and-now. In order to bind past and future behaviors with the knowledge of here-and-now one must introduce semiotic constructs by which such bindings can be made (through representations) by the knowing subject (in the manner expressed by Morris 1946).

Another key assumption in LEGOL/NORMA is the invariability thesis. Agents must rely on invariants to act in a coordinated manner and to communicate in the constantly changing conditions of social reality. In performing any action the familiarity with what is biologically and socially significant to those who share that same reality permits predictable and stable behavior.

This can be expressed as:

AGENT . . . . Invariant

Here the concept names an invariant in the behavior of the agent who is responsible for establishing the existence and limits of the invariant. Invariants are recurrent patterns of behaving and acting.

Invariants are informally established, or, when necessary, codified in law. Information and business system development lie in between these two 'extremes'. Moreover, agents in any environment express numerous invariant behaviors (you could also call them action schemes or strategies). LEGOL/NORMA refers to these as affordances (or realizations) in the case of a single agent, whereas for a group of agents the invariant behavior is called a norm.

The principal concern in refining LEGOL/NORMA has been to develop methods of representing formal specifications of invariant behaviors which lend themselves to systematic and rigorous analysis. In order to do this in a disciplined fashion, an addition to NORMA has been developed — a language called LEGOL (Stamper 1983). LEGOL forms a manipulation language for norm based NORMA-representations. Operators in LEGOL are time based as they depict the start and end times of affordances. When forming expressions to describe a fragment of reality we can thus combine affordances with the LEGOL operators like while, orwhile, whilenot, and whenever. In the following we shall examine some of the major constructs in LEGOL/NORMA and clarify how they can be used to express and analyze rules that underlie IS use.

7.3.5.2 Basic LEGOL/NORMA constructs

A crucial task in using LEGOL/NORMA is semantic analysis which aims at establishing agreed upon meanings for linguistic terms (concepts) in a problem or application domain. The semantic analysis is carried out following six analysis steps (Liu and Stamper 1989; Backhouse even identifies 10 steps in his detailed specification of the technique to derive a semantic schema). Through these steps a systematic model of business semantics is gradually built.

Semantic analysis is carried out by analyzing texts and conversations that deal with or describe the analysis domain. The analysis focuses on different types of lexical units (through lexical analysis) such as nouns, verbs, adjectives and adverbs and links them back to specific agent behaviors in the analysis domain. The result of this is called a semantic model. It describes agents and their possible actions in terms of ontological relationships. These are the fundamental relationships which form the socially constructed 'structure' of reality. In addition, the semantic model captures norms which specify details of possible behaviors, e.g. the conditions where the action must happen, or where they are actually impossible. These norms are written in LEGOL. In LEGOL/NORMA these norms are regarded as less stable than the fundamental ontological relationships, because they are less determined by the underlying culture (or forms of life), and more by organizational expediency.

Stamper notes that the semantic model represented in LEGOL/NORMA appears to be 'a special kind of schema, although it is not primarily intended for database design' (Stamper 1990, p. 1). Therefore it provides a stable basis for database implementation and derivation of programs (through detailed analysis and refinement of norms). At the same time it can be seen as a representation of users' requirements in the formal NORMA syntax.

In constructing the semantic model LEGOL/NORMA relies on what might be considered a complicated set of primitives for the specification of: agents and affordances, universals and particulars, generic–specific structures, whole-part structures, role-carrier and role-name structures, determiners, and ontological relation structures (Liu and Stamper 1991, Backhouse 1989). Each of these will be briefly explained so as to give an idea of how to read a LEGOL/NORMA specification (*cf.* figure 7.3).

Agent-affordance

In LEGOL/NORMA all phenomena in the analyzed social system can be classified into two categories: agents who can do actions, and affordances which are actions or results of actions. The agents construct the social world; the agent can hold responsibilities for their actions. Examples of agents are 'Administration', 'Person', 'Garage'. Examples of affordances are 'Ownership', or 'Tax Bill'. LEGOL/NORMA also distinguishes a special class of affordances which result in signs. These affordances are represented by double quotes. For example the form A"Ax" as in John "John Hungry", would

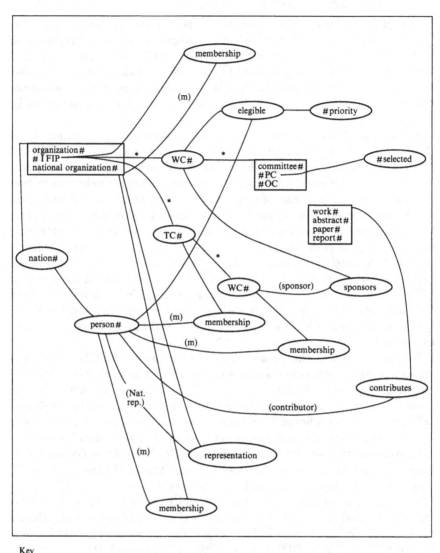

Key

WG	Working group
WC	Working conference
PC	Program committee
OC	Organization committee
TC	Technical committee
(m)	member
Nat. rep.	National representative
IFIP	International federation of information processing

Figure 7.3: Semantics for a system to support the running of international conferences (adapted from Stamper *et al.* 1991, p. 78)

mean that John realizes a sign type that means "John is hungry". Also joint affordances with several agents are allowed as 'getting married.'

Universal–particular

This concept pair is similar to the type–instance distinction in the fact-based approaches. One should describe properties of types of things, rather than of particular instances, unless some particulars are so unique and so important that they have to be described specially. For example 'Land Tax' and 'John Doe' are examples of particulars.

Generic–specific

Many phenomena in a social world fall into a generic–specific structure. This is similar to is-a relationships and generalizations in fact-based data modeling. The specific concepts inherit the properties of generics. For example, 'Land Parcel' is a generic concept, while 'Agricultural Parcel' and 'Urban Parcel' are specifics of the generic concept of 'Land Parcel'.

Whole–part

Some phenomena can only exist as parts of a whole, through which we come to know them - this is the idea of a whole-part relationship. For example in the case of an administrative structure, a 'district' is a part of a 'province', and a 'village' is a part of 'district'. However, in the case of geographical areas the parts pre-exist the administrative areas, and in this case we do not have the whole–part relationship, but simply an assembly of components described by ontological dependencies.

Role carrier–role name

Some agents may be involved in certain affordances, where the agents are the role–carriers and have certain role names. For example, 'Person' may own one or more land parcels (or cars), which makes him 'an Owner' of the parcel. The relationship between the 'Person' and the 'Parcel' is called an 'Ownership' (affordance).

Determiners

These are generalizations of the concept of measurement and hence determine an important type of behavior. They function to partition instances of realizations along various criteria. Hence, determiners are the affordances of quantity and quality that permit us to compare one instance of a realization to others. A standard (norm) is always involved. An example of a determiner is 'Tax-Rate'. Determiners are prefixed with # in ontology charts (see below). It is important to note that problems with individuality, discreteness and identity are represented in LEGOL/NORMA by determiners. For example, identity is behavior that enables an agent consistently to select the same individual (denoted for example as Agentperson#).

Ontological structure relations

Discovering ontological dependencies between the phenomena in the business domain is the most essential step in the semantic analysis. The basic idea is the following: if one thing y exists only while x does, then the dependency between them is defined as an ontological dependency. In NORMA this is depicted as

$$x \ldots \ldots y$$

indicating that y ontologically depends on x. For example, all invariants are ontologically dependent on some agents (the basic postulate of the LEGOL/NORMA philosophy). The ontological chart should be read from left to right: the item on the right is dependent, whereas the item on the left is antecedent.

Using the NORMA syntax the ontological relationships between the semantic units can be modeled as several fragments represented in figure 7.3.

The idea behind generating an ontological chart (as shown in figure 7.3) is to put each linguistic term in its context with respect to ontological constraints. This serves the goal of assigning each term a clear meaning (with necessary affordances). The ontological chart is a graphical description of the resulting 'semantic schema'.

Transforming ontological charts to database schemata

LEGOL/NORMA provides a simple and well-defined technique by which ontological charts can be translated into relational database schema implementations (Liu and Stamper 1989). This standard format which keeps information about agents and affordances is called a surrogate structure and all surrogates in this implementation share a uniform data structure.

A prototype system is also available which can parse the semantic model, transform it into a time-based database schema, help to capture data (in conformance with the semantic model), and to query and report the database using LEGOL. A unique feature of this transformation is that it incorporates time semantics automatically (start and finishing times), automatically adds identifiers for each individual, maintains knowledge of the types of affordances (such as universal/particular/determiner), sorts of affordance (such as 'Person' as a type of universal), alias names, antecedents, and authorities which define allowable start and finish times. Hence a running prototype of the specified system represented in an ontological chart can be implemented in a short time.

Norm specification

The semantic analysis is completed with a norm specification. Stamper (1980) distinguishes two types of norms: action norms which direct or permit action, and structure norms which define the hierarchical norm structure and say when the norms directing action should be applied. Action norms are further divided into:

(1) Standing orders

These change states in the world. An example would be

The owner of a parcel of land should be sent a bill for the tax on that parcel at least four weeks before the tax is due.

Hence, standing orders state conditions under which some action should, should not, or may take place. A computer can also perform this action. There is, however, a difference between the physical act of sending the bill (and producing it) and what this action means in the social world of obligations.

(2) Status norms

These change the social world and define the legal and social status of the agents and actions. For example:

If a parcel is owned by more than one person, the owner having the largest share shall be the principal owner, otherwise any one of them can be designated as principal owner.

(3) Powers of intervention

These invoke or inhibit the existing norms and allow parts of laws or norms to be brought into action or taken out of the operation. Hence, they allow parts of the normative networks to be 'switched on' or 'switched off'. For example:

Agricultural parcels which suffer from erosion, upon application by the owner, may be exempted from land tax at the discretion of the district land tax inspector.

(4) Powers of legislation

These change the norm structure itself and can be illustrated by the following norm:

A District Land Tribunal shall specify locally appropriate procedures for the conduct of appeals concerning exemptions from tax liability.

Structure norms

These are norms about the norms. The most obvious one is: 'The first rule is that there are rules'. Hence structure norms consist of a condition clause determining when a set of norms should be applied. Structure norms are categorical and do not depend on discretion — they simply reflect powers that be, i.e. a logical structure of the norm hierarchy.

Use of norms in database implementation

The specified norms can be stored in the 'Normbase' implementation and thereby linked to relevant agents and affordances. The resulting norm specifications can be used for several purposes:

(1) as constraints to check operations on the data items (such as during or
     after database transactions);

(2) as triggers to prompt actions. These actions can be of two kinds. First
     they can be used to automatically change data in the database. For
     example, if there is a tax-calculation norm written in LEGOL attached
     to a tax-rate, the tax-rate can then be calculated automatically accord-
     ing to the updated information about the parcel, which is kept in the
     system. Second they can trigger action to produce messages to users to
     prompt action in the business domain (such as automatically producing
     a tax-bill four weeks before the tax due date).

The resulting complete semantic model expresses the agreed upon meanings of terms (if agreement is possible) and how these terms are used in defining and imposing norms that govern agents' behaviors in certain domains.
The idea is that a LEGOL/NORMA specification allows the inhabitants of
the informal system to impose formal structures on the technical domain.
In the fact-based school the opposite is the case: the structures in the technical domain implicitly impose formal structures on the social domain often
calling for unified ontological structures. The goal of LEGOL/NORMA, in
contrast, is to carefully respect the differential semantics of the user groups
and let them decide for themselves in which 'ontology' they want to work.

7.3.5.3 Summary of LEGOL/NORMA achievements

The complicated and sometimes confusing nature of LEGOL/NORMA has
stymied its recognition (in addition to the fact that the results of the project
are not easily accessible in major publication outlets). Nevertheless it has
many interesting properties which deserve proper recognition because it is
still one of the few real implementations of a data modeling language which
clearly transcends naive realism. Foremost among the LEGOL/NORMA
features are:

(1) The approach makes explicit the concept of time, i.e. each affordance
     (realization) has a period of existence by the specification of its starting
     and ending time.

(2) Rules, which describe the conditions and deontic operators for actions
     performed in the social system, are permitted to change. This dy-
     namism is a major advantage over the static constraints specified by
     other data models.

(3) Semantic primitives are defined in terms of behaviors which partition
     phenomena in the social domain into different types of structures. This
     distinction neither accepts ontological differences between entities, at-
     tributes and relationships (as all these are in fact dependent on our
     social invariants and not on some persistent concrete structure), nor
     follows the notion of a fact and its correspondence with a state-of-
     affairs. Instead, the approach distinguishes between agents and affor-
     dances (invariants), and how social affordances link into larger systems.

It retains all these in a standard representation scheme. Thus, the approach does not face the potential dilemma of defining an object as an entity, attribute or relationship because such decisions are guided by analyzing the behaviors in which agents can engage. Neither does LEGOL/NORMA have to deal with problems of object identity and transformation as the fact-based school.

(4) The existence of the 'operational criterion of meaning' concept in LEGOL/NORMA permits the link between data and reality to be established on a more concrete level. This is done by comparing various statements made about affordances, i.e. rules used to describe the organization. Stamper (1979) claims that:

> the data model which arises from the application of this criterion serves as a road map showing how one must travel to obtain ever more reliable evidence until ideally the routes terminate at common place objects (realizations) which can be described in reliable ways.

In this sense LEGOL/NORMA offers a powerful means to analyze and understand a complicated web of behaviors which link different data items into a rich array of varying phenomena in a socially constructed world. Several applications of the method have shown that it helps to achieve more stable, extendable and flexible data models (Liu and Stamper 1989).

The weaknesses of LEGOL/NORMA (in addition to its complexity and somewhat overwhelming and opaque vocabulary) is its sole focus on how the ontology of the social world is crafted. This leads the approach to largely ignore, or to deal with only in a superficial manner, the following important issues of requirements specification and the definition of data meaning:

(1) what are the actual impacts of data on behaviors in the business domain? (in contrast to those one would expect to perceive by studying norms and invariants)

(2) how can LEGOL/NORMA account for differences in the interpretation of data in specific contexts and what issues can explain these differences? (i.e. how far are the horizons of meanings of different user groups from one another)

(3) in what way can semiotic affordances (speech acts) affect the design of the IS? In other words how can invariances in the uses of data be used to understand and capture requirements for retaining and storing data — such as with a file of standing orders?

All these issues need further clarification and elaboration, but so far have mostly been ignored by the LEGOL/NORMA approach. With the first issue, the approach has not developed any empirical or practical guidelines as to which 'representations' are relevant and result in changes in behaviors with various individuals, or groups in different situations. This, however, is necessary in determining the boundaries of the semantic analysis and in assessing its potential value.

For the second issue, the approach seems to assume that once the semantic model has been agreed upon all problems of 'different' interpretations would disappear. Stamper *et al.* (1991) call this the process of increasing mutual understanding which it can, indeed be. But how can one know how 'close' or 'far' these understandings are from each other and how stable they are? If we were to take Gadamer's philosophical hermeneutics seriously we would claim that the goal of unified interpretations is an illusion, and we would argue that no formal or rigorously fixed description such as a LEGOL/NORMA schema can resolve the problem (and challenge) of understanding differently. Therefore, communication through an IS emerges as a historical process of interpretation and reinterpretation. When time and resources foreclose, an action is taken on the basis of current understandings, but not dictated by some formal specification (within LEGOL/NORMA). Yet, in our opinion no systematic guidelines have yet been developed to deal with this issue (see also Stamper and Lee 1986). Interestingly, the LA view has been specifically focussed on this issue.

7.3.6 The language action view

The language action (LA) view shares the belief with the LEGOL/NORMA project that data modeling is basically concerned with modeling the rules of human communication, but it differs quite radically in the underlying philosophical framework. Some proponents of the LA view explicitly relate its foundations to the critical social theory of Jurgen Habermas and the speech act theory of Searle and Austin. Moreover, several researchers in this school have applied discourse theories to study symbolic interactions through the IS.

The LA view proposes that information systems development serves the three knowledge interests recognized in Habermas' critical social theory (Habermas 1972): technical control over inanimate and social objects, improvements in communication among participants, and emancipation from unnecessary social or natural constraints in human life. From this perspective the central goal of data modeling is to overcome the barriers to consensual symbolic action by improving the conditions for human communication. This is most effectively done, according to the LA view, by modeling data in terms of speech act concepts and exploring rules which facilitate intelligible and undistorted human expression through speech acts. This in turn is seen as the most important prerequisite for emancipation — the realization of the potential of each human being and the community as a whole.

7.3.6.1 Background and basic goals

The central idea of the LA view is to look upon IS use as one form of social action. In this sense it has much similarity with LEGOL/NORMA, as it denies the existence of knowledge and information without an acting subject. Yet, it differs quite substantially in the manner it uses the notion of social action, because in the LA view the underlying concept is borrowed from sociological theories developed by Weber and Habermas.

Influenced by the Frankfurt school of social action theory, in particular by the critical social theory of Habermas (1972, 1979, 1982; also McCarthy 1982), the LA view proposes that a distinction can be made between two types of social action: irrational and rational. Irrational actions are based on group think, myth, mass hysteria or the like. Rational action is founded on reason as evidenced through knowledge of proper evidence as established by maximal criticism in informed debate. Such a debate is said to be the grounds of knowledge. Basically there are three sources which undermine the rationality of social action: subjective bias (which includes lack of understanding), inability to obtain proper information due to physical constraints (e.g. distance, time pressures, mechanical calculation errors, etc.) and distortion of information by social conditions, in particular by the effects of hierarchy and power on the human willingness to communicate accurately (i.e. to engage in and contribute to an informed debate). Information system development is ultimately aimed at fighting all of these sources of misinformation. The basic research strategy of the LA view is to bring to bear the insights of both language and social action theory and philosophy on the issues arising from the need to 'rationally ground' organizational (social) action.

Crucial for achieving a rational grounding is the improvement of the modes of evidence generation and exchange. This suggests a focus on the process by which evidence for or against certain courses of action is elicited and checked by means of arguments. Therefore the LA view speaks of improving the exchange of meanings in rational human discourse. With this the LA view simply refers to the exchange of data and information in day to day business operations and policy debate. It covers such a simple message as a credit correction memo or a lengthy report to the president about the tax ramifications of a complete reorganization of the company. For the purpose of analyzing such messages, be they oral, in writing, diplomatic gestures, or whatever, the LA view proposes to apply the concepts of communication theories.

The LA view analyzes human communications with the belief that there exists a general theory of communicative human action (which is a form of social action aiming at creating a common understanding) and that speech act theory is the most promising avenue to follow for the development of such a theory. Speech act theory differs from its rival theories, e.g. truth based semantics or generative grammar theories of language (for a general introduction to linguistic theory see Lyons 1977) by the assumption that meaning cannot be grasped fully without analysis of the human intent behind communication. The LA view proposes to apply this principle to data modeling as well. Moreover, data processing is a subset of human communicative action.

The general concept of social action adopted in the LA view is best explained with the help of an example. The fact that most employees of a bank will use a certain format and stationary for writing a report, or will apply similar criteria in processing loan requests, etc., cannot be explained by 'free choice', but only by the influence of social 'forces' and constraints. All action that is taken under the influence of social constraints is social action. Seen together, these constraints form a conceptual and behavioral system which guides the action of individuals (this is a similar fundamental notion as the set of invariants in LEGOL/NORMA). The information needs of people to a large extent are also constrained by 'preprogrammed' social behaviors, and the information system itself becomes a component of the social action system in the LA view.

The LA view proposes that the basic concern of any IS is to support the rationality of symbolic interactions. Such interactions are called rational if they are justified by reasons which can stand the test of critical, informed debate. If the regularities which channel individual behavior are themselves not based on valid reasons, for instance if they are based on vested interests or mere conventions, they cannot stand the test of a universal, informed debate. Therefore, consensual human discourse is crucial for creating the knowledge which alone can distinguish between rational and merely 'accepted' social action. The mere fact that social action is based on agreement cannot guarantee 'rationality', since agreements can be fallacious or illegitimate (and often are).

The LA view suggests that information systems should be designed in such a way that they help to 'ground' social action on valid reasons through improving communication. Information systems are thus defined as 'formal linguistic systems for communication between people which support their actions.' (Goldkuhl and Lyytinen 1982a, p. 14; emphasis added).

There are two important implications of this definition:

(1) information systems development is concerned with modeling a subset of the language which is the medium of expression for human communication. The elementary unit of human communication in natural language is called a speech act. Data are stored in computer-based systems for the purpose of generating or reproducing speech acts, in lieu of direct human interaction. (The approach to modeling speech acts is discussed below.)

(2) Since there exists a number of barriers to effective communication, the LA view notes that rational social action needs to be 'supported' or 'grounded' through special efforts of ISD and data modeling. To achieve this, the 'intersubjective intelligibility' (or understanding) of messages needs to be achieved by some means. Such means include:

(i) improving the social conditions for communication,

(ii) improving the language (or message formalisms) used by the social actors, and

(iii) improving the means through which the information needs of the individuals can be modeled and dealt with. In most cases all three means need to be incorporated into the ISD effort.

The rationality principles of the communications are clarified using Habermas' theory of 'ideal speech'. According to Habermas, for undistorted communication to occur, four types of validity claims (Habermas 1979; 1984) must be respected and defended. That is, for ideal interaction to be carried out, communication must be 'intelligible', 'truthful', 'adequate', and 'appropriate'. 'Intelligible' implies that what is being said makes sense for the audience. The state of 'truthfulness' is the belief by an individual that what he states to be true is true, whereas 'veracity' (Habermas 1979) is whether a statement is correct in relation to the external world. In other words: communication is adequate if its claims meet either veracity tests or means tests. 'Appropriate' implies that the utterance complies with social norms which define what can/cannot or should/should not be said. A situation in which all use their best efforts to test whether these validity claims can be passed under all circumstances is called an ideal speech situation. Communications carried out under an approximation of the conditions of ideal speech form what Habermas calls a rational discourse.

The LA view sees that in reality several barriers typically block the way to a rational discourse:

(a) subjective bias which results in the lack of understanding or motivation to participate;

(b) inability to obtain proper information due to physical constraints (e.g. distance, time pressures, mechanical calculation errors, etc.); and mental constraints (information processing capability, inability to follow and accept the logic of the argument), and

(c) the distortion of information due to unjust or unequal social conditions, in particular due to conflict of interest and misuse of power.

A first step to creating the conditions of rational discourse is to improve the intersubjective intelligibility of messages. If the meaning of a messages is — intentionally or unintentionally — obscured, it is all the more difficult to check veracity and validity claims. Evidence generation and exchange is impaired. Consequently, the LA view proposes to model the rule governed meanings of messages in social action, something which conventional approaches to data modeling largely, if not totally, ignore.

In principle, the analysis strategy proceeds similarly to other methodologies by proposing fields of analysis with associated methods and tools. In doing so the LA view makes, however, a very distinct assumption which differs from the more traditional fact-based methods: it presumes that human communication is governed by social rules some of which are followed by the human species as a whole, and some of which are more local and contin-

gent. The species dependent ground rules of communication are called rules
of universal pragmatics (*cf.* Habermas 1979). The LA view argues that the
ISD efforts must recognize some of these universal rules of communication,
and moreover, it must clarify the local rules by changing the users' implicit
'knowing how' of linguistic communications to explicit 'knowing that' (Ryle
1949).

ISD need not specify all rules, but only a 'relevant' set by applying 'fruitful abstractions' of linguistic behavior. Goldkuhl and Lyytinen clarify this
principle as follows:

> By fruitful we mean in this context that the abstractions applied con-
> tribute to systematic reconstruction (see below, authors) and devel-
> opment of existing communicative competence. ... We aim, when de-
> veloping our methodology, to base different IA–tasks (IA: Information
> Analysis = data modeling) on a conscious selection of ... abstractions
> .... Primarily used abstractions are: (abstractions) ... from concrete
> place and time of communication (so called type-token distinction, see
> Lyons 1977), ... from a direct context ... (concrete participants, con-
> crete situation, concrete utterances) ... and finally abstractions from
> different aspects of speech acts (syntax, semantics and pragmatics),
> .... These abstractions form a hierarchy, where we abstract gradu-
> ally more and more from actual communications ... in an information
> system. Goldkuhl and Lyytinen (1982b), pp. 8–9.

The LA view further argues that in deploying these abstractions the developers must engage in activities to describe their intuitively mastered
linguistic knowledge. In other words, the activities aim to reveal how language is intuitively used in social situations. The designers and users must
'reconstruct' the underlying rules which govern symbolic action. Therefore,
the LA view suggests that principles of 'rational reconstruction' (Habermas
1979) can act as a model for deriving valid knowledge during the data modeling process. Rational reconstructions aim at systematically revealing and
describing users' intuitive linguistic knowledge which is needed to understand the purpose, structure and context of symbolic interactions enabled
by the IS. This means making explicit how users can 'speak', 'understand'
and 'act' at all.

An important conclusion of this insight is that the designers of the IS
need some theoretical framework in which to express their reconstructions.
Symbolic logic and Chomsky's theory of generative grammars are examples
of such frameworks which help to elicit our 'know-how' of making valid inferences and generating syntactically correct sentences, respectively. Other,
less rigid attempts to reconstruct our understandings of human action are
Wittgenstein's theory of language games, and the theory of speech acts.
The LEGOL/NORMA approach can also be interpreted as such an example, even though it never clearly says so. In the LA view the most prominent

role in deriving rational reconstructions has been given to speech act theory, and the theory of discourses. The motivation for this is that the LA by using such theories can express the pragmatic rules that guide communication (symbolic action) when mediated through an IS. These theories will be discussed next.

7.3.6.2 Basic LA constructs: speech act and discourse theories

Speech act theory is concerned with the systematic study of linguistic regularities and the meaning of utterances. The basic idea in the theory is that people do things with words to achieve purposes which are expressed intentions. The basic tenet of the theory is that in order to analyze how people do things with words, it is necessary to describe the conventional generic intent (the intention of the act) behind communication. Hence a classification of generic intentions which people pursue with using words is fundamental to a theory of language. Examples of such generic intentions are to assert a fact, to make a promise or threat, etc. Depending on the intent with which they are communicated the same words can mean different things and so will also differ in their consequences which one can expect from their utterance. This contrasts sharply with the fact-based viewpoint which holds that the meaning of messages (propositions) can be derived solely from the syntactic elements of speech, e.g. words and phrases and their universal semantic 'assignment' functions. In consequence, the data modeling efforts in the fact-based school are confined to represent basic ontological primitives (values, entities), and their compositions (attributes, relations) which are seen to form messages in the IS. It is not possible here to describe in detail how the LA theory of ISD proposes to formalize professional languages using concepts of speech act theory and discourse theories as reconstructive devices. However a brief outline of the LA approach to data modeling follows.

The LA view takes speech acts as the basic units of communication. Making a speech act involves several types of 'subacts': utterance acts, propositional acts, illocutionary acts, and perlocutionary acts. These are considered on four levels of analysis in data modeling.

An utterance act is the act that a speaker performs by uttering (producing) an expression. For example, the expressions 'John loves Mary' and 'Mary is loved by John' when uttered are different utterance acts. Describing utterance acts leads to modeling of syntax and typography of data produced in the IS. Hence, on this level data modeling is concerned with the rules which determine if a message is correctly structured and encoded. Data models provide a mechanism by which well-formed and ill-formed messages can be distinguished. If messages are ill-formed, they may still be intelligible, but their integrity is in jeopardy. The specification of 'well-formed' utterance acts is similar to deriving checking rules for well-formed formulae in logic and mathematics. Other uses of data models on this level involve code checking, higher level data transmission protocols, and some integrity constraints that define value ranges (e.g. that a person's salary must be of a certain data type). Hence, modeling utterance acts is concerned with the rules which differentiate well-formed messages from invalid ones.

A propositional act expresses the propositional content of an utterance and it covers acts of denotation (identification) and predication. Examples of acts of identification are 'John' and 'Mary' in the above sentence. An example of predication is 'x loves y'. Describing propositional acts in speech acts leads to modeling of the semantics (propositional content) of the produced data. Hence on this level data modeling is concerned with the rules by which messages are associated with objects to which they can be said to refer and with the rules which state what types of predications can be applied to identified objects.

Traditionally, data dictionaries and data model primitives (entities, attribute values) have attempted to specify the applicable rules of reference through characterizations of object and attribute types. Closely associated are rules of predication which constrain the kind of attributes which entity types are allowed to have, and how they can be related to other entity types. Specification of the rules for propositional content is very similar to defining the semantics of theorems in predicate logic which will hold in different 'worlds'. Typical problems of data modeling on this level involve solving problems of naming, typing, hyponymy, synonymy and homonymy, derivation of inference rules, and clarification of necessary and shared assumptions and presuppositions about the communication topic (Goldkuhl and Lyytinen 1982b).

An illocutionary act is the basic unit of meaningful human communication: it is always performed when one utters a certain expression with an intention. For example, one can perform illocutions 'I promise to write a letter', or 'I refuse to pay a bill'. Here the illocutionary acts involved are described by such 'indicators' as 'I promise' or 'I refuse'. When the intention is recognized by the hearers, the illocutionary act has been successful, and we can say that the meaning of the uttered expression has been understood. This also implies that a commitment has been created which binds future behaviors of all parties and pledges them to certain activities/expectations. Describing the illocutionary acts in speech acts leads to describing the intentions which underlie the symbolic interactions through an IS. This involves describing the speakers, the hearers, the context and the purpose and meaning of communications. In speech act theory propositional acts are always subsidiary acts of illocutions. Therefore, on this level the propositions are tied to some socially recognized purposes of 'using' the proposition which can be for example 'asserting', 'predicting', 'promising', or even 'condoling'. Illocutionary acts are described more formally and systematically using primitives of illocutionary logic (see below). Perlocutionary acts produce the speech effects of feelings, attitudes, and subsequent behaviors of hearers. In general, perlocutionary effects are 'caused' by perlocutionary acts which can be expressed by verbs such as 'persuading', 'assuring', 'clarifying' etc. One example of a perlocutionary effect is to get somebody to write a letter upon a request. Unlike utterance, propositional and illocutionary acts, perlocutionary acts are not rule-based but contingent, empirical phenomena. Therefore, their description and analysis differs markedly from the three other acts involved in speech acts. Yet, in the data modeling context perlocutions play a vital role as they are analyzed and described when predicting, anticipating or describing the actual effects of data on IS users such as a decision makers. We shall omit them in the following as these concerns relate more directly to initial statements of information requirements and their representations (for a survey see e.g. Cooper and Swanson 1979; Yadav 1983) and not to the subsequent formalizations and representations of symbolic interactions which is the primary focus of LA based data modeling.

Illocutionary acts are modelled in the LA view with a fairly complicated and differentiated vocabulary the details of which must be omitted here (but see Lehtinen and Lyytinen 1986, Auramaki *et al.* 1988, Auramaki *et al.* 1992a who summarize some of the most fundamental concepts). In general an illocutionary act is expressed in the form:

illocutionary act (⟨context⟩, ⟨content⟩, ⟨illocutionary force⟩)

This means that an illocutionary act consists of an illocutionary force and a propositional content performed in some context. All these constituents are essential in grasping the meaning of a message. Also relationships of these constituents are worth considering, e.g. understanding the content can depend on understanding the context and the illocutionary force; sometimes the context can only be constructed by understanding the content. An important observation is that all these constituents can vary independently of each other and this will change the meaning of the message. For example, different illocutionary forces can be assigned to the same propositional content, and vice versa.

The context is defined by the terms: speaker, hearer, time, place and the world of the utterance. Hence data modeling in the LA view always captures the agents (who 'utters' to whom, their environment, etc.) in the context of an utterance. Clearly, all these help in imagining what the speaker might say and mean. The most fundamental concept in speech act oriented data modeling is that of illocutionary force. It expresses two notions:

(a) the kind of commitment a speaker makes when he says something, and

(b) the way in which the direction-of-fit is assigned between the world and 'word' (word is shorthand for the propositional content of what is said in the speech act).

Both of these notions are most easily illustrated by examples. For example in assertives, when a speaker claims that something is the case, s/he becomes committed to providing evidence in support of the assertion. Another type of commitment is associated with a promise (to do in the future what one says now). As can be seen, the word 'commitment' is understood here more widely than in everyday usage. Commitments are associated with all types of illocutionary forces: assertives (speaker notes some existing state of affairs), directives (speaker asks for performance of an act), commissives or promises (speaker becomes committed to future performance of an act), declaratives (speaker brings about a (new) state of affairs), expressives (speaker expresses his attitudes/feelings about a state of affairs).

The direction-of-fit can also be illustrated by an example: a purchase order has a world-to-word direction-of-fit as it is intended to change the world, and the speaker commits himself to the future action of paying an invoice in return for receiving some goods or services.

Both these notions are fundamental for the LA view of data modeling. The concept of commitment suggests that information systems should be seen as communication networks which create, maintain and fulfill commitments. The illocutionary force can be defined using more elaborate concepts of illocutionary point (defining the direction-of-fit), propositional content conditions (what kinds of propositions can be associated with the illocutionary force), and preparatory conditions (what kinds of states of affairs are a prerequisite for making a certain illocutionary act 'felicitous', i.e. successful).

The modeling of illocutionary forces is usually accomplished in the LA view by applying an exhaustive classification of possible 'illocutionary forces' to communications supported in the IS. The following five illocutionary forces proposed by Searle and Vanderveken (1985) are usually applied:

(1) Assertives, i.e. communications can be said to be true or false; direction is word-to-world, i.e what is said must correspond to what is the case in the world.

(2) Directives, i.e. communications can be said to be valid or invalid, e.g. if not performed by the right person or incorrect if they do not accomplish what they are supposed to; direction-of-fit is world-to-word as a certain state of the world is to be obtained by obeying the directive.

(3) Declaratives which can be said to be effective or ineffective. Examples of declarations are promotion announcements, giving notice, formal acceptance of an agreement; in general any institutional act which creates a new state of affairs, e.g. 'I pronounce you man and wife'; direction-of-fit is world-to-word (by declaring a valid marriage a new state is created in the world).

(4) Commissives can be said to be felicitous or infelicitous (e.g. a promise extracted by presenting false evidence); for a valid promise the direction-of-fit is world-to-word.

(5) expressives which can be said to be sincere or insincere. Frequent examples can be found in memos where concerns are expressed, e.g. I feel that. Direction-of-fit is undefined by Searle (Habermas 1984 points out

that it should be word-to-world because what is said needs to correspond to the true state of the speaker's feelings if he is sincere.)

How then do these concepts apply to data modeling? This can be illustrated by considering a simple example of processing a purchase order. A stored purchase order records a result of a speech act called a purchase order. The propositional act of a purchase order is represented by a number of data items stored in various data fields of the record. Examples of such propositions are 'An item x is to be delivered in quantity y on a day z to location w'. This proposition is associated with the illocutionary force of a 'request' which captures the fundamental idea that a purchase order is not a prediction but a directive for delivering some items to a specific location at a certain time (it has a world-to-word direction-of-fit). This request also implies the change in ownership of those items and a promise to pay for the delivery upon a matching request, the invoicing. Moreover, this propositional content is repeated for all items ordered. The illocutionary force of the purchase order hence expresses that this is a directive and not for example a prediction that a delivery will in some likelihood take place on day w (yet some other stakeholders will interpret the proposition in this way). The context parameters define who can be a speaker, to whom this act can be performed, what things must be true in the world so that the act is recognized as a purchase order, and what dates are possible (one would not, e.g. consider purchase orders as valid which are 10 years old).

The perlocutionary act involved in the purchase order example creates expectations in both communication partners which are partly communicated and agreed upon using a second speech act following a purchase order: an order confirmation (a commissive). These expectations concern the behaviors of transferring goods and money using means that are agreed upon by both parties. Perlocutionary aspects of communication go beyond these.

Legally a purchase order is a promise to deliver the goods with a matching promise to pay. Within a larger fabric of social conventions and behaviors this information can be used to further coordinate and make possible other types of activities. For example, for the production department a valid purchase order is a prediction of a future state of affairs, i.e. a forecast that such and such quantity of certain materials will be available at a certain date. For marketing it may provide evidence to make promises to customers about the possibility of delivering these goods. Now if the order goes bad, e.g. the supplier sends a memo asking for a later delivery date, the perlocutionary effects of this communication are radically different for these language communities: the legal department may 'threaten' with damage claims to uphold the former date, while the production department treats the delay as an annoying fact (a more precise 'prediction') and simply revises its production schedules. This observation points to one of the advantages of action based data modeling, namely to capture the multiple meanings of one speech act as recorded by a single database record type. Fact-based theories of data modeling have no way to explicitly capture these different meanings which the same data can convey to different people. Instead, they assume that users are to interpret and use data correctly and that automation has no negative consequences for this. But this is fallacious because computer-based applications often change communication paths inadvertently and interrupt the personal communication between different user groups through which the background knowledge needed for interpretation is maintained. The result is that computer applications often feed data into social contexts in which some or all of their meanings are neither self-evident nor easily articulated.

Our example also illustrates that there are necessary interrelationships between various speech acts. A purchase order and order confirmation make sense only in pairs; one without the other leads to confusing and socially inappropriate behaviors (although such mishaps do take place to the misfortune of all of us). This observation is also applied in the LA view which emphasizes that illocutionary acts seldom occur alone and therefore they cannot be adequately understood unless they are described as members of ordered speech act sequences. One reason for this is that a preceding speech act usually changes the context, and thereby affects the interpretation of subsequent speech acts.

Sequences of contextually related speech acts are called conversations in the LA view. Conversations are understood as generic types of discourses or message-forms which define specific linguistic behaviors taking place in an organization. The characteristic feature of a conversation is that it connotes a larger unit of communication serving some social goals. One example of such a unit is order processing. In analyzing conversations the LA view builds on discourse theories (Brown and Yule 1984) and pragmatic theories of language (Levinson 1983).

The LA view provides several methods and tools to analyze sequences of speech acts if they form systematic regularities and possess important properties such as coherency, completeness and relevance. All these are assessed so that the communications through the IS are socially useful, appropriate and clear (and hence can pass some of the validity claims). The LA view also focuses on interactions and dependencies between conversations which are important in an organization (such as budgeting and investment conversations).

7.3.6.3 Summary of LA view achievements

The LA view leads to a fairly sophisticated, but also complicated analysis which has stymied its recognition. Its critics claim that it is not clear how the complicated language analysis (reconstruction) can help in specifying 'better' IS which are socially more satisfactory than those that could be developed by conventional approaches. By and large the LA view has not achieved wide recognition as a data modeling approach. It has met with more success when used as a basis to develop group oriented communication tools which can 'add value' to the functionality of the electronic mail. Even in this area, the outcomes are mixed. An example is Winograd's and Flores' (1986) Coordinator (TM) tool which is probably the first and most widely debated software package the design of which is based on speech act theory. The most visible problems of the LA view are:

(1) The concepts of conversations and speech acts, though illuminating are not necessarily sufficiently well-defined to guarantee a well-behaved design process. In particular, it is not clear, how the linguistic representations can be matched with more technical design decisions, i.e. does the LA approach, when implemented, really lead to different types of systems. Some researchers have cast serious doubts over the applicability of speech act concepts, in general, in analyzing human communications.

(2) It is not clear what the practical implications of the philosophical turn into critical social theory are. While Habermas' arguments regarding the negative effects of distorted communication are theoretically convincing, their connection to the practice of applying the LA view remain obscure. Though proponents of the LA view have put forward such features as 'full-blown participation', 'greater user responsibility' as major results of adopting the rational reconstruction strategy, these are mostly guesses rather than established accomplishments. For example, none of the papers in the LA view points out how Habermas' four validity claims connect to the practice of modeling speech acts and conversations (with the possible exception of Lyytinen and Hirschheim 1988).

All in all, the LA view suggests an insightful, but nevertheless largely unproven method for specifying information systems. However, there are some reasons which make it likely that the interest in analyzing communications, commitments and coordination problems through LA concepts will grow in the future. One reason is that currently more attention is paid to business structures, processes and social communications and to understand their subtleties. This requires greater socio-theoretical sophistication than is provided by structured methods and object-oriented analysis. Another reason is that the drive towards higher levels of organizational integration (such as in total quality management) will bring to the surface many of the problems which were already theoretically anticipated in the LA view (such as the differences of the meaning of data in different contexts, the social implications of interpreting data in a specific way and so on). Hence the time may arrive soon, when the LA action view is no longer a theory in search of an application, but a welcome framework which helps to articulate and address the problems which are experienced in practice.

7.3.7 Possible directions for improvements

A number of the major weaknesses of the rule-based approaches have been outlined above. These concern the internal complexity and opaque vocabulary of the rule-based approaches, their weak integration, lack of explicit guidelines on how to implement (in a modeling context) a hermeneutic perspective, and their weak operationalization. As reflected in these observations, the rule-based school does not need more theory and abstract analysis of data modeling concepts, but rather advances in concrete methods and guidelines that will help to make them more applicable and useful for practicing systems analysts. This requires that the methods and principles are simplified, their connections spelled out more clearly and also that the school tries to analyze the implications of its hermeneutic assumptions on such practical issues like information architectures, application architectures and approaches to determine information requirements. For example, there is a large body of literature on hermeneutic and text interpretation (exegesis) that should be expanded and clarified to form a set of methods and guidelines that could be applied in data modeling exercises. The same applies to principles and theories of discourse analysis (see e.g. Goguen and Linde 1991). There is also a clear need to test and apply rule-based methods in field environments to develop new insights into how they could be strengthened and supported with tools.

7.4 Summary and Conclusions

As defined in chapter 2, data modeling involves a change process with respect to a set of object systems perceived in terms of linguistic phenomena. This change process is conceived in radically different ways in the rule-based and fact-based approaches to data modeling. In the fact-based school the primary focus is on designing a language which would faithfully and clearly depict states and invariances of a reality which is presumed as objective. A data modeling language is designed to remove defects and errors in the representational functions of user languages. Data modeling is mostly conceived as a Cartesian rationalistic enterprise which strives for formal exactness and rigor. Therefore, the fact-based modeling approaches put emphasis on rigorous methods and tools and derive their conceptual foundations from scientific theory building and analytical philosophy and logic.

In the rule-based approaches the primary focus is on cyclical hermeneutic processes by which reality is socially constructed through language as to make significant acting possible in that constructed reality. Hence the focus is on agreeing upon and reconstructing a set of shared rules as to make joint action possible through language and to continually extend our shared understandings of our socially constructed world. A data modeling language is designed to improve action or to change it, and to help users in their language to define what counts as reality in new ways. Data modeling is an interpretive social activity which strives for shared understanding, enactment and legitimation of invented norms. Therefore the rule-based data modeling approaches emphasize processes and practices which make joint interpretation possible and improve the clarification of data meanings. These include modeling methods and representation forms, tools, etc., but also social practices such as participation issues, role models and organizational change considerations. In accordance with this, rule-based approaches derive their conceptual foundations from the sociology of knowledge, pragmatics, hermeneutical and critical philosophy, and the language philosophy of ordinary speaking.

Our analysis points out that so far, the major emphasis in the IS research community has been on the fact-based approaches. This is natural because computers as such put a premium on formalization and exactness. Yet, our analysis also reveals that the pendulum is shifting towards wider acceptance of the premises of the rule-based approach. This is also natural because computer systems are now more widely seen as general communication media the analysis and application of which cannot avoid subtle issues of interpretation, sense-making and human understanding. We continue this line of reasoning in the next chapter.

8
Conclusions

8.1 Introduction

In this book we have tried to provide insights into information systems development and data modeling through a philosophical and conceptual analysis. More specifically, we have sought to meet the two goals articulated in chapter 1:

(1) to trace systematically the complexity of IS development to a set of beliefs about its domain of change; and

(2) to point out that IS development cannot be reduced to 'technological fixes'.

The first goal was addressed by demonstrating how a wide range of IS methodologies and data modeling approaches take radically different stances about the nature of the organization, data, information system, and what it means to change them. A careful analysis of the differences led us to perceive the inherent complexity of social change which is associated with IS development. The second goal was addressed by pointing out that there is inherent complexity in the social condition and environment of systems development which escapes technological solutions; indeed, such complexity is often amplified through such technological solutions. We hope that the reader, having taken the time and pains to consider our ideas, agrees with our initial position that the IS community should not ignore the philosophical controversies which have raged over the social sciences during the past decades as they fundamentally impact upon our understanding of IS. These controversies are also reflected in the debate which has arisen about the nature of computer science and information systems as disciplines. This debate is beneficial to the IS community because it helps us to become critically aware of the limitations of all our approaches in the face of the pluralistic and complex reality of IS development. This book is an attempt to add one viewpoint into the evolution of this debate. In this chapter we wish to focus on the terrain which this book commands in this debate, and elaborate upon its implications for the academic and practitioner communities. We start with a look at the academic community and its view about the nature of IS research.

8.2 Conflict about the Nature of IS Research

In the research literature on information systems development, it has been recognized for some time that the assumptions made in ISD are of fundamental practical and theoretical importance, because assumptions affect the way information systems are developed (the process), their design features (the product), or the way they are used (contributing to system success, undesirable consequences or even failure). However, earlier work tended to focus on very specific assumptions. For example, Hedberg and Mumford (1975) examined the analysts' assumptions about users and themselves using McGregor's (1960) Theory X, Theory Y framework. Bostrom and Heinen (1977) focused on the causes of system failures and identified seven specific assumptions that designers tend to make about users and the scope of analysts' responsibilities. A similar line of thinking was applied in Lyytinen and Lehtinen (1987).

Of special importance here is that the debate has recently taken a new turn by recognizing the need to explore the most fundamental foundations from where assumptions arise. Whereas some fundamental works addressing this are classics in the field (Churchman 1971; Kling 1980; Checkland 1981), the debate has recently intensified by focusing more clearly on the assumptions that characterize different paradigms or schools of thought in systems development (Winograd and Flores 1986; Hirschheim 1986; Klein and Hirschheim 1987b; Lyytinen 1987; Oliga 1988; Hirschheim and Klein 1989; Iivari 1991; Kerola and Simila 1992; Goguen 1992).

In principle, one side in this debate seeks to develop a science of software engineering in the image of the established natural sciences, believing that the success of the natural sciences can be repeated in the area of applied systems development if software engineering emulates the methods of the natural sciences. To a very large extent, this view is still held by the majority of computer scientists, industrial engineers and academics in the area of information systems. This is reaffirmed by the recent report of the *Task Force on the Core of Computer Science* (Denning *et al.* 1989). It identifies three 'major paradigms, or cultural styles, by which we approach our work'. The first of this is theory, and rooted in mathematics. The second is abstraction and rooted in the experimental scientific method, and the third is design and rooted in engineering (Denning *et al.* 1989, p. 10):

> The discipline of computer science is the systematic study of algorithmic processes that describe and transform information: their theory, design, efficiency, implementation, and application. The fundamental question underlying all of computing is 'What can be (efficiently) automated? (Denning *et al.* 1989, p. 12)

This report (Denning *et al.* 1989) appears to presume a unified ontology, ignoring that qualitative differences may exits in different application domains. For example, the question in some applications might not be what can be efficiently automated, but what can contribute to better mutual understanding. If the belief in the unified ontology could be upheld it would imply that software development can follow the same principles regardless of whether the design requirements arise from physical or human-social application domains. In a unified ontology there is no fundamental difference between an operator whether human, machine, or animal as long as the same function is performed.

However, the view that software development is a branch of applied mathematics primarily concerned with the study of algorithms is in conflict with several well-established lines of research. For example, a transaction cost analysis of organizational behavior suggests that data are used opportunistically to influence colleagues and superiors (Ciborra 1987). Hewitt (1986) and Gerson and Star (1986) show the need to manage ambiguity, inconsistencies and conflict in system specifications. Empirically, the political nature of software development has been demonstrated in Keen (1981) through documented cases of counter-implementation strategies (*cf.* Markus 1983; Hirschheim and Newman 1988). An impressive base of facts and theory gives ample evidence for the social character of software development (Kling 1980; Hirschheim 1985b; Hirschheim and Newman 1991).

Therefore the opponents of what might be considered a 'unified ontology' view (as exemplified in the Denning *et al.* (1989) report) argue that the objects of inquiry in information systems development are different from those in the natural sciences, because users, developers and other stakeholders are not natural objects but conscious subjects. Consciousness is a quality with which the natural sciences so far have not been able to deal satisfactorily. Consciousness is important for data modeling because information system design is aimed at developing social communication systems and these are conscious sense-making systems. They are formed around shared meanings. Therefore, the design of an information system is like the design of human communities which requires a different approach than is practiced in mathematics and the natural sciences because they cannot deal with the significance and ethics of differing forms of life.

A similar point of view emerges from modern systems theory in that natural systems as studied in physics and chemistry or artificial systems (machines) as studied in traditional engineering or computer science are not 'self-referential', that is they do not rely on communication with peers to maintain images of themselves to maintain their internal structures and to distinguish themselves from the environment. For self-referential (or autopoietic, *cf.* Goguen 1992) systems, either communication or action are the fundamental building blocks and this differs from the 'elements' and subsystems as typically defined in engineering and the natural sciences. Recent systems theory makes clear ontological distinctions between machines, organisms, social and psychic systems (*cf.* Luhmann 1987). In the preceding chapters, we have tried to build on the results that the recent radicalization of this debate has produced.

8.3 Conflict about the Nature of IS Practice

Apart from our concern about the nature of IS research we note an interesting aspect of IS practice. Although our criticism of functionalist IS has mainly been based on an interpretation of the research literature, many of the central tenets of this book may have a familiar ring to the seasoned practitioner. Moreover, this is all the more surprising since newcomers to the practice of ISD typically are not taught the alternatives to functionalist methodologies. There certainly are approaches to ISD which embrace a number of the principles of social relativism, and to a lesser extent radical structuralism and neohumanism. But they are documented mostly in the research literature and even there they are much less developed than functionalism. The research literature by and large continues to promote one paradigm: functionalism in ISD and objectivism in data modeling.

Moreover, if one looks at the textbooks on data modeling and IS development which form the basis of university teaching, they are virtually entirely functionalist in orientation: functionalist methodologies, adopting functionalist ontological and epistemological assumptions and a functionalist mode of thinking. So the academic community perpetuates, consciously or unconsciously, functionalism. We teach it to our students since only functionalist textbooks are available. The students upon graduation, in turn, apply it in practice. However in applying it to practice, it is likely that the shortcomings of functionalist approaches surface. Reality is not the neat picture painted by functionalist writers: different user communities have very different views about the nature of the environment (reality) the information systems is supposed to support. Acquiring knowledge about the user world does not necessarily follow the tenets of positivist thought: knowledge and understanding is socially constructed, continuously emerging and defies simple cause–effect relationships. Interestingly enough, these are, by and large, the attitudes and practices of seasoned practitioners to whom many of the central tenets of this book may have a familiar ring. How come?

If our philosophical journey — metaphorically speaking — to reach beyond functionalism has any merit, it is because many practitioners have also embarked on a journey arriving at the same place, but they do not know where they are or how they got there. They just got there, driven to it by struggling with and confronting the complexity of systems development. Indeed, these practitioners have learned, often intuitively and through learning from experience, that functionalist tenets are an insufficient basis on which to develop and implement information systems. In this sense, our book acts as a guide so that they — and the academics who study them — can locate the place where they ultimately landed and why they got there.

It turns out that systems development in practice is heavily influenced by insights from other paradigms, particularly that of social relativism but not entirely. Some organizations, such as Texaco (Hirschheim and Miller 1993), have embraced the ideal of emancipation (through empowerment) and use systems development to facilitate the implementation of worker empowerment. They are not alone — many organizations we are familiar with have adopted similar strategies. This leads us to ask: why is it that academia seems to confine itself within the boundaries of functionalism when the practitioner community appears to have already moved on? Shouldn't we as academics learn from our practitioner colleagues? Shouldn't we move on from our apparent strangle-hold on functionalism to embrace alternative paradigms and in particular, the new insights that these paradigms promote?

Many academics are still stuck on the closed shores of functionalism, but some may be eager to chart the new territory which many practitioners have crossed on their meandering journey; for the academics the previous chapters may suggest how to go about refining the map. Of course, whether there will be any interest in budging from the entrenched positions most IS researchers appear to be in, is anyone's guess. Let's hope so.

It is our belief that the task of map refinement is a critical one, because as our technological sophistication grows so will the level of social complexity. With this level of increased complexity, future journeys in unmapped territories are likely to fail more often than now as new undocumented, unforseen hurdles await the travellers. Such hurdles include technologies like high speed information networks, distributed databases spanning organizational boundaries, EDI, knowledge agents, knowledge engineering, and image processing. These will increase the anxiety level of issues such as privacy, surveillance, location of decision authority, security, protection against fraud, increased stress and other frustrations created by information intensive environments to new unprecedented levels. An informed approach to these issues will require that careful social analyses form an integral part of any systems development effort. This book has introduced some of the fundamental philosophical foundations upon which such future approaches to ISD can build. On the one hand, these philosophical foundations bring order to chaos by providing an intellectual structure to grasp ISD. On the other hand, these foundations concomitantly create new seeds of chaos through a criticism of the dominant ideology of ISD. Dealing with this dialectic is the true mark of creativity.

Appendix A: Summaries of Selected Methodologies

In these summaries of selected methodologies, it should be noted that in the case of the structured methodologies and prototyping, we are really describing a 'family of methodologies' rather than a single approach.

In order to provide a sense of consistency throughout these summaries, the methodology descriptions consist of four parts:

(1) an analysis of the reasons why the particular methodology was proposed (its purpose and rationale);

(2) a concise examination of the key ideas underlying the methodology by which it hopes to achieve its stated purpose (its focus);

(3) a characterization of the methodology's principal stages and their sequence (its phase structure); and

(4) a list of its special methods and tools with their intended purpose.

In order to highlight the special features of each methodology, in some cases we relate these features to the classical system life-cycle (*cf.* the systems analysis textbooks of Kendall and Kendall 1988; Yourdon 1989).

A1. Structured Methodologies

Purpose and rationale

The most common forms of structured methodologies can be traced to the classic works of Gane and Sarson (1979), DeMarco (1978) and Yourdon (1989). They were introduced to cope with the complexity of analysis and design and problems which the complexity caused with descriptions used in the classical life-cycle approach. The latter lacked a clear focus and organization for the analysis and predefined formats for describing and filing the myriad of details that a development exercise collects during the systems development process beginning with vague descriptions of the problem and ending (hopefully) with detailed program specifications and user documentation. As a result, system descriptions formats were ad hoc, very verbose and difficult to read like a 'Victorian novel'. There was no assurance that the documentation was in any sense of the word complete or consistent. This produced many specification errors through omission and multiple interpretations. In addition, it is practically impossible to keep conventional life-cycle documentation up to date, because it is too time consuming and costly to track down all changes in a lengthy document that is redundant and uses ambiguous, often inconsistent terminology. Classical life-cycle approaches also failed to clearly separate functional requirements from implementation options and constraints. This led to confusion between logical and physical design details further compounding the system documentation problem.

Focus

Structured methodologies tried to resolve these issues by proposing specification and diagramming standards and a new organization of the life-cycle (see the phase structure section). In order to more effectively organize system documentation four documentation standards were proposed:

(1) A set of levelled diagrams documenting work processes with their inputs and outputs (data flows) and intermediate data storage needs (i.e. files, directories and the like) in a set of interlinked data flow diagrams.

(2) The details of the processes and data flows and data stores are recorded in a project data dictionary. For each type of entity in the system documentation (e.g. data flows, data stores, external entities and processes) a standard format is proposed to record the details. This results in a special, concise, semi-formal notation for system description; hence the notion of a special system description language arises.

(3) Data flow diagrams break processes down until they can be documented on one page. Again semi-formal notation like decision tables or Nassi-Schneidermann diagrams are used to describe the processes which during implementation provide the input to defining program modules. Process documentations are part of the project data dictionary.

(4) Program designs are documented via the tools of structured design such as structure charts that allow one to formulate models with strong cohesion that are only loosely coupled.

Phase structure

The specification phase of the fully structured life-cycle has five stages which are then followed by coding, testing and implementation. In each of the stages a special system model is built: in stage 1 the problem is formulated by building a model of the existing system. Based on this a logical model of the existing system is built in stage 2. In the more recent Yourdon (1989) version, an 'essential model' describes the key functional requirements which replaces the physical and logical model of the existing system. By now the requirements are thoroughly understood (at least in theory) and a logical model of the new systems is built in stage 3. The results of the logical specification stages are also used to identify hardware options. Stage 4 deals with the physicalization of this model describing implementation details. In stage 5 the specification is 'packaged' by filling in deferred details (such as processing error messages, performance considerations) and key user interfaces. Stage 6 uses this information to create program and hardware specifications.

This last stage of structured analysis and design deals with coding, testing and implementation.

Special methods and tools

The structured approach was instrumental in recognizing the importance of information systems modeling and the special methods and tools which support it. Methods include effective conventions for representing systems (i.e. data flow or state transition diagrams) and maintaining descriptions, i.e. data dictionary formats for processes and data. Most recently the ideas underlying the original methods and tools have been refined and incorporated into computer-aided software environments — complex computer packages that support all phases of the structured life-cycle. They include graphic editors, a central data repository, word processing and document generation facilities. In the most advanced versions, software tools can use the information collected in the data repository to generate database schemas and skeleton program, i.e. to support the generation of structured program code.

A2. Prototyping

Purpose and rationale

Prototyping, sometimes referred to as the 'iterative-adaptive' (Keen 1980) or 'evolutionary' (Hawgood 1982; Budde at al. 1984) approach to systems development, specifically attempts to address the difficulties with formulating and articulating requirements reliably and completely before proceeding with system design and implementation. It seems to have emerged at about the same time in a number of different countries (*cf.* Earl 1978; Keen and Scott-Morton 1978; Courbon and Bourgois 1980; Naumann and Jenkins 1982). It was an attempt to overcome several limitations of the system life-cycle methods which were a direct consequence of the life-cycle's rigidity. In situations that are very volatile or full of uncertainties, it simply is impossible to specify reliable requirements in advance as all learn the 'real' requirements as work proceeds. Often users do not know or cannot articulate their requirements and modeling the existing system is impossible or prohibitively difficult. In particular this is the case with systems that support creative problem solving and planning. In such cases neither users nor analysts can specify the requirements in advance. Modeling the existing system even if possible may be undesirable because it perpetuates unsatisfactory ways of information processing. The only way for improvement may be through experimentation with a working prototype, i.e. a system that delivers some promising functions, but is not developed in full detail. Basically, prototyping allows the user to experiment with partially completed systems that can be 'patched together' quickly. The prototype is a scaled down version of the full system which delivers a sufficient subset of the functions to allow the users to understand and modify the full systems' capabilities. Two principal ways are usually considered: A horizontal prototype provides the interfaces to give the user a 'feel' for the interaction patterns without much computational functions. In cases where computational power is essential to judge the potential of a new system, a vertical prototype provides some of the functionality by implementing a connected subset of functions that solves some real problems, but is constricted in scope. In either case, one of the main benefits of prototyping is that it permits the users to get a feel for the system through hands-on experience without the delays of systems development normally associated with life-cycle methodologies.

Focus

Prototyping forgoes the idea that detailed specifications must be developed before coding starts. Rather it aims at identifying some essential, but basic user requirements such as can be elicited by an informal conversation and documented in some casual notes. The prototype, a system exhibiting the essential features of a possible solution to the initial requirements, is then implemented quickly — typically within a few days. This initial solution is then presented to the user in the spirit of an experiment. The analyst assists the user in running the prototype and the user is encouraged to experiment with it. In this way it is learned what the initial prototype can do for him and in which way it is unsatisfactory. On the basis of what the analyst and the user learn from using the prototype, the requirements are refined and a second prototype is developed. This process is repeated until (hopefully) the user is satisfied. The last version of the prototype is documented and implemented more carefully to make it run efficiently and provide the user with a better interface.

Phase structure

Prototyping as originally proposed (Naumann and Jenkins 1982; Courbon and Bourgois 1980) essentially involves five phases leading to stepwise refinement so that 'the prototype becomes the system':

(1) Identify some of the basic requirements without any pretensions that these are either complete or not subject to drastic changes.

(2) Develop a design that meets these requirements and implement it.

(3) Have the user experiment with the prototype (possible with the developer acting as a chauffeur if the implementation is not robust) noting good and bad features.

(4) Revise and enhance the prototype accordingly thereby redefining and gradually completing the requirements and also improving the interface and reliability.

(5) Repeat steps 3 and 4 until the user is satisfied or time and money foreclose on further revisions. At this point 'the prototype becomes the system' (Lantz 1986, p. 5).

Special methods and tools

As noted above, there are two primary types of prototype (Floyd 1984, p. 4): 'horizontal' which is a mock-up of the user-system interfaces that allows the users to develop an appreciation of the interaction patterns of the system although without many computational functions; and 'vertical' which offers full computational power but limited functionality by implementing a carefully selected subset of functions in their intended final form solving some real problems, but which are constricted in scope.

As prototyping requires rapid implementation, very high level code generators, on-line screen design programs and the like are needed. Such tools also keep the cost of frequent recoding manageable. Often they are more suited for horizontal prototypes and less so for vertical prototypes that need a high degree of computational power. An exception to this is Iverson's APL. It is an early very high level language that was used for vertically prototyping mathematically oriented applications. More recently, database languages like SQL, query-by-example, spreadsheets, hypercard and graphic packages have been used. Some CASE tools have special prototyping features such as screen generators and journaling of screen designs.

A3. Soft System Methodology

Purpose and rationale

Checkland's (1981) goal was to develop a general methodology, termed soft system methodology (SSM) which could be used for information systems analysis but is not specific to IS. He views SSM as a meta-methodology that should guide a systematic approach and is tailored to a specific situation. This kind of meta-methodology is more concrete than a general philosophy for analyzing the world, but broader and more flexible than a specific professional method that is usually limited to a predefined problem domain. Checkland states that SSM was designed for use in broad problem-solving situations, but its relevance to systems analysis is clear. He sees information systems within the realm of social systems which he states are composed of rational assemblies of linked activities and sets of relationships. He refers to these as 'human activity systems'. SSM adopts the viewpoint that human activity systems possess goals which are not quantifiable. In human activity systems, problems are manifestations of mismatches between the perceived reality and that which is perceived might become actuality.

Focus

Checkland's methodology is different from the traditional approaches in that it does not prescribe specific tools and techniques, only general problem formulating approaches. It is a framework which does not force or lead the systems analyst to a particular 'solution', rather to an understanding. The seven steps (or 'stages') within the methodology are categorized as 'real world' activities and 'systems thinking' activities. The steps in the former are executed by the people in the real world or problem situation; the steps in the latter attempt to provide a conceptual model of the real world which is in turn modified by discussion with the people concerned. It is therefore a highly participative approach.

Phase structure

Although the characterization of the general form of SSM has recently been
somewhat modified (Checkland and Scholes 1990), as noted earlier in section
5 of chapter 5, the following refers to the version presented in Checkland
(1981).

(1) Stages 1 and 2: Expressing the problem situation

The function of these stages is to outline the situation so that a range of
possible and relevant views can be revealed. The first stage is concerned
with the problem situation unstructured and the second attempts to 'express the problem situation' such that many different perceptions of the
problem situation, from people with a wide range of roles, are collected.
The views will, hopefully, reveal patterns of communication (both formal
and informal), power, hierarchy, and the like. These early stages should not
attempt to 'define' the problem, only to build up an understanding of the
'situation in which there is perceived to be a problem' without imposing
any particular structure on it or assuming any structure exists.

(2) Stage 3: Root definitions of relevant systems

By the conclusion of stage 2, different perceptions of the problem situation
should have been sufficiently clear to enable 'notional systems' to be named.
These are systems which are relevant to the problem. Stage 3 is concerned
with choosing the appropriate notional systems from the stated systems in
stage 2. The choice is done through the help of what is known as a 'root
definition' — a concise description of a human activity system that captures
a particular view of it. To put it differently, it is a definition of the basic
nature or purpose of the system thought by a particular actor to be relevant
to the problem at hand. The construction of the root definition is at the core
of the methodology. Checkland offers a six-element checklist which all root
definitions should explicitly contain, known conveniently by the acronym
CATWOE, which stands for:

   Customer — clients, beneficiaries, or victims of the system's activities;

   Actors — the agents who carry out, or cause to be carried out, the
   transformation activities of the system;

   Transformation — the process by which defined inputs are transformed
   into defined outputs;

   Weltanschauung — an outlook, framework, image, etc. which makes
   the particular root definition a meaningful one;

   Ownership — the agents who have a prime concern for the system,
   systems owners, system control or sponsorship; and

   Environmental Constraints — environmental impositions; features of
   the environment or wider system which have to be taken as given.

(3) Stage 4: Making and testing conceptual models

Conceptual models are models which will accomplish what is defined in the root definition. If the root definition is viewed as an account of what the system is, then the conceptual model is an account of the activities which the system must perform in order to be the system named in the definition. Conceptual models are not descriptions of any part of the real world, only the structured set of activities sufficient to account for the system as defined by the root definition.

(4) Stage 5: Comparing conceptual models with reality

At this stage, conceptual models are compared with the problem situation analyzed in stage 2. There are four approaches for making such a comparison:

(i)   use the conceptual model as a basis of ordered questioning — in particular, to open up a debate about change;

(ii) trace through the sequence of events that have produced the present problem situation and compare what had happened with what would have happened if the conceptual models had been implemented;

(iii) ask what features of the conceptual models are particularly different from the present reality, and why; and

(iv) develop an alternative conceptual model of the problem situation with the same 'form' as the first, then 'overlay' one onto the other revealing mismatches which are the sources of discussion of change.

The purpose of the comparison stage is to generate debate about the possible changes which might be made within the perceived problem situation.

(5) Stages 6 and 7: Implementing 'feasible and desirable' change

Checkland states that the changes likely to be recommended through his methodology will probably be more modest in nature than what would be recommended by a 'hard' methodology . (The latter is likely to advocate the creation and implementation of a new system.) Changes should be desirable as a result of the insight gained from building and selecting root definitions, and creating conceptual models. They should be culturally feasible taking into account the characteristics of the situation, the people in it, and their shared experiences and beliefs. Changes generated from this stage are debated by those people in the problem situation who care about the perceived problem. Once changes have been agreed, they can be implemented. This process may be straightforward or problematic — in which case the methodology itself may be used to help in the implementation process.

Special methods and tools

Checkland offers a number of methods and tools which are specific to SSM. For example, the notion of CATWOE as a vehicle for making sure alternative root definitions are sensible descriptors of the problem situation; rich pictures for describing the problem situation in an imaginative and creative fashion; making and testing conceptual models which abstract from the real world; human activity systems which describe the nature of what is studied; and what might be thought of as SSM's dualistic ontology which allows the separation of the conceptual and real world spheres.

A4. UTOPIA

As UTOPIA is not a methodology but rather a specific project it cannot be written up in the same structure as above. The UTOPIA project was an attempt at developing a computer-based system for typesetters in the newspaper industry in Sweden. The project invoked a number of interesting tools and techniques in the systems development exercise. Here, we briefly describe the nature of the industry and then how the systems development proceeded.

Traditional newspaper production involves four major processes: writing, editing, typesetting and printing. Reporters and columnists write individual copy which is then edited by editorial staff. Typesetters take the edited copy, including the relevant pictorial material, and lay out pages. Printers take the results and print the newspapers. Typical systems designs focus on rationalizing newspaper production by combining tasks which can logically be done on the same electronic device, such as editing and formatting. Page layout is conceived as a natural extension of formatting. A requirements analysis along these lines suggests that the editorial staff can perform the typesetting function because computers already aid the editors with handling page layout as well as editing. Editors can embed typesetting commands directly in the final copy. Page layout is done on screen and sent to phototypesetting equipment. The editors become responsible not only for editing but also for page makeup. High resolution screens, electronic cut, paste and scaling facilities, and previewing apparatus permit the typesetting function to be assigned to the editors.

In the UTOPIA project (Ehn *et al.* 1983; Howard 1985) an alternative approach was tried at one newspaper company. The system development team consisted of union representatives and typesetters. Their goal was the establishment of an electronic typesetting support system which enhanced the position of the typesetting craft in the newspaper industry. Union involvement in the design team was required because the typesetters by themselves possessed neither the know-how nor the resources necessary to complete such a systems development project. Union resources were used to employ computer scientists and consultants to educate and advise the project team. The newspaper's management was not included in the design team so that typesetters' interests were given primacy in all design decisions. Existing turn-key systems were considered inappropriate because they had built-in design constraints and management biases that did not take into account the unique requirements of the typesetting craft. These management biases emphasized cost savings, efficiency and control leading to deskilling, job losses and an aesthetically inferior end product. Data processing specialists assumed an advisory role serving the typesetters' interest. In the requirements analysis, the design team viewed typesetting as an essential task requiring specialist skills which would be lost by its integration with editing. Two types of requirements were established:

(1) the transforming of edited texts into made-up pages; and

(2) the creating of an aesthetically pleasing product: the newspaper.

Typesetting skills were different from editorial skills which were responsible for content. (Editors are in charge of substance, typesetters are in charge of form.) The crafts' interest was to retain the quality of typesetting and to possibly enhance the productivity of typesetters. To retain quality, systems design options focused on providing the flexibility and diversity of the traditional tools of the typesetting trade by electronic means. For meeting this objective, the team found it necessary to use hardware mock-ups in order to overcome the limitations of the then available technology. While this is similar to prototyping, the use of hardware mock-ups overcame the bias inherent in the technology used for prototyping. The available prototyping tools were unable to accommodate the craft skills which were used to meet the aesthetic requirements of newspaper page layout. To enhance the quality of typesetting output, additional system capabilities were added such as fine-tuning the contrast of pictures, scaling of pictures, etc. which were not available before. The UTOPIA approach resulted in an electronic typesetting support system that enhanced the typesetters' skills and productivity.

Development process differences

Process differences relate to the decisions made during system development. In the UTOPIA project, the development team made a conscious decision to retain and enhance the craft, not to include management representatives, and not to be bound by the then available page layout technology. The rationale for these decisions can be traced back to the paradigmatic assumptions which guided the development team. For example, the assumption that conflict is endemic to society in the radical structuralist paradigm, motivated the project team to focus on the conflict between typesetters and management. The denial of the possibility of the system developer being a neutral expert, committed them to bolstering the position of the worker in the perceived social struggle and to enhancing the craft of the typesetters. This led to an emphasis on union leadership which put control of systems development in the hands of a single group. It also heightened the sensitivity to the effects of ideological, managerial bias in that the existing typesetting systems would make the craft largely redundant thereby enhancing management control over workers. Moreover, they believed the ideological bias was manifest in the components of the technology itself: the social neutrality of technology was denied. As Kubicek (1983) notes: 'This approach is based on the assumption that EDP-knowledge is not impartial to the interests of capital and labor but rather biased by the perspective of capital and management' (p. 9). If available technology had limitations that would not allow the enhancement of the craft's future, then it would not be in the interest of the workers to accept existing technology as a design constraint. In the words of Ehn *et al.* (1983, p. 439): 'The trade unions' ability ... is limited in an increasing number of situations to a choice between yes or no to the purchase of 'turn-key packages' of technology and organization'.

A5. ETHICS

Purpose and rationale

ETHICS, an acronym for Effective Technical and Human Implementation of Computer Systems, is a methodology developed by Enid Mumford at the Manchester Business School and has been evolving over the past fifteen years (Mumford 1983). It is quite different from the traditional approaches to information system development in that it is based on the ideals of socio-technical systems (STS). A key aspect of the methodology is that it views participation not only as a necessary device to obtain valid requirements, or stimulate commitment, but as an intrinsic right or end in itself. Consequently users play a very large and important role in systems development. While user involvement is important in any methodology, it is absolutely vital in ETHICS.

Focus

While the participative nature of ETHICS is often written about in the literature, this facet of the methodology should not be overemphasized. The methodology is a serious attempt at operationalizing the key aspects of the socio-technical systems philosophy. In particular, two design teams are formed each with a different focus of attention. One is concerned with the technical design of the system, the other with its social design. Another important aspect of ETHICS is its focusing on the job satisfaction needs of the system users. ETHICS's social orientation is clearly visible throughout the methodology.

Phase structure

The ETHICS methodology contains six stages which are further divided into twenty-five steps (*cf.* overview in figure A1)

Stage 1: Essential systems analysis

Stage 1 is the preliminary phase of the ETHICS methodology. The procedures carried out here have much in common with the more conventional methodologies. For example, in this stage the problem to be solved is identified, its boundaries are noted, the current system is analyzed and described, and key objectives and tasks are identified. After the establishment of key objectives and tasks, it is necessary to pinpoint key information needed to accomplish these objectives and tasks. Subsequently, a diagnosis is made of efficiency needs and job satisfaction needs, and a future forecast ('future analysis') is undertaken. The final step in the first stage is an exercise in

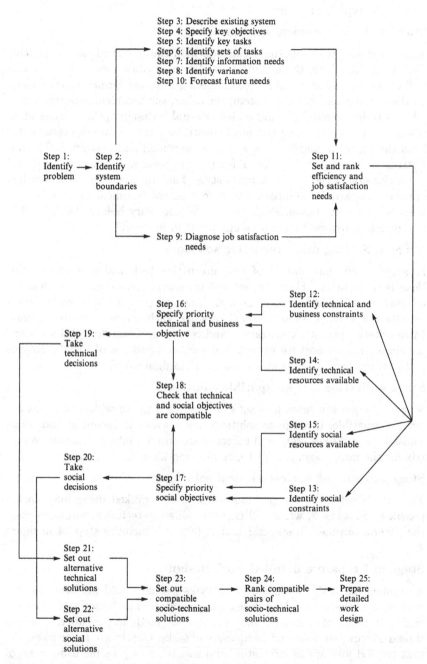

Figure A1: stages of the ETHICS methodology

which all interest groups rank the list of objectives on a scale of 1–5. (Stage 1 includes steps 1–11 in figure A1.)

Stage 2: Socio-technical systems design

Stage 2 tries to reconcile the social side with the technical side of systems design. In this stage, the technical and business constraints are set out as well as the social constraints. Two different groups are formed (one focusing on the social aspects of the system; the other, the technical aspects) whose job it is to find technically and socially desirable design options. After identification of the social and technical constraints, the resources available for both the technical and social system are identified and examined. The objectives and tasks set in stage 1 for the technical and business side, and the social side are set out in priority style. The objectives (in ranked order) are then checked for compatibility before actual technical and social systems decisions are taken. Revision may be necessary before this final step is completed. (Stage 2 includes steps 12–20 in figure A1.)

Stage 3: Setting out alternative solutions

In stage 3, an examination of any alternative technical and social solutions is undertaken. These are set out in matrix form evaluating possible advantages and disadvantages as well as overall compatibility with the established objectives. As in the previous stage, each will be evaluated against three criteria: priority, constraints, and resources. Once doubtful solutions are eliminated, a short list of technical solutions and one of social solutions is drawn up. (Stage 3 includes steps 21–22 in figure A1.)

Stage 4: Setting out compatible solutions

Stage 4 merges the short lists set out in stage 3 to see which solutions are most compatible. Incomplete solutions are discarded. Technical and social solutions found to operate well together are entered into an evaluation matrix for the next stage. (Stage 4 includes step 23 in figure A1.)

Stage 5: Ranking socio-technical solutions

The matrix set up in the previous stage is now ranked using information generated in stage 3, while still ensuring all socio-technical solutions meet the criteria outlined in stages 1 and 2. (Stage 5 includes step 24 in figure A1.)

Stage 6: Prepare a detailed work design

A detailed list and description of all tasks people would perform under a particular socio-technical solution's implementation is drawn up. Tasks are ranked in terms of simplicity and attempts are made to provide a balanced spread of required skills and complexity of tasks. Checks are made to ensure that created jobs are as interesting and satisfying as possible using a set of 'issues of concern'. If the highest ranking socio-technical solution scores high on these issues while achieving the technical objectives, it is accepted as the final solution. If this is not the case, another short listed solution is tried in the same manner. (Stage 6 includes step 25 in figure A1.)

Special methods and tools

ETHICS adopts a number of special methods for systems development. For example, there is a special diagramming method used for describing work layout. There is also a job diagnostic questionnaire which is used to elicit views on the job situation. More importantly perhaps, ETHICS employs a facilitator who seeks to find a consensus on the systems development exercise using special questionnaire instruments.

Another special feature is the use of dialectics to stimulate the generation of socially and technically desirable alternatives. Mumford noted that managers often varied technical solutions after the fact at the implementation stage. She observed that much more could be accomplished to meet social requirements if they were considered at a stage when design was not yet frozen. At that time, social objectives could often be met with little or no extra cost. This gave rise to the split of the development team described in stage 2 and the explicit consideration of social and technical design objectives as described in stages 3 and 4.

Bibliography

Abrial, J. R., 1974, Data Semantics. In Klimbie J. and Koffeman K. (eds.), *Data Base Management*. North-Holland, Amsterdam, 1–60.

Agresti, W. W., 1986, *New Paradigms for Software Development*. IEEE Computer Society Press, North-Holland, Amsterdam.

Alavi, M., 1984, An Assessment of the Prototyping Approach of IS Development. *Communications of ACM*, **27** (6), 556–563.

Albrecht, J., and Lim, G.-C., 1986, A Search for Alternative Planning Theory, Use of Critical Theory. *Journal of Architectural Planning Research*, **3** 117–131.

Alexander, J., (ed.), 1985, *Neofunctionalism*. Sage Publications, Beverly Hills, CA.

Alter, S., 1980, *Decision Support Systems: Current Practice and Continuing Challenges*. Addison-Wesley, Reading, MA.

Alvarez, R. and Klein, H. K., 1989, Information Systems Development for Human Progress?. In Klein, H. K. and Kumar, K. (eds.), *Systems Development for Human Progress*. North-Holland, Amsterdam, 1–19.

Andersen, N., Kensing, F., Lundin, J., Mathiassen, L., Munk-Madsen, A., Rasbech, M. and Sorgaard, P., 1990, *Professional Systems Development: Experience, Ideas and Action*. Prentice Hall International, Hemel Hempstead.

Andersen, P.-B., 1991, A Semiotic Approach to Construction and Assessment of Computer Systems. In Nissen, H.-E., Klein, H. K. and Hirschheim, R. (eds.), *Information Systems Research: Contemporary Approaches and Emergent Traditions*. North-Holland, Amsterdam, 465–514.

Andersen, P.-B. and Holmqvist, B. 1995, *The Semiotics of the Workplace.*, Walter de Gruyter, Berlin.

ANSI/X3 SPARC, 1975, *Study Group on Data Base Management Systems*, Interim Report. FDT–Bulletin **7** (2).

Apel, K., 1980, *Towards a Transformation of Philosophy*. Routledge and Kegan Paul, London.

Argyris, C., 1971, Management Information Systems: the Challenge to Rationality and Emotionality. *Management Science*, **17** (6), 275–282.

Argyris, C., 1982, *Learning and Action: Individual and Organizational*. Jossey-Bass, San Francisco, CA.

Argyris, C. and Schoen, D., 1974, *Theory in Practice*. Jossey-Bass, San Francisco, CA.

Argyris, C. and Schoen, D., 1978, *Organizational Learning: A Theory of Action Perspective*. Addison-Wesley, Reading, MA.

Assche, F. van, Moulin, B. and Rolland, C., (eds.) 1991, *Object-oriented Approach in Information Systems*. North-Holland, Amsterdam.

Auramaki, E., Lehtinen, E. and Lyytinen, K., 1988, A Speech-act Based Office Modeling Approach. *ACM Transactions on Office Information Systems*, **6** (2), 126-152.

Auramaki, E., Hirschheim, R. and Lyytinen, K., 1992a, Modelling Offices through Discourse Analysis: The SAMPO Approach. *The Computer Journal*, **35** (4), 342-352.

Auramaki E., Hirschheim R. and Lyytinen K., 1992b, Modelling Offices through Discourse Analysis: a Comparison and Evaluation of SAMPO with OSSAD and ICN. *The Computer Journal*, **35** (5), 492-499.

Austin, J., 1962, *How to do Things with Words*. Clarendon Press, Oxford.

Avison, D. E. and Fitzgerald, G., 1988, *Information Systems Development: Methodologies, Techniques and Tools*. Blackwell Scientific, Oxford.

Avison, D. E. and Wood-Harper, A.T., 1990, *Multiview: An Exploration in Information Systems Development*. Blackwell Scientific, Oxford.

Backhouse J., 1991, *The Use of Semantic Analysis in the Development of Information Systems*. PhD Dissertation, Department of Information Systems, London School of Economics.

Baier, V. E. and March, J. G., 1986, Implementation and Ambiguity. *Scandinavian Journal of Management Studies*, May, 197-212.

Banbury, J., 1987, Towards a Framework for Systems Analysis Practice. In Boland, R. and Hirschheim, R. (eds.), *Critical Issues in Information Systems Research*. Wiley, Chichester, 79-96.

Bansler, J., 1989, *Systemudvikling: Teori og Hitorie i Skandinavisk Perspectiv*. Studenttliteratur; as referenced and summarized in J. Bansler, Systems Development Research in Scandinavia: Three Theoretical Schools. *Scandinavian Journal of Information Systems*, **1** 3-20.

Bansler, J. and Havn, E., 1991, The Nature of Software Work. In Vanden Besselaar, P., Clement, A., and Jarvinen, P. (eds.), *Information System Work and Organizational Design*. North-Holland, Amsterdam, 145-152.

Banville, C., 1990, *Legitimacy and Cognitive Mapping: An Exporatory Study of a Social Dimension of Organizational Information Systems*. PhD Thesis, Faculté des Sciences de L'Administration, Université Laval, Quebec.

Bardach, E., 1977, *The Implementation Game*. MIT Press, Cambridge, MA.

Bariff, M. and Ginzberg, M., 1982, MIS and the Behavioral Sciences. *Data Base*, **13** (1), 19-26.

Barwise, J., 1983, *Situations and Attitudes*. MIT Press, Cambridge, MA.

Baskerville, R., 1991, Practitioner Autonomy and the Bias of Methods and Tools. In Nissen, H.-E., Klein, H. K. and Hirschheim, R. (eds.), *Information Systems Research: Contemporary Approaches and Emergent Traditions*. North-Holland, Amsterdam, 673-697.

Batini, C., Lenzerini, M. and Navathe, S., 1986, A Comparative Analysis of Methodologies for Database Schema Integration. *Computing Surveys*, **18** (4), 323-364.

Batra D., and Davis J., 1989, A Study of Conceptual Data Modeling in Data Base Design: Similarities and Differences between Expert and Novice Designers. In *Proceedings of 10th International Conference on Information Systems*. Janice DeGross, John C. Henderson, Benn Konsynski (eds.), ACM, Baltimore, MD.

Batra, D., Hoffer J. and Bostrom R., 1988, A Comparison of User Performance Between the Relational and the Extended Entity Relationship Model in the Discovery Phase of Database Design. In *Proceedings of the 9th International Conference on Information Systems*. Minneapolis, MN.

Berger, P., and Luckmann, T., 1967, *The Social Construction of Reality: A Treatise in the Sociology of Knowledge*. Doubleday, New York.

Biller, H., 1979, On the Notion of Irreducible Relations. In Bracchi G. and Nijssen, G. (eds.) *Database Architecture*. North-Holland, Amsterdam.

Biller H. and Neuhold, E., 1978, Semantics of Databases: The Semantics of Data Models. *Information Systems*, **3** (1), 11–30.

Bjerknes, G. and Bratteteig, T., 1984, The Application Perspective – Another Way of Conceiving Systems Development and EDP-based Systems. In Saaksjarvi, M. (ed.), *Proceedings of the Seventh Scandinavian Research Seminar on Systemeering*. Helsinki, August 1984.

Bjerknes, G. and Bratteteig, T., 1985, FLORENCE in Wonderland – Systems Development with Nurses. Paper presented at the Conference on Development and Use of Computer Based Systems and Tools, August, Aarhus, Denmark.

Bjorn-Andersen, N. and Davis, G., (eds.), 1986, *Information Systems Assessment: Issues and Challenges*. North-Holland. Amsterdam.

Bjorn-Andersen, N., Earl, M., Holst, J. and Mumford, E., (eds.), 1982, *Information Society: For Richer For Poorer*. North-Holland, Amsterdam.

Blair, David C., 1990, *Language and Representation*. Elsevier, New York.

Bleicher, J., 1980, *Contemporary Hermeneutics – Hermeneutics as Method Philosophy and Critique*. Routledge and Kegan Paul, London.

Bleicher, J., 1982, *The Hermeneutic Imagination: Outline of a Positive Critique of Scientism and Sociology*. Routledge and Kegan Paul, London.

Blumenthal, S., 1969, *Management Information Systems: A Framework for Planning and Development*. Prentice Hall, Englewood Cliffs, NJ.

Bodker, S. and Groenbaek, K., 1989, Cooperative Prototyping Experiments – Users and Designers Envision a Dentist Case Record System. In Bowers, J. and Benford, S. (eds.), *Proceedings of the First European Conference on Computer–Supported Cooperative Work*. EC-CSCW, London, 343–357.

Bodker, S., Ehn, P., Kammersgaard, J., Kyng, M. and Sundblad, Y., 1987, A UTOPIAN Experience: On Design of Powerful Computer-Based Tools for Skilled Graphic Workers. In Bjerknes, G., Ehn, P. and Kyng, M. (eds.), *Computers and Democracy: A Scandinavian Challenge*. Avebury, Aldershot, 251–278.

Boehm, B., 1976, Software Engineering. *IEEE Transactions on Computers*, December, 225–240.

Boehm, B., 1981, *Software Economics*. Prentice Hall, Englewood Cliffs, NJ.

Boehm, B. W., 1988, A Spiral Model of Software Development and Enhancement. *Computer*, **21** (5), May, 61–72.

Boland, R. J., 1978, The Process and Product of System Design. *Management Science*, **28** (9), 887–898.

Boland, R. J., 1979, Control, Causality and Information System Requirements. *Accounting, Organizations and Society*, **4** (5), 259–272.

Boland, R. J., 1985, Phenomenology: A Preferred Approach to Research in Information Systems. In Mumford, E., Hirschheim, R., Fitzgerald, G. and Wood-Harper, T. (eds.), *Research Methods in Information Systems*. North-Holland, Amsterdam, 193–202.

Boland, R. J., 1987, The In-Formation of Information Systems. In Boland, R. and Hirschheim, R. (eds.), *Critical Issues in Information Systems Research*. Wiley, Chichester, 363–380.

Boland R. J. 1989, Metaphorical Traps in Developing Information Systems for Human Progress. In Klein H. and Kumar K. (eds.), *Systems Development for Human Progress*. North-Holland, Amsterdam, 277–290.

Boland, R. J., 1991, Information System Use as a Hermeneutic Process. In Nissen, H.-E., Klein, H. and Hirschheim, R. (eds.), *Information Systems Research: Contemporary Approaches and Emergent Traditions*. North-Holland, Amsterdam, 439–458.

Boland, R. J. and Day, W., 1982, The Process of System Design: A Phenomenological Approach. In Ginzberg, M. and Ross, C. (eds.), *Proceedings of the Third International Conference on Information Systems*. Ann Arbor, MI, 31–45.

Bolour, A. and Dekeyser, L., 1983, Abstractions in Temporal Information. *Information Systems*, **8** (1), 11–30.

Bostrom, R. and Heinen, S., 1977, MIS Problems and Failures: A Sociotechnical Perspective – Part I: The Causes. *MIS Quarterly*, **1** (3), 17–32.

Bracchi G. and Lockeman P., (eds.), 1980, *Database Architecture*. North-Holland, Amsterdam.

Brancheau, J., Schuster, L. and March, S., 1989, Building and Implementing an Information Architecture. *Data Base*, **20** (2), Summer, 9–17.

Braverman, H., 1974, *Labor and Monopoly Capital*. Monthly Review Press, New York.

Briefs, U., 1983, Participatory Systems Design as Approach for a Workers' Production Policy. In Briefs, U., Ciborra, C. and Schneider, L. (eds.), *Systems Design For, With, and By the Users*. North-Holland, Amsterdam.

Briefs, U., Ciborra, C. and Schneider, L., (eds.), 1983, *Systems Design For, With, and By the Users*. North-Holland, Amsterdam.

Brinkmann, H., 1986, Autonomous Areas in Comprehensive Office Systems – A Perspective of Human Work in Organizations. In *Proceedings of the IFIP WG 9.1 Working Conference on Systems Design for Human Development and Productivity*. Berlin.

Brodie, M., 1978, *Specification and Verification of Database Semantic Integrity*. PhD Dissertation, University of Toronto.

Brodie, M., 1979, Data Quality in Information Systems. *Information & Management*, **3** (4), 245–258.

Brodie, M., 1980, The Application of Data Types to Database Semantic Integrity. *Information Systems*, **5** 287–296.

Brooks, F., 1975, *The Mythical Man-Month*. Addison-Wesley, Reading, MA.

Brown, G. and Yule, G., 1984, *Discourse Analysis*. Cambridge University Press, Cambridge.

Bubenko, J. A., 1977a, IAM: An Inferential Abstract Modeling Approach to Design of Conceptual Schemas. In *Proceedings of the ACM SIGMOD*, 62–74.

Bubenko, J. A., 1977b, Validity and Verification Aspects of Information Modeling. In *Proceedings of the Third International Conference on Very Large Data Bases*, 556–565.

Bubenko, J. A., 1978, *Database Design in the Perspective of Information Systems Development*. Chalmers University of Technology, Department of Computer Sciences, Report ADB–HT–78.

Bubenko J. A., 1979, On the Role of "Understanding Models" in Conceptual Schema Design. In *Proceedings of the Fifth International Conference on Very Large Data Bases*. IEEE Society Press.

Bubenko J. A., 1980, Information Modelling in the Context of System Development. In Lavington, H. A. (ed.), *Proceedings of the IFIP World Congress*. North-Holland, Amsterdam, 395–411.

Bubenko, J. A., 1983, Information and Data Modeling – State of the Art and Research Directions. In Kangassalo, H. (ed.), *Proceeding of the Second Scandinavian Research Seminar on Information Modeling and Data Base Management*. University of Tampere, Tampere, Finland, 9–28.

Bubenko, J. A., 1986, *Information Systems Methodologies – A Research View*. SYSLAB Report No. 40, The Systems Development and Artificial Intelligence Laboratory, University of Stockholm, Sweden.

Budde, R., Kuhlenkamp, K., Mathiassen, L. and Zullighoven, H., (eds.), 1984, *Approaches to Prototyping*. Springer-Verlag. Berlin.

Burch, J. and Strater, F., 1974, *Information Systems: Theory and Practice*. Wiley, New York.

Burns, A., 1981, *The Microchip: Appropriate or Inappropriate Technology*. Ellis Horwood, Chichester.

Burnstein, D., 1980, *BIAIT – An Emerging Management Engineering Discpline*. BIAIT International Inc., Petersburg, NY.

Burrell, G. and Morgan, G., 1979, *Sociological Paradigms and Organizational Analysis*. Heinemann, London.

Canning, R. 1956, *Electronic Data Processing for Business and Industry*. Wiley, New York.

Capurro, R., 1986, *Hermeneutic der Fachinformation*. K. Alber Verlag, Munich.

Capurro, R., 1992, Informatics and Hermeneutics. In Floyd, C., Zullighoven, H., Budde, R. and Keil-Slavik, R. (eds.), *Software Development and Reality Construction*. Springer-Verlag, 363–375.

Carlson, J., Ehn, P., Erlander, B., Perby, M. and Sandberg, A., 1978, Planning and Control from the Perspective of Labor: A Short Presentation of the DEMOS Project. *Accounting, Organizations, and Society,* **3** (3/4).

Carnap, R., 1956, *Meaning and Necessity.* Harvard University Press, Cambridge, MA.

Carroll, D.C., 1965, *Man–Machine Cooperation on Planning and Control Problems.* Paper presented at the International Symposium on Long Range Planning for Management, UNESCO, Paris, September 20–24.

Carroll, D. C., 1967, Implications of On–line, Real Time Systems for Management Decision Making. In Myers, C. A. (ed.), *The Impact of Computers on Management.* MIT Press, Cambridge, MA.

Chaffee, E., 1985, Three Models of Strategy. *Academy of Management Review,* **10** (1), 89–98.

Chase, S., 1956, Foreword to Carroll, J.B., (ed.), *Language, Thought, and Reality: Selected Writings of Benjamin Lee Whorf.* MIT Press, Cambridge, MA.

Checkland, P., 1972, Towards a Systems-Based Methodology for Real-World Problem Solving. *Journal of Systems Engineering,* **3** (2), 9–38.

Checkland, P., 1981, *Systems Thinking, Systems Practice.* Wiley, Chichester.

Checkland, P., and Scholes, J., 1990, *Soft Systems Methodology in Action.* Wiley, Chichester.

Chen, P., 1976, The Entity-Relationship Model: Toward a Unified View of Data. *ACM Transactions on Database Systems,* **1** (1), 9–36.

Chen, P., 1977, The Entity–Relationship Model: a Basis for the Enterprise View of Data. In *Proceedings of the National Computer Conference.* Dallas, TX **46** 77–84.

Chen, P., (ed.) 1980, *Entity–Relationship Approach to Systems Analysis and Design.* North-Holland, Amsterdam.

Chen, P. 1981, Entity–Relationship Approach to Information Modeling and Analysis. In *Proceedings of the Second International Conference on E-R Approach.* Washington, Oct. 12–14, 1981, published by E-R Institute.

Chomsky, N, 1966, *Syntactic Structures.* Mouton, The Hague.

Chua, W. F., 1986, Radical Developments in Accounting Thought. *The Accounting Review,* **61** (4), 601–632.

Churchman, C. W., 1971, *The Design of Inquiring Systems.* Basic Books, New York.

Ciborra, C. U., 1981, Information Systems and Transactions Architecture. *International Journal of Policy Analysis and Information Systems,* **5** (4), 305–323.

Ciborra C. U., 1987, Research Agenda for a Transaction Cost Approach to Information Systems. In Boland, R. and Hirschheim, R. (eds.), *Critical Issues in Information Systems Research.* Wiley, Chichester, 253–274.

Cleland, D. and King, W., 1975, *Systems Analysis and Project Management.* McGraw-Hill, New York.

Coad, P. and Yourdon, E., 1990, *Object-Oriented Analysis.* Prentice Hall, Englewood Cliffs, NJ.

CODASYL, 1961, An Information Algebra Phase I Report. *Communications of the ACM*, **5** (4), 190–204.

Codd, E. F., 1970 A Relational Model of Data for Large Shared Data Banks. *Communications of the ACM*, **13** (6), 377–387.

Codd, E. F., 1972, Relational Completeness of Database Sublanguages. In Rustin, R., (ed.), *Data Base Systems: Courant Sixth Computer Science Symposium*. Prentice Hall, Englewood Cliffs, NJ, 33–64.

Codd, E. F., 1979 Extending the Data Base Relational Model to Capture More Meaning. *ACM Transactions on Data Base Systems*, **4** (4), December, 397–403.

Colter, M., 1982, Evolution of the Structured Methodologies. In Couger, J. D., Colter, M. and Knapp, R. (eds.), *Advanced System Development/Feasibility Techniques*. Wiley, New York, 73–96.

Cooper, R. and Swanson, E.B., 1979, Management Information Requirements Assessment: the State of the Art. *Data Base*, **11** (2), 5–16.

Coser, L., 1956, *The Functions of Social Conflict*. Free Press, New York.

Cotterman, W. and Senn, J., (eds.), 1992, *Challenges and Strategies for Research in Systems Development*. Wiley, Chichester.

Cotterman, W., Couger, J. D., Enger, N. and Harold, F., (eds.), 1981, *Systems Analysis and Design: A Foundation for the 1980s*. North-Holland, Amsterdam.

Couger, J. D., 1973, Evolution of Business System Analysis Techniques. *ACM Computing Surveys*, September, 167–198.

Couger, J. D., 1982, Evolution of Systems Development Techniques. In Couger, J. D., Colter, M. and Knapp, R. (eds.), *Advanced System Development/ Feasibility Techniques*. Wiley, New York.

Couger, J. D., Colter, M. and Knapp, R., 1982, *Advanced Systems Development/Feasibility Techniques*. Wiley, New York.

Courbon, J.C., and Bourgois, M., 1980, The IS Designer as a Nurturing Agent of a Socio-technical Process. In Lucas, H., Land, F., Lincoln, T. and Supper, K. (eds.), *The Information Systems Environment*. North-Holland, Amsterdam, 139-148.

Dahlbom, C. and Mathiassen, L., 1993, *Computers in Context*. Blackwell Scientific, Oxford.

Daniels, A. and Yeates, D., (eds.) 1969, *1971: Systems Analysis*. American edition, Palo Alto, 1971. (Original title: *Basic Training in Systems Analysis*. National Computing Centre, England 1969).

Date, C. J., 1975, *An Introduction to Database Systems*. Addison-Wesley, Reading, MA.

Davenport, R., 1979, Logical Database Design – from Entity Model to DBMS Structure. *The Australian Computer Journal*, **11** (3).

Davis, G., 1982, Strategies for Information Requirements Determination. *IBM Systems Journal*, **21** (1), 4–30.

Davis, G. B. and Olson, M., 1985, *Management Information Systems-Conceptual Foundations Methods and Development* (2nd edition). McGraw-Hill, New York.

Deen, S., 1980, A Canonical Schema for a Generalized Data Model with Local Interfaces. *The Computer Journal*, **23** (3), 201–206.

DeMaio, A., 1980, Socio-technical Methods for Information Systems Design. In *The Information Systems Environment*. Lucas, H., Land, F., Lincoln, T. and Supper, K. (eds.), North-Holland, Amsterdam, 105–122.

DeMarco, T., 1978, *Structured Analysis and Systems Specification*. Yourdon Press, New York.

DeMarco, T., 1979, *Structured Analysis and Systems Specification*. Prentice Hall, Englewood Cliffs, NJ.

Denning, P., Comer, D., Gries, D., Mulder, M., Tucker, A. Turner, A. J. and Young, P., 1989, Computing as a Discipline: Final Report of the Task Force on the Core of Computer Science. *Communcations of the ACM*, **32** (1), 9–23.

Dhar, V. and Jarke, M., 1988, Dependency Directed Reasoning and Learning in Systems Maintenance Support. *IEEE Transactions on Software Engineering*, **14** (2), 211–227.

Dickson, G. W., 1981, Management Information Systems: Evolution and Status. In Yovitz, M. (ed.), *Advances in Computers*, **20** Academic Press, New York, 1–29.

Dickson, G. W., Senn, J. and Chervany, N., 1977, Research in Management Information Systems: the Minnesota Experiments. *Management Science*, **23** (9), 913–923.

Dietz, J. L. G., 1994, Business Modelling for Business Redesign. In *Proceedings of the Hawaii International Conference on Systems Sciences*, **27** IEEE Press.

Dietz, J. and Widdershoven, G., 1992, A Comparison of the Linguistic Theories of Searle and Habermas as a Basis for Communication Supporting Systems.. In van de Riet, R. and Meersman, R. (eds.), *Linguistic Instruments in Knowledge Engineering*. 121–130.

Dobson, J., Martin, M., Olphert, C. and Powrie, S., 1991, Determining Requirements for CSCW: the ORDIT Approach. In Stamper R., Kerola P., Lee R. and Lyytinen, K. (eds.), *Collaborative Work, Social Communications and Information Systems*. North-Holland, Amsterdam, 333–354.

Donaldson-Dewitz S., 1991, Contracting on a Performative Network: Using Information Technology as a Legal Intermediary. In Stamper R., Kerola P., Lee R. and Lyytinen, K. (eds.), *Collaborative Work, Social Communications and Information Systems*. North-Holland, Amsterdam, 271–294.

Dowty, D., Wall, R. and Peters, S., 1981, *Introduction to Montague Semantics*. Reidel, The Hague.

Dreyfus, H., 1982, *What Computers Can't Do*. Harper & Row, New York.

Dreyfus, H. and Dreyfus, S., 1986, *Mind over Machine – the Power of Human Intuition and Expertise in the Era of the Computer*. Basil Blackwell, Oxford.

Dumdum, U. R., 1993, *An Approach to Problem Formulation in Information Systems Development*. Unpublished PhD thesis, State University of New York at Binghamton, NY.

Dummett, M., 1981, *Frege: Philosophy of Language* (2nd edition). Duckworth, London.

Earl, M., 1978, Prototype Systems for Accounting Information and Control. *Accounting, Organizations and Society*, **3** (2), 161–172.

Ehn, P., 1988, *Work-Oriented Design of Computer Artifacts*. Arbetslivscentrum, Stockholm.

Ehn, P., 1990, Scandinavian Design – on Participation and Skill. Invited Paper at the Conference on Technology and the Future of Work, 28–30.

Ehn, P. and Kyng, M., 1987, The Collective Resource Approach to Systems Design. In Bjerknes, G., Ehn, P., and Kyng, M. (eds.), *Computers and Democracy: A Scandinavian Challenge*. Avebury, Aldershot, 17–57.

Ehn, P. and Kyng, M. 1991, Card Board Computers: Mocking-it-up or Hands-on the Future. In Greenbaum, J. and Kyng, M. (eds.), *Design at Work: Cooperative Design of Computer Systems*. Lawrence Erlbaum Associates, Hillsdale, NJ, 169–195.

Ehn, P., Kyng, M. and Sundblad, Y., 1983, The Utopia Project: on Training, Technology, and Products viewed from the Quality of Work Perspective. In Briefs, U., Ciborra, C. and Schnieder, L. (eds.), *Systems Design For, With and By the Users*. North-Holland, Amsterdam, 439–449.

Ehn, P. and Sandberg, A., 1983, Local Union Influence on Technology and Work Organization: Some Results from the DEMOS Project. In Briefs, U., Ciborra, C. and Schneider, L. (eds.), *Systems Design For, With and By the Users*. North-Holland, Amsterdam, 427–437.

Ehn, P. and Sjogren, D. 1991, From System Descriptions to Scripts of Action. In Greenbaum, J. and Kyng, M. (eds.), *Design at Work: Cooperative Design of Computer Systems*. Lawrence Erlbaum Associates, Hillsdale, NJ, 241–268.

Ellul, J., 1964, *The Technological Society*. Vintage Books, New York.

El Masri, R. and Wiederhold, G., 1985, The Entity Category Relationship Model. *Data and Knowledge Engineering*, **1** (1), 75–116.

Engles R. W., 1972, A Tutorial on Data Base Organization. *Annual Review of Automatic Programming*, **7** 1–64.

Episkopou, D., 1987, *The Theory and Practice of Information Systems Methodologies: A Grounded Theory of Methodology Evolution*. Unpublished PhD Thesis, University of East Anglia, UK.

Faia, M., 1986, *Dynamic Functionalism: Strategy and Tactics*. Cambridge University Press, Cambridge.

Falkenberg, E., 1976, *A Uniform Approach to the Data Base Management*. PhD Dissertation, University of Stuttgart, Report No. 1.

Falkenberg, E., 1977, Concepts for the Co–existence Approach to Data Base Management. In Morlet, P. and Ribbens, H. (eds.), *Proceedings of the International Computing Symposium, Liege*. North-Holland, Amsterdam.

Fay, B., 1975, *Social Theory and Political Practice*. George Allen & Unwin, London.

Feldman, M. and March, J., 1981, Information in Organizations as Signal and Symbol. *Administrative Science Quarterly*, **26** 171–186.

Feyerabend, P., 1975, *Against Method*. New Left Books, London.

Finkelstein, C., 1989, *An Introduction to Information Engineering: From Strategic Planning to Information Systems*. Addison-Wesley, Reading, MA.

Flores, F. and Ludlow, J. J., 1980, Doing and Speaking in the Office. In Fick, G. and Sprague, R. H. Jr. (eds.), *Decision Support Systems: Issues and Challenges*. Pergamon Press, Elmsford, NY.

Flores, F., Graves, M., Hartfield, B. and Winograd, T., 1988, Computer Systems and the Design of Organizational Interaction. *ACM Transactions on Office Information Systems*, **6** (2), 153–172.

Floyd, C., 1984, A Systematic Look at Prototyping. In Budde, R., Kuhlenkam, K., Mathiassen, L. and Zullighoven, H. (eds.), *Approaches to Prototyping*. Springer-Verlag, Berlin, 1–18.

Floyd, C., 1987, Outline of a Paradigm Change in Software Engineering. In Bjerkness, G., Ehn, P., and Kyng, M. (eds.), *Computers and Democracy: A Scandinavian Challenge*. Avebury, Aldershot, 191–212.

Floyd, C., Zullighoven, H., Budde, R. and Keil-Slavik, R., (eds.), 1992, *Software Development and Reality Construction*. Springer-Verlag, Berlin.

Fodor, J., 1977, *Semantics: Theories of Meaning in Generative Grammar*. The Harvester Press, Boston, MA.

Fodor, A. and Katz, J., 1964, *The Structure of Language: Readings in the Philosophy of Language*. Prentice Hall, Englewood Cliffs, NJ.

Forester, J., 1989, *Planning in the Face of Power*. University of California Press, Berkeley, CA.

Frege, G., 1952, On Sense and Reference. In *Translations from the Philosophical Writings of Gottlob Frege*. Translated by Geach, P.T. and Black, M. Basil Blackwell, Oxford.

Freire, P., 1971, *Pedagogy of the Oppressed*. Herder & Herder, New York.

Friedman, A. and Cornford, D., 1989, *Computer Systems Development: History, Organization and Implementation*. Wiley, Chichester.

Gadamer, H., 1975, *Truth and Method*. Translated by Barden, G. and Cumming, J. Seabury Press, New York.

Gadamer, H., 1976, *Philosophical Hermeneutics*. University of California Press, Berkeley, CA.

Gadamer, H. G., 1980, *Vernunft im Zeitalter der Wissenschaft*. Suhrkamp, Frankfurt.

Gane, C. and Sarson, T., 1979, *Structured Systems Analysis: Tools and Techniques*. Prentice Hall, Englewood Cliffs, NJ.

Gane. C. and Sarson, T., 1981, *Structured Systems Analysis*. Prentice Hall, Englewood Cliffs, NJ.

Garfinkel, H., 1967, *Studies in Ethnomethodology*. Prentice Hall, Englewood Cliffs, NJ.

Gerson, E. M. and Star, L. S., 1986, Analyzing Due Process in Organizations. *ACM Transactions on Office Information Systems*, **4** (3), 257–270.

Glans, B., Holstein, D., Meyer, W. and Schmidt, R., 1968, *Management Systems*. Holt, Rinehart and Winston, New York.

Goguen, J., 1992, The Software Project as an Autopoietic Being. In Floyd, C., Zullighoven, H., Budde, R. and Keil-Slavik, R. (eds.), *Software Development and Reality Construction*. Springer-Verlag, Berlin.

Goguen, J. and Linde, C., 1991, Techniques for Requirements Elicitation. In *Proceedings IEEE Symposium on Requirements Engineering, San Diego, CA*, 152–164.

Goldkuhl, G., 1984, ISAC Omvörderat. In Nissen, H.-E. (ed.), *Systemutvecklingav vem, für Vem och Hur?* Institutionen für Informationsbehandling-ADB, Lund Universitet, Sweden.

Goldkuhl, G. and Lyytinen, K., 1982a, A Language Action View of Information Systems. In Ginzberg, M. and Ross, C., (eds.), *Proceedings of the Third International Conference on Information Systems, Ann Arbor, MI*. 13–30.

Goldkuhl G. and Lyytinen K., 1982b, A Disposition for an Information Analysis Methodology based on Speech Act Theory. In Goldkuhl, G. and Kall, C.–O. (eds.), *Proceedings of the Fifth Scandinavian Research Seminar on Systemeering Models*. Department of Information Processing, University of Gothenburg, 201–238.

Goldkuhl, G. and Lyytinen, K., 1984, Information System Specification as Rule Reconstruction. In Bemelmans, T. (ed.), *Beyond Productivity – Information Systems for Organizational Effectiveness*. North-Holland, Amsterdam, 30–55.

Goldkuhl, G. and Rostlinger, A., 1987, *Forandringsanalys*. Studentlitteratur, Lund, Sweden.

Goodhue, D., Kirsch, L., Quillard, J. and Wybo, M., 1992a, Strategic Data Planning: Lessons from the Field. *MIS Quarterly*, **16** (1), 11–34.

Goodhue, D., Wybo, M. and Kirsch, L., 1992b, The Impact of Data Integration on the Costs and Benefits of Information Systems. *MIS Quarterly*, **16** (4), 293–311.

Gorman, K. and Choobineh, J., 1991, Object-Oriented Entity–Relationship Model. *Journal of Management Information Systems*, **7** (3) 41–65.

Grant, D., 1991, *Towards an Information Engineering Approach for Computer Integrated Manufacturing Information Systems*. PhD Dissertation, State University of New York at Binghamton, NY.

Grant, D.A., Klein, H. K. and Ngwenyama, O., 1991, *Modeling for CIM Information Systems Architecture Definition: An Information Engineering Case Study*. Working paper, School of Management, State University of New York at Binghamton, NY.

Greenbaum, J. and Kyng, M., 1991, Introduction: Situated Design. In Greenbaum, J. and Kyng, M. (eds.), *Design at Work: Cooperative Design of Computer Systems*. Lawrence Erlbaum Associates, Hillsdale, NJ.

Grewlich, K., and Pedersen, F., (eds.), 1984, *Power and Participation in an Information Society*. Commission of the European Communities, Brussels.

Grice, H. P., 1975, Logic and Conversation. In Cole, P. and Morgan, J., *Syntax Semantics 3, Speech Acts*. Academic Press, New York.

Griethuysen, J. van, (ed.), 1982, *Concepts and Terminology for the Conceptual Schema and the Information Base*. ISO Report, ISO/TC97/SC5/N695, March.

Groenbaek, K., 1989, Extending the Boundaries of Prototyping – Towards Cooperative Prototyping. In Boedker, S. (ed.), *Proceedings of the Twelfth IRIS: Part I, DAIM PB-296-I, Aarhus*. 219–238.

Grudin, J., 1989, The Case Against User Interface Consistency. *Communications of the ACM*, **32** (10), 1164–1173.

Gutting, G., (ed.), 1980, *Paradigms and Revolutions*. University of Notre Dame Press, South Bend, IN.

Habermas, J., 1967, *On the Logic of the Social Sciences*. German edition. Here quoted from translation by Nicholsen and Stark, fourth printing 1991, MIT Press, Cambridge, MA.

Habermas, J., 1971, *Towards a Rational Society*. Heinemann, London.

Habermas, J., 1972, *Knowledge and Human Interest*. Translated by Shapiro, J., Heinemann, London.

Habermas, J., 1973, *Theory and Practice*. Beacon Press, Boston, MA.

Habermas, J., 1979, *Communication and the Evolution of Society*. Heinemann, London.

Habermas, J., 1982, Reply to My Critics. In Thompson, J. B. and Held, D. (eds.), *Habermas Critical Debates*. MIT Press, Cambridge, MA, 219–283.

Habermas, J., 1984, *The Theory of Communicative Action. Volume I: Reason and the Rationalization of Society*. Beacon Press, Boston, MA.

Habermas, J., 1987, *The Theory of Communicative Action. Volume II: The Critique of Functionalist Reason*. Beacon Press, Boston, MA.

Harsanyi, J. C., 1962, Measurement of Social Power, Opportunity Costs and the Theory of Two-person Bargaining Games. *Behavioral Science*, **7** 67–80.

Hawgood, J., (ed.), 1982, *Evolutionary Systems Development*. North-Holland, Amsterdam.

Hedberg, B. and Jonsson, S., 1978, Designing Semi-confusing Information Systems for Organizations in Changing Environments. *Accounting, Organizations and Society*, **3** (1), 47–64.

Hedberg, B. and Mumford E., 1975, The Design of Computer-based Systems: Man's Vision of Man as an Integral Part of the System Design Process. In Mumford, E. and Sackman H. (eds.), *Human Choice and Computers*. North-Holland, Amsterdam, 31–59.

Hedberg, B., Nystrom, P. and Starbuck, W., 1976, Camping on See-saws: Prescriptions for Self-Designing Organizations. *Administrative Science Quarterly*, **24** 40–63.

Heidegger, M., 1962, *Being and Time*. Basil Blackwell, Oxford.

Held, D., 1980, *Introduction to Critical Theory: Horkheimer to Habermas*. University of California Press, Berkeley, CA.

Hewitt, C., 1986, Offices are Open Systems. *ACM Transactions on Office Information Systems*, **4** (3), 271-287.

Hirschheim, R. A., 1983, Assessing Participative System Design: Some Conclusions From an Exploratory Study. *Information & Management*, **6** (1), 317–327.

Hirschheim, R. A., 1985a, User Experiences with and Assessment of Participative Systems Design. *MIS Quarterly*, **9** (4), 295–303.

Hirschheim, R. A., 1985b, *Office Automation: A Social and Organizational Perspective*. Wiley, Chichester.

Hirschheim, R. A., 1986, The Effect of A Priori Views on the Social Implications of Computing: The Case of Office Automation. *Computing Surveys*, **18** (2), 165–195.

Hirschheim, R. and Klein, H., 1989, Four Paradigms of Information Systems Development. *Communications of the ACM*, **32** (10), 1199–1216.

Hirschheim, R. and Klein, H., 1991, A Research Agenda for Future Information Systems Development Methodologies. In Cottermann, W. and Senn, J. (eds.), *Systems and Design: A Research Agenda*. Wiley, Chichester.

Hirschheim, R. and Klein, H. 1994, Realizing Emancipatory Principles in Information Systems Development: The Case for ETHICS. *MIS Quarterly*, **18** (1) March, 83–109.

Hirschheim, R. and Miller, J. 1993, Implementing Empowerment Through Teams: The Case of Texaco's Information Technology Division. In Tanniru, M. (ed.), *Proceedings of the 1993 ACM SIGCPR Conference, St. Louis, MO*. 255–264.

Hirschheim, R. and Newman, M., 1988, Information Systems and User Resistance: Theory and Practice. *The Computer Journal*, **31** (5), 1–11.

Hirschheim, R. and Newman, M., 1991, Symbolism and Information Systems Development: Myth, Metaphor and Magic. *Information Systems Research*, **2** (1), 1–34.

Hirschheim, R., Klein, H. and Lyytinen, K. 1991, *Control, Sense–Making and Argumentation in Information Systems*. Information Systems Research Center (ISRC) Working Papers Series, University of Houston, TX.

Hirschheim, R., Klein, H., and Newman, M., 1991, Information Systems Development as Social Action: Theoretical Perspective and Practice. *Omega*, **19** (6), 587–608.

Holmqvist, B. and Andersen, P.-B., 1987, Work Language and Information Technology. *Journal of Pragmatics*, **11** 327–357.

Hopper, Paul, 1987, Emergent Grammar in General Session and Parasession on Grammar and Cognition. In Aske, J., Beery, N., Michaelis, L. and Fili, H. (eds.), *Proceedings of the Thirteenth Annual Meeting of the Berkeley Linguistics Society*. Berkeley Linguistics Society, Berkeley CA, Feb. 14–16.

Hopper, T. and Powell, A., 1985, Making Sense of Research into the Organizational and Social Aspects of Management Accounting: a Review of its Underlying Assumptions. *Journal of Management Studies*, **22** (5), September, 429–465.

Howard, R., 1985, UTOPIA: Where Workers Craft New Technology. *Technology Review*, **28** (3), 43–49.

Hull, R. and King, R., 1987, Semantic database modeling: survey, applications, and research issues. *ACM Computing Surveys*, **19** (3), 201–260.

Iivari, J., 1982, Taxonomy of the Experimental and Evolutionary Approaches to Systemeering. In Hawgood, J. (ed.), *Evolutionary Information Systems*. North-Holland, Amsterdam, 105–119.

Iivari, J., 1984, Prototyping in the Context of Information Systems Design. In Budde, R., Kuhlenkam, K., Mathiassen, L. and Zullighoven, H. (eds.), *Approaches to Prototyping*. North-Holland, Amsterdam, 261–277.

Iivari, J., 1989, A Methodology for IS Development as Organizational Change: A Pragmatic Contingency Approach. In Klein, H. and Kumar, K. (eds.), *Systems Development for Human Progress*. North-Holland, Amsterdam, 197–217.

Iivari, J., 1991, A Paradigmatic Analysis of Contemporary Schools of IS Development. *Europena Journal Information Systsems*, **1** (4), 249–272.

Iivari, J. and Koskela, E., 1983, The Object System Model in the PIOCO Metamodel of the Data System. *Acta Universitatis Tamperensis Ser. B,*, **19** University of Tampere, Tampere, 29–70.

Israel, J., 1979, *The Language of Dialectics – The Dialectics of Language.* Munksgaard, Copenhagen.

Ives, B., Hamilton, S. and David, G., 1980, A Framework for Research in Computer-based Management Information Systems. *Management Science,* **26** (9), 910–934.

Jackson, M. C., 1975, *Principles of Program Design.* Academic Press, London.

Jackson, M., 1983, *System Development.* Prentice Hall, Englewood Cliffs, NJ.

Jacobson, I. 1992, *Object-Oriented Software Engineering: a Case Driven Approach.* Addison-Wesley, Reading, MA.

Jardine, D. A. and Reuber, A. R., 1984, Information Semantics and the Conceptual Schema. *Information Systems,* **9** (2), 147–156.

Jepsen, L., Mathiassen, L. and Nielsen, P., 1989, Back to Thinking Mode: Diaries for the Management of Information Systems Development Projects. *Behavior and Information Technology,* **8** (3), 207–217.

Kahn, B. S., 1982, LDDM – A Structured Logical Database Design Methodology. In Yao, S., Navathe, D., Weldon, J. and Kunii, T. (eds.), *Database Design Techniques I: Requirements and Logical Structures.* Springer-Verlag, Berlin, 31-55.

Kangassalo, H., 1982, On the Concept of a Concept in a Conceptual Schema. In Kangassalo, H. (ed.), *First Scandinavian Research Seminar on Information Modeling and Data Base Management.* Acta Universitatis Tamperensis, Series B **17**.

Kapp, E., 1942, *Greek Foundations of Traditional Logic.* Free Press, New York.

Kaula, R., 1990, *Open System Architecture.* PhD Dissertation, State University of New York at Binghamton, NY.

Kay, A., 1984, Software. *Scientific American,* **251** (3), 41–47.

Kay, A., 1985, Software's Second Act. *Science,* November, 1022–1026.

Keen, P., 1980, Adaptive Design for Decision Support Systems. *Data Base,* **1/2** Fall, 15–25.

Keen, P., 1981, Information Systems and Organizational Change. *Communications of the ACM,* **24** (1), 24–33.

Keen, P. and Scott-Morton, M., 1978, *Decision Support Systems: An Organizational Perspective.* Addison-Wesley, Reading, MA.

Kendall, K. and Kendall, J., 1988, *Systems Analysis and Design.* Prentice Hall, Englewood Cliffs, NJ.

Kent, W., 1978, *Data and Reality.* North-Holland, Amsterdam.

Kent, W., 1983a, A Simple Guide to Five Normal Forms in Relational Database Theory. *Communications of the ACM,* **26** (2), 120–125.

Kent, W., 1983b, Fact-based Analysis and Design. In Davis, C. *et al.* (eds.), *Proceedings of the Entity–Relationship Approach to Software Engineering.* Elsevier, Amsterdam, 3–53.

Kent, W., 1986, The Realities of Data: Basic Properties of Data Reconsidered. In Steel, T. and Meersman, R. (eds.), *Data Semantics I*. North-Holland, Amsterdam, 175–187.

Kerola, P., 1985, On the Fundamentals of a Human-centered Theory for Information Systems Development. In *Report of the Eighth Scandinavian Seminar on Systemeering August 14–16, Aarhus*. Part I, 192–210.

Kerola, P., 1987, Integration of Perspectives in the Conception of Office and its Systems Development. In Jarvinen, P. (ed.), *The Report of the Tenth IRIS Seminar*. University of Tampere, Tampere, Finland, 369–392.

Kerola, P. and Simila, J., 1992, Information Science. In Floyd, C., Zullighoven, H., Budde, R. and Keil-Slavik, R. (eds.), *Software Development and Reality Construction*. Springer-Verlag, Berlin.

Kerschberg, L., Klug, A, and Tsichritzis, D., 1976, A Taxonomy of Data Models. In Lockemann, P., Neuhold, E., (eds.), *Systems for Large Databases*. North-Holland, Amsterdam, 43–64.

Kim, W. and Lochovsky, F., 1990, *Object-Oriented Concepts, Databases and Applications*. ACM Press, New York.

Kimbrough, S. and Lee, R., 1986, On Illocutionary Logic as a Telecommunications Language. In *Proceedings of the Eighth International Conference on Information Systems*. San Diego, CA, December, 15–26.

King, W. R. and Srinivasan, A., 1987, The Systems Life Cycle and the Modern Information Systems Environment. In Rabin, J. and Jackowski, E.M. (eds.), *Handbook of IS Resource Management*. Basil Marcel Inc., New York, 325–343.

Kirsch, W. and Klein, H. K., 1977, *Management Information Systems II: On the Road to a New Taylorism?*. Kohlhammer, Stuttgart, Urban-Taschenbuecher. (Translated from *Management Information Systems II: Auf dem Weg zu einem neuen Taylorismus?*)

Kleijnen, J. P. C., 1980, *Computers and Profits – Quantifying Financial Benefits of Information Systems*. Prentice Hall, Englewood Cliffs, NJ.

Klein, H. K., 1984, Which Epistemologies for Future Information Systems Research. In Saaksjarvi, M. (ed.), *Report of the 7th Scandinavian Research Seminar on Systemeering (part l)*. Helsinki Business School, Helsinki, 60–90.

Klein, H. K. and Hirschheim, R., 1983, Issues and Approaches to Appraising Technological Change in the Office: A Consequentialist Perspective. *Office: Technology & People*, **2** (1), 15–42.

Klein, H. K. and Hirschheim, R., 1985, Fundamental Issues of Decision Support Systems: a Consequentalist Perspective. *Decision Support Systems*, **1** (1), 5–23.

Klein, H. K. and Hirschheim, R., 1987a, Social Change and the Future of Information Systems Development. In Boland, R. J. and Hirschheim, R. (eds.), *Critical Issues in Information Systems Research*. Wiley, Chichester, 275–305.

Klein, H. K. and Hirschheim, R., 1987b, A Comparative Framework of Data Modelling Paradigms and Approaches. *The Computer Journal*, **30** (1), 8–73.

Klein, H. K. and Hirschheim, R., 1991, Rationality Concepts in Information Systems Development Methodologies. *Accounting, Management and Information Technologies*, **1** (2), 157–187.

Klein, H. K. and Hirschheim, R., 1993, The Rationality of Value Choices in Information Systems Development. Information Systems Research Center Working Paper 08-92-01, University of Houston, TX.

Klein, H. K. and Lyytinen, K., 1985, The Poverty of Scientism in Information Systems. In Mumford, E., Hirschheim, R., Fitzgerald, G. and Wood-Harper, T. (eds.), *Research Methods in Information Systems*. North-Holland, Amsterdam, 131–161.

Klein, H. K. and Lyytinen, K., 1992, Data Modeling: Four Meta-theoretical Assumptions. In Floyd, C., Budde, R. and Zuellinghoven, H., *Software Development and Reality Construction*. Springer-Verlag, Berlin.

Klein, H. K. and Truex, D. 1994, Discourse Analysis: a Scientific Approach to the Investigation of Organizational Emergence. In Andersen, P.-B. and Holmqvist, B. 1995, *The Semiotics of the Workplace.*, Walter de Gruyter, Berlin.

Kling, R., 1978, Value-conflicts and Social Choice in Electronic Funds Transfer Developments. *Communications of the ACM*, **21** (8), 642–657.

Kling, R., 1980, Social Analyses of Computing. *ACM Computing Surveys*, **12** (1), 61–110.

Kling, R., 1985, Computerization as an Ongoing Social and Political Process. In *Proceedings of Conference Development and Use of Computer-Based Systems Tools*. August 19–23, Aarhus, 309–328.

Kling, R., 1987, Defining the Boundaries of Computing Across Complex Organizations. In Boland, R. and Hirschheim, R. (eds.), *Critical Issues in Information Systems Research*. Wiley, Chichester, 307–362.

Kling, R. and Iacono, S., 1984, The Control of Information Systems Development After Implementation. *Communications of the ACM*, **27** (12), 1218–1226.

Kling, R. and Scacchi, W., 1980, Computing as Social Action: The Social Dynamics of Computing in Complex Organizations. In *Advances in Computers*, **19** Academic Press, New York.

Kling, R. and Scacchi, W., 1982, The Social Web of Computing: Computer Technology as Social Organization. In *Advances in Computers*, **21** 2–90, Academic Press, New York.

Kolakowski, L., 1972, *Positivist Pholosophy*. Penguin, Harmondsworth.

Kolf, F. and Oppelland, H., 1980, Guidelines for the Organizational Implementation of IS: Concepts and Experiences with the PORGI Implementation Handbook. In Bjorn-Andersen, N. (ed.), *The Human Side of Information Processing*. North-Holland, Amsterdam, 69–87.

Kraft, P., 1977, *Programmers and Managers*. Springer-Verlag, New York.

Kraft, P. and Bansler, J., 1988, The Introduction of New Technologies in Danish Workplaces. Paper presented at the Third Technological Literacy Conference, Arlington, VA.

Kraft, P. and Bansler, J., 1992, The Collective Resource Approach: The Scandinavian Experience. In Muller, Kuhn and Meskill (eds.), *PDC'92: Proceedings of the Participatory Design Conference*. Stanford, CA, 127-135.

Kubicek, H., 1983, User Participation in Systems Design: Some Questions about Structure and Content Arising from Recent Research from a Trade Union Perspective. In Briefs, U., Ciborra, C., and Schneider, L. (eds.), *Systems Design For, With and By the Users.* North-Holland, Amsterdam, 3–18.

Kuhn, T., 1970, *The Structure of Scientific Revolutions.* (2nd edition), University of Chicago Press, Chicago, IL.

Kutchera, F. von, 1975, *Philosophy of Language Revolutions,* (2nd edition). University of Chicago Press, Chicago, IL.

Kyng, M., 1989, Designing for a Dollar a Day. *Office: Technology and People,* **4** 51–170.

Kyng, M., 1991, Cooperative Design: Bringing Together the Practices of Users and Designers. In Nissen, H.-E., Klein, H. and Hirschheim, R. (eds.), *Information Systems Research: Contemporary Approaches and Emergent Traditions.* North-Holland, Amsterdam, 405–416.

Kyng, M. and Ehn, P., 1985, STARDUST Memories: Scandinavian Tradition and Research on Development and Use of Systems and Tools. Paper presented at the Conference on Development and Use of Computer-Based Systems and Tools, August, Aarhus.

Kyng, M. and Mathiassen, L., 1982, Systems Development and Trade Union Activities. In Bjorn-Andersen, N., Earl, M., Holst, J. and Mumford, E. (eds.), *Information Society: For Richer For Poorer.* North-Holland, Amsterdam.

Lakoff, G. and Johnson, M., 1980, *Metaphors We Live By.* University of Chicago Press, Chicago, IL.

Lakatos, I. and Musgrave, A., (eds.), 1970, *Criticism and the Growth of Knowledge.* Cambridge University Press, Cambridge.

Land, F., 1989, From Software Engineering to Information Systems Engineering. In Knight, K. (ed.), *Participation in Systems Development.* Kogan Page, London, 9-33.

Land, F. and Hirschheim, R., 1983, Participative Systems Design: Rationale, Tools and Techniques. *Journal of Applied Systems Analysis,* **10** 91–107.

Langefors, B., 1963, SomeAapproaches to the Theory of Information Systems. *BIT,* **3** 229–254.

Langefors, B., 1970, *Theoretical Analysis of Information Systems* (2nd edition). Studentlitteratur, Lund, Sweden.

Langefors, B., 1973, *Theoretical Analysis of Information Systems.* Auerbach, Philadelphia, PA.

Langefors, B., 1977, *Hermeneutics, Infology, and Information Systems.* TRITA–IBADB No. 1052, University of Stockholm.

Lantz, K., 1986, *The Prototyping Methodology.* Prentice Hall, Englewood Cliffs, NJ.

Lanzara, G. and Mathiassen, L., 1984, Mapping Situations within a System Development Project – an Intervention Perspective on Organizational Change. DIAMI PB–179, MARS Report No. 6, November, University of Aarhus, Denmark.

Lee, B., 1978, *Introducing Systems Analysis and Design: Vols. I and II.* National Computing Centre, Manchester.

Lee, R., 1983, Epistemological Aspects of Knowledge-Based Decision Support Systems. In Sol, H. G. (ed.), *Processes and Tools for Decision Support.* North-Holland, Amsterdam, 25–36.

Lee, R., 1984, Automating the Red Tape—the Informative vs. the Performative Role of Bureaucratic Documents. *Office-Technology and People*, **3** (1).

Lee, R., 1988, A Logic Model for Electronic Contracting. *Decision Support Systems*, **4** (1), 27–44.

Lee, R. and Donaldson-Dewitz, S., 1990, Finding International Contracting Opportunities: AI extensions to EDI. In DeGross, J., Alavi, M. and Oppelland, H. (eds.), *Proceedings of the 11th International Conference on Information Systems, Copenhagen*. ACM Press, New York, 1–14.

Leech, G., 1974, *Semantics*. Penguin Books, Harmondsworth.

Lehtinen, E. and Lyytinen, K. 1983, *The SAMPO Project: A Speech–Act Based Information Analysis Methodology with Computer Based Tools*. Report WP-2, Department of Computer Science, Jyväskylä University, Finland.

Lehtinen, E. and Lyytinen, K., 1984, Discourse Analysis as an Information System Specification Method. In *Proceedings of the 7th Scandinavian Research Seminar on Systemeering*. Helsinki, August 26–29.

Lehtinen, E. and Lyytinen, K., 1986, Action Based Model of Information Systems. *Information Systems*, **13** (4), 299–317.

Leibniz, G.W., 1875, *Die Philosophischen Schriften von Leibniz*. In 7 volumes edited by Gerhardt, C. I., Berlin (1875–1890).

Leibniz, G.W., 1890, *The Philosophical Works of Leibniz*. Translated with notes by Duncan, G. M., Yale University Press, New Haven, CT.

Lessnoff, M., 1974, *The Structure of Social Science*. George Allen & Unwin, London.

Levinson, S., 1983, *Pragmatics*. Cambridge University Press, Cambridge.

Lewis, D., 1969, *Convention*. Harvard University Press, Cambridge, MA.

Licklider, J. C. R., 1960, Man–computer Symbiosis. *IEEE Transactions on Human Factors in Electronics*, HFE-1. 4.

Licklider, J. C. R., 1968, Man–machine Communication. *Annual Review of Information Science and Technology*. Cuadra, C. A., (ed.), Chicago, IL, 201.

Lindgreen, P., 1984, Abstract Entities and Entity Existence. In Kangassalo, H. (ed.), *Third Scandinavian Research Seminar on Information Modeling and Data Base Management*. University of Tampere, Tampere, Finland, 201–214.

Liu, K. and Stamper, R., 1989, Semantic and Normbase approach to Development of Land Resources Information Systems. Paper presented on the Applications of Remote Sensing and Geographic Information Systems to Urban–Rural Planning and Management, May 2–9, Wuhan, China.

Lucas, H. C., 1975, *Why Information Systems Fail*. Columbia University Press, New York.

Lucas, H. C., 1978, Empirical Evidence for a Prescriptive Model of Implementation. *MIS Quarterly*, **2** (1), 27–41.

Lucas, H. C., 1981, *Implementation: The Key to Successful Information Systems*. Columbia University Press, New York.

Luhmann, N., 1987, *Sociale Système*. Suhrkamp, Frankfurt.

Lundberg, B., 1982, *Contributions to Information Modeling*. PhD thesis, Department of Information Processing, University of Stockholm, Sweden.

Lundeberg, M., Goldkuhl, G. and Nilsson, A., 1981, *Information Systems Development – A Systematic Approach*. Prentice Hall, Englewood Cliffs, NJ.

Lyons, J., 1977, *Semantics, Vols. I-II*. Cambridge University Press, Cambridge.

Lyytinen, K., 1981, *Language Oriented Development of Information Ssystems – Methodological and Theoretical Foundations*. Unpublished licentiate thesis, Department of Computer Science, University of Jyväskylä, Finland.

Lyytinen, K., 1982, Predicative Analysis of Databases. In Kangassalo, H. (ed.), *Report of the First Scandinavian Research Seminar on Information Modeling and Data Base Management*. Acta Universitatis Tamperensis, Ser B, **17** 39–78.

Lyytinen, K., 1985, Implications of Theories of Language for Information Systems. *MIS Quarterly*, **9** (1), 61–74.

Lyytinen, K., 1986, *Information Systems Development as Social Action-Framework and Implications*. PhD Dissertation, Jyväskylä Studies in Computer Science, Economics and Statistics **8** University of Jyväskylä, Finland.

Lyytinen, K., 1987, Two Views of Information Modeling. *Information and Management*, **12** (1), 9–19.

Lyytinen, K., 1992, Information Systems and Critical Theory. In Alvesson, M. and Wilmott, H. (eds.), *Critical Management Studies*. Sage Publications, Beverly Hills, CA, 159–180.

Lyytinen, K., 1993, Reality Modeling Considered Harmful – The Need for a Linguistic Framework. In Bubenko, J. (ed.), *Information Modeling*. Studentlitteratur, Stockholm, 170–222.

Lyytinen, K. and Hirschheim, R., 1987, Information Systems Failures: A Survey and Classification of the Empirical Literature. *Oxford Surveys in Information Technology*, **4** 257–309.

Lyytinen, K. and Hirschheim, R., 1988, Information Systems as Rational Discourse: An Application of Habermas's Theory of Communicative Action. *Scandinavian Journal of Management*, **4** (1/2), 19–30.

Lyytinen, K. and Klein, H., 1985, The Critical Social Theory of Jürgen Habermas (CST) as a Basis for a Theory of Information Systems. In Mumford, E., Hirschheim, R., Fitzgerald, G. and Wood-Harper, T. (eds.), *Research Methods in Information Systems*. North-Holland, Amsterdam, 219–232.

Lyytinen, K. and Lehtinen, E., 1984, On Information Modeling through Illocutionary Logic. In *Proceedings of the Third Scandinavian Research Seminar on Information Modeling and Data Base Management*. Tampere, Finland.

Lyytinen K. and Lehtinen E., 1987, Seven Mortal Sins of Systems Work. In Docherty, P., Fuchs-Killowski, K. and Mathiassen L. (eds.), *Information Systems for Human Productivity – Participation and Beyond*. North-Holland, Amsterdam.

Macksey, R. and Donato, E., (eds.), 1972, *The Structuralist Controversy: The Language of Criticism and the Sciences of Man*. Johns Hopkins Press, Baltimore, MD.

Maddison, R., Baker, G., Bhabuta, L., Fitzgerald, G., Hindle, K., Song, J., Stokes, N. and Wood, J., 1983, *Information System Methodologies*. Wiley-Heyden, Chichester.

Madsen, K.H., 1989, Breakthrough by Breakdown. In Klein, H. and Kumar, K. (eds.), *Information Systems Development for Human Progress in Organizations*. North-Holland, Amsterdam, 41–53.

Maier, D., 1989, Why Isn't There an Object-Oriented Data Model? In Ritter, G. (ed.), Information Processing **89** North-Holland, Amsterdam, 793–799.

Malone, T., Grant, K., Lai, K. Y., Rao, R. and Rosenblitt, D., 1988, Semistructured Messages are Surprisingly Useful for Computer–Supported Coordination. *ACM Transactions on Office Information Systems*, **5** (2), 115–131.

Markus, M. L., 1983, Power, Politics and MIS Implementation. *Communications of the ACM*, **26** (6) 430–444.

Markus, M. L., 1984, *Systems in Organizations: Bugs and Features*. Pitman Press, Mansfield, MA.

Martin, J. C., 1983, *Managing the Database Environment*. Prentice Hall, Englewood Cliffs, NJ.

Martin, J., 1984, *An Information Systems Manifesto*. Prentice Hall, Englewood Cliffs, NJ.

Martin, J. and Odell, J., 1992, *Object Oriented Analysis and Design*. Prentice Hall, Englewood Cliffs, NJ.

Mathiassen, L., 1981, *Systems Development and Systems Development Method*. DAIMI PB-136, Department of Computer Science, Aarhus University, Denmark.

Mathiassen, L. and Anderson, P.-B., 1985, Systems Development and Use: a Science of the Truth or a Theory of Lies. In *Proceedings of the Working Conference on Development and Use of Computer-Based Systems and Tools, August, Aarhus Part II*.

Mathiassen, L. and Nielsen, P.A., 1989, Soft Systems and Hard Contradictions – Approaching the Reality of Information Systems in Organizations. *Journal of Applied Systems Analysis*, **16** 75–88.

Mathiassen, L. and Nielsen, P., 1990, Organizational Competence: Soft Systems and Hard Contradictions. In Bjerknes, G. and Dahlbom, B. (eds.), *Organizational Competence*. Studentlitteratur, 101–210.

Mathiassen, L., Rolskov, B. and Vedel, E., 1983, Regulating the Use of EDP by Law and Agreements. In Briefs, U., Ciborra, C. and Schneider, L. (eds.), *Systems Design For, With, and By the Users*. North-Holland, Amsterdam, 251–264.

Mattos, M. M., Meyer-Wegener, K. and Mitschang, B. 1992, A Grand Tour around Concepts for Object-Orientation from a Database Point of View. *Data & Knowledge Engineering*, **9** (3), 321–352.

McCarthy, T., 1978, *The Critical Theory of Jürgen Habermas*. MIT Press, Cambridge, MA.

McCarthy, T., 1982, Rationality and Relativism: Habermas's 'Overcoming' of Hermeneutics. In Thompson, J. and Held, D. (eds.), *Habermas: Critical Debates*. MIT Press, Cambridge, MA, 57–78.

McCorduck, P., 1979, *Machines Who Think*. Freeman, San Francisco, CA.

McGregor, D., 1960, *The Human Side of Enterprise*. McGraw-Hill, New York.

McLean, E. and Soden, J., 1977, *Strategic Planning for Management Information Systems*. Wiley, New York.

McMenamin, S. and Palmer, J., 1984, *Essential Systems Analysis*. Yourdon Press, New York.

Mead, G., 1934, *Mind, Self and Society*. University of Chicago Press, Chicago.

Meersman, R. and Steel, T. B., (eds.), 1985, *Database Semantics (DS-1)*. North-Holland, Amsterdam.

Millington, D., 1978, *Systems Analysis and Design for Computer Application*. Ellis Horwood, Chichester.

Mingers, J., 1981, Towards an Appropriate Theory for Applied Systems Thinking: Critical Theory and Soft Systems Methodology. *Journal of Applied Systems Analysis*, **7** (1), 41–49.

Minsky, M., 1968, *Semantic Information Processing*. MIT Press, Cambridge, MA.

Minsky, M., 1975, A Framework for Representing Knowledge. In Winston, P. (ed.), *The Psychology of Computer Vision*. McGraw-Hill, New York.

Misgeld, D., 1977, Discourse and conversation: The Theory of Communicative Competence and Hermenutics in the Light of the Debate between Habermas and Gadamer. *Cultural Hermeneutics*, **4** 321–344.

Mitroff, I., 1980, Towards a Logic and Methodology for 'Real World' Problems. In Bjorn-Andersen, N. (ed.), *The Human Side of Information Processing*. North-Holland, Amsterdam, 187–195.

Mitroff, I., 1983, *Stakeholders of the Organizational Mind*. Jossey-Bass, San Francisco, CA.

Mitroff, I. I., Mason, R. O. and Barabba, V. P., 1982, Policy as Argument – a Logic for Ill-structured Decision Problems. *Management Science*, **28** (12), 1391–1404.

Montague R., 1974, *Formal Philosophy: Selected Papers of Richard Montague*. Edited by Thompson, R. H., Yale University Press, New Haven, CT.

Morgan, G., (ed.), 1983, *Beyond Method: Strategies for Social Research*. Sage Publications, Beverly Hills, CA.

Morgan, G., 1986, *Images of Organizations*. Sage Publications, Beverly Hills, CA.

Morris, C., 1946, *Signs, Language and Behavior*. Prentice Hall, Englewood Cliffs, NJ.

Mowshowitz, A., 1984, Computers and the Myth of Neutrality. In *Proceedings of the 1984 Computer Science Conference*, Philadelphia, February 14–16, 85–92.

Mulder, M., 1971, Power Equalization Through Participation? *Administrative Science Quarterly*, **16** (1), 31–38.

Mumford, E., 1981, Participative Systems Design: Structure and Method. *Systems, Objectives, Solutions*, **1** (1), 5–20

Mumford, E., 1983, *Designing Human Systems – The ETHICS Method*. Manchester Business School, Manchester.

Mumford, E., Hirschheim, R., Fitzgerald, G. and Wood-Harper, T. (eds.), 1985, *Research Methods in Information Systems*. North-Holland, Amsterdam.

Murphy, W. and Rawlings, R., 1981, After the Ancien Regime. *The Modern Law Review*, **44** November, 617–657.

Mylopoulos, J. 1981, A Perspective on Conceptual Modeling. In Brodie, M. L. and Zilles, S. (eds.), *SIGPLAN Notices*, **16** (1), 98.

Nagel, E., 1961, *The Structure of Science: Problems in the Logic of Scientific Explanation*. Harcourt, Brace and World, New York.

Naumann, J. and Jenkins, M., 1982, Prototyping: The New Paradigm for Systems Development. *MIS Quarterly*, **6** (3), 29–73.

Naur, P., 1985, Programming as Theory Building. *Microprocessing and Microprogramming*, **15** 254–261.

Navathe, S. B., 1980, Schema Analysis for Database Restructuring. *ACM Transactions on Database Systems*, **5** 157-184.

Newell, A. and Simon, H. A., 1972, *Human Problem Solving*. Prentice Hall, Englewood Cliffs, NJ.

Newman, M. and Noble, F., 1990, User Involvement as an Interaction Process: A Case Study. *Information Systems Research*, **1** (1), 89–113.

Newman, M. and Rosenberg, D., 1985, Systems Analysts and the Politics of Organizational Control. *Omega*, **13** (5), 393–406.

Ngwenyama, O., 1987, *Fundamental Issues of Knowledge Acquisition: Toward a Human Action Perspective of Knowledge Acquisition*. PhD Dissertation, Watson School of Engineering, State University of New York, Binghamton, NY.

Ngwenyama, O., 1991, The Critical Social theory Approach to Information Systems: Problems and Challenges. In Nissen, H.-E., Klein, H. and Hirschheim, R. (eds.), *Information Systems Research: Contemporary Approaches and Emergent Traditions*. North-Holland, Amsterdam, 267–280.

Nijssen G. M., 1976, A Gross Architecture for the Next Generation Database Management Systems. In Nijssen, G. M. (ed.), *Modelling in Data Base Management Systems*. North-Holland, Amsterdam.

Nijssen, G. M., 1977, Current Issues in Conceptual Schema Concepts. In Nijssen G. M. (ed.), *Architecture and Models in Data Base Management Systems*. North Holland, Amsterdam, 31–66.

Nijssen, G. M., 1980, Towards and Ideal Conceptual Model for Data Base Management. In Deen, S. and Hammersley, P. (eds.), *Proceedings of the International Conference of Data Bases, Aberdeen*.

Nijssen, G.M., and Bracchi, G., 1979. In Bracchi, G. and Lockeman, P. (eds.), *Database Architecture: IFIP 2.6 Proceedings*. North-Holland, Amsterdam.

Nissen, H.-E., 1980, Towards a Multisubject Group Conception of Information Systems. In Lyytinen, K. and Peltola, E. (eds.), *Report of the Third Scandinavian Seminar on Syste-*

meering Models, (IRIS). Department of Computer Science, University of Jyväskylä, 141–175.

Nissen, H.-E., 1989, Information Systems Development for Responsible Human Action. In Klein, H. and Kumar, K. (eds.), *Systems Development for Human Progress*. North-Holland, Amsterdam, 99–115.

Nissen, H.-E., Klein, H. K. and Hirschheim, R., (eds.), 1991, *Information Systems Research: Contemporary Approaches and Emergent Traditions*. North-Holland, Amsterdam.

Nygaard, K. and Haandlykken, P., 1981, The System Development Process – Its Setting, Some Problems and Needs for Methods. In Hunke, H. (ed.), *Software Engineering Environments*. North-Holland, Amsterdam, 157–172.

Nygaard, K., 1975, The Trade Unions: New Users of Research. *Personnel Review*, 4 (2), 5–10.

Ogden, C. and Richards, I. A., 1949, *The Meaning of Meaning*. Routledge and Kegan Paul, London.

Oliga, J. C., 1988, Methodological Foundations of System Methodologies. *Systems Practice*, 1 (1), 87–112.

Olle, T. W. and Sibley E., (eds.), 1986, *Information System Design Methodologies – Improving the Practice*. North-Holland, Amsterdam.

Olle, T. W., Sol, H. G. and Verrijn-Stuart, A. A., (eds.), 1982, *Information Systems Design Methodologies: A Comparative Review*. North-Holland, Amsterdam.

Olle, T.W., Sol, H. G. and Tully, C., (eds.), 1983, *Information System Design Methodologies: a Feature Analysis*. North-Holland, Amsterdam.

Olle, T. W., Verrijn-Stuart, A. A. and Bhabuta, L., (eds.), 1988, *Information Systems Design Methodologies: Computerized Assistance During the Information Systems Life-Cycle*. North-Holland, Amsterdam.

Oppelland, H., 1984, Participative Information Systems Development. In Bemelmans, T. (ed.), *Beyond Productivity: Information Systems Development for Organizational Effectiveness*. North-Holland, Amsterdam, 105–125.

Oppelland, H. and Kolf, F., 1980, Participative Development of Information Systems. In Lucas, H., Land, F., Lincoln, T. and Supper, K. (eds.), *The Information Systems Environment*. North-Holland, Amsterdam, 238–249.

Orlikowski, W. and Baroudi, J., 1991, Studying Information Technology in Organizations: Research Approaches and Assumptions. *Information Systems Research*, 2 (1), 1–28.

Palmer, R., 1969, *Hermeneutics: Intepretation Theory in Schleiermacher, Dilthey, Heidegger, and Gadamer*. Northwestern University Press, Evanston, IL.

Parnas, D. L. and Clements, P. C., 1985, A Rational Design Process: How and Why to Fake It. In Ehrig, H. *et al.* (eds.), *Formal Methods and Software Developement*. Springer-Verlag, Berlin.

Pava, C., 1983, *Managing New Office Technology: An Organizational Strategy*. Free Press, New York.

Peckham, J. and Maryanski, F., 1988, Semantic Data Models. *ACM Computing Surveys*, 20 (3), 153–189.

Peirce, C., 1960, *Collected Papers, Volumes 5 & 6*. Edited by Hartshorne, C. and Weiss, P., Harvard University Press, Cambridge, MA.

Pettigrew, A., 1973, *The Politics of Organizational Decision Making*. Tavistock, London.

Pettigrew, A., 1985, *The Awakening Giant: Continuity and Change in Imperial Chemical Industries*. Basil Blackwell, Oxford.

Pfeffer, J., 1981, *Power in Organizations*. Pitman Press, Boston, MA.

Pitkin, H., 1973, *Wittgenstein and Justice*. University of California Press, Berkeley, CA.

Popper, K., 1965, *Conjectures and Refutations*. Basic Books, New York.

Popper, K., 1972, *Objective Knowledge*. Clarendon Press, Oxford.

Pressman, R. S., 1987, *Software Engineering: a Practioner's Approach* (2nd edition). McGraw-Hill, New York.

Quine, W. V., 1960, *Word and Object*. MIT Press, Cambridge, MA.

Quine, W. V., 1963, *From a Logical Point of View*. Harper Torch Books, New York.

Quine, W. V. and Ullian, J., 1970, *The Web of Belief*. Random House, New York.

Reason, P. and Rowan J., 1981, *Human Inquiry – A Sourcebook of New Paradigm Research*. Wiley, Chichester.

Richter, G. and Durcholtz, R., 1982, IML-inscribed High-level Petri Nets. In Olle, T. W., Sol, H. G. and Verrijn-Stuart, A. A. (eds.), *Information Systems Design Methodologies: A Comparative Review*. North-Holland, Amsterdam, 335–368.

Robey, D. and Markus, M. L., 1984, Rituals in System Design. *MIS Quarterly*, **10** (1), 5–15.

Rocfeldt, A. and Tardieu H., 1983, MERISE: an Information System Design and Development Methodology. *Information & Management*, **6** 143–159.

Rosove, P., (ed.), 1967, Developing Computer-based Information Systems. Wiley, New York.

Rovner, P. and Feldman, J., 1969, The LEAP Language and Data Structure. In *Information Processing (IFIP World Conference)*. **68** North-Holland, Amsterdam, 579–585.

Rumbaugh, J., Blaha, M., Premerlani, W., Eddy, F. and Lorensen, W., 1991, *Object–oriented Modeling and Design*. Prentice Hall, Englewood Cliffs, NJ.

Russell, B., 1929, *Our Knowledge of the External World*. Open Court, Chicago, IL.

Russell, B. and Whitehead, A. N., 1950, *Principia Mathematica*. Cambridge University Press, Cambridge.

Ryle, G., 1949, *The Concept of Mind*. Penguin Books, Harmondsworth.

Sackman, H., 1967, *Computers, System Science, and Evolving Society*. Wiley, New York.

Sandberg, A., 1985, Socio-technical Design, Trade Union Strategies and Action Research. In Mumford, E., Hirschheim, R., Fitzgerald, G. and Wood-Harper, A. T. (eds.), *Research Methods in Information Systems*. North-Holland, Amsterdam, 79–92.

Scacchi, W., 1985, Applying Social Analysis of Computing to System Design. In *Proceedings of Conference Development and Use of Computer-Based Systems Tools August 19–23, Aarhus*. 477–499.

Schafer, G., Hirschheim, R., Harper, M., Hansjee, R., Domke, M. and Bjorn-Andersen, N., 1988, *Functional Analysis of Office Requirements: A Multiperspective Approach.* Wiley, Chichester.

Schmid, H. A., 1983, A Comparative Survey of Concepts for Conceptual Information Models. In Bubenko, J. A. (ed.), *Information Modeling.* Studentlitteratur, Lund, 6–102.

Schneiderman, B., 1987, *Designing the User Interface: Strategies For Effective Human-Computer Interaction.* Addison-Wesley, Reading, MA.

Schon, D., 1983, *The Reflective Practitioner. How Professionals Think in Action.* Basic Books, New York.

Schutz, A., 1967, *Phenomenology of Social World.* Northwestern University Press, Evanston, IL.

Schutz, A. and Luckmann, T., 1974, *The Structures of Life World.* Heinemann, London.

Scott-Morton, M. S., 1967, Interactive Visual Display Systems and Management Problem Solving. *Ind. Management Review,* (9) 69.

Scott-Morton, M. S., 1971, Strategy for the Design and Evaluation of an Interactive Display System for Management Planning. In Kriebel, C. H., Van Horn, R. L. and Heames, T. J. (eds.), *Management Information Systems: Progress and Perspective.* Carnegie Mellon University, Pittsburgh, PA.

Searle, J., 1969, *Speech Acts, An Essay in the Philosohy of Language.* Cambridge University Press, Cambridge.

Searle, J., 1979, *Expression and Meaning.* Cambridge University Press, Cambridge.

Searle, J. and Vanderveken, D., 1985, *Foundations of Illocutionary Logic.* Cambridge University Press, Cambridge.

Senko, M., 1975, Information Systems, Records, Relations, Sets, Entities, and Things. *Information Systems,* **1** (1), 3–13.

Senko, M., 1977, Conceptual Schemas, Abstract Data Structures, Enterprise Descriptions. In Morlet, A. and Rihbens, G. (eds.), *Proceedings of International Computing Conference.* North-Holland, Amsterdam, 28–39.

Senko, M. E., Altman, E., Astrahan, M. and Fehder, P, 1973, Data Structures and Accessing in Data Base Systems. *IBM Systems Journal,* **12** (1), 30–93.

Senn, J., 1989, *Analysis and Design of Information Systems,* (2nd edition). McGraw-Hill, New York.

Sernadas, A., 1982, Temporal Aspects of Logical Procedure Definition. *Information Systems,* **5** (3).

Shaw, M., 1990, Prospects for an Engineering Discipline for Software. *IEEE Computer,* **7** (6), 15–24.

Sheth, A. and Larson, J. 1990, Federated Database Systems for Managing Distributed, Heterogeneous and Autonomous Databases. *ACM Computing Surveys,* **22** (3), 183–236.

Shlaer, S. and Mellor, S., 1992, *Object Lifecycles – Modeling the World in States.* Yourdon Press, New York.

Silverman, D., 1970, *The Theory of Organizations*. Heinemann, London.

Smith, J. and Smith, D., 1982, Principles of Database Conceptual Design. In Yao, S., Navathe, S., Weldon, J. and Kunii, T. (eds.), *Database Design Techniques: Requirements and Logical Structures*. Springer-Verlag, Berlin.

Solvberg, A., 1977, *A Model for Specification of Phenomena, Properties and Information Structures*. RJ2027(28348), IBM Research Laboratory, San Jose, CA.

Solvberg, A. and Kung, C., 1984, An Exercise of Integrating Data Base Design Tools. In Kangassalo, H. (ed.), *Third Scandinavian Research Seminar on Information Modeling and Data Base Management*. University of Tampere, Tampere, Finland, 277–298.

Solvberg, A., Aanstaad, P., Johansen, T. and Skylstad, G., 1978, An Experiment in Computer-aided Information Systems Development. In Bracchi, G. and Lockeman, P. (eds.), *Information Systems Methodology*. Lecture Notes in Computer Science 65 Springer-Verlag, Berlin.

Somogyi, E. and Galliers, R. 1987, From Data Processing to Strategic Information Systems – A Historical Perspective. In Somogyi, E. and Galliers, R. (eds.), *Towards Strategic Information Systems*. Abacus Press, Tunbridge Wells, Kent, UK, 5–25.

Sowa, J., 1984, *Conceptual Structures in Mind and Machine*. Addison-Wesley, Reading, MA.

Stachowitz, R. A., 1985, A Formal Framework for Describing and Classifying Semantic Data Models. *Information Systems*, **10** (1), 77–96.

Stamper, R., 1973, *Information in Business and Administration Systems*. Batsford, London.

Stamper, R., 1979, A Logic of Social Norms for the Semantics of Business Information. In Meersman, R. (ed.), *Database Semantics*. North-Holland, Amsterdam.

Stamper, R., 1980, Towards a Semantic Normal Form. In Bracchi, G. and Lockeman, P. (eds.), *Database Architecture*. North-Holland, Amsterdam.

Stamper, R., 1983, Information Analysis in LEGOL. In Bubenko, J. (ed.), *Information Modeling*. Studentlitteratur, Lund, Sweden, 565–596.

Stamper, R., 1985a, A Logic of Social Norms for the Semantics of Business Information. In Steel T. B., Meersman R., and Stamper, R. (eds.), *Knowledge and Data*. North-Holland, Amsterdam.

Stamper, R., 1985b, Management Epistemology: Garbage In, Garbage Out. In Methlie, L. B. and Sprague, R. H. (eds.), *Knowledge Representation for Decision Support Systems*. North-Holland, Amsterdam, 55–80.

Stamper, R., 1987, Semantics. In Boland, R. J. and Hirshheim, R. A. (eds.), *Critical Issues in Information Systems Research*. Wiley, Chichester, 43–78.

Stamper, R., 1989, *A Guide to the LEGOL/NORMA*. Project papers, Department of Information Systems, University of Twente, Netherlands.

Stamper, R., 1990, Language and Computing in Organised Behavior. Unpublished Working paper, University of Twente, Netherlands.

Stamper, R. and Lee, R., 1986, *Doing Business with Words: Performative Aspects of Deontic Systems*. Working Paper, Department of Information Systems, London School of Economics.

Stamper, R., Althaus, K. and Backhouse J., 1988, MEASUR – Method for Eliciting, Analysing and Specifying User Requirements. In Olle, T.W., Verrijn-Stuart, A. A. and Bhabuta, L. (eds.), *Computerized Assistance During the Information Systems Life-Cycle*. North-Holland, Amsterdam, 67–116.

Stamper, R., Liu, K., Kolkman, N., Klarenberg, P., van Slooten, F., Ades, Y. and van Slooten, C., 1991, From Database to Norm Base. *International Journal of Information Management*, **11** (1), 67–84.

Steel, T., 1975, Data Base Standardization: A Status Report. In Douque, B. and Nijssen, G. (eds.), *Data Base Description*. North-Holland, Amsterdam, 183–195.

Steel T. B. and Meersman R., (eds.), 1983, *Database Semantics (DS-1)*. North-Holland, Amsterdam.

Stocker, P., Gray, P. and Atkinson, M., (eds.) 1984, *Databases – Role and Structure*. Cambridge University Press, Cambridge.

Suchman, L., 1987, *Plans and Situated Actions – The Problem of Human-Machine Communication*. Cambridge University Press, Cambridge.

Sundgren, B., 1973, *An Infological Approach to Data Bases*. PhD Dissertation, Statistiska Central Byra, Urval No 7, Stockholm.

Swanson, E. B., 1987, Information Systems in Organization Theory: a Review. In Boland, R. and Hirschheim, R. (eds.), *Critical Issues in Information Systems Research*. Wiley, Chichester, 181–204.

Tagg, J., 1989, Postmodernism and the Born-Again Avant-Garde. In Tagg, J. (ed.), *The Cultural Politics of Post-Modernism*. SUNY Binghamton MRTS, Binghamton, NY.

Tarski, A., 1956, The Concept of Truth in Formalized Languages. In *Logic. Semantics. Metamathematics*. Clarendon Press, Oxford.

Teichroew, D. and David, G., (eds.), 1985, *System Description Methodologies*. North-Holland, Amsterdam.

Teichroew, D. and Hershey, E., 1977, PSL/PSA: A Computer Aided Technique for Structured Documentation and Analysis of Information Processing Systems. *IEEE Transactions on Software Engineering*, **SE-3** (1), January, 41–48.

Teichroew, D., Macasovic, P., Hershey, E. and Yamamoto, Y., 1980, Application of the Entity–Relationship Approach to Information Processing Systems Modeling. In Chen, P. P. (ed.), *Entity–Relationship Approach to Systems Analysis and Design*. North-Holland, Amsterdam, 15–38.

Tenenbaum, E. and Wildavsky, A., 1984, Why Policies Control Data and Data Cannot Determine Policies. *Scandinavian Journal of Management Studies*, November, 83–100.

Teorey, T., Yang D. and Fry J., 1986, A Logical Design Methodology for Relational Data Bases using the Extended Entity–Relationship Model. *ACM Computing Surveys*, **18** (2), 197–222.

Toffler, A., 1980, *The Third Wave*. Pan Books, London.

Truex, D., 1993, *Information Systems Development in the Emergent Organization*. PhD Dissertation, Thomas J. Watson School of Engineering, SUNY, Binghamton, NY.

Truex, D. and Klein, H., 1991, Rejection of Structure as a Basis for Information Systems Development. In Stamper, R. and Lee, R. (eds.), *Collaborative Work, Social Communications and Information Systems*. North-Holland, Amsterdam.

Tsichritzis, D. and Lochovsky F., 1982, *Data Models*. Prentice Hall, Englewood Cliffs, NJ.

Twining, W. and Miers, D., 1976, *How to do Things with Rules – a Primer of Interpretation*. Weidenfield and Nicholson, London.

Ulrich, W., 1983, *Critical Heuristics of Social Planning*. Werner–Haupt, Bern.

Ulrich, W., 1988, Systems Thinking, Systems Practice and Practical Philosophy: A Program of Research. *Systems Practice*, **1** (1), 137–163.

Van Maanen, J., 1979, Reclaiming Qualitative Methods for Organizational Research: a Preface. *Administrative Science Quarterly*, **24** (4) December, 520–526.

Vitalari, N. P., 1984, Critical Assessment of Structured Analysis Methods: A Psychological Perspective. In Bemelmans, T. M. A. (ed.), *Beyond Productivity: Information Systems Development for Organizatlonal Effectiveness*. North-Holland, Amsterdam, 421–434.

Vitalari, N. P., 1985, Knowledge as a Basis for Expertise in Systems Analysis: An Empirical Study. *MIS Quarterly*, **9** (3), 221–241.

Wagner, I., 1993, A Web of Fuzzy Problems: Confronting the Ethical Issues. *CACM*, **36** (4), June, 94–101.

Wand Y. and Weber R., 1990, Toward a Theory of Deep Structure Information Systems. In DeGross, J., Alavi, M. and Oppelland, H. (eds.), *Proceedings of the 11th International Conference on Information Systems*. ACM Press, New York, 61–72.

Wasserman, A. I. and Freeman, P. 1983, ADA Methodologies: Concepts and Requirements. *Software Engineering Notes*, **8** (1), 33–50.

Weber, M., 1947, *The Theory of Social and Economic Organization*. Free Press, Collier MacMillan, London.

Weigand, H., 1991, the Linguistic Turn in Information Systems. In Stamper, R., Kerola, P., Lee, R. and Lyytinen, K. (eds.), *Collaborative Work, Social Communications and Information Systems*. North-Holland, Amsterdam, 117–132.

Weinberg, G., 1981, Can Technology Replace Social Engineering. In Teich, A. J. (ed.), *Technology and Man's Future*. St. Martin's Press, New York, 29–39.

Weinberg, V., 1980, *Structured Analysis*. Prentice Hall, Englewood Cliffs, NJ.

Welke, R., 1983, IS/DSS: DBMS Support for Information Systems Development. In Holsapple, C. and Whinston, A. (eds.), *Data Base Management: Theory and Application*. Reidel, Dordrecht, 195–250.

Whitaker, R., Essler, U. and Ostberg, O., 1991, *Participatory Business Modeling*. Lulea University, Sweden, Research Report Tulea 1991: 31, ISSN 0347-0881.

Wilensky, H., 1967, *Organizational Intelligence, Knowledge and Policy in Government and Industry*. Basic Books, New York.

Winch, P., 1958, *The Idea of Social Science and its Relation to Philosophy*. Routledge and Kegan Paul, London.

Winograd, T., 1980, What Does It Mean to Understand Language. *Cognitive Science*, **4** (4), 209–241.

Winograd, T. and Flores, F., 1986, *Understanding Computers and Cognition*. Ablex Publishers, Norwood, NJ.

Wittgenstein, L., 1922, *Tractatus Logico-Philosophicus*. Routledge and Kegan Paul, London.

Wittgenstein, L., 1958, *Philosophical Investigations*. Basil Blackwell, Oxford.

Wittgenstein, L., 1972, *Lectures and Conversations on Aesthetics, Psychology and Religious Belief*. Edited by Barrett, C., University of California Press, Berkeley, CA.

Wood-Harper, A. T., Antill, L. and Avison, D., 1985, *Information Systems Definition: The Multiview Approach*. Blackwell Scientific, Oxford.

Wood-Harper, A. T. and Fitzgerald, G., 1982, A Taxonomy of Current Approaches to Systems Analysis. *The Computer Journal*, **25** (1), 12–16.

Wright, G. H. von, 1963, *Norm and Action*. Routledge and Kegan Paul, London.

Wright, G. H. von, 1963, *An Essay in Deontic Logic and General Theory of Action*. Acta Philosophica Fennica **23** North-Holland, Amsterdam.

Wright, G. H. von, 1971, *Explanation and Understanding*. Routledge and Kegan Paul, London.

Yadav, S., 1983, Determining an Organization's Information Requirements: a State of the Art Survey. *Data Base*, **14** (2), 3-20.

Yager, R, and Zadeh, L., 1987, *Fuzzy Sets and Applications*. Wiley, New York.

Yao, S. B., Navathe, S. B. and Weldon, J., 1982, An Integrated Approach to Database Design. In Yao, S. B., Navathe, S. B., Weldon, J. L. and Kunii, T. L. (eds.), *Data Base Design Techniques: Requirements and Logical Structures*. Springer-Verlag, Berlin.

Young W. and Kent, T., 1958, Abstract Formulation of Data Processing Problems. *Journal of Industrial Engineering*, Nov–Dec, 471–479.

Yourdon, E., 1982, *Managing the System Life Cycle*. Yourdon Press, New York.

Yourdon, E., 1989, *Modern Structured Analysis*. Prentice Hall, Englewood Cliffs, NJ.

Yourdon, E. and Constantine, L., 1979, *Structured Design: Fundamentals of a Discipline of Computer Program and Systems Design*. Prentice Hall, Englewood Cliffs, NJ.

Index

281